In your hands is a key . . .

a key that will unlock many doors. No work has ever contained the practical and scientific explanations on the workings of your self and your universe that are presented in this volume.

You will find herein the wisdom of the ages, knowledge of a different kind—knowledge that has been withheld from the masses, knowledge that has been guarded in the retreats of the Masters for thousands of years. Here you will learn the code of your Identity, of Nature, and of Life itself.

"We all have our eyes fixed on the same goal, and we agree that there is but one summit to reach. Unfortunately we differ on what road to take. Guides come forward and we follow them. Some go one way, others choose different paths. All are convinced that their trail is the best, and all are sincere.

"By following them we approach the one goal, but when the groups which started from different points meet, instead of uniting, they seek to convince each other mutually that it is they who have discovered the best road, and they sometimes end by throwing insults and stones at each other. Yet they know that one day, provided they never stop ascending, they must all meet at the top of the mountain and that the road to reach it matters little."
—*Lecomte du Noüy*

On the ancient temple walls these words were inscribed: "Man, know thyself!" In order to know himself, man must discover that which is false and that which is true, that which is synthetic and that which is real. Having done this, he can follow the Path that will lead him into all Truth.

Children of the Light, pursue this knowledge and be free! Children of the Light, awake! The day of victory is at hand! The Golden Age is nigh!

Climb the Highest Mountain

BOOK ONE

And I will give power unto my two witnesses, and they shall prophesy a thousand two hundred and threescore days, clothed in sackcloth.

These are the two olive trees, and the two candlesticks standing before the God of the earth.

Revelation

MARK L. PROPHET

ELIZABETH CLARE PROPHET

Climb
the Highest
Mountain

BOOK ONE

The Path of the Higher Self

Mark L. Prophet · Elizabeth Clare Prophet

The Everlasting Gospel

SUMMIT UNIVERSITY ◍ PRESS®

We wish to express our heartfelt gratitude to all who have made possible the publication of this volume—our heavenly Father, our beloved Masters Jesus Christ, Saint Germain, and El Morya; Mother Mary, Archangel Michael, and the hosts of Light without number; our faithful staff, our dedicated co-workers and friends throughout the world, and our patient children:

To all who have stood with us as the sentinels of a new age—a Golden Age of opportunity for the children of the Light—to all now ascended who "loved not their lives unto the death" we say,

Thank You.

And I saw another angel fly in the midst of heaven, having the Everlasting Gospel to preach unto them that dwell on the earth, and to every nation, and kindred, and tongue, and people,

Saying with a loud voice, Fear God, and give glory to him; for the hour of his judgment is come: and worship him that made heaven, and earth, and the sea, and the fountains of waters.

Revelation

Contents

Illustrations

Authors' Message to the Reader

To You Who Would Climb the Highest Mountain:

Ralph Waldo Emerson said, "Truth is the summit of being."[1] We have called that summit God—indeed, the God of all Truth—and it is to that Summit that we would direct your consciousness through the writing in this book.

"No matter what our religion," observed Lecomte du Noüy, "we are all like people at the bottom of a valley who seek to climb a snowy peak that dominates the others. We all have our eyes fixed on the same goal, and we agree that there is but one summit to reach. Unfortunately we differ on what road to take. Guides come forward and we follow them. Some go one way, others choose different paths. All are convinced that their trail is the best, and all are sincere. By following them we approach the one goal, but when the groups which started from different points meet, instead of uniting, they seek to convince each other mutually that it is they who have discovered the best road, and they sometimes end by throwing insults and stones at each other. Yet they know that one day, provided they never stop ascending, they must all meet at the top of the mountain and that the road to reach it matters little."[2]

We uphold, as God does, the right of every man to choose the path he shall take to the Summit of his own being. Although we cannot make the journey for him, we would offer a hand to help him on the way. The climber will need ropes and picks to scale the jagged heights. These we have provided, together with maps and charts to assist him in avoiding the pitfalls and unmarked ways where danger lurks and where those who have "words without knowledge"³ may perish.

Before you embark upon your expedition to the top, it is advisable that you practice the techniques and test the equipment. The helps we present in the following pages have been successfully used by the summiteers who have preceded you. The experts, who are familiar with the markings on the trail, also recommend that you employ a trained guide who is qualified to show you how to overcome the unmerciful elements of wind and cold, ice or broiling sun that greet the climber sphinxlike, unyielding.

No matter what his faith, his creed, or his religion, the seeker can profit from the experience and the know-how of those who have gone before him on the Path. Many look to Jesus as the wayshower; others follow the Eightfold Path of the Buddha or the law of Moses. In the West they have pursued the calling of Saint Francis and Clare, of the Little Flower of Jesus and the Virgin Mother; in the East they hail Maitreya, Lord Krishna, Lao-tse, and Confucius. These and countless others have demonstrated the principles of Truth and left a record of exemplary lives. But whomever the seeker follows, it is results that count! If a man's philosophy does not make him a better man, capable of contributing something of worth to his friends and to his society, then either he or his philosophy has failed.

We may well ask as we look at the world around us, Has Christianity failed or have men failed the

Christ? Our answer would be that men have failed because the complete teachings of the Master of Galilee, of John the Baptist, and of the prophets who preceded them have not been made available to the multitudes. These we must make plain. These we must free from the shroud of dogma. These we must set forth that the day might come which Micah foresaw when every man should sit "under his vine and under his fig tree"[4] to be self-taught by the Great Mediator of the Word.

In your hands is a key—a key that will unlock many doors. No work has ever contained the practical and scientific explanations on the workings of your self and your universe which are to be presented in the volumes of *The Everlasting Gospel.* You will discover how you can work out your salvation not only with "fear and trembling,"[5] as Paul said, but also with the love and dominion of the Christ.

Once you have put together the cosmic jigsaw puzzle—the pieces of which you will find one by one in the thirty-three chapters of the total work—you will possess not only the hieroglyph of living Truth but also the blueprint of your fiery destiny. If you take the Teaching apart piece by piece, making it a smorgasbord of concepts and ideas, you will deprive yourself of the magnificent comprehension of the whole. But if you dare to pursue the totality of the Teaching, you will soon realize the full value of the key.

Some of the facts contained in the writing will be familiar to you; others will not. The elimination of what is known to one reader and not to another would jeopardize the worth of the instruction. The concepts unfold "precept upon precept, line upon line";[6] and if carefully followed, they will lead you to your life's destination. This is your destiny: to realize the divine gnosis, the universal saga of your Being, and to become one with all Life. By following the most up-to-date road map to the Summit of your identity, you will see rising before you the foothills of your own Everest and behind you a cosmic panorama never before beheld by humanity in any age.

You will be shown mysteries[7] that will no longer be mysteries—secrets of the ages that will nevermore be secrets. You will find a linking-together of the whole tapestry of Truth in each multiform part. The glossing over of these parts may well abort the embryonic ideas that are intended to germinate in your consciousness until they unfold the magnificence of your own soul's comprehension of the laws of Cosmos. These laws are made known in signs from far-off worlds, from the Pleiades as well as from the sun of our own solar system, from the sands of the Sahara and the tall pines of Darjeeling.

You will find herein the wisdom of the ages, the thoughts of a Christ, a Buddha, and the many savants and servants of the Word—all of whom are one in the Lord who said, "Other sheep I have, which are not of this fold; them also I must bring, and they shall hear my voice; and there shall be one fold, and one shepherd."[8] You will find knowledge of a different kind—knowledge that has been withheld from the masses, knowledge that has been guarded in the retreats of the Masters for thousands of years. In the words of the Apostle, "We speak the wisdom of God in a mystery, even the hidden wisdom, which God ordained before the world unto our glory."[9]

We are concerned with the coming of the vanguard of Light upon the planetary body, "kings and priests unto God"[10] who have heard the whisperings of the universe in heart and soul, who have brooded with the Great Spirit over the rites of creation—those who have been cast in the cosmic drama, reenacting the ritual of a cosmos, a rose, a cell, or a conception in the Mind of Christ. These are they who are unafraid to involve themselves in Reality and thereby secure the mastery of self, of destiny.

As Diogenes with his lantern roamed the streets in search of an honest man, so we invite you, the reader, to raise the torch of your mind and without bias seek Truth within these pages; for here you will learn the code of your identity, of Nature, and of Life itself. And in the process you will find the power of the Holy Spirit by which each man becomes the king of his own kingdom and the priest of his own temple in response to the fiat of the Logos "Take dominion over the earth!" [11]

Please recognize that we, as Messengers for the spiritual Hierarchy, have been commissioned to speak the unspeakable, to utter the unutterable, and to set forth in writing what no man has written. We have had to make plain in earthly tongue what heretofore has been penned in the tongues of angels. Words consisting of the twenty-six letters of the English alphabet, concepts boxed in by the dictionaries of men—these we have formed into sentences and paragraphs in an attempt to make plain the eternal precepts of Love.

At times feeling inadequate to the task, we have stood before the burning bush and asked our Lord as Moses did: "Behold, when I come unto the children of Israel, and shall say unto them, The God of your fathers hath sent me unto you; and they shall say to me, What is his name? what shall I say unto them?" As God revealed himself to Moses saying, "I AM THAT I AM," so he has said to us, "Thus shalt thou say unto the children of Israel, I AM hath sent me unto you." [12]

And so we have sought to spell out the pathos of a cosmos even as God has sought to create in you the awareness of himself. Not by our own authority, but by the power of the living Word have we spoken the words of the Son of man who said, "Heaven and earth shall pass away: but my words shall not pass away." [13]

Within these seven hundred pages you will discover mandalas of Truth, conceptions from the heart of the Solar Logoi who declared to John: "I AM Alpha and Omega, the beginning and the end. I will give unto him that is athirst of the fountain of the water of Life freely. He that overcometh shall inherit all things; and I will be his God, and he shall be my son." [14]

Through the written word you will be made aware not only of the intellectual concepts of Truth but also of the feelings of those concepts. As the positive and negative aspects of self, as mind and heart, these spell out the whys and wherefores of man's need both to understand and to devote himself to the divine plan and to his reason for being. It would be folly to make the claim that these concepts are confined to these pages; for these were in the very breath of Life itself which in the beginning God breathed into man's nostrils when "man became a living soul." [15]

Your newfound freedom will come not only from the formed but from the unformed as well, not just from what is said but from what remains unsaid. For words are but cups into which the mind must pour the substance of experience and devotion, the distillations of soul-knowing and the formulations that are idling just beneath the surface of awareness waiting to be energized by the Christ Mind.

If by living up to the full measure of your active understanding of Truth you "show yourself approved unto God, a workman that needeth not to be ashamed, rightly dividing the word of Truth," [16] you will expand mankind's consciousness of the Law of Life and serve as an avant-garde messenger of hope to all generations.

The Christ, whom so many proclaim and so few

understand, is not confined to a nation, to a people, or to a person. Christ is the Light emanation, the Solar Logos, the living Word by whom all things were made and without whom was not anything made that was made.[17] You are a fragment of the Lord's Body, a measure of his attainment, destined to be a chalice for his Light that you might give a cup of living water to a humanity waiting to be filled.

The "key of knowledge" which was "taken away"[18] is yours for the knowing. As the scribes and Pharisees lay in wait for Jesus and sought "to catch something out of his mouth, that they might accuse him,"[19] so some will analyze this work with one purpose in mind: to destroy it. Others will take the key and open the door to the Christ who calls: "Behold, I stand at the door, and knock: if any man hear my voice, and open the door, I will come in to him, and will sup with him, and he with me."[20]

Inevitably, the profitable servant will enter into the joy of the Lord and the unprofitable servant will be cast into outer darkness.[21] Those who forsake dogma for Christ, bigotry for love, and ignorance of the Law for wisdom (wise dominion) will find the answers to life's questions which they have long sought. And they will know the dominion of the overcomers: "To him that overcometh will I grant to sit with me in my throne, even as I also overcame, and am set down with my Father in his throne. He that hath an ear, let him hear what the Spirit saith unto the churches."[22]

As the word of God was spoken by Jesus in parable, so the words of *The Everlasting Gospel* are hieroglyphs charged with both an inner and an outer meaning that can change your life and your world into the beauty and perfection which God intended you to manifest. You must take these hieroglyphs and eat them up—assimilate them into your consciousness—as the angel told John to take the little book and eat it up, warning him that it would make his belly bitter, but that it would be in his mouth sweet as honey.[23]

If the prejudices and precepts of the world have kept you from the divine design, then these must be set aside, at least temporarily, while you explore this virgin forest where Truth lies waiting to be acclaimed in towering oak and tiny acorn, in bubbling brook and nodding flower. Instead of comparing each joyous burst of Life you find with the relics of civilization that you have left behind, savor each new concept for its own intrinsic worth; ponder and absorb a new comprehension and a new freedom.

To properly discern Truth, you will have to lay aside your preconceived ideas—even your most cherished beliefs—and give God the opportunity to lead you "in the paths of righteousness for His name's sake."[24] Above all, remember Jesus' words "Whosoever shall not receive the kingdom of God as a little child shall in no wise enter therein."[25]

The enemy of righteousness may seek to impress upon you the need to immediately accept or reject our instruction. Be not mocked! True progress always manifests to those who in patience possess their souls.[26] Therefore, reserve your judgment until you have read the last word of the last chapter.

The purpose of The Summit Lighthouse is to publish the Teachings of the Ascended Masters, to shed light on the lost or distorted Teachings of Christ, and to provide humanity—every man, woman, and child, bar none—with the knowledge of Cosmic Law which, when applied, will lead him to freedom, to self-mastery, to the fulfilling of his divine plan, and to the reunion of his soul with God.

The Summit Lighthouse is not out to capture souls for membership, to tell people what to do and what not to do, or to confine their worship of the one God within the narrowness of man-made doctrine and dogma. The Masters who sponsor this organization seek not to bind men through fear and ignorance, but to lead them through enlightenment on the true path of discipleship where each man gives answer solely to his God.

Pearls of Wisdom are letters written each week by the Ascended Masters to their disciples throughout the world, dictated to us as Messengers appointed by the Lord. They are sent "without money and without price" to all who ask for them. Those who desire systematic and graded instruction in Cosmic Law and who at the same time are willing to dedicate themselves in the service of humanity may receive the Keepers of the Flame Lessons sponsored by Saint Germain, the Knight Commander of the Keepers of the Flame Fraternity, together with the Maha Chohan, the Representative of the Holy Spirit, and the Seven Chohans of the Rays.

The Summit Lighthouse was founded to be an outer arm of the Great White Brotherhood. This spiritual order of Hierarchy is an organization of the Ascended Masters and their disciples united for the highest purposes of the brotherhood of man under the Fatherhood of God. The word *white* refers not to race, but to the white light of the Christ that surrounds the saints and sages of all ages who have risen from every nation to be counted among the immortals.

Thus, The Summit Lighthouse is a fount of the living Word to which the prophet Isaiah called the people saying: "Ho, every one that thirsteth, come ye to the waters, and he that hath no money; come ye, buy, and eat; yea, come, buy wine and milk without money and without price."[27]

On the ancient temple walls these words were inscribed: "Man, know thyself!" In order to know himself, man must discover that which is false and that which is true, that which is synthetic and that which is real. Having done this, he can follow the Path that will lead him into all Truth.

Children of the Light, pursue this knowledge and be free! Children of the Light, awake! The day of victory is at hand! The Golden Age is nigh!

In the service of those who have climbed the highest mountain and those who are beginning the ascent, we remain

Mark L. Prophet

Elizabeth Clare Prophet

Mark and Elizabeth Prophet
for the Darjeeling Council
of the Great White Brotherhood

The Royal Teton Ranch
Thanksgiving Day
November 27, 1986

TELL THEM

Tell them,
Ancient Fires,
How the strata of the rock
Cooled and formed the surface
Of a verdant sphere to be.

Tell them,
Ancient Waters,
Of the coolants of the deep—
Mighty cycles of perfection,
Marine world now we see.

Tell them,
Mighty Atmosphere,
Of blue inspired veil,
Of lacy white cloud cover
Curtained Cosmos does unveil.

Tell them of Creation
That like clockwork telling time
Shows the intricacy of Nature
In a network so sublime.

Tell them of a seedling
Filled with patterned destiny.
Tell them of a cedar tall
That through sunshine was to be.

Tell them of a whisper
That was heard within the soul.
Tell them, Ageless Wisdom,
Nature's blessed goal.

Tell them of Reality
That plays hide and seek with men.
Tell them of a Golden Age
That cometh once again.

Tell them of the Buddha
And of Christ upon the hill.
Tell them Truth, Reality
That hungry souls do fill.

Tell them of electric spark
That flashes 'cross the sky.
Speak of Immortality that cradles our humanity—
That one day none shall die.

Speak of Truth
That out the mouth of Christ did manifest,
That Pilate heard and questioned,
That now in truth is blessed.

Speak it loud and speak it long;
Tell in poetry and song
That tall upon the hills of time
An ageless wisdom now does chime—

Carillon bells from celestial towers
Rung by other hands than ours,
Angel voices chiming in
Raise an anthem now to win.

Tell them how that we who read
Can in faith plant vital seed,
Watch them push their shoots right through
Soil and rock and obstacle too—

Thrusting roots into the earth,
Seeking vital essence' worth
And reaching to the sun to claim
That I AM real in God's own Name!

Tell them, then, that darkest night
Waits the first dawn's early light,
That man may see and catch the thought
That God in truth has to us brought
An opportunity so fair—
An answer to a child's own prayer.

Our Father, help us now to be
Selflessly engraft' in Thee—
That our nature then shall be
Like a father's heart of love;
Seeds from heaven up above
Scattered here in garden fair—
Sun and rain in falling there
Can assist the planned delight
And the victory for the right!

Tell them, Father, Ageless One,
Of Thy Nature's Golden Sun.
Tell them of Thy Name and Spirit!
Tell them so that all may hear it!
Tell them so that none may fear it!
Tell them so that all revere it!
Tell them so that none may lose
Life or gift—that all may choose
Now and without fail to see
That only Truth can ever be
Clad with Immortality.

In the days of the voice of the seventh angel, when he shall begin to sound, the mystery of God should be finished, as he hath declared to his servants the Prophets.

And the voice which I heard from heaven spake unto me again, and said, Go and take the little book which is open in the hand of the angel which standeth upon the sea and upon the earth.

And I went unto the angel, and said unto him, Give me the little book. And he said unto me, Take it, and eat it up; and it shall make thy belly bitter, but it shall be in thy mouth sweet as honey.

And I took the little book out of the angel's hand, and ate it up; and it was in my mouth sweet as honey: and as soon as I had eaten it, my belly was bitter.

Revelation

Chapter One
Your Synthetic Image

Your Synthetic Image

But there went up a mist from the earth, and watered the whole face of the ground. And the LORD God formed man of the dust of the ground, and breathed into his nostrils the breath of Life; and man became a living soul.   *Genesis*

Because that, when they knew God, they glorified him not as God, neither were thankful; but became vain in their imaginations, and their foolish heart was darkened. Professing themselves to be wise, they became fools, and changed the glory of the uncorruptible God into an image made like to corruptible man.   *Romans*

AN ALLEGORY

ONCE UPON A TIME the synthetic image of you was created, and darkness moved upon its face. Yet the Spirit of God-*Good* was the vital energy used to create its very shadowed form. Darkness veiled the radiant face of the Light within, and your synthetic image came into existence and moved upon the human sea. The counterfeit likeness waxed strong and took dominion over the earth. Its patterns became accepted as natural, and the way to the paradise of true happiness was almost entirely lost and forgotten.

With the veiling of the divine radiance in flesh and the coming into prominence of shadowed illusion, an unfortunate event took place: the Real became progressively ethereal and took on the quality of the unreal, until at last its wondrous tones seemed but muffled echoes coming from the corridors of ancient memory; whereas the unreal took on body and substance, and illusion filled the mind and consciousness of man.

Whirling electrons, dancing in joyous freedom within the body cells, became fixed as orbiting planets around nuclei suns in miniature systems. Alas, these sparks of individuality were imprisoned in imperfect matrices, and the atomic structure of man no longer mirrored the splendor of the true, the free, and the brave. Instead, a dense molecular abortion came into being which, although fearfully and wonderfully organized, was, in effect, but a systematized miasma of matter.

The human diorama became a microcosmic nightmare interspersed with periods of joyful ecstasy 'neath the sun and blue sky, midst the verdure of the earth. The minds and feelings of men were now full of fleeting phantoms—flashes of crimson emotion, the blackness of despair. And the disciplines of the cult of achievement were legion.

The patterns of human experience were locked in a long chain of events leading through stages of infancy, childhood, adolescence, and adult years. The pressures of environment continued to mold and shape the personal personality. Home, school, church, and nation, parents, teachers, and friends—all exerted their influences upon the plastic nature of the evolving soul.

Subtle inner pressures were also at work. At subliminal levels the individual came into contact with the mental musings of the great and the small, the debased and the exalted. The outreach of the subconscious mind was far greater than man ever knew; and while he wandered in a maze of whirling impressions, the problems of his existence amid the social complexities of life became more and more intricate. According to the law that like attracts like, minds attuned with minds whose frequencies were akin to their own. Thus, the rich became richer, the poor became poorer, and the depressed entered new lows of depression.

The cumulative thoughts and feelings of mankind all too frequently caused the individual to gravitate toward the negative, and it became easier for him to descend in a downward spiral than to ascend toward the Light. Meanwhile, heavenly bodies and solar orbs banded together in fixed wonder of the cosmic plan. In contrast to the vast simplicity of stellar design, the individual's own internal sense of struggle created the complexity that was a friction of worlds within worlds against worlds that were without. And the truism was so true: we had nothing to fear but fear itself.

Freedom, or escape, as some called it, from all of the binding, blinding worries of day-to-day existence was sought in a change of scenery, travel, new climate, new clothes, or new acquaintances. But the only permanent change that ever took place in anyone was that which was wrought by a permanent change of thought.

The Quest for Reality

We shall attempt in this volume to weave a tapestry of life—your life—and to provide viable answers to those questions that everyone has asked at least once: Who am I? Where did I come from? Where am I going? How do I go about getting there?

We all came forth from the Source of Oneness, and to it we shall all one day return—with or without our individuality. But at this point in time we see neither the beginning nor the end of our existence. Both are remote in the distant past and future.

Having lost the perspective of both shores, we try to fashion meaning out of relativity. Actors on a stage, playing many roles, we are no longer able to distinguish "the real me." We make merry and join clubs, playing the games people play; and if we dare to think, we attempt to find a rationale for our weltanschauung which at best is incomplete. Then, when we think we have found the logic of "the way," we close our minds to all other interpretations, dismissing them as heresy.

We become so insulated by the contraptions of a synthetic society and the convictions of our own minds that we have no link to Reality, hence no means of escape. We have forgotten our wondrous origin and our glorious destiny. We grovel in the dark; we continue in the rounds of a senseless existence; we ask, "Why?" Many voices with many answers fail utterly to satisfy our soul's longing for Truth.

We go to bed at night, we dream, and when we awaken we are relieved that "it was only a dream." We have no remorse for the unreal. We dismiss it and we go on. Thus we distinguish the night from the day. But we fail to realize that there is a synthetic world that is also a dream from which we must one day awaken. What's more, the transition from unreality to Reality will be just as natural as our awakening from an unpleasant dream.

Much of the world's knowledge we may do without, especially in an age of increasing specialization. As individuals we can be quite content without having the slightest idea of how an atom is split, what makes our TVs and electrical appliances function, our cars run, satellites orbit, or rockets escape the pull of gravity. Whether or not the moon is made of green cheese is, after all, not a question of life and death.

We can survive without the knowledge of such complexities, but can we survive without the knowledge of Reality? Little do we know how necessary to our everyday life is the faculty of discrimination—the ability to distinguish the Real from the unreal. Without it, it is impossible to determine our beginning or our end. Light and Darkness, white and black, Good and Evil—where does one leave off and the other begin?

We may do all things, but we will never reach the shores of immortal Life until we have mastered this art. Others may build our homes, service our cars, manage our finances, treat our ailments, and spoil us with gadgets, but no one in heaven or on earth can fulfill our destiny for us. This we must do by ourselves, each man with his God; for He—call him Infinite Intelligence, Divine Love, or Science, if you will—is essential to the plan.

It is vital that we have in hand accurate knowledge of the laws governing our destiny. For only with the knowledge of the Law can we develop the ability to distinguish the Real from the unreal, to wield the Flaming Two-Edged Sword, and to answer the question that has been asked a thousand times, What is Truth? Once we have this knowledge and its attendant skill, Life is ours to command; Principle is ours to apply. Love is there waiting to be realized, and we become progressively more real as we behold Reality.

We offer this work to those who are tired of the long sojourn in the rapids of a half-real existence, to those who would get on with the journey, to those who have the courage to approach the jagged rocks of Truth, though the ship of unworthy concepts be dashed into pieces. They know it is possible to reach the Shore while the tides and the winds are in their favor; they remember the words that beckon them onward and the Poet who stands upon the Shore, waiting to throw the line with a mighty heave of welcome:

> Onward, courage!
> Then blame not the Bard
> When the wind and the gale
> Sweep o'er the moor
> And bow down the sail,
> For the ship shall move on
> And the Port be obtained
> If the courage be high
> And the will be maintained!

THE SOUL: A LIVING POTENTIAL

God is a Spirit and the soul is the living potential of God. The soul's demand for free will and its separation from God resulted in the descent of this potential into the lowly estate of the flesh. Sown in dishonor, the soul is destined to be raised in honor to the fullness of that God-estate which is the one Spirit of all Life. The soul can be lost; Spirit can never die.

> Never the Spirit was born;
>   the Spirit shall cease to be never;
> Never was time it was not;
>   End and Beginning are dreams!
> Birthless and deathless and changeless
>   remaineth the Spirit for ever;
> Death hath not touched it at all,
>   dead though the house of it seems![1]

The soul, then, remains a fallen potential that must be imbued with the Reality of Spirit, purified through prayer and supplication, and returned to the glory from which it descended and to the unity of the Whole. This rejoining of soul to Spirit is the alchemical marriage which determines the destiny of the self and makes it one with immortal Truth. When this ritual is fulfilled, the highest Self is enthroned as the Lord of Life and the potential of God, realized in man, is found to be the All-in-all.

"God hopes for the soul," the Ascended Master Kuthumi (whose most beloved Christian embodiment was that of Saint Francis of Assisi) once wrote to his followers. "Man must identify with the hopes of God. And then, as the tolling of a great bell, the death knell of the finite self will make no mournful sound; but it will sing to the soul in cadences of immortality. Through these cadences man shall come to understand the golden meaning of Reality, and the revelation of worlds unknown shall also be his own. Stretching as an endless column of beautiful trees, the landmarks of the Real point the way from present circumstances to the very footstool of Reality, the rainbow of ascendancy, the Spirit Most Holy where man is crowned with the Life that is God."[2]

The allegory of the synthetic image has become a way of life for millions of souls caught in the labyrinth of a mass accumulation of their own synthetic creations. They do not know that their thoughts and feelings are clothed with the realities that they have given them; they have not thought upon the words of the scribe "As a man thinketh in his heart, so is he."[3]

It is true that the unreal is often made to appear real, while that which is genuine and sustaining is relegated to the background of life, often stereotyped as charlatanism, cultism, or heresy. Moreover, the crystal-clear realities of the universal Mind are weighed down by dogma and doctrine and ridiculed by the popular people of the day.

In the synthetic society the blind leaders of the blind perpetuate a fraudulent existence and receive therefore the scathing denunciation of the Christ:

"Woe unto you, lawyers! for ye have taken away the key of knowledge: ye entered not in yourselves, and them that were entering in ye hindered!"[4]

Since the "slaying of the Lamb from the foundation of the world,"[5] the "scribes and pharisees" have barricaded man's progress by their cunning hypocrisy. They have not afforded man his rightful freedom to think, to believe, and to create; neither have they opened the door to his understanding of the universe and its fathomable mysteries.

And so the LORD has sent his prophets and servant-sons and commanded them saying, "Comfort ye, comfort ye my people. . . . Prepare ye the way of the LORD, make straight in the desert a highway for our God."[6]

While man carries on his mundane affairs, the soul within cries out for Truth as a beggar in the street. Its pleas are seldom heeded by the outer mind that rushes madly to and fro, fulfilling the patterns of an existence it has not defined. And so the soul is left to starve until one day the din of life recedes; the self, no longer entranced by the glamour of the world, looks around for the beggar in the street and sees standing in his place an old man with a shepherd's crook pointing to an alley somehow not seen before.

Pausing a moment to eye the curious figure, the self turns and follows the way. "No different from a hundred other side streets in the city—why did he send me here?" Suddenly at the far end atop the hill he notices a door; his pace quickens as he approaches nigh. There is a stirring from within his soul, and then a rustling from behind the door. Excitedly, expectantly, almost ecstatically he cries out:

> What is this pearly door before which I stand?
> Is this some realm of dream
> Where lurks a shadowed band?

Nay, for that face I see so clearly now,
Peeping out from behind the open door,
Is an angel face
That I have known in long ago before.

Reflecting upon his departure from Reality, he realizes how far the soul must go to regain that God-awareness it once knew:

My thoughts slid down the finite spout
And all the light of hope went out—
The rope I broke
And fear of icy desolation seized me round
'Til I was then completely bound
In all delusions' cords and vanities.

Now once again I rise,
Pulsation toward the skies
Where God and home as fires of love do glow,
Renewing courses raised to Sources
All divine.

My soul begins again to climb
The stairway ladder where
Each meaning comes
So tender, sweet, and pure—
It makes me to know
That God's own plan secure
Will hold me when the world
Seems nigh to fall apart.

For after all there is but one great heart
Which beats our own,
And we must rise to fairer realms
Where we atone,
At one with all that really lives;
For paradise is Life that gives
Nobility of efforts just
To counteract the concept of the dust

From which God did make in hope
A living soul—
And through the fragrant mists
Reveals the Goal
Of paradise to come.[7]

The understanding of the living potential of the soul—where to find it, how to recognize it when you find it, how to amplify its powers for good—all of this and much more can be found in the Teachings of the Ascended Masters, those saints and sages of all time who have successfully passed the tests of life, and whose souls have regained that living potential with which every man and woman was also endowed.

Having graduated from the schoolrooms of experience in this world, these masterful Spirits are rejoined with the Image of Reality; and they stand with the elder brother of the race, the Lord Jesus, ready to assist from exalted heights those who have not yet pierced the veil of the synthetic image. To them we owe our own souls' illumination and the wisdom of this little book. Through them you, too, can discover the Truth that waits beyond the veil even while you solve the dilemma of the synthetic image.

"In the seeming struggle between Good and Evil," the Master Meru of the Andes said, "there are negative forces that seek to hide from the eyes of man his Real Image and to glorify the pseudoimage. This they do in order that they may control men by warping their motives and by surrounding them with fear. But the key to escape is simple.

"You must understand first that the image* that appears is not real; second, that the Image that does not readily appear but that *is* real is often hidden; and third, that this hidden Image is the Image that God

image, from the Latin *imitari* 'to imitate': a reproduction or imitation of the form of a person or thing; esp. an imitation in physical form.

did make and that he saw was good. The subtle forces of the serpent that roam the planet—whether they act through a fraudulent theology, through psycho-political treachery, or through an invasion of the minds of men, producing obsessions—will continue to down-grade the individual by amplifying his supposed or actual errors; and they will continue to seek to hide the beautiful Image of God in whose likeness each man was made."[8]

The manipulations of these forces will continue only so long as man identifies with the synthetic consciousness. Therefore, in order to escape the foe without, man must conquer the foe within. The latter is identified as man's synthetic, or false, image of himself; the former is the synthetic society he has created based upon the vain imaginings he sees mirrored in the synthetic image.

THE DETHRONING OF THE SYNTHETIC IMAGE

The foreground of your life is the screen of your conscious awareness; your attention is the lever which selects and directs the images that are projected upon the screen. These make up the composite that people identify as the real you, saying, "This is your life," when it is not at all; for the synthetic you, made in the image of mortality, is never the Real You—the being who affirms, "I AM."

The synthetic you is accustomed to making such statements as "I am sick," "I am tired," "I am poor," "I am lonely." These claims synthesize the unreal you and give rise to those soul-hampering conditions which are never true of the Real Self, who would not and could not utter such binding blasphemy. It is ever the synthetic masquerader—the impostor, the counter-feiter of the Real Man—who thus affirms, whose habit patterns are composed on the one hand of the false reasoning of the carnal mind and on the other of the emotional torrents that flood the mainstream of the race consciousness.

The crude menagerie of thoughts and feelings spawned in the subconscious minds of the populace forms a mass entity whose name is Legion.[9] A synthesis of synthetic images, this entity is stamped out of the mold of the mass effluvia. Conforming to the lowest common denominator of the human consciousness, this legion is incapable, by reason of its origin, of paying allegiance to the natural perfection of the universe and its immutable laws. This conglomerate glob of nightmarish energies is the betrayer of each lifestream and of the divine plan for this earth, and it has delayed the spiritual fruition of the golden age, long envisioned by men and angels.

Deliverance from the hordes of darkness must come first to the individual before it can come to the planet as a whole. And each man must win his own freedom by disengaging his consciousness—his thoughts and his feelings—from the unbalanced and chaotic forces of mass conformism which are ready at any moment to sweep him into the undercurrents of fear, depression, obsession, mental confusion, and emotional insanity. When the individual makes an about-face to challenge the synthetic image, it seems as though he is confronting the entire world. And so he is, for in the synthetic society, the Real is no longer seen for what it is, but as the figment of some men's imaginations; and he who aligns himself with the Real finds his enemies to be of this world and his allies to be of the next.

Here in the mainstream of planetary life, the power of the various communications media to mold public opinion and to keep alive the synthetic image is almost total. Books, magazines, newspapers, television, radio, theater, and movies exert a tremendous influence over the minds of men, controlling their tastes, their morals, their fads, and even their politics in the manner of a mass hypnosis. Rightly used, such media can assist man's spiritual as well as his material development; but wrongly used, they can become a monster of sadistic creation, threatening to reduce the individual to an animal and civilization to an "animal farm."

Whereas the molding factors of life, including the artifacts of science, ought to be a slave creation obediently serving their creator, man, the reverse has been the case. Man has been made the slave not only of the atomic age but also of his environment and of his inherited traits and attitudes. The synthetic image has dethroned the Real Man and now stands in the place of his master. This is the "abomination of desolation," prophesied by Daniel, "which standeth in the holy place where it ought not." [10] Thus has it been well spoken of the relationship between God and man, "Thou art the potter, I am the clay"; but too often we have made it to read, "I, the potter, and Thou, the clay." [11]

Because of the existence of so many conflicting centers of influence and the attendant pressures that these exert upon the human psyche, the type of life that is presently being lived upon earth and the quality of consciousness that registers in the minds of its people do not reflect the true purpose of life as it was planned by the Creator. At a dizzying pace these influences present to souls young and old a kaleidoscope of synthetic thoughts and feelings composed of the conscious and unconscious creations of the mass mind. Certainly this is not the Reality which you were intended to be and which inwardly the soul knows that you are—for that portion of you which was created in the Divine Image always knows who "I AM."

There is a cure for the synthetic image, but its discovery is dependent upon the recognition by each person of the environmental and hereditary factors that must be counteracted ere the Real Image can appear.

"The only way out is through the door of Reality," advises Meru, who has parted the veil for the sixth root race at his retreat at Lake Titicaca. "This is the escape hatch which has been provided so that the body of destructivity created by man's own negativity can be transmuted and overcome. As long as men remain involved in the ego, no matter what religious study they undertake, no matter what devotion they temporarily manifest, no matter how many good works they do, no matter what level of striving they attain, they will never be free from the illusion of the self that pursues them as a wanton ghost of struggling identity.

"Only when they escape through the door (I AM the door) into the understanding that the eternal Being of God is the 'doer,' into the realization that God can act in them to remove hampering influences, to transmute their darkness, and to translate their consciousness from Darkness into Light, will they begin to know the freedom of the self [soul] to achieve without limit.

"Let all see and know for all eternity that the not-self, the shadowed-self, the named-self, the personality-self, is and always has been the snare of the ego, and that the man or woman who lives in that consciousness must die in it. There is no possibility for flesh and blood to inherit eternal Life.[12] Men seek eternal Life because it is their true nature, the nature of God and of the Divine Image. Eternal Life is formed independently of the vehicle of self through the process of translation, that man should no longer see death but be translated into that Life which is the Divine Nature.

"The statement that man should die daily[13] to the finite, egoistic self must be followed by another—that he should live daily to the progressive glory of his eternal Self and the apprehending of all the Reality which that Self can and does bring. This is the Sun we face that casts no shadow.

"This concept is far more than an index of words. It is a flow of the vital seed-idea into the consciousness of man whereby the consciousness itself is transformed into its natural glowing Presence. This is the Presence of God which identifies the individual, through his sense of expanding Reality, with the universal consciousness of God, yet never takes from him one erg of his energy or of his true selfhood."[14]

THE ENTHRONING OF THE REAL IMAGE

Having realized through honest reckoning the truth about the synthetic image, everyone that is born of God should determine to dethrone all the potentates that masquerade as his Real Self and to enthrone in their place the image of Truth that man is intended to be—the manifestation of the Divine Nature.

The scriptures record that God made man in his own "image and likeness" and, further, that he saw the creation which he had made and beheld it as "very good."[15] This creation which God hath made is your Real Self. It is that inner lodestone of goodness and perfection, that archetypal pattern of the Infinite which is intended to mold the outer form and consciousness in the divine likeness ordained by God.

Your Real Self is the permanent atom of your identity, the rock of ages that remains unmoved by the restless tides of life. It is the wholly natural man who

came forth from God, eternally vibrant and pure as a
ray of Light from the heart of the Sun. Your Real Self
is your conscience, which speaks its own name with
the voice of authority and does thereby honor the
name of God, I AM.

One cannot deny that in contrast to the Real
there is an overwhelming manifestation of unreality
upon this planet; and yet, it would be folly to affirm
that mortal error has permanence, for its temporary
existence stems solely from mass acceptance in the
minds of men. All should recognize that the vacuum
we call darkness, which blankets interstellar space, is
but an absence of Light—that virgin territory which is
our opportunity to expand the kingdom. All should
realize that Darkness can also be a misqualification of
Light, and as such it forms the *energy-veil* we call *evil.*
Thus all should see that in Light is the Presence of
God-Good. Therefore, evil cannot declare with valid-
ity, "I AM"; for evil is a transitory shadow that must
pass away. It is the counterfeit of the Life that is God;
it is *live* spelled backwards.

While we can say that darkness is the absence of
Light, we cannot say that error is the absence of Truth.
Error is a misqualification of Truth just as evil is a misqualification of Light. Jesus' statement "If the Light
that is in thee be Darkness, how great is that Darkness!"[16] tears the mask from the synthetic image and
points out man's tendency to misqualify the Light that
is in him.

The lie of the serpent, or carnal, mind lends cre-
dence to error by creating dogmas and then saying,
"Fall down and worship me."[17] Thus, error is founded
upon the darkness of a self-centered existence and
must be uprooted by scientific investigation as well
as by progressive revelation. In every age man must

rediscover Truth and thereby be renewed; "for now we see through a glass, darkly; but then face to face: now I know in part; but then shall I know even as also I am known." [18]

Only the Light of man's being—the *Christos*—can stand in the Presence of God and affirm Truth. The claims of evil are annihilated by the power of Truth which affirms—for all to hear, to know, and to be—the Reality of perfection's image. The statement "I AM Good" refers to the power of God who created man to be the perfection which God is, the power that conveys happiness and grace to those who acknowledge Truth and bow their knees to the supremacy of the Divinity within.

As the consciousness of man is disconnected from the sense that he is the doer, there is a diminishing of the power of the human ego and a corresponding increase of the power of the Light of Reality within the individual. The statement "I AM the door" shows that the God within must be the only acting (and activating) power in man. When the dynamic, spiritually regenerative act of affirming "I (the lesser self) and my Father (the I AM—the Greater Self) are one" is accomplished, the Presence of God can take dominion in the life of the individual and restore the law of grace and truth to its rightful place.

As John the Baptist spake concerning Christ, "He must increase, but I must decrease," [19] so the power of God, when invoked by the individual who understands that God is the doer, the arbiter of his destiny, increases the potential of his life until the whole man begins to express the greater reality of his original Self. This is the breaking-down of the partition between man and God. [20] This is the dethroning of the synthetic image and the fulfilling of the ancient Mosaic law

"Thou shalt have no other gods before Me,"[21] written in the Book of Life as "Thou shalt not place the synthetic image before My infinite Reality."

When the power of God, the Almighty I AM Presence, is enthroned as the governing authority for the individual's every act, he is freed from the synthetic image. His consciousness is transformed until he can stand as Moses did on the desert of Sinai (which depicts the wasteland of the synthetic human consciousness) and there behold the bush which is aflame but not consumed.[22] This phenomenon teaches that Nature herself outlasts the synthetic image in almost infinite degrees, for the bush remains long after it has turned to dust.

The Flame that is God imparts the knowledge that behind the visible creation is the essential spark of Life which comes forth from the Creator and must be claimed by each of his servant-sons. Man, standing in awe of the Creator and the creation, takes off his shoes from his feet, symbolizing his recognition of the omnipotence of Truth that speaks out of Spirit's own essence and declares, "I AM THAT I AM."[23]

The first commandment, paraphrased by Jesus when he said, "Be ye therefore perfect, even as your Father which is in heaven is perfect,"[24] reminds us that no man should honor another above the Divine Presence which is within him. For the Presence is the inner guiding Light which will lead him through the wilderness of human thought and the maze of bewildering experience into the promised land of spiritual opportunity. Here the soul is fattened on the heavenly manna of divine Truth in the joyous seeking of a universally scientific Creator and creation; and man, by his God-given creativity, evolves through the Christic Light toward oneness with Reality.

THE WAY OF LOVE

From Love I came, to Love I go;
And all this swing both to and fro
Alters not any jot
Of cosmic purpose I forgot.

I reach out now, to Truth I vow;
To Love in all I ever bow.
The universe is one alone—
No clash of multifacet tone.

The chime I hear is ever near;
'Tis Love that casts out every fear.
Where'er I AM Thy Love lives too
To free the many and the few.

Command perfection, Love's great Law!
Command perfection, Love's great Light!
Thy glowing beauty through the night
As Star eternal, Light supernal,
Woos us all by present might.

For Love I AM and Love I live;
This is the allness that I give.
To each Manchild the spark is given—
'Twill rend the veil and bring to heaven.

Chapter Two

Your Real Image

Your Real Image

*And God shall wipe away all tears from their
eyes; and there shall be no more death, neither
sorrow, nor crying, neither shall there be any more
pain: for the former things are passed away.*
Revelation

THE LIGHT EMANATION OF ETERNAL PURPOSE

IN THE BEGINNING the Real Image of you was created
and Light gave it birth! This Light was the only begotten of the Father, full of grace and truth. This Light
was the Christ by whom all things were made, the
emanation of eternal purpose, the Son radiance from
the heart of Cosmos.

> The heavenly Image is the thought
> God used as blueprint plan,
> As architectural demand upon the universe
> To fabricate and design
> A perfect man, a holy sign,
> Symbol of the Flame encased in form,
> The dual Paraclete reborn.
> As Holy Spirit manifest in men,
> This is the visit of our God again
> To world that 'waits the dawn.[1]

The fires of creation burned brightly on that memorable day when, born out of the flaming consciousness of the Creator, the spirit of man danced for joy and the morning stars sang together. The fiat of the Almighty rang clear: Go forth, sons and daughters of the infinite Mind, Go forth to fulfill thy immortal destiny!

It was God-Good whose vital energy revealed the glowing face of his potential, as billions of Spirit-sparks spiraled through Cosmos,* trailing clouds of glory and chanting, "Lo, I AM come to do thy will, O God!"[2] And so the Spirit of man was born, and so God was borne in man, and so the soul descended into form and took dominion over the earth.[3]

Contemplating the wonder of its origin and its fiery destiny, the soul hears the triumph of the ages echoing in the sweet symphony of the Father-Mother God: "I AM Alpha and Omega, the Beginning and the End."[4] Contacting the rejuvenating cycles of the very center of Being, the soul is infused with a new burst of Life! Apprehending the flame of its internal greatness, like unto the Flame from whence it came, it no longer fears immersion in the baptismal font of the sacred fire. Nay, it pursues total identification with God and the universe.

Suspended within the dimensions of time and space, the soul touches Reality; and body and mind are electrified with a burst of light and holy awe. Beholding past, present, and future—as though standing atop the moving train of life—the truth dawns upon the outer mind: the living potential of the soul is not related to name, to genealogy, to flesh and blood, or even to the world to which it is tethered. The humble as well as the great can possess it. Those of lowly

*When capitalized, *Cosmos* means the totality of the Spirit-Matter universes, the All of God manifest and unmanifest in whom we live and move and have our being.

and high estate can "mount up with wings as eagles"[5] and win their immortality.

The dominant aspect of the Spirit is its universal availability. The Spirit enlivens the soul and enables each Life expression to come forth from the tomb of the synthetic image and to live. Wherever there is a receptive heart—a receiving center, an identity that can relate a universe within to a universe without— there Spirit makes contact and rushes in to fill the chalice of being with light, energy, and hope. This is the theme of immortal Life to which the soul is the rightful heir.

"I AM come that all might have Life, and that they might have it more abundantly!"[6] This statement of cosmic purpose gains meaning for the individual— wherever he is, whoever he is—as he realizes that the abundance of his life consists not of the things of the world that he possesses.[7] It is enough to know that God has made him. His Father is the Eternal One who stretched forth the Pleiades, whose harmony fills all space and turns the radiant spheres in their appointed rounds. He is a son of God; and as long as he is willing to claim his identity through the Real Image, he will know what it means to live in the consciousness of Reality and to be a "joint heir with Christ."[8]

"I AM come that all might have Life, and that they might have it more abundantly!" The fiat of the Master Jesus is intended to be fulfilled in every part of Life. As universes expand, the sons and daughters of God increase the abundant Life, apprehending the Real Image and evolving thereby the microcosmic kingdom.

By cosmic law the offspring of the Most High are intended to experience the abundant Life—to experience the abundant consciousness of God-Good expressed in myriad orbs which, like themselves, are also made in His image and likeness. As their sensitivity to

the Real Image of other sons and daughters of the
Flame heightens (simultaneously as their empathy with
the synthetic image lessens), the joy of universal sharing, of mutual givingness, is discovered; and souls
become one with each other, even as they are one with
Him in the abundant Life.

With feet upon the ground and hands reaching
for the stars, the soul, attuned to its fiery destiny, is
filled with the love of cosmic purpose. There is meaning to life: it will find the way; it will discover the master
plan; it will come to know the why, the whence, the
wherefore. With a sigh of relief and a glow of gratitude
for just being, it lifts a mighty prayer to the Infinite:

> LORD God of Hosts, LORD God of Hosts—
> Thou who hast strung out the Pleiades
> And gladdened eyes of little child—
> The wise and foolish all are Thine,
> The cruel and the mild;
> There is no greater urge or goal
> Than holding freedom in the soul
> Of all the world and every man!
>
> Let us do, then, what we can
> And daily make an effort greater;
> By God's great love let all walk straighter
> On the Path as Freedom's friends—
> Beauteous hearts who will defend
> Value line and worthy mission
> By the power of Christ-decision.
>
> Christ before me, light my way!
> Christ behind me all the day!
> Christ above me as I pray!
> Christ within me lives today!
>
> Freedom's flame where'er He goes—
> Holy Spirit, like a rose
> Opening its tiny bud;

Its scent releases all Thy love
And hallows mind and being all—
By Love's great service
For which I call.[9]

THE SPIRIT: BIRTHLESS, DEATHLESS, ETERNAL

According to the record in the Book of Genesis, man was created in the image of God. If God is a Spirit and man was made in his image, then man is also a Spirit, pure and holy in his sight. Like his Creator, he has both conscious self-awareness and unlimited cosmic potential; and, like his Creator, he is able to reach the realm of the miraculous.

The destiny of the real man, therefore, cannot be aught but spiritual. Possessing the latent Cosmic Consciousness of the One in whose likeness he was made, man is truly blessed with immortal opportunity. One with his Creator, he is omnipresent, omniscient, and omnipotent. Ever in contact at inner levels of his being with all others who were also made in the image of immortal Spirit, he is yet involved in the ritual of becoming, through his mastery over the cycles of time and space in Matter.

Whereas the soul is the living potential of God which man by his intelligent use of free will can immortalize, the Spirit is that permanent atom of Being which is birthless, deathless, and eternal. While man may lose his soul and become a castaway,[10] the Spirit is inviolate—birthless in the sense that it had preexistence in the Mind of God even before it separated from the Great Fiery Ovoid; deathless in that its identity is preserved as an individualized focus of the Flaming One that never dies; eternal in that it is forever an idea in the Mind of God.

The soul is a drop in the vast ocean of Being, a cell in the Body of God. The Spirit-spark that ignited its potential was endowed with the Life-giving Image of the Divine One and contains the creative potential of its Source. Thus the soul came forth from the Spirit to preserve in form the geometric energies of a higher world unsung.

"The Ocean could have chosen to remain the Ocean; but, by separating the tiny luminous drop from the Whole and holding it up to the glorious rays of the sun of illumination, a new ocean was begun. And so the individual consciousness was given dominion over his own world. And so man, made in the image of his Creator, also became a creator."[11] Why creation "in the beginning," if not to evolve the Creator's intent? Why destiny, if not that Deity be established in you? Why man, the manifestation, if not to become all that God is?

Long ago the Master Jesus declared himself to be the Son of God, and truly he was. The Sadducees and the Pharisees found fault with his statement, saying, "He blasphemes!" Jesus did not remain silent on this issue. He spoke to them with the authority of the Law, "If he [Moses] called them gods to whom the word of God came, and the scripture cannot be broken, say ye of him, whom the Father hath sanctified and sent into the world, Thou blasphemest, because I said, I AM the Son of God?"[12]

Through communion with his Real Image, Jesus was able to acknowledge his oneness with his Source— even as the everlasting stream that issues from the fountain of Life sings all the day, "I and my Father are one! I and my Father are one! I and my Father are one!" Through this intimate awareness of his own Real Image—that Spirit of the living God, that essential Identity of every man and woman which makes all one under the canopy of Christ—Jesus was also aware of your Real Image.

Yes! The Son of God who declared, "Before Abraham was, I AM,"[13] also knew your own Divine

Identity that existed before the worlds were framed; and he was not afraid to proclaim it for you and for all—yea, to give his very life, if necessary, in order that the Real Image might live.

> You are a child of the Light,
> You were created in the Image Divine,
> You are a child of Infinity,
> You dwell in the veils of time,
>   You *are* a Son of the Most High!
>
> I AM is the name of the Father,
> I AM is the name of the Son,
> I AM is the Spirit Most Holy—
> Ye all are clothed by the One.
>
> He will guide and guard you forever,
> He will carry you far in his arm,
> He hides himself from the clever,
> He enshrines the poor with his charm.
>
> God lives in your soul, the image of Self—
> To know it will change your view.
> God lives in the Light that shines from within,
> He breaks his bread with the few.
>
> He hears our calls and answers,
> His love is the Light of men.
> Accept, then, his understanding—
> Your wonderful way to win.
>
> I AM is the name you must call on—
> 'Tis Being so broad and true.
> For the narrow confinements of selfhood
> Can only hide from view
>
> The Face of Forever in heaven
> Unfolding within the soul.
> His bread is the precious leaven
> To raise us all to our goal.[14]

The true teachings of Christ restore the soul to its lost estate, to its rightful place in the cosmic peerage of the sons and daughters of God. They free man from the shackles of a false theology that weighs him down with the weight of sin. In the chambers of the night where death is sweet relief and misericord the arm of fate, a single ray of hope filters through the darkened sky: the Angel of Deliverance trumpets no mournful cry, but the prolonged note of victory for each one. And the shell is broken—the degradation of that serpentine lie "In sin did my mother conceive me." [15]

Man has not correctly understood the immaculate concept that relates each conception in reality to the Divine. "That holy thing which shall be born of thee shall be called the Son of God" [16] is also spoken to each mother and father who can accept the injunction of the Most High as their opportunity to become cocreators with divine Perfection, thus sharing in the joy felt by Mary as the Mother of one whose glory was of "the only begotten of the Father, full of grace and truth," [17] immaculately held in heart and mind. Through the understanding of the immaculate conception of the sons and daughters of God, each man and each woman can raise high his head to behold the Sun glory from whence he came. Each pilgrim on the shore of life can look up and live.

Let the condemnation of the father of lies be upon his own head and upon his own generation! "As for me and my house, we will serve the LORD." [18]

Man's origin is in God. Where, then, original sin? Only in the synthetic image that is no more. There is no sin in the generation of the sons and daughters of God. There is no shame in the regeneration of the soul and the soaring of the Spirit from the center of God's Being to the periphery of universal manifestation. As in heaven the Father-Mother God brought forth their firstborn Son, the Christ, the Real Image in you all, so on earth the son of God comes forth through father-mother flames who await in veils of flesh the coming of the first ray of the dawn.

> Life in heaven and on earth
> Is sacred still;
> Life, the Spirit of God, his worth,
> Does work his will.
>
> Where'er the radiance of his Flame
> Does kindle spark,
> Cosmic arrow's aim
> Heightens Perfection's mark.
>
> Spirit endows creative love
> To sweetly flow—
> No thought the image mar Above
> Nor here below.
>
> For Life's sacred bark
> Sails on forever free,
> And none shall break the arc
> Of our blest liberty.

GOD THE MACROCOSM, MAN THE MICROCOSM

Individual life is the doorway to the Infinite. Thus the admonishment was written on the ancient temple walls: "Man, know thyself!"—which is to say, "Man, know thy Self as God!" To know the Real Self is to know God—God, not as the tyrant that so many dread, that some have forsaken and others have proclaimed as dead, but God as the *Geometry of Divinity* (G-O-D), the Geometry of *your* Divinity.

The control of consciousness leads to the knowledge of Self, and the knowledge of Self leads to greater and greater control of consciousness. Such control must necessarily involve the discipline of mind and heart as well as the harnessing of one's energies. This is accomplished through the correct apprehension of your Real Self, which may also be called the *Superconscious Ego.* The relationship of the Superconscious Ego to the ego, which yet identifies with the synthetic image, depends, therefore, upon one's acquaintance with the Real Self. "Acquaint now thyself with him, and be at peace: [19] . . . that ye may know that I AM LORD [that the I AM is the LORD]." [20] In our examination of Reality, then, let us first consider this relationship of the Superconscious Ego to the ego.

Just as it appeared to Kipling that "East is East, and West is West, and never the twain shall meet," [21] so it seems there is no meeting ground between the Superconscious Ego and the ego, between the Real Image and the synthetic image. Yet both are present in man until the hour of his perfectionment when he experiences total reunion with Reality.

The problem of duality, of good and evil tendencies in man, is one that must be squarely faced; for although our souls are an essential part of his Spirit, we find that for a time our existence is confined to the bonds of flesh. The meeting ground between our Real Self, that high ideal we aspire to become, and the synthetic image we have accepted in its place is to be found in the *Super Ego.* Also known as the Christ Self, the Super Ego is the mediator of our duality who stands at the crossroads between God and man. A comparison which will help each one to understand these three levels of his consciousness—(1) the Superconscious Ego which is aware of Reality, (2) the ego which is aware of unreality, and (3) the Super Ego which is aware of both—is that of the Macrocosm and the microcosm.

We understand the Macrocosm to be the entire warp and woof of creation, known and unknown, visible and invisible, stretching forth and holding within its framework the entire schema of universes, galaxies, stars and sun systems, planets and monadic worlds within worlds. We understand the microcosm to be man himself—the epitome of the creation confined within a framework of individuality. Examining the origin of these two words, we find that the prefix *macro* is taken from the Greek *macros,* meaning long or great; *micro* is taken from the Greek *micros,* meaning little; and *cosm* is a derivative of *kosmos,* meaning world. Thus, we speak of the Macrocosm, the "great world," and of the microcosm, or "little world."

The Macrocosm can be illustrated by drawing an imaginary circle of infinite size, which we shall call the Body of God and into which we shall place all that he has created, both spiritual and material, including the Spirit and soul of man. Whereas literally billions of spiritual-material universes are contained within the infinite circle of the Macrocosm, which itself endures forever as a perfect idea in the Mind of God, the microcosm is the circle which God has drawn around his Spirit-sparks in the desire to impart individuality to the infinite parts of the infinite Whole.

Each microcosmic world is a cell in the Macrocosm, a crystal fragment of the Greater Crystal, reflecting a portion of his glory. Each man is a *mani*festation of God (a manifest action of God), the image of the higher *Cosm* reflected in the lower *cosm.* The key to infinity is won through the mastery of the lesser self (the microcosm) by the power of the Greater Self (the Macrocosm). This is the power of the Superconscious Ego over the ego, of God the Macrocosm over man the the microcosm. Through man's correct use of the sacred gifts of Life, including free will, his consciousness in the microcosm can identify with the fullness of God's consciousness in the Macrocosm. But first it is essential that he learn how to make the contact, how to establish and maintain his relationship with the Superconscious Ego.

The figure-eight pattern is used to illustrate the principle of exchange between the macrocosmic world *Above* and the microcosmic world *below*. At the nexus, the point where the lines in the figure eight cross, the virtues of the *Greater Reality* of oneself, of the Superconscious Ego, flow downward into the microcosm, and the aspirations of the *lesser reality* of oneself, of the ego, flow upward into the Macrocosm. This exchange is accomplished through the consciousness of the Christ, the Super Ego, who, positioned in the center of the cross, is the agent of the alchemical transformation that takes place between the energies of God and man.

The principle underlying this process is easily understood if one compares it to that of a Silex coffee maker. When the water boils in the lower pot, the pressure of the steam forces it to rise into the upper receptacle where it combines with the coffee. When the pot is removed from the heat, the brew descends to the lower part, ready for serving.

In man it is the heat of fervent desire to become Godlike which causes his energies to rise into the upper sphere of his identity. There they mingle with the ingredients of perfection and are transformed into an elixir of liquid light. The vacuum that is created through the giving of one's all to the Reality of one's Highest Self forces the return of a portion of the Spirit of Reality into the empty vessel of one's consciousness; and so the purified energies descend. The superiority of the Higher Self can thus be evoked and retained by the strong desire of the lower self to manifest the larger potential of being.

The *Higher Self* is the Real Man who dwelleth not in temples made with hands,[22] whose house is eternal in the heavens,[23] and who is, in effect, like unto God, everywhere present. The *lower self* is that portion of individuality which cannot be called the Real Man because it is yet in the *state of becoming* the Whole—wholly one with the Real Self. The lower self is that portion of the Real Man which dwelleth in the body temple, finite in the earthly house, confined to time and space.

"Understand thy Highest Self, then, as the God of very gods," says the Master of the Temple of Illumination. "As you face this concept, the lower self falls upon its knees [the ego surrenders when the soul consciousness accepts the Real Self as God]. As the Christ, the eternal Mediator, bows to the Father, Good becomes All-in-all [Good becomes the Higher Self expressed in the lower self]. Man enters the sudden stream of overcoming Self-realization. He fears no merge, for he sees that the blackened image of the synthetic self that has sought to cast down his immortal birthright is not real! Therefore, he quickly replaces it with the Divine Image and humbly holds himself in the consciousness of the son who awaits his divine inheritance."[24]

THE INVASION OF THE MICROCOSMIC CIRCLE

So saturated with the smoke of illusion have the garments of man's consciousness become through the centuries of his involvement with mortality, that there is no possibility for the penetration of his being by the pranic winds of the Holy Spirit unless he first sheds his mourning garb and puts on the clean white linen of the wedding garment.

Mankind's rejection of the promptings of the Real Self and his failure to become acquainted with the Superconscious Ego have resulted in the damming of the flow of Life between the Macrocosm and the microcosm. The consequence of this cutting-off of the vital energies from the source of Reality is the ego impoverished, emaciated, and self-destroyed—a mere skeleton of that which man is destined to become, of that which he already *is* in his Real Image.

Jesus referred to those who by their own free will had thus separated themselves from the fountain of eternal Life in the heart of the Macrocosm as "whited sepulchers, full of dead men's bones." [25] Of these saith the Amen, the faithful and true witness, "Because thou sayest, I am rich, and increased with goods, and have need of nothing; and knowest not that thou art wretched, and miserable, and poor, and blind, and naked: I counsel thee to buy of me gold tried in the fire, that thou mayest be rich; and white raiment, that thou mayest be clothed, and that the shame of thy nakedness do not appear; and anoint thine eyes with eyesalve, that thou mayest see." [26]

Thus the "living dead" know not their plight. The invasion of the microcosm has taken place so gradually that man knows neither the hour nor the day when his consciousness slipped into the mist of the synthetic image. Having gradually replaced the Real with the unreal, he fears not his loss, he senses not his doom; he knows not that his soul requires salvation.

The moment man turns his attention from the pure, flowing radiance of his True Self, he forfeits the protection of the Light focused through the lens of its perfect image. Whereas the circle of the Macrocosm is perfect, hence inviolable, the circle of the microcosm is incomplete unless it reflects the circle of the Macro-cosm. The microcosm is intended to mirror the Macro-cosm; thus the transfer of the Real Image to the soul occurs naturally when the soul is allowed to absorb the patterns that are released from the plane of the Superconscious Ego in place of those that originate in the plane of the ego.

The invasion of the microcosmic circle can occur only when men relinquish their right to both con-scious and subconscious control of their energies and worlds by admitting, in place of the perfect ideas of God, the thoughts and feelings of the mass synthetic consciousness. Filling, as it were, brightly colored bal-loons of myriad shapes, these *thought* and *feeling forms*—which can be seen at astral levels by those who are clairvoyant—are actually floating grids and force-fields of the mass mind.

The invasion of the microcosm, then, takes place in the following manner: First, man opens the lens of his consciousness to imperfect images, which are sometimes seen and sometimes felt. Second, he allows his attention to focus upon them, whether consciously or unconsciously. Third, over his attention flow the energies of the Macrocosm, filling the molds of the synthetic patterns that make his world vulnerable to the influences of a synthetic society. By thus misdirect-ing the energies of the Macrocosm, man sustains im-perfection in the microcosm.

This acceptance of hypnotic suggestions that pass through the atmosphere from one human being to the next—unless checked—results in the violation of man's being. Thus the microcosm is bombarded with a flow of race memory patterns which enter man's world sometimes on the surface of his mind and then again at subterranean levels of consciousness. These are magnetized by the presence of similar vibrations—

similar imperfect thought and feeling patterns—which he has previously admitted, either consciously or unconsciously.

When man is ignorant of this fact and he fails to maintain vigilance in affirming his immutable Reality, he suffers the consequence of being the target of imperfect emanations. These enter the subconscious mind and are recorded there until by an act of will he invokes the divine power that will erase every unrighteous and unlawful marking in his Book of Life.

"Just as there are cosmic rays of a benign influence that continually shower the world of the individual," explains another of mankind's teachers, "so there are subtle emanations coming from other lifestreams which also reach his world. One might compare these emanations to a moving belt on which egglike containers are conveyed into the consciousness or form of the lifestream. When these containers are ruptured and divested of their contents—whether those contents be of good or ill—a penetration of the substance of man's four lower bodies (see Chapter Four) almost certainly occurs.

"This accounts for the strange feelings that people sometimes have which they recognize to be foreign to their natural disposition, yet over which they seem capable of exercising little control. These feelings are the result of the very subtle penetration of their form and consciousness by emanations or projections of energy sent from others, either consciously or unconsciously.

"Now, those who suffer from mental disorders such as paranoia (wherein delusions of persecution and of one's own greatness are experienced) often send forth erratic charges of desultory energy which carry sharp and jagged patterns. When these are dislodged from one human form and driven into another, they can do serious damage unless they are controlled. Therefore, it is essential that the initiate learn how to protect himself against the penetration of his substance and form by any and all harmful influences."[27]

MANIFEST IMMORTALITY: PUTTING ON THE NEW MAN

By the law of free will, each man is the authority for his own world and has the right to determine that which shall be admitted to his sphere of consciousness. Inasmuch as the thoughts and feelings of the synthetic image—his own as well as those that are abroad in the world—are the mortal enemies of his Real Image, man must keep the watch upon the wall of being, ready at any moment to sound the alarm and summon his forces to defend the citadel of his consciousness.

Ignorant of the divine decree that has made him the arbiter of his destiny, man often allows the pressures of the thoughts and feelings of the masses to close the door to the best side of himself. Regarding his life as the product of fate or the whimsy of an unjust god, instead of realizing that it is the product of his own thoughts, words, and deeds, man fails to exercise his opportunity in the microcosm to polarize the energies of God-Good. Instead, he waits for things to "happen"; to him life is a spectator sport, and while he watches the world go by, he allows himself to be rubber-stamped with those synthetic images that deny his expression of the Real Man—the great, God-free, God-created Image, in all of its light and buoyancy and unlimited potential.

The original covenant of the Law established between God and man—the very principle which makes possible the interchange between the Macrocosm and the microcosm—secures man the full protection of cosmic law, if he will obey the commandments of God and "keep himself unspotted from the world."[28] The breaking of the first commandment, "Thou shalt have no other gods before Me," and the second which is like unto it, "Thou shalt not make unto thee any graven image, or any likeness of anything that is in heaven above, or that is in the earth beneath, or that is in the water under the earth. . ."[29] nullifies this covenant between God and man and shatters the hourglass pattern that once enabled the sands of righteousness to flow freely between Creator and creation—between the Ocean and the drop.

As Gideon threw down Baal's altar,[30] so man must tear the veil from the synthetic image; once and for all the idol he has placed upon the altar of being must be shown for what it is and then broken. Through absolute devotion to the living God, man must determine to joyously manifest his own immortality, to be peace and purity in action, and to achieve the great cosmic dream of God which the Real Self will never withhold. In thought, in word, and in deed, man must determine to keep his sacred covenant with his God by allowing only the impressions of the Real Image to pass through the gate of his consciousness. All else is idolatry.

But devotion and determination are only the first steps. Man must have knowledge and a sword. The sincere may well ask, How is the mandate of perfection to be fulfilled? Did God really intend that man should pursue a perfect standard in an imperfect world?

Through fervent invocation to the Spirit of Reality, the Real Image of God can be drawn down from the great reservoir of the Macrocosm into the pool of the microcosm. Allowing the energies of his two worlds to flow freely over the figure-eight pattern, man finds a unique transformation taking place: as the energies from the microcosm enter the Macrocosm, they take on the image or qualification of the Real Self. These purified energies then return to the microcosm via the figure eight to reestablish in the world of form man's original identity which was his "in the beginning." This is the ritual of putting off the old man and putting on the new, "renewed in knowledge after the image of Him that created him."[31]

Jesus taught his disciples this law and how to make it work through the power of the spoken Word and the name of God, I AM. He gave them the following transfiguring affirmations which all can use to magnetize the love of the one great Source of Life that unlocks the living, breathing potential of the soul:

I AM that I AM
I AM the Open Door which no man can shut
I AM the Light which lighteth every man
    that cometh into the world
I AM the Way
I AM the Truth
I AM the Life
I AM the Resurrection
I AM the Ascension in the Light
I AM the Fulfillment of all my needs and
    requirements of the hour
I AM abundant Supply poured out upon all Life
I AM perfect Sight and Hearing
I AM the manifest Perfection of Being
I AM the illimitable Light of God made manifest
    everywhere
I AM the Light of the Holy of Holies
I AM a Son of God
I AM the Light in the Holy Mountain of God

When man speaks the name of God in this manner, as an affirmation of his true Being, he is acknowledging in the microcosm the macrocosmic potential of his Real Image. He is demonstrating the principle of cosmic coexistence—of the Spirit of God dwelling in the soul of man. He is proving the fact that right where he is, right where he has self-conscious awareness, there God can be experienced. The name of God releases the power of the Macrocosm wherever it is spoken in the microcosm; and man becomes more Godlike as he says, "Where I AM, there God is, and where God is, there I AM."

What *is* in a name? Everything! In the name of God is the Light of man's being whereby the microcosm puts on the Macrocosm and the "soul doth magnify the LORD." [32]

Each time man speaks the word "I AM," he is offering his energies to the Real Self and he becomes progressively more real; for the law of cycles assures him that he will receive in turn more than he has sent out. "Cast thy bread upon the waters: for thou shalt find it after many days." [33] The creative potential of the energies that descend from the Macrocosm for man's use in the microcosm increases as the energies which ascend from the microcosm are purified. "And every man that hath this hope in Him purifieth himself, even as He is pure." [34]

"Little by little," the Apostle said, "the Christ is formed in man"; little by little the synthetic image is replaced by the Real Image. "Precept upon precept, line upon line," [35] man awakens from the dream of mortality to the living awareness of his immortal identity as a son of God; and the tides of illusion that have been running against his spirituality are reversed in their course.

Vestiges of the Synthetic Image
Replaced by Real-Eye Magic

Although our souls are imbued with the knowledge and the spirit of overcoming victory, we see all around us vestiges of the synthetic image working together to tear down the magnificent Reality of man. Hereditary and environmental influences, together with the mortal sense of limitation molding social and educational patterns, permeate every facet of man's thinking and existence. As a result of this veritable maelstrom of conflicting forcefields, he is often confused as to the real purpose of life.

Living in this twentieth century, with all of its burgeoning materialism, scientific wonder, and intellectual challenge, man does not appreciate nor does he feel any need to pursue his mystical Reality. Everywhere the mingling of the natural with the artificial makes him wonder whether he is a mechanical creation or the mere product of a biological evolution or—dare he hazard the guess—a son of the Most High God.

Even though he knows that the span of his earthly life is comparatively short and filled with pitfalls and temptations, man seldom concerns himself with what will happen when the curtain is drawn on the final act and he must retire to the wings until he is cast in another role in another life. Entertaining instead a warped sense of immortality, he may look to his offspring for a continuation of his personality; he may seek to live in the memory of the race by erecting monuments to personal achievement; or, conditioned by erroneous doctrine, he may remain satisfied in the belief that another has already secured his immortality for him.

Paul, writing to the Corinthians, said, "Flesh and blood cannot inherit the kingdom of God."[36] What, then, is the purpose of the creation of flesh and blood? It is written that the LORD God clothed Adam and his wife with coats of skins.[37] Is man mere flesh and blood? Or is he much more? Is he but an animal among other animals? Or is he simply an energy system as some modern physicists have suggested?

Every now and then one in a crowd steps to the periphery of the human jungle and sees that he is trapped in a maze of synthetic images which sooner or later he will find are all calculated to divert his attention from his Real Image. He feels like an animal in a cage. Not knowing where to go, he roams the streets of his consciousness in search of understanding, crying, "Who am I? What is all this for?" Surrounded on every side by the pressures and demands of worldly life, he loses what little faith he may have had in the great universal Reality of true Being. In times of stress he finds it even more difficult to apprehend who or what he really is.

The cause of man's little faith lies in the fact that his senses are dulled by the drone of the appearance world. Without the vision of the higher way, he perishes in the "sub-ways" of greater suburbia. Whether his lack of the abundance of the "good life" is in material things, in human happiness, health, or success, he unquestioningly pursues the goals set up by a synthetic society. While he dresses his form in the height of fashion, his soul takes on the black mourning garb of sackcloth and ashes. He does not realize that the greatest crisis of his consciousness is the spiritual impoverishment of his soul. Not finding the answers to his questions, there is nothing to do but lose himself in the human jungle. Sliding down the negative spiral of the mass consciousness and the blank acquiescence of the crowd, he once again becomes despondent.

The vital idea of man as Spirit, created by God in his own image and coexisting now and forever with him, is the first fresh wind of hope that lifts him out of the socket of sense impressions, of billboards, neon signs, and bawdy "flicks" and provides a method in place of a madness whereby he can pass through the portals of Reality and discover the laws that will enable him to master the world that has thus far mastered him.

Crossing the threshold, man enters for the first time the realm of the Real Image; he breathes deeply of the air of freedom for which his soul has always longed. The weight of the world drops from his shoulders—all of his worries and his concerns, all that has ever kept him from the real truth about himself. Having emptied the cup of worldly desire, he sees clearly that the hunger of the real man of the heart will never be satisfied until the cup of his soul's consciousness is filled with the knowledge of the vital truth of eternal Life. He drinks the elixir of freedom handed to him by angel ministrants; he dines at the Lord's table; and he is fed the heavenly manna that quickens his mind and charges every cell of his body and consciousness with newness of life and purpose.

Just when it seems that his cup can contain no more, he is conducted into an oval chamber where others are already gathered to hear one whom he will come to know as simply "the Old Man of the Hills." The Master is speaking: ". . . The basic fact that I am 'I' and not another leads to the realization that the real 'I' which 'I AM' has a peculiar individuality, a peculiar raison d'être. Beholding Life in the Macrocosm and in the microcosm, everywhere he turns, man is confronted with the inexplicable gift of identity. What to do with this gift, how to use it wisely and well, will become more and more apparent as he climbs the highest mountain of the Ascended Masters' teachings.

"Now you shall be given a basic and vital key, which, if properly used, will enable your aspiring mind to leave the vestiges of the synthetic image in the foothills as you make your way up the narrow trail, seeking higher Truth. This key is the faculty with which your own soul or *solar* consciousness was endowed by the Spirit. This key is that *real-eye magic* which you must make your own.

"One of the greatest gifts of identity, which the conscious [outer] mind little dreams of, is this latent ability to realize the image of the eye. This science of the immaculate concept is practiced by every angel in heaven. It is that law which is written in the inward parts of man, known by his very heart of hearts, yet dim in the memory of his outer mind. It is based on the visualization of a perfect idea which then becomes a magnet that attracts the creative energies of the Holy Spirit to his being to fulfill the pattern held in mind.

"Having seen what he is in Spirit and what is the potential of his soul, man must retain that image of Reality in his thoughts and feelings, for the Image is a natural repellent to all that opposes his Reality in manifestation. This he does through the real eye of his soul—his inner eye that knows as it sees and sees as it knows.

"The eye magic of the soul is the *I-mage* or image of Reality which man plants in his consciousness and waters with the pure energies that flow freely from the Macrocosm. The increase of the abundant Life that follows is the LORD's, or the Law's; for those who follow the scientific principle of the real-eye magic find that they are rewarded by the same. As Saint Paul said, 'I have planted, Apollos watered; but God gave the increase.'[38] And so God is expressed impersonally in the outworking of his immutable laws, all of which are corollary to the one great law of Being in Cosmos. The science of the immaculate concept, then, is the knowledge of how to use pure ideas to transform the world of the microcosm into a macrocosmic wonder— *as Above in God, so below in man.*

"Beauty and Truth have a geometry all their own, a symmetry that allows the energies of God to flow freely through their ideations and then to coalesce in form. Pure ideas and noble forms are the archetypal patterns of the Real Image; they are seeds of Light which, when planted in the subconscious and conscious domains of the fertile mind, bring forth after their kind.

"Without these kernels of Light, rooted and nourished in the very substance of his soul, man cannot hope to express perfection in his world. Each one is a lodestone of God-desire to become without, all that which is within. Each one is a magnet that attracts from God Above to man below the creative essence of the universe. And if these monads be abundantly scattered throughout his consciousness—each one a nucleus of Reality, each one a forcefield of fervent faith, hope, and charity—then man can indeed look to *outpicture* (bring forth) in the microcosm that which he has thought to be 'the impossible dream, the unreachable star.'

"Each time the soul beholds the sun, the clouds, the wind in the trees, a rose, a perfect leaf, a pebble, or a wave and then tucks the design in the folds of memory, he is adding to his treasure of those perfect ideas which are the building blocks of his Reality. Each time the fingers of his mind trace the lines of a Michelangelo, the strokes of a Raphael, the movements of a symphony, the cadences of a ballet, the formations of the birds that cross the sky, the soul takes in the patterns of the Mind of God on which hang the entire schemata of his microcosmic universe.

"Beholding the universe and even our own planetary home, we observe how Nature upholds the law of perfection and shrugs off imperfection. Truly, the very stones that cry out[39] in praise of the Christ do uphold more earnestly than man his mandate 'Be ye therefore perfect, even as your Father which is in heaven is perfect.'[40] How beautifully the Lord has placed all around us in the natural kingdom these links to eternity and to the invisible world of realities which we perceive only in the substance of things hoped for—these precious evidences of things not seen! . . ."[41]

Thus, after alternate periods of living in the synthetic world and then in the real, man comes to the feet of the Masters of Wisdom where he learns that Life is to be found only in reverence for all that lives. Returning to the abode of his own thoughts, he seeks to recapture the realization of that unity which he now knows must exist within the heart of the universe and even within the heart of a cell. He begins to turn within to tap the reservoirs of Nature. He must explore the unknown as well as the known!

THE DISCOVERY OF THE REAL SELF IN THE NATURAL ORDER

The Ray

I AM beholding
 Nature where'er I look,
The Tree of Life I shook—
 And tumbling down,
Visions of Source reveal
 Sunflowers God's radiance steal.
Shells of restless tides reveal
 The golden ratio
In universes twinkling from afar.

Life in me beats freely.
    I see a tree or man
Walking into Reality
    As robin's egg in spring,
Holding Cosmos all inside,
    Does bring to mind a sun.
The warmth of love from Above
    Makes me sing of Source
Far greater than I understand.

And covering land, I see
    A million snowflakes blending bland
Into a million faces,
    Daisies in the field of earth
Gazing spherelike.
    A billion grains of sand, of worth
Do lead me to a sunbeam,
    Raylike with its Light,
A Golden Thread—

From heart to mountain height
    Does lead me to my Home delight
Where each ray ne'er alone
    Does find aright
The palm of God, our goal—
    Perfection bright,
Dazzling white!
    Serenity—
The balm of Victory!

The universal Mind of God has spun a blueprint of Light that blazes just behind the screen of Nature, and he has endowed the natural order with a wisdom which man calls instinct or intuitive knowledge. Right where he is, man can begin to penetrate the natural order and to discover there and beyond, in the blueprint of Light, the knowledge of the Real. Through communion with the Spirit of God in Nature, he can learn to identify with his invisible Self, with the powerful spiritual consciousness that is his birthright.

If he would know Truth, man must go to Nature's archives where Truth is indelibly written. But alas, even here error has been superimposed, layer upon layer. Therefore he must record and discard, record and discard, record and discard. Through scientific research he must demand empirical proof as well as supersensory verification of his findings. He must reexamine all hypotheses in the light of his expanding knowledge about himself.

No mere dogmatic speculation must substantiate his probe into Reality, for his very existence is at stake. Explorations of the past were based on a set of conceptual relations and experience patterns that have been antiquated by a higher science and a higher religion. Therefore, he must base his investigations upon the truth of immortal Being, which every son of God holds to be self-evident; his proof must be found in the natural order of the universe that is reflective of the omnipresent One; his data must be collected from Nature, from the intuitions of the heart, and from the thunderings of Sinai that declare irrefutably, "I AM WHO I AM—I WILL BE WHAT I WILL BE."

God is not dead! But unless man holds awareness of being alive in God, he himself is dead! Let him seek, then, to live to apprehend universal purpose and to invoke assistance from extraterrestrial sources. Are there those who can aid him on earth? Are there highly evolved beings, angels, and wise men of the ages who are qualified to assist him in his search? If earth is populated with the visible creation of God in imperfect form, does it not follow that heaven is populated with a creation of perfect form and perception?

In attempting to prove the existence of his own Reality, man echoes the observation of Descartes,

"I think, therefore I am." But well might the premise be reversed: "I AM! therefore I think." In any case, thinking and being are both primal factors of identity. Without these factors there is no basis for existence or self-conscious awareness. Both originate not in man but outside of him. Man cannot cause himself to be; neither can he cause himself to think; but through the misuse of free will he may cause himself not to be and not to think.

Scientists may create animal and even human life in a test tube, but they will never be able to create the substance out of which all things are formed—"the stuff that dreams are made of." They will only be able to transform energy from one of its myriad manifestations to another—never to create or destroy it. Although they wrest the secrets of Nature, they must still bow before the Creator of all energy and life. The fact that something cannot come from nothing leads the seeker for Reality to probe the cause behind the world of effect in which we live.

Now, when we consider that by definition creation implies creator, even as effect implies cause, whether some choose man as creator while others see only God as Creator does not matter; for man is destined to become a co-creator with God. The fact that man can create does not disprove the existence of the Supreme Creator, nor does it make His existence unnecessary. On the contrary, the fact that it is necessary for man to create only confirms the great principle of Being, that in order for man to be, to think, or to create, someone had to do so before him. That One was fully known by him who declared, "Before Abraham was, I AM." Therefore he created. And he left a record for the ages—for all who would go and do likewise.

Sometime, somewhere, in the evolution of every soul, the great Source of being makes known to it its preexistence. The Real Image antedates all being, thinking, and creation in form. It is the blueprint of each one's identity; it is the identity of each one's blueprint. It is the cause behind the effect we see in manifestation; yet it can become that effect even as God's energy is continuously undergoing transformation throughout the spiritual-material universe.

The search for the pattern of existence is an individual matter. It must be accomplished by everyone who would be master of himself and his world. We suggest that the seeker proceed from the basis of known facts taken from the world of effect and that from these he induce the unseen realities of the world of cause. His assumptions might well be the following:

1. that man was created by a Being greater than himself (our orientation with life tells us that the lesser must proceed out of the greater)
2. that man was fashioned after an image held in the consciousness of his Creator even as the clay must resemble the idea held in the mind of the potter
3. that the Creator could not create anything unlike himself even as all species generate after their kind
4. that if one can determine the true nature of the creation, he can thereby induce the true nature of the Creator
5. that man in his present state is not reflecting the Real Image, but rather has taken on the synthetic image
6. that one can discover the true nature of man in the synthetic image only insofar as any original work of art can be detected in a copy
7. that he must, therefore, look to Nature to discover the secrets of man and his Creator that cannot be traced in the synthetic image
8. that the archetypal patterns found in Nature reflect a vast geometry, a natural order of selection, and a

law of the survival of the fittest that point to a standard of perfection

9. that the standard of perfection reflected in Nature is the basis of the entire creation that we perceive in the world of effect, including man.

A study of Nature reveals the scientific accuracy of its processes and the exhaustless skill of the Mind that conceived it. Without further elaboration of the wonders of the material universe, which may be investigated through any of the branches of the physical sciences, we shall make our final generalizations regarding Creator and creation based on the testimony of the natural order:

A. that the Creator of man and his physical environment transcends the creation both in expressed consciousness and planned infinitude; that his nature, being transcendental, is capable of transcending itself and is ever reaching for a more expansive manifestation of his own expanding Identity. Because of this inherent ability to transcend being, we call the Creator a Spirit, and his creation, endowed with the same attribute, we call spiritual. Man is a Spirit-spark who, like his Creator, continually gathers unto himself more of the fires of creation

B. that the one quality which can be consistently applied to Creator and creation, regardless of all material evidence to the contrary, is that of perfection. The perfection of which we speak is synonymous with goodness and includes all virtue and wisdom, all science and truth: its presence is universal and all-powerful. Inasmuch as the Creator includes the infinite qualities of perfection within the vast reaches of his Identity, man has access to these qualities as he invokes them within the confines of the microcosm. As he does so, he is putting

on the Real Image, becoming a co-creator and fulfilling the command "Be ye therefore perfect, even
as your Father which is in heaven is perfect"

C. that the purpose of creation was to expand the
Creator's Identity (his kingdom) through the objectification of his Self-awareness. Through the
creation the Creator gains expression. The sons of
God are therefore outposts of the Mind of God,
receiving and transmitting waves of creative energies which manifest fragments of the one creative
Mind. Man is the objective realization of the Mind
of God. His is the form that provides expression
for the Formless One. Man in his pristine state is
the image of Reality.

Using the foregoing assumptions and generalizations as the basis for his investigations, the seeker
should proceed to examine the evidence which confirms his hypotheses as well as that which tends to
refute them. Then, like Job, he will have to draw his
conclusions and make his own determination. Will he
accept the trials and tribulations of human existence
as proof either that God does not exist or that he is an
unmerciful tyrant? Or will he see them as a chastening—self-imposed—that is the design of an impersonal
law, formed by a personal God who desires to draw
his children closer to the Real Image?

The modern Job must cast aside unwanted ideas,
but he must also exercise care that his rejection be not
abrupt. He may bypass unfruitful endeavors of the
past, but he must also approach with reverence his
own Reality. He must perceive that the hand of his
Creator has not left him comfortless or without the
fruit of honest labor. The intellect must not be allowed
to force the issues or to override the heart; for the
inductive and intuitive faculties of the mind and heart
working together will provide the missing link in this

the greatest discovery of the ages—the discovery of the Real Self in the natural order.

Men have always rejected inventions that have broken the comfortable pattern of the norm, laughing at those who have probed the unknown and then made practical their findings. Yet there is an inner sense in man that reaches out to discover how he may become more than man—how he may become more real. And in his quest for Reality, he is willing to follow any clue, any hunch, even the promptings of the inner voice that will not let him rest until he has wrestled with the angel and pried the secrets of the universe.

The Real Self-Mastery of the Natural Order

"Two thousand years ago when Christ walked upon the waters of the Sea of Galilee," explains Saint Germain, "his demonstration was a manifestation of the natural law of levitation, operating within an energy framework of cohesion, adhesion, and magnetism—the very principles which make orbital flight possible. The light atoms composing the body of Christ absorbed at will an additional quantity of cosmic rays and spiritual substance whose kinship to physical light made his whole body light, thereby making it as easy for him to walk upon the sea as upon dry land.

"His body was purely a ray of light shining upon the waters. The most dazzling conception of all was his ability to transfer this authority over energy to Peter through the power of Peter's own vision of the Christ in radiant, illumined manifestation. By taking his eyes temporarily from the Christ, however, Peter entered a human fear vibration and vortex which immediately densified his body, causing it to sink partially beneath the raging seas. The comforting hand of Christ, extended in pure love, reunited the alchemical tie; and the flow of spiritual energy through his hand raised Peter once again to safety.

"The further example of the Master Jesus releasing a flow of energy—as in the case of the woman who touched the hem of his garment without his knowledge aforehand—shows the impersonal love of God which responds equally to the call of faith from any of those creatures he has fashioned so wonderfully and so purely in the supreme hope of absolute cosmic freedom for all." [42]

The Nazarene Master, possessing the power to change the water into wine, to heal the sick, and to raise the dead, disappeared from the midst of those who sought to harm him. He walked upon the water and prepared food for his disciples on the shore, saying, "Come and dine." At the close of his mission, he not only raised his body by the power of the resurrection flame, but forty days later he exhibited the most dramatic of all accomplishments: he rose into the air in the glory of the ascension. Surely this was a victory of victories. This was a demonstration of mastery over substance, passion, and prejudice; this was triumph over life and death. This was the Real Self-mastery of the natural order whose laws he first discovered and then demonstrated.

As he rose into the air and was received out of mortal sight, a cloud of radiant light veiled his Real Image from those who had not severed their ties with the synthetic consciousness. But all heard his parting words, "Lo, I AM with you alway, even unto the end of the age," [43]* signifying the continuity of his mission

*An age in cosmic history may be reckoned as thousands or even millions of years. Ages are measured according to the fulfillment of the cycles of the Christ consciousness in peoples, in nations, and in worlds.

to the present day and beyond. The life of Jesus was an example of the manifestation of the Real Image in the life of one man. Think what a different world it would be if greater numbers were able to refute the synthetic creation through the realization of that Real Image!

The tracings of the intent of God for every man to earn this selfsame immortality are nowhere more significantly revealed than in the latent or subconscious memory of a perfection he once knew. If man can realize the cumulative effects of his misdirected acts and perceive the consequences of his selfishness that has encased his soul in a mold of unworthiness, he can also perceive the great freeing power of heaven. He can contemplate the power of the wind of the Holy Spirit to blow through the chinks of his mind and to inspire the very substance thereof to glow with the fervor of possibility.

Once he realizes his present potential, man no longer strings his energies as skull-shaped beads of inevitable death upon the strands of time, crowded into jagged space. He knows that he is with God, a Spirit, the commander of his destiny—and of time and space. He knows that he wields all power in heaven and earth because the Father has given it to him,[44] and he obediently accepts the covenant which stipulates that in the use of this power he must exercise prudence and responsibility and that he must live by the Golden Rule.

Now he considers the possibility of the ascension for himself. Eternal Life is a goal that is attainable. He grovels no more in the condemnation of sin or the desire to do unworthy deeds that serve the cause of the synthetic image. He reaches toward the Light; he raises his head; his eyes seek the face of the Infinite.

As a follower of the Light of regeneration upon earth, he comes to the place where as an adept, a follower of the Master himself, he can do "the works that I do. . . and greater works."[45]

As the master of his destiny, man becomes more than man. He becomes the Real Image and he understands at last the meaning of the words "To this end was I born, and for this cause came I into the world that I should bear witness unto the Truth of my Real Self!"[46]

ADORATION TO GOD

Beloved Mighty I AM Presence,
Thou Life that beats my heart,
Come now and take dominion,
Make me of thy Life a part.
Rule supreme and live forever
In the flame ablaze within;
Let me from Thee never sever,
Our reunion now begin.

All the days proceed in order
From the current of Thy power,
Flowing forward like a river,
Rising upward like a tower.
I AM faithful to Thy love ray
Blazing forth light as a sun;
I AM grateful for Thy right way
And Thy precious word "Well done."

I AM, I AM, I AM adoring Thee.
O God, You are so magnificent.
I AM, I AM, I AM adoring Thee.

Moving onward to perfection,
I AM raised by Love's great grace
To thy center of direction—
Behold, at last I see Thy face.
Image of immortal power,
Wisdom, love, and honor, too:
Flood my being now with glory,
Let my eyes see none but You!

O God, You are so magnificent.
I AM, I AM, I AM adoring Thee.
O God, You are so magnificent.

My very own Beloved I AM, Beloved I AM, Beloved I AM.

Chapter Three

A Heap of Confusion

A Heap of Confusion

Lo, this only have I found, that God hath made man upright; but they have sought out many inventions.   *Ecclesiastes*

ORDER: THE FIRST LAW OF BEING

FROM THE CENTER OF BEING God geometrized, and the geometry of your Divinity was born. What noble symmetry excelled in all the earth and in all the heavens! The design foursquare in the earth, the spherical reality in the heavens, the starry wonder of cellular life—what could be more exalting, more beautiful, more free! Supreme order is the wonder of worlds aborning within and without—mathematical precision that liberates the soul to soar and sing, that makes the heart a winged thing. Ah, sweet order of the universe and man, reveal through Love the holy plan!

Alas, the world into which we have descended full of hope is but a heap of confusion. Contrary to the Creator's intent and the bent of every soul, earth is not a golden ball of joy, abundance, and brotherly love. Everywhere we look, error is piled upon error; and our future, rising from an insecure foundation, is unknown. The plumb line of Truth by which the Great Geometer calculates the measure of a man must also be applied to nations and to planets at the hour of judgment. And they must not be found wanting.[1]

Although man is ready to discard traditional authorities as unsafe and unsound, he does not always know how to replace them with a Golden Rule standard and the knowledge of higher law that reveals the relativity of past and present and future as points of reference for the evolution of the soul within a given environment.

It is more comfortable to live in a familiar world than in an unfamiliar one, to follow the well-traveled highways than to explore the byways of life. Yet human nature often desires change for the sake of change itself. And the excitement of the new often makes the old seem dull and uninteresting. The challenge of the unexplored captivates men and nations to embark upon a course of action that may lead not to a reign of glory but to ruination.

Some desire change in government and society for selfish reasons, to reenact the age-old dramas of personal and national glory, wealth, and the control of power blocs; others desire change as a means of liberating peoples from strange oppressions; and for the same reasons many will rally to preserve the status quo. Some feel that the process of change must come about gradually by evolution; others advocate revolution and the violent overthrow of existing institutions.

Now we survey a world that man—not God—has made, and we are not altogether pleased with what we see. The grasping greed of war, the hypocrisy and injustice of the times, the impersonal, mechanical treatment of the cells in the body politic, the blare of an unreal existence—all of these are anathema to our souls.

We rise up in righteous indignation to do battle against the foe, only to find that the iron walls that bastion the false values of an established order—which at times is not an order but a chaos—will not be moved. Our efforts frustrated, we sink back into our routine, waiting for the moment of our destiny, which we know will surely come because the flame of hope that never dies whispers in the heart, "Be willing just to listen and to labor and to wait."

Rebirth and revolution—flames that leap into the air—are kindling minds and hearts here and there. Men are looking for renewal, and in the process they are wont to kick over the traces of their karmic violations. "There is a renaissance coming all right, and there is a revolution coming," commented Saint Germain, the master strategist of freedom, "but these need not have as their objective the destruction of the sovereign governments of the free powers of the world. Let change take place first within the heart and soul of man, creating there that determination which will enable him to overcome all negative hereditary and environmental influences; then, having mastered himself, let him introduce a kingdom of spiritual values where Life and Light and Love under brotherhood will at last bring in a golden age of understanding and peace *because man wills it so.*"[2]

Between the dark of the synthetic image into which man fell and the daylight of the Founding Image in which he was created, there is a discrepancy of color, light, sound, and symmetry. And out of the chaos of this contrast has arisen a monolith of human vanity, a veritable heap of confusion which man has inflicted upon his environment and which his environment has in turn inflicted upon him. The discrepancy between the Real and the synthetic image is nowhere more apparent than in a world groaning in travail to give birth to a golden age and in the agony of the soul longing to be born into its native purity.

Man's authority to govern himself, to organize his life, and to be a co-creator with God is derived from the spiritual edict "Take dominion over the earth!"[3] Man's failure to understand the meaning of free will, of taking the reins of authority and ruling majestically in the footstool kingdom,[4] has brought down upon his head the heap of confusion that always results from the misapplication of cosmic principle.

Having heard and seen the testimony of the natural order, having moved upon the foaming waters and danced atop the tallest, loneliest pines, the soul is convinced that the beauty and the abundance of life, so variegated yet so perfect, are not based upon confusion or a random interplay of energy systems, but upon a supremely ordered ritual of creation from the center to the periphery of an atom or a cosmos. The wondrous unfoldment of the embryo within the womb and the perfection of the physical body of man—of the parts in relation to the whole—remind us that the Supreme Intelligence that created man and placed him in the womb of Matter planned all things wisely and well.

But everywhere this man whom God hath made—and whom man hath remade—is confronted with confusion and complexity, spewing from minds unwise and unwell. His psyche and his society are both so vast and so involved as to be almost ungovernable. The freedom that his soul knows must exist— else man has no reason for living—"is an airy creature of the heart," the Master says, "ever rising, ever moving forward; but if the outer man will not keep pace with the advancements of his own soul, he may find himself 'tail ending it' and falling to rise no more. The soul will go on. It is a flaming radiance from the heart of God. It has beckoned and called; it has patiently sought to glorify in man the Divine Nature and that loving-kindness in all man's doings which is promoted by the spirit of holiness and righteousness."[5]

Although his mind reels at the problems confronting his nation, his world, his family, and himself, man feels the inner mandate to reorder his life, to reconstruct his world after the spirals of perfection. And he knows that his time is running out.

Truly it has been said, "Without vision, the people perish."[6] Truly it is the vision of the immaculate concept—the pure idea held in the Mind of God for every man and every woman fashioned in his likeness—that must be retained. Men die to the Spirit when they let go of the thread of contact that tethers the mind to this vision—to this sphere of Reality, this brilliant ball of purpose, this intricacy of exquisite design—that contains the master blueprint of identity.

In this chapter we shall trace the long-forgotten history of man in the ideal society, his subsequent departure from the state of holy innocence, and the transfer of his mental and emotional impurity to his environment. We shall see that man himself is the crucible for alchemical transformation—for good or for ill—and that whatsoe'er he decrees for his microcosm will sooner or later appear upon the horizon of the Macrocosm. First the violation of man's being was plotted and executed; then came the violation of his world. But none of this could have taken place without his consent to a standard and a practice that were far below the golden mean of perfection.

Once the wall of Light was broken, there was nothing to hold back the hordes of Darkness. The invasion of the citadel of man's consciousness and his civilization was swift and sudden. The coming of the Luciferians and the laggards is the price man paid for partaking of the fruit of the tree of the knowledge of good and evil. The warping of his vision, his subjection to psychic domination, the preponderance of his own error became a weight upon his soul, a burden so great as to make him cry out, "How long, O LORD, ere freedom be trumpeted over the whole world? How long, O LORD, before the victory of the Light?"

To all who have longed for freedom Saint Germain

replies: "You must remember that never in recent history has the world enlisted the aid of the total body of humanity in the defense of freedom. The relatively few have consistently held for the many the balance of spiritual power by which marvelous accomplishments have been made upon earth and by which the quality of man's life has been correspondingly enhanced."[7]

Now we see that the return of the many to a golden age of enlightenment and peace is the only alternative to the tightening strategies of control which, unless challenged and exposed by all of the people, threaten to enslave the evolutions of earth in a Luciferian superstate. In this chapter we open the curtain on the colossal fraud that has been perpetrated against mankind and carefully concealed through the long night of human bondage; and in the remaining chapters we present the Teachings of the Ascended Masters that, if correctly applied by the many, will give to the individual and society the victory over the enemy that is both within and without.

"The key to the redemption of the social system," observes Lord Lanto, instructor in God-government at the Royal Teton Retreat, "lies in the victory of divine law in the being of individual man. What the individual man becomes, the collective world is. Through a wholehearted entering into the kingdom of God and his righteousness and through participation in those spiritual exercises that strip man of the false and clothe him with the Real, the individual and his world can and must become the fullness of all that God intended from the beginning."[8]

THE IDEAL SOCIETY

Just as man has a Divine Image, so the society in which he evolves also has a Divine Image, based on the architectural design of the New Jerusalem recorded by John in the Book of Revelation.⁹ The ideal society exists as "Thy kingdom come" when every member of the group identifies with his Real Self and strives to outpicture the blueprint that God has ordained as the master plan for individual creative expression within a given community of souls destined to evolve as a hierarchical unit.

The outer memory of past golden ages has long faded in the race consciousness, but the desire of the people for social progress and good government points to the inner memory of souls who know that there is a better way because they have experienced that way firsthand. The records of golden-age civilizations have been buried not only with the continents that sank beneath the Atlantic and Pacific oceans and with the remains of other civilizations that have been destroyed through cataclysm, but also in the subconscious recesses of all evolving on this planet; in addition, these records have been impressed upon the ethers, upon that substance and dimension known as *akasha,* where they can be read and studied by the clairvoyant.

Although man has been evolving upon the planet earth for hundreds of thousands of years—as will be scientifically proved in the not too distant future by archaeologists, geologists, and oceanic explorers working hand in hand with those whose senses can probe akasha—his current knowledge of history goes back five to ten thousand years at the most. Therefore, except for those extraordinary men of vision such as Plato, who wrote the *Republic,* Sir Thomas More, who wrote the *Utopia,* and Francis Bacon, who wrote the *Novum Organum,* the bulk of the people perpetuate the erroneous concept that the perfect society is only a dream, an ever receding goal that man may approach but never attain.

The commandment of Jesus "Be ye therefore perfect, even as your Father which is in heaven is perfect"[10] applies to nations as well as to individuals; and it is possible of attainment because perfection is the natural estate of man toward which the soul ever gravitates, and because it has been attained before. Just how individuals and nations can meet this standard will unfold throughout this work.

Now let us examine the golden-age civilizations that rose on Lemuria and Atlantis.[11] These were composed of lifewaves who came forth as Spirit-sparks from the Great Central Sun and whose souls descended into form for the purpose of gaining self-mastery in time and space, where they were destined to manifest in denser spheres the immaculate concept of the Real Image locked within their beings by the Almighty Logoi. During three golden ages, these lifewaves lived in purity and in that childlike innocence of which Jesus spoke so often to his disciples as necessary to their "entering in"[12]—innocence of harm and selfish motivation, innocence of duality and carnal desire, innocence of the synthetic consciousness and its energy veil.

Although some may find it hard to believe, the total absence of the element of evil within these golden ages did not lessen the variety and spice of life! On the contrary, the activities and creative opportunities of these evolutions were heightened by the infinite variegation and shadings of Truth and the unlimited potential for scientific discovery and artistic expression inherent within the Real Image, to which all had direct access. The challenge of initiation in the cosmic order of Hierarchy kept millions happily spiraling up the ladder of greater and greater self-mastery, each step unfolding new worlds to conquer.

When God made man and the universe, he did not include evil as essential to the plan, as a necessary backdrop for Good, or the night as contrast for the day. "And the city had no need of the sun, neither of the moon, to shine in it: for the glory of God did lighten it, and the Lamb is the Light thereof." [13]

Under the tutelage of Cosmic Beings and the Manus of their races, these civilizations reflected the highest cultural and scientific standards upheld in the City Foursquare. The joy that quickens with individual self-mastery, the freedom that comes with dominion over the elements as the result of the disciplines of the laws of God—these qualities were recognized by all as essential ingredients of their universal destiny.

Brave souls in a brave new world saw their beginning and their end, their origin and their ultimate, to be the manifestation of the Universal Christ. Thus they strove to magnify the Light of the eternal Christos each day throughout the cycles of their sojourn in the dimensions of Matter; they understood the meaning of the "testing of the mettle," and they were willing to prove their proficiency in precipitation of the arts and sciences, of the handiworks of God. They knew that thereby they would earn the right to expand their dominion in the domain of Spirit, ultimately attaining their immortal freedom and proceeding on to higher worlds in the endless opportunities of the Father's many mansions. [14]

These citizens of earth never lost sight of the vision of their Reality. They saw the Christ in one another and loved all with whom they shared the goal of becoming more of God. They loved a man for his intrinsic worth and the unique design of his lifestream even before the God-idea matured.

These three golden ages existed before the Fall of Adam and Eve, which is presented allegorically in the Book of Genesis. Prior to his descent into the consciousness of duality and into the sense of sin and separation from his Source, man's attention and hence his energies were God-centered: his life was God's Life, and by the intelligent use of free will he dedicated God's energies to the lowering of the patterns made in the heavens into the patterns made in the earth.[15] The covenants between God and man had not been broken; therefore, as man surrendered his all to God, God surrendered his all to him. Truly this was the perfect balance between the Macrocosm and the microcosm: as Above, so below.

The family, embodying the Trinity of Father, Son, and Holy Spirit, is the basic unit of the divine society. The Atlantean origin of the word *family* is father-mother flames in loving union. In the early golden ages the father held the focus of the Spirit of God, of his authority and Fatherhood over all. The mother as the homemaker held the focus of the Holy Spirit and its descent into Matter, kindling the heavenly energies of AUM. Eve, the mother of all living, was designed to be the perfect expression of the Motherhood of God. Through the loving union of father-mother flames, the body temples of descending souls were formed and the Christ flame was nourished in the sons and daughters of God. This trinity of faith (Father), hope (Son), and charity (Holy Spirit) that begins at home is the foundation for all that is built in the ideal society and in every golden age, where life is a joyous unfoldment of the God flame within the heart of each Spirit-spark, each flame a spiral rising and undulating to blend with the sweet mysteries of Life.

Government and education in the ideal society are instruments for the development of the individual potential of man in harmony with all members of the community. All institutions, public and private, stress the unity of Life through its triune aspects of faith, hope, and charity, embraced as the Power, Wisdom, and Love of God. Here the Trinity in action and a striving for excellency in all things are the motivating forces.

"Learn to love to do well, and you shall!" was the advice given by Casimir Poseidon, ruler of an ancient civilization that flourished at the site of the Amazon Basin. Adherence to this principle kept each soul striving to excel beyond the attainment of yesterday; every form of activity from athletics to mutual service was seen as recreation, the re-creation of the qualities of the Holy Spirit in man and Nature.

Competition between peoples was never a factor of motivation; the only competition that man knew was that competition which he practiced with himself in order that he might transcend his former attainment through the invocation of more light and through greater mastery of the energies and talents entrusted to his care. If man could realize today a more perfect union with Life than he did yesterday, his reward was with him and his cup was full.

Contrary to the lie that man is a sinner and gravitates to the baser elements of his nature, man is inherently Good; he polarizes to Good and to the highest representatives of God-Good. Therefore, the relationship of the individual to the Whole—of the part of Good to the All of Good—is kept in proper perspective in the ideal society as the spokes are to the wheel of Life. The relationship of the individual parts to one another is likewise honored, even as the Whole acknowledges the autonomy of the parts within a given frame of reference. Thus the Golden Rule is the keynote of social relations in the ideal society. Contact with the Center of God's Being gives all men a reason for being, a path to follow, a spiral of direction leading to the very Hub of Life. Thus a sense of expectancy prevails and man responds to his ability, God-ordained, to *become* all that he really *is*.

From the foundation of the Pyramid of Life rises the balance of the Christ consciousness as the ideal that all are to attain no matter what their calling from God. Although all are created with equal opportunity, all do not remain equal in the ideal society. For as each one multiplies his God-given talents, he ascends the scale of Hierarchy; as each one proves himself faithful over a few things, he earns the right to rule over those of lesser attainment and to educate those who are following in his footsteps.

The leaders of the ideal society are priest-king-scientists; for there is no separation between government, science, and religion, which are seen as a manifestation of the tripartite flame of Power, Wisdom, and Love. Positions of authority in the temples and in governmental, educational, and scientific institutions are awarded to those initiates who have passed certain degrees of self-mastery and who are thereby qualified to rule and make decisions on behalf of those still going through the tests and initiations which all must eventually pass in order to win their immortality.

The laws of the ideal society are based on that cosmic law which the Creator put in the "inward parts" of man, carefully wrote in his heart, [16] and then sent his angels to record in the archives of universal Truth. These have been guarded to the present hour in the retreats of the brotherhood of Ascended Masters who have already passed through this or other planetary schoolrooms.

The most advanced initiate within a golden-age civilization who masters these three branches of cosmic law becomes the ruling authority for the planet under the Ascended Masters and Cosmic Beings who have charge of the planet at inner levels. He is the pillar who stands at the nexus of the figure eight because he has mastered his own world and taken dominion over the earth; for him the microcosm is the planetary body and the Macrocosm is the entire Cosmos. (Thus we see that whatever portion of God's energy man masters becomes his microcosm, and he becomes centered as the God-presence of that world.) His consciousness is the Super Ego, the Christ personified on behalf of billions of lifestreams who have not yet evolved to the point of complete manifest action of their own Christ-potential. Through his consciousness flow the energies from the heart of the Sun; and he holds the balance of Power, Wisdom, and Love for all evolving on the planet as they outpicture the cosmic blueprint of the City Foursquare.

Holding this office, he is responsible for teaching the people likewise to attune with the flow of energy from the one great Source of Life. Being a master of cycles and of the very rhythm of the universe, he teaches them how to govern the ebb and flow of energy within their individual forcefields, gradually to transfer this mastery over the individual microcosm to mastery over the planetary microcosm, and finally to identify with the Macrocosm through the interchange of energies—as Above, so below. The total identification of the ruler with his Real Self is the basis of his mastery, won over long periods of study and application of the laws of the universe. To him the people give obeisance as the highest living expression of the Deity; for to them he is the will, wisdom, and love of God incarnate.

Those who acknowledge the authority of *God over man* thus have the right to rule as *God's overmen* in the ideal society; and this is the twofold meaning of the word *government*. Thus, as the Christ is the head of every man [17] and the chief cornerstone [18] in the temple of Being, so is he the head of the ideal society. And whoso embodies the greatest measure of the Christ consciousness is most qualified to rule. Therefore, the manifestation of the Universal Christ is recognized as the highest goal of all members of the society. Without common adherence to that goal, a golden-age civilization cannot endure. Because the people of earth do not presently share this goal, the ideal society does not exist upon the earth today.

In golden-age societies souls newly come into the world of form go through a very exacting program of discipline and education. In early years they are taught the rudimentary science of the psyche, how to develop their senses to contact physical and metaphysical dimensions of Reality, and how to expand the faculties of the soul to probe Cosmos through Nature. They are taught communion with all life through the focusing of their attention within the heart and establishing an arc to the heart of all things living, to the hearts of plants and trees and flowers, the very elements, and the fiery core of the atom. The mastery of levitation, precipitation, and the science of alchemy are also part of the curriculum in the early years of soul development. Higher education is based on a series of initiations leading to cosmic mastery whereby individuals then qualify for positions in government, science, education, and temple service.

The flaming sword is the symbol of divine wisdom that stands before the institutions of learning to keep the way of the sacred energies of the Tree of Life in all who enter there. The sword symbolizes the dividing of the way between the Real and the unreal. In the ideal society the concept of unreality is taught in allegory, since the evolving souls have no direct experience with the synthetic image that is produced when man lowers his gaze from perfection to imperfection.

Thus a study of cosmic history is required, and the akashic records of other systems of worlds are carefully reviewed. The initial causes and the far-reaching consequences of individual and collective failure to uphold the standard of unity on other planets afforded ample proof to those evolving in the first three golden ages as to why they should use their free will to invoke the will of God and his kingdom come upon earth.

The powers wielded by those lifestreams who were the first to walk upon the virgin soil of Terra, who never knew the feeling of limitation or struggle or even the burden of a dense, physical form such as we now wear, would be considered miraculous by those whose memory scans only the relatively short period in which the planet has been immersed in a synthetic civilization and consciousness. Souls sustained life in one body for as long as a thousand years; and when they reembodied, they retained the memory and faculties of former lives, including the mastery they had attained.

The entire planet was a veritable Garden of Eden, and man ate every fruit and herb that was charged by Nature's helpers with the essence of the immortal Spirit to energize and revivify his mind and form. The ground was transparent like crystal, and the rays from the sun in the center of the earth glowed softly beneath man's feet. During the period of rest when the souls of men, together with their lower vehicles, were recharged for another round of service, there was an ever-present radiance from the white fire core like an aurora borealis. Thus total darkness was unknown, and evil as the energy veil was no more real than a fairy tale. To the Almighty man gave the glory for each accomplishment. The Sun that ruled the day was the focus of his adoration, symbol of the unfoldment of the only begotten Son of God, whose promise would be fulfilled in each one. The stars defined intervals of time and space and were the giant reflectors of man's blissful adoration of the One Supreme Being. Crystal coordinates marking his courses past, present and future, they magnified his mystical feelings of heavenly joy that rippled across the antahkarana of Cosmos.

More than fifty thousand years ago Saint Germain ruled an ancient civilization that reached great heights where the Sahara Desert now is. Here, while men acknowledged their God Source, true cosmic freedom was known by every individual—a freedom that has not even been dreamed of by men and women of the twentieth century, who champion rights and causes and movements but know not the freedom of the soul. In the latter days, men began to forget the Source from whence their energies came; and they forgot to acknowledge their talents as originating in Him who is ever the author and finisher of every perfect work realized by and through man. This civilization fell when, after repeated warnings from the Ascended Masters who had guided its destiny, the people continued in their separatist ways.

Inevitably, when man attributes his victories and his accomplishments to the plane of the ego instead of to the plane of the Superconscious Ego, he eclipses the light of the Cosmic Sun within his being; and his power, his wisdom, and his love are correspondingly diminished. Thus the curtain closed on another era of Light and the abundant Life. The Hierarchs withdrew, and the people went down into the consciousness of duality that always brings toil and suffering as the scourge of individual and group karma that is intended to spur a renewed search for the pristine state.

The moral of the story of "paradise lost" and of every civilization fallen into ruin is that man must consider God as the origin of all things—then he will never confuse the fountain with the stream. As Jesus said, "My Father worketh hitherto, *and I work.*"[19] Thus he taught the true relationship that must be maintained between God and man in the ideal society. When this relationship breaks down, the ideal society cannot long endure.

Never tiring in his service to humanity, Saint Germain remains dedicated to the reawakening in the souls of men of the lost art of freedom and of their ancient heritage as kings and priests unto God. In his dissertations on alchemy,[20] he points out that man must defend his freedom to create because man by divine right is a co-creator with God. He indicts the false sense of the synthetic consciousness, of a "far-off and future Good," as the villain in the piece; and he affirms that Real Life is abundant here, now, and forever, wherever you are. It needs only to be tapped. This correct sense of the ever-present availability of Good is the key to the golden age that lieth even at the very door.

"Truly, 'eye hath not seen, nor ear heard, neither have entered into the heart of man, the things which God hath prepared for them that love him'"[21] says he, quoting Saint Paul. "What a pity that more cannot shed this false sense of a far-off and future Good! The secrets of Life are to be found here below, as Above. The changing of base metals into gold would produce only earthly beauty and earthly wealth. But the changing of the base nature of man into the refined gold of the Spirit enables him not only to master the world of the Spirit but also to take dominion over the material world.

"If all power in heaven and earth is given unto me,[22] then I can give it to whomsoever I will. Yet would I will to give it to those who would abuse and misuse it to the hurt and harm of their brothers? Why was the flaming sword placed at the east of Eden?[23] Why was the continuity of existence interrupted by death? Why did illness, warfare, and brutality flash forth and take hold in human consciousness? Why was anger sustained? Was it not because people have been afraid of loss—loss of self-respect, loss of individuality, loss of relativity? Actually, what have they to lose? Nothing but their fears, nothing but their negatives. For that which is tethered to Reality can never be lost.

"Let men learn to empty themselves completely of their attachments to the earth; so shall they begin to enter into the childlike mind and spirit of creative innocence. The greatest angels who keep the way of the Tree of Life cannot deny those who have reunited with the wholly innocent Mind of God access to Eden. How can they then deny it to the divine Alchemist in man, who in honor reaches forth to take the fruit of the Tree of Life that he may indeed live forever?[24]

"The meaning of the allegory is quite simple: so long as man lives according to the 'earth, earthy,' according to the concepts of 'flesh and blood,' he cannot inherit the kingdom of heaven;[25] he cannot sustain the heavenly consciousness. But when in childlike innocence he enters into the divine domain, he finds that all of the universe is his; for now he belongs to all of the universe.

"This sweet surrender to the mighty currents of cosmic law and purity shows him the need to transfer from the higher octaves of light into the lower ramifications of self the power and the glory, the victory and the overcoming, the transmittal and the transmutation. He must shed the glitter and the glamour; he must replace it by light and purity and do all things well. He must seek for the spirit of excellence; he must forget limitations and all things that are behind. He must have faith in that which he cannot yet see and know that Nature herself holds a cornucopia of loveliness and light, waiting to be showered upon him when the magic word is spoken. . . .

"Humanity are bored, they are frustrated, they are ungentle. Through what you would call the 'hoopla' of life, they have taken on the phoniness that the dark powers have created, spread abroad, and popularized as worldly sophistication—the antithesis of the child-like consciousness. 'Ye are the salt of the earth: but if the salt have lost his savour, wherewith shall it be salted?'[26] We reiterate the Master's statement because it reminds us that the essential flavor of living is in the cultivation of the inner sense of beauty and Reality.

"That which the individual son receives from God is never denied to anyone; men only deny it to themselves in their ignorance. We all have a responsibility to encourage the Light to expand in all people, but each one must open the door for himself. Each one must enter into the realization that the divine Redeemer is the divine Creator and that since man's descent into the lower octaves of human consciousness the Lord of Light has continued to emanate his radiance everywhere.

"He is available, yet hidden.
He is Real, yet cloaked with unrealities
By the minds of men and their life experiences.
He is Light, sometimes covered over
With the darkness of men's misqualifications.
He is the Great Supplier
Of every good and perfect thing.
He combines the green shoot and the crystal snow.
He combines the ethereal in the sky that glows
With fiery Sun from solar center.
His loving Heart bids all to enter:

'Take upon you, precious child,
Garments of mastery, meek and mild.
Dominion need not bluster,
Yet dominion e'er shall muster
Each required grace
To help the world keep pace
With cosmic legions when facing senile moments.
Youth and Light appear when facing time's election.
Shed, then, all your fears and glow,
Eternal fires of youthful cosmic innocence!'" [27]

DEPARTURE FROM INNOCENCE

When man ceased to identify with his Super Ego, the Christ consciousness, when he ceased to live in the similitude of his Superconscious Ego, the God consciousness, his existence became ego-centered at the level of the human consciousness. This shift in the polarity of man's consciousness marked his departure not only from innocence but also from the ideal society. The tearing of the veils of innocence that had insulated man's world with sheaths of righteousness, light, and fervent devotion took place as man consented to the serpentine lie projected into his thought and feeling processes by the fallen Luciferians.

"Who told thee that thou wast naked?" [28] Man and woman knew they were naked, for the seamless garment had dropped from their shoulders the moment they forsook the Christ consciousness.

The first to fall were the high priests whose subtle sense of superiority over the people yielded to spiritual pride. Then began spiritual competition in true Luciferian fashion as they vied with one another for position, power, and prestige. Hurling invectives, they used their momentums of invocation to work spells on their rivals and to create grotesque images, the remnants of which can be seen on Easter Island. The war of the priests was well under way.

And then "there was war in heaven: Michael and his angels fought against the dragon; and the dragon fought and his angels, and prevailed not; neither was their place found any more in heaven. And the great dragon was cast out, that old serpent, called the Devil, and Satan, which deceiveth the whole world: he was cast out into the earth, and his angels were cast out with him."[29]

Thus the Luciferians were cast down into the earth. Through pride and ambition they had fallen from their state of heavenly grace, and many among them were required to take embodiment upon the planet earth to work out the karma they had made through the corruption of the holy innocents. The latter, having been betrayed by the high priests, were disillusioned with all in positions of authority; and with the passing of time they became susceptible to the sympathetic magnetism with which the fallen angels sugarcoated their defections from Principle.

Once "Adam and Eve," archetypes of the common people, partook of the fruit of the tree of the knowledge of good and evil—under the influence of Lucifer himself, who is portrayed by "the Serpent"—the departure from innocence through Original Sin spread throughout the Motherland. Now penetration of the veils of innocence was complete; the downward spiral was irrevocable. The long night of mankind's travail in the endless astral valleys of the synthetic consciousness began; gradually the memory of earth's golden ages faded into the distant past.

The evolutions of the first three root races won their immortal freedom through absolute obedience to cosmic law and total identification with the Real Self. It was during the time of the fourth root race on the continent Lemuria that the allegorical Fall of Man took place. The story of the introduction of evil to the earth through the Luciferians, who themselves were traduced by one known as Peshu Alga, the first rebel against God, is given in Chapter Twenty-Six as it was read to us from the Book of Life by the Keeper of the Scrolls.

The subsequent coming of the laggards and their mechanical creations[30] caused the consciousness of mankind to further descend almost to subhuman levels, all because man departed from the innocence that he had when his consciousness was attuned solely to the Mind of God and his All-Seeing Eye. Modern biologists, anthropologists, and archaeologists trace man's history only as far back as this low point in his cosmic evolution; and then from incomplete data they draw the conclusion that he descended from the ape. Actually, the era of the caveman marked the depths of man's descent into duality, from which he is destined to rise to that oneness and high estate he knew as a son of God before his departure from innocence.

The root of all mankind's problems is his ego-centered existence. Instead of holding dominion in the central axis of the figure eight in the plane of the Super Ego, man allowed himself to descend in a negative spiral of self-centeredness. And once he had descended to the very bottom of the figure eight, the lowest plane of the ego, he could no longer rise to the Center of Being.

Dictating from his retreat at Lake Titicaca, Meru commented on man's plight: "The first stirrings of Reality outside of the lost Edenic state moved in the darkness, in the void of not-knowing; these stirrings of purpose were soon translated into outer action, but the fabrications of social contact unfortunately dedicated themselves to egoistic expression and a sense of struggle.

"Man's rise seemed to be proportionate to his dominion, not over self, but over others and over his environment. The overcoming of environment was valid. The wreaking of destruction upon others was not. Therefore, the tribunal of justice known as the Karmic Board came into being in order to record and govern the interaction of man's humanity or inhumanity to man.

"The sense of struggle mounted. Involvement in the ego became a snarl of inverted spirals, structuring within the consciousness of mankind a kaleidoscopic reverie so complex as to make the consciousness to recoil. The simple forms of grace were forgotten in the astral melodrama. Man seemed to live without, but actually he lived within the snares of his own creation; now he was infecting others with his own dilemma, and the power of contagion banished him from the heavenly state."[31]

Saint Germain, who as the prophet Samuel had railed, "Rebellion is as the sin of witchcraft, and stubbornness is as iniquity and idolatry. Because thou hast rejected the word of the LORD, he hath also rejected thee from being king!"[32] said in a recent discourse on the alchemical secrets of the Tree of Life:

"Man's disobedience to cosmic law, his hesitancy in matters of the Spirit, his gathering momentums of destructivity upon earth—these have necessitated the curbing of his activities in heaven. In a very real sense, then, man has been confined to the earth to work out his destiny. Eden, the Garden of God, and the secrets of Life contained therein have been denied him because he would not heed the divine injunction 'In the day that thou eatest thereof, thou shalt surely die!'"[33]

No longer fulfilling their divinely ordained function as mediators between the Macrocosm and the microcosm, the priests turned to methods of deceit and hypocrisy to turn the people away from the immaculate design of the Real Self focused through the image of the All-Seeing Eye of God enshrined upon the temple altars in the center of the six-pointed star. For, as we shall see, in order to control them it was necessary to destroy the Real Image. And just as they foresaw, without the vision of the Christ the people perished.

Thus man lost his innocence and his childlike mind, his openness to the Divine and his ability to create after the heavenly design. Simultaneously, he forfeited his protection from evil. Truly, this was the invasion of the microcosmic world of the individual and of the entire planetary body. It was the rending of the protective sheath that had enveloped the world consciousness sealed by the flame of purity, which from afar could be seen blazing in the great urns of the sacred temples and felt in the hearts of all the inhabitants of Mu. Having first penetrated the consciousness of the innocents from astral planes, the Luciferians now moved into the physical plane, leading the people further and further astray until they danced before the golden calf and broke the commandments of the Sacred Covenant.

When man partook of the knowledge of good and evil he acquired a double standard; therefore he was no longer qualified to draw the line between the two, for his reference point in Reality was lost. Thus his sin did not appear to him as sin; as a wise ruler once said, "There is a way which seemeth right unto a man, but the end thereof are the ways of death." [34]

"The despoiling of the pristine state," says Paul the Venetian, "came about as the result of man's violations of the unwritten law—for the perfect Law of Love between God and man does not require recording without; it was already recorded within the soul of man from the founding moment when his Creator gave him individualized existence.

" 'The strength of sin,' as Saint Paul says, 'is the law.'[35] Therefore, once man had broken the Law inscribed in the heart and made his sin the law of his world, the Great Law was enforced as the ordinance of God that would keep man within the bounds of order and decency."[36]

Man's communion with Nature and Nature's God was gradually lost as the logic of the carnal mind was substituted for the direct perceptions of his Christlike innocence. The serpentine force, personified by the fallen angels, intervened as the false mediator between the mind of man and the Mind of God. Truly this was antichrist come in the flesh, whose cunning allure the holy innocents were ill prepared to handle.

Not at all content in having caused the rape of a planet, the fallen angels had as their goal the thorough indoctrination of the people into their philosophy and the enmeshing of their consciousness in an idolatrous way of life, so that when the Christ should come to save their souls from perdition, they would no longer recognize him as the archetype of their own God-identity and the exemplar of that mission which they had failed to fulfill. They would either reject him totally or worship his personality as one who could do for them that which they had no right to do for themselves.

Once the infiltrators succeeded in making man feel separate from his God and therefore separate from His will, His wisdom, and His love, they were able to divert his attention and to make him base his society upon this ego-centered existence instead of upon a Christ-centered existence. When God is remote, all that proceeds from His heart is also remote. Eventually the screen of *maya,* of illusion, becomes so thick that man completely forgets his God. This consciousness is reinforced by the Luciferians, who proclaim themselves as better able to adjudicate the affairs of man in the world of form since they are closer to man's needs and consciousness than "this God" who is so far removed from the world order that no one even knows whether He is alive or dead.

While man walks and talks with God in a perfect society, his energies are polarized in his heart, head, and hand as a triune action of the sacred fire. The significance of the term "fall" in connection with the departure from innocence is that it denotes the fall of man's energies from the centers of Christ-awareness above the heart to the misqualification of his energies in the centers of soul-awareness below the heart—the base-of-the-spine, the solar-plexus, and the seat-of-the-soul chakras—now completely under the domination of the carnal mind and the pleasure cult.

Because man's energies are sacrificed upon the altar of the Goat of Mendes, in whose image they are locked through misqualification in the centers below the heart, the pull of carnal pleasure becomes greater than the divine magnetism of the One Source. Having trapped man's energies in this ungodly thoughtform, the Satanists have no trouble in convincing him that he shall not "surely die"[37] if he commits the sin of partaking of the knowledge of good and evil. In fact, they pervert all sacred ritual, based on man's communion with God through the upper chakras, into the black mass, based on his communion with dark forces through the desecration of the lower chakras.

Man's withdrawal from his Real Self is so subtle that he knows not that the frail bark of his identity is drifting farther and farther out into the astral sea. Once man crosses the bounds of his habitation, he invokes upon his head the karmic edict that shortens his life span and his sphere of influence. He has spilled his life energies upon the ground,[38] and withal he has lost the art of self-regeneration. Practice of the science of the immaculate concept gradually fades, and the people are unable to distinguish the Real from the unreal in themselves or in their leaders.

The teachings of the spiritual elders of the race became unacceptable to the children of Mu; they laughed at their solemn warnings of impending retribution and followed instead the lure of the black magicians who wielded hypnotic powers to amplify the forcefield of their egos as focal points for swaying the masses. So universal was the departure of the people from the covenants of God, so horrendous were the misuses of power by the priests of the sacred fire, that Nature was forced to repel the impositions placed upon her; the sinking of the continent of Lemuria was Nature's way of balancing the impurities of man.

With the sinking of Mu, the scientific achievements and culture of hundreds of thousands of years was lost; and worst of all, the Mother flame anchored upon her sacred soil went down—"cast down, but not destroyed."[39] Thanks to the vigil kept by the guardians of mankind, this flame, invoked in the Retreat of Illumination in the Andes Mountains near Lake Titicaca, has been burning there ever since, tended by those devotees of the sacred fire who hold the balance of the Feminine Ray for the earth and her evolutions.

The remnant of the people who managed to escape the holocaust gradually forgot the personification of God as Mother and Father, and their image of him degenerated to that of an unjust tyrant or a race god who favored one group over another; a god of wrath and vindication, punishing the sins of the fathers unto the third and fourth generation;[40] a god of hellfire and brimstone who suffered the eternal damnation of his children (for their ancestors had seen with their own eyes the destruction wrought upon Mu and the flames that raged until they met the sea in a burst

of steam); a jealous god that could be moved to favor
by animal sacrifice and even the human sacrifice of
his own children; a god whose moods could be seen
reflected in the violent, changing patterns of Nature.
And so man created a god in his own image; in the
image of fallen man created he him. An anthropo-
morphic god was born, and the image waxed strong
and took dominion over the earth.

By and by, the monstrous god that mankind
evolved became so overbearing and so unlike the true
nature of his soul that he sought effective means of
doing away with his creation. And what could be more
effective than to proclaim him dead! The mind of
man, conditioned to respond to the false in place of
the True, was incapable of replacing the synthetic god
with the living God. Having dismissed the last vestiges
of his perverted "conscience," he seized his "freedom" and became his own god, a law unto himself.

Where every man is his own god, anarchy prevails and the focal point for law and order in society—
the Christ-standard—is nowhere to be found. Such is
the idolatrous society that replaces the ideal society.
Here there are gods many—one for every human. Here
the ego reigns supreme, and the degeneration of the
life-force from the center of illumination in the brain
to the base of the spine makes animalism inevitable.
When all of man's daily allotment of energy is focused
in the centers below the heart, all spirituality is lost
and the era of the caveman begins. Such conditions
prevailed for centuries after the fall of Mu.

And so the idol that man had erected became the
idol that man tore down, and in its place there appeared
gods many. His soul could no longer relate to the
synthetic god invented by the synthetic consciousness
into which mankind had fallen; but neither could it
relate to the ego, which had usurped the authority of

the high priest in the temple of man's being, the Holy Christ Self. Refusing to bow down and serve the ego, the soul retired into latency. When the souls of mankind withdrew from a hostile environment, leaving man as the shell of his former self, the Luciferians knew they had succeeded in severing man's tie to Reality and in destroying the last remains of what was once the Age of Glory.

"Now and always," Saint Germain reminds us, "man must understand that when he partakes of the consciousness of evil, he becomes subject unto the laws of mortality."[41] These are not created by God: they are created by man. Therefore it is man who must undo the wrong he has done; and he must not blame the Almighty for his plight, but invoke the laws and practice the science that will right all wrong. The God of the Real Image, who is the same yesterday, today, and forever, stands waiting for man to return to Eden and to that consciousness of holy innocence which truly knows Him and can therefore affirm His omnipotence, His omnipresence, and His omniscience.

THE COMING OF THE LAGGARDS

When man lost his perfection, he lost his protection. As like attracts like, so the level to which his consciousness had descended became a magnet for any interplanetary consciousness vibrating at the same level. Had man not departed from innocence, the protective sheaths which sealed the planet from interplanetary invasion should never have been rent and the earth would never have become host to laggard souls who had failed to fulfill their divine plan on schedule on their home star.

The asteroid belt between Mars and Jupiter is all that remains of Maldek, the tenth planet of our solar system—a stark reminder of what can happen when a people forsake their God. Two thirds of the evolutions of Maldek—who dared to deny the power of the Creative Spirit of pure Being—went through what is known as the second death, the penalty for having waged total war and brought about total nuclear annihilation of their planetary home. The remaining third, a remnant of souls considered salvageable because they had taken a stand against the evil ways of their brethren, were allowed to embody on earth to work out their karma and hopefully to walk once more in the ways of righteousness and Truth. For in the far distant past they, too, had known the Edenic state; they, too, had come from God; they, too, had departed from innocence. And among them were talented artists and artisans whose peaceful and constructive efforts had been drowned by the din of their more warlike and destructive brethren.

It was considered by the Lords of Karma that the laggards, together with the Luciferians who had also known a higher way, and the innocents who were no longer innocent, had ample opportunity right here on earth to choose Good and shun evil. But this even the most advanced laggards and fallen angels were not wont to do, despite the mercy of heaven and the infinite patience of the LORD of Hosts, despite the great momentum for overcoming afforded by the akashic records of spiritual victory and the mastery of self and environment from earth's previous golden ages.

The majority of laggards, although highly evolved materially and scientifically, had willfully refused to use their talents and their free will to glorify God and to execute his plan on Maldek. The momentums that they had developed and that had caused the destruction of their planetary home were brought with them; and here on earth they have continued to lag behind the spiritual evolution of the race and their God-ordained destiny. In addition to the arts of Cain and Tubal-cain, the laggard scientists taught the less experienced evolutions of this planet how to split the atom and harness nuclear power for peaceful as well as destructive purposes, how to create various forms of life in a test tube, and how to use ultrasonic waves, laser beams, and astral rays as implements of healing and conquest. Their advancements in aeronautics, space travel, and many other branches of science were far ahead of those of the scientists of today.

Because of their greater development and longer experience in the physical plane, the laggards soon gained complete control of the materialistic society they built on Atlantis, holding key positions in gov-ernment, religion, science, the economy, the arts, and the media, which they dominated with their recalcitrant consciousness that sought after wealth and power as an end in itself rather than as the means to implement spiritual values. Thus by their efficiency in material things, they reinforced the Luciferian lie that man does not need God because he can do all things for himself; and although the innocents, joined by the best of the Maldekians, desired to return to their lost estate, they soon fell under almost total domination of these more advanced lifewaves, whose every effort, no matter how socially progressive, was intended to preserve the status quo and to prevent the spiritual enlightenment of the race. Jesus' commentary on their aggressive activities was simply "The children of this world are wiser in their own generation than the children of Light."[42]

The student of higher Truth must be careful to identify the laggards and the Luciferians by their actions and not by their religion, nationality, or race; for these advocates of antichrist have infiltrated every

walk of life, and no church, no government, and no
nation can claim immunity from their presence. They
are the tares that the enemy has sown in the fields of
human endeavor, growing side by side with the wheat,
which the Lord has said will not be separated until the
harvest. Any attempt to label, classify, or categorize
these dark ones can only be met with failure; and to
do so is to fall prey to their schemes of dividing and
conquering the people. From the outer standpoint
there is no clear-cut line of demarcation between the
sons of Belial and the sons of God. Therefore, let us
study cosmic law and cosmic truth and follow in the
footsteps of the Master who said, "By their fruits ye
shall know them."[43]

The law "I AM my brother's keeper" is based on
the principle that all evolutions upon this planetary
home have their origin in God. Their very life is his.
Their bodies are composed of his energy spirals con-
densed in Matter. Their desire to live is God's desire,
for he is Life. Their desire to love, to pursue Truth, to
master Life's energies, and to excel—all originate as
the desire of God to manifest more of himself as Love,
as Truth, as creative potential. Though this desire be
perverted through centuries of allegiance to Darkness,
those who are keeping the flame on behalf of their
brethren must never forget that at any moment the
divine energy system that is the being of man can be
polarized to God and, in the twinkling of an eye, can
declare supreme allegiance to the one great Source of
all Being.

Because all have free will, all can choose Good;
hence all can be saved. Man is predestined to be Good
if he wills it so, for God has already chosen to make
man in his own image—in the image of God-Good.
Therefore, to wage war upon the Luciferians or the
laggards is to forget that "we wrestle not against flesh

and blood, but against principalities, against powers, against the rulers of the darkness of this world, against spiritual wickedness in high places."[44] Our warfare is against perverted concepts, against the energy veil we call evil, and against all that prevents man from exercising his free will to choose Good.

It is our job, then, to expose the lie that man does not have free will and that he is predestined to sin, to disintegrate, and to die. It is our job to invoke in every man the light and the image of the Real Self that will clear the way for all to choose Good because they themselves are inherently God-Good. However, those who persist in embracing the lie must be exposed as the enemies of righteousness; and inasmuch as they have personified evil by aligning their energies with evil, they must not be allowed to impose themselves or their evil ways upon the world order.

The laggards' misuse of the sacred fire included the creation of vile forms of life—half man and half horse—distortions of the Christ not in keeping with the Father's plan. Imprisoned as they were in these grotesque bodies, the souls of the innocents were not free to evolve spiritually. Perversions of the divine art destroyed the Real Image in man, and the pure ideas and noble forms necessary to his practice of real-eye magic were replaced by fractionalized concepts, jagged forms, upside-down images. Finally, even the beings of the elements were imprisoned in distorted animal forms. Thus, through these *ani-mal* (animated evil) forms, the seeds of rebellion and sensuality were planted in the holy ground of man's subconscious mind; and man, shorn of his God-identity, became an unwitting tool that could be conditioned to respond to evil minds.

Whereas Lemuria went down in smoke and fire, Atlantis was destroyed by earthquake and tidal wave, recorded in the Book of Genesis as the Flood of Noah.

The miscreations of the laggards were destroyed as Nature shrugged off the imbalances imposed upon her by a wayward generation. And the edict went forth: "Henceforth every seed shall bear after its kind." The possibility of crossing animal and human life was thus forbidden by divine decree.

At one point in earth's long, dark history, cosmic councils decided that the planet should be destroyed; for its evolutions no longer emitted enough light to maintain its balance in the solar system. It was the intercession of Sanat Kumara, Hierarch of Venus, and his self-imposed exile upon Terra that spared the planet and her evolutions. Remembered by biblical writers as the Ancient of Days,[45] this great lover of humanity served with the elder brothers of the race, the Ascended Masters, who had withdrawn to octaves of purity. From invisible heights, those who in olden days had walked and talked with unascended man attempted again and again to lead the people into the knowledge of the Law as the foundation for building great empires of light in various parts of the world.

The city of Ur of the Chaldees, the lands of ancient China and Egypt, civilizations of North and South America that existed even before the golden age of the Incas are examples of the ideal society patterned after the City Foursquare. These empires rose under the inspiration of Cosmic Beings ministering unto the needs of a planet; and they fell as a result of the evil influences of the foreign invaders who took advantage of mankind's increasing preference for Darkness rather than Light.

From the beginning, the alliance between the Luciferians and the laggards had one objective: the overthrow of all God-oriented societies and the removal of the sons of God from the control of the governments of the nations and the education of the youth. Nimrod's Tower of Babel was a monolith of Luciferian pride, the archetype of world control. The impersonal Law of Love returned upon their own heads the evil intent of those who looked to mammon instead of to God, and their own misqualified energies were used to "confound their language." And "the LORD scattered them abroad from thence upon the face of all the earth"[46] to thwart the multiplication of their evil ways by thwarting their ability to communicate evil. Thus, when men forsake the Law of Love, they lose contact not only with their Source but also with one another as rays emanating from that Source. And when the leaders of the people no longer stand at the nexus of the figure eight between the Macrocosm and the microcosm, the true relationship between man and God and between man and man is denied.

Thus when the LORD (through the impersonal law of karma) scattered the nations, the enemy capitalized on people's differences and made their separation more important than their unity by isolating the children of God into opposing camps by means of their "divide and conquer" tactics. To this day, this has been the principle strategy of the sons of Belial, who down through the centuries have ridden the wave of mankind's own returning karma, taking advantage of cosmic law which exacts of humanity a just recompense for his violations of the sacred covenants.

Once they convince the children of the same Father-Mother God that hatred and war are justified, the sons of Belial have no need to engage in the slaughter of the innocents; for by creating two opposing philosophies or systems and rallying blocs of people around both, it takes very little to convince them of the need to defend the sovereignty of "their" system or "their" philosophy, which soon becomes inseparable from their egos and their ego-centered civilizations. Goaded to war in defense of false ideals, the children of God effectively wipe each other out, leaving the dark ones in control of both sides, which they conveniently play against the middle whenever it suits their ends.

The manipulation of mankind's energies, of his thoughts, and even his feelings at an individual and a mass level has been the principal tactic of these dark spirits, whose goal is the total domination of man and society. Just why this is their goal and what they plan to do when they have achieved it will unfold in subsequent chapters. At this juncture, the instruction of the Persian Master known as Cha Ara will help us to understand the problem of Good and evil arrayed in society today:

"As there is Darkness in the world, so there is Light. As there is Truth, so there is error. As physical light banishes physical darkness, so spiritual Light banishes the ignorance of spiritual error.

"There are many who have said that man was made in the image of God. Let it be known, then, that as man was made in the image of God, so he was also made in the image of creative opportunity—he was given the great opportunity *to create himself in the image of God.*[47] But it is not enough to be created in the Divine Image; man must also direct his life patterns toward the outpicturing of that Image. To assist him in that goal, the Great Mediator, the living Christ, was given to man as the spiritual Light that would banish Darkness and ignorance from his consciousness.

"The Indian Council has asked me to apprise the students that there are upon the planet sons of Belial,[48] just as there are sons of God. These sons of Darkness have reappeared throughout the ages, desiring the slaughter of the innocents. In the time of Moses they were there, making it necessary to hide him in the bulrushes; in the time of Christ Jesus they were also there, making it necessary for him to be taken in the arms of his Mother across the desert in the flight into Egypt.

"Many are these sons of Belial scattered among humanity who would corrupt the perfection of the soul of man, who would obscure the Divine Image. These are the harbingers of destruction that you read about in your papers. Although their goals have remained the same, their methods of executing them have changed with the times.

"One day, by reason of the false patterns they have adopted in their lives, by reason of the Darkness they allow to lodge within them, they will be no more. Yet while the sun shines upon the just and the unjust, they continue their machinations as though there were no standard of decency in the universe. They lament their lot as well as the plight of humanity. Seeking solution in the hand of flesh, they deny the pervading order of Spirit.

"Some have not considered the parable of the tares and the wheat in terms of the children of Darkness and the children of Light, as Jesus explained it to his disciples privately. [49] Some have not even thought upon the problem of embodied evil. It is not our intention that any should become unduly upset upon discovering those evil elements in society which have been present for generations. All should recognize the operation of the law of cycles, the inevitability of the harvest when the tares will be gathered in bundles and burned. At the same time, they should be vigilant in defense of the Christ Light, seeking to curb the nefarious influences of the sons of Belial upon their children, upon their governments, and upon the educational systems of the world. . . .

"Those who yield their lives to Him, who are content to follow His plan as a magnificent reaching-out of spiritual opportunity, will always receive a just recompense for their efforts and devotion. Naught can stay the onward hand of Life when cosmic progress impels the stream of rippling happiness to cast down every idol in its course, to break down every barrier, to pursue every worthy goal, and to see the hand of God not as an illusive, vanishing dream, but as an invisible but real guardian of man's life.

"Unless spiritual opportunity be recognized, you may find only in part that which you seek. But when the hand of spiritual opportunity is seen behind all events as a conspiracy of Light calculated to adorn the soul with garments of greatness—in order that each man might be clothed upon with the proper spiritual thoughts and feelings—then you shall draw near to your own eternal design, then Christ shall come to live in you. On the other hand, your rejection of your own potential can temporarily destroy your spiritual opportunities for attunement with those great cosmic friends of Light who would bring your life into perfect balance.

"You are creations of vastness, but unless the cup of your consciousness be rightly enlarged, you remain as unborn sons. When you accept as your very own the authority of the divine Master of Life, the eternal Spirit in whose image you were made, then true inner progress can occur; for in his hands are wrought such marvelous wonders as man seldom dreams of in his earthly state. But when he embarks upon the higher goal as the fires of imagination intensify, he sees with holy reason that the real purpose of life is to bring each man through the veil to the place where his spiritual merger makes him the author of his own destiny.

"Thus, one by one do all transcend the dust, and day by day rise triumphant into the all-enfolding progress of a higher realm, right while their feet pursue the pilgrim path on earth below." [50]

The conflict between the sons of God and the forces of Darkness has continued to the present day. History is strewn with the rise and fall of civilizations, governments, nations, political systems, and philosophies. Because the Luciferians and the laggards have effectively removed the records of golden ages and of the Real Image from the scriptures and archives of the world, it has been easy for them to dominate the masses. Nevertheless, as soon as man receives from the Angel of the LORD the sword of living Truth that cleaves asunder the Real from the unreal, their plots are exposed and their lies self-destroyed.

Jesus Christ, surveying the wicked generations of the dark ones and the mingling of Truth and error in man and society, declared his intent with fiery zeal: "I came not to send peace, but a sword!"[51] The sword of which he spoke and its scientific use as an instrument of cosmic liberation to a planet and its evolutions—regardless of their historical background—will be fully explained in this little book.

The key to overcoming the evils of a synthetic civilization is the same key that is used to overcome the synthetic image in individual man. That key is man's consciousness, which can be either his chief advocate or his chief adversary as he allows his consciousness to be dominated either by the forces of Light or by the forces of Darkness. Whoever controls man's consciousness, which is the origin of his thoughts, his feelings, and his actions, controls the man. Whoever controls the consciousness of the race controls the planet. And it is the control of the planet that the Luciferians are after—which control is the rightful inheritance of the sons and daughters of God.

"Unfortunately," continues Cha Ara, "the sons of perdition do not recognize the law of transference of authority given to the sons and daughters of God as filial dominion. Being of the 'bad seed,' they do not recognize the God-given responsibilities of the Christed offspring to hold dominion over Nature. Nor do they see that the beautiful rose appears thorn-crowned not as a divine act, not even as a manifestation of protection, but as the result of man's wrong thoughts, his sharp feelings, his bitterness and hatred toward his brothers.

"Nature is a champion mimic, always desiring to design as man thinks, as man feels. Being a reflection of the world of man, the world of Nature is at the present time dangerously divided and unbalanced. Bowed down with the pollutions of mankind's consciousness, elemental life can no longer provide the vehicle for the pristine power of the comfort flame, as was intended by God.

"The feelings of the masses, side by side with reasoning minds, vie for control of men's lives. In most cases, neither the feelings nor the thoughts of men are imbued with perfection; yet it is possible for man to so endow them, if he will. Let men understand that even the emotions in all their turbulence can come under the command of the inner power of the Christ Light, the Light of spiritual dominion.

"Peace, be still! The waves of mass emotion, choppy, engulfing, and humanly erratic, are quieted by the command of the Christ, becoming thereby a calm reflector of the splendor of the Light. The mind can also be stilled, becoming the bearer of good tidings and holy wisdom as the Mind of Christ or of God. Unfortunately, even the justice of human knowledge does not always appear to win in the battle between fact, opinion, and feelings; for man is more often moved by his feelings of happiness, fleeting though they be, by his emotions and his opinions of himself or others, than he is by logic and fact.

"Now, let us call upon the powers of Light; and let us divest the whole self, as each man is able to surrender, of these undesirable fluctuations that prevent him from realizing God as Spirit, enfolding all and teaching all to mimic the divine plan and to avoid contact with the arm of flesh and those worldly spirits that wraithlike, demonlike, bring man into a sea of emotional turmoil.

"The day side of beauty and illumination lives. It is abundance and compassion. The night side wallows in alternating harsh and tender dreams, from time to time crushing the aspiration of the young student. May I then urge all who would run with the strong to make provision for spiritual fortitude in their lives. Do not allow yourselves to be thrust from side to side, and then upwards and downwards, *making your experiences to be yourself—or yourself to be your experiences.* After all, is not your life of greater value, of a more enduring nature, than either your perilous or your ecstatic moments? Is not your life able to become a vehicle of expression of such infinite love, of such infinite wisdom, as to be eventually enveloped with the infinite power you seek?

"So many would put on the pole of power before they are given the gift of wisdom and the gift of beautiful love. Yet spiritual man must be unafraid to burn his own Darkness, to burn his bridges behind him, and to continue with the utmost determination on the spiritual path, come any wind of hatred from any source, come any destructive emotion or thought into his mind. His life is an opportunity so vast and so utterly filled with divine compassion that nothing shall choke the tender young seed, although it be surrounded by a sea of monstrous emotion or suppressed by the boulders of intellectual pride.

"Let the specters of fear and avarice go back into the dark whence they came! Let these fade as phantoms of the night! But let each dawn bring the angels' songs of forgiveness and love into your heart. For there where God lives, in the garden of inner delight, man can become invulnerable like a diamond or lustrous like a pearl of great price, shining either within the heart of the earth or within the heart of the oyster. His soul consciousness is sometimes uncut or unpolished, but it is ever expanding through those experiences which will one day make possible the tender and skillful art of the Master Jeweler who will cut, refine, and polish it, even as he is wont to do this hour." [52]

THE WARPING OF MAN'S VISION

The distortion of Reality blinds man not only to his God but also to the Real Image of his individual and collective destiny in the ideal society. The plot behind all plots is to deprive man of his vision—his vision of the World of Cause behind the world of cause and effect in which he moves.

Within the forehead of man is the focus of the All-Seeing Eye of God, which keeps the way of the Tree of Life within him and preserves the purity of the immaculate conception of his soul held within the Spirit of God. Before his departure from innocence, man's third eye was active as the faculty of his extrasensory perception. Through this holy orb he saw worlds within and worlds beyond the ken of earthly senses. But with his departure from innocence came the loss of his whole-eye consciousness, the loss of the vision of his inner self and of wonders and beings beyond the veil of flesh. Having lost the vision of his Origin, of his divine heritage, and of his relationship to his I AM Presence, man was reduced to the level of *Homo sapiens*. Without the influence of the Superconscious Ego and the Super Ego, man remains an animal among other animals until he reconnects with his inner being and once again begins to fulfill his fiery destiny.

Without his native purity and soul faculties, man becomes a Ping-Pong ball that bounces back and forth between the fatalism of the heap of confusion and the misconception of who and what he is, fed to him by the manipulators of the synthetic society. Year after year, embodiment after embodiment, the Ping-Pong ball bounces back and forth; and the soul is trapped in a game of life, entirely divorced from true existence. Having once deprived man of the knowledge of his Source, these self-styled overlords keep his attention bound in a round of diversions—social, economic, and political. Their goal is to distort his remaining faculties of perception and their modus operandi is custom-made for every situation.

Without the vision of the higher way, the people perish in mass conformism to the schemes of the manipulators. This spell can and shall be broken in this age by those who take up the sword of living Truth in defense of the Real Image. A mass conformism to the designs of the City Foursquare shall replace this hypnotic control when mankind en masse return to the state of holy innocence typified in the childlike mind, and when they relinquish their childish ways and maturely accept the responsibility of building the ideal society.

Unraveling the snarls of the strategists, we find that at the bottom of the heap of confusion is the perversion of the childlike mind. Of this mind Saint Germain said: "The child mind is the greatest mind because its innocence is its best and sure defense, because it is not surrounded by crowding concepts and because it is free to develop symmetry, color, sound, light, and new ideas. In short, it is free to create and its supreme goal is to spread happiness in all of its forms and manifestations, all the while maintaining the purity and harmlessness of the child.

"Let me say, however, that the idea of harmlessness

is applicable only to the world of human beings, for how can there be a need for harmlessness unless there first exist harm? When you destroy harm, you no longer have need to create harmlessness. In the absence of harm or harmlessness, the innocence of childhood prevails, enabling the souls of men to commune gently with Nature and Nature's God." [53]

No wonder the enemies of man's freedom base their entire schemes upon the destruction of his child-like consciousness! As the child mind matures, it becomes the fullness of the Christ consciousness that forms the square at the base of the Great Pyramid of Life. Without the Christ, the pyramid of being cannot rise and man's energies cannot coalesce around the flame in the center of the pyramid. Where the flame of the Christ consciousness is not sustained, man's energies pile into a heap of distortion, discrimination, degeneration, and division—distortion of the divine geometry, discrimination among brethren, degeneration of the moral code, and division within society.

Worldly sophistication and the material reasoning of the carnal mind are the slayers of the Christ child in every man. As the Master said, "Smite the shepherd, and the sheep shall be scattered." [54] When the mind and emotions of man, the memory, and their physical coordinates are no longer guided by the Christ, their energies are scattered to the four winds; and immediately the Satanists assume control of these phases of man's consciousness, individually and collectively, by dividing and conquering every area of his life.

The Luciferian rebels have deluded the people into thinking they can reject the Christ and be king of the mountain. But alas, such is not the case, for when Christ is barred from the inn of being, Satan enters in and dominates the soul of man. Therefore, in order to reverse the trends of spiritual blindness that beset the age, man must declare supreme allegiance to the Light. In the words of Joshua, "Choose you this day whom ye will serve. . . ."[55] Once the Satanists gain entree to the heart of man, they create splits within his personality, for they know that society can rise no higher than the individual.

A literal dump of emotional and intellectual refuse buries the real man. Only the sacred fire that consumes in man all that is unlike the Christ can raise the soul, enabling it to soar into that freedom of spirit which is necessary for the mastery of life. The manufactured complexities of the world, the bewildering confusion of diverse philosophies, the screen of maya that rises as a mist over the densely populated areas, the energy veil of evil, the negative spirals of world and individual karma, the confrontation of the soul with the ways of the world—all of this is designed to perpetuate a synthetic society in which man assumes the identity of the synthetic image simply because he cannot see the Real Image.

As order is heaven's first law, so order is the principle by which the City Foursquare is lowered into manifestation from the spiritual to the material universe as "Thy kingdom come." It is precisely that order which reflects the very mathematics of Cosmos itself which the legions of Darkness seek to tear down through their many plots against the orderly consciousness of the Christ—the pivot point of creativity in man and in society.

To accomplish the breakdown of order, it is necessary to invert every other quality of God in man and in society: love must be turned into hatred; peace into war; truth into error; faith into doubt, fear, and suspicion; and the sweet wine of Holy Communion into the bitter fruit of psychic intercourse. These perversions are systematically enforced through infiltrating

God-government, education, science, and religion, the family, the church, and the community with the warped concepts of warped minds. The authors of these perversions of the God flame have one goal in mind: the destruction of man and society through the dethroning of the Real Image.

By employing distraction and confusion as alternate weapons, the very few have turned the many upon this planetary home away from the main issues of life and the central order of the universe. The masterminds who brought down the children of Africa and an ancient civilization of great light that once flourished on what has come to be known as "the dark continent," did so through the perversion of its sacred rituals and art forms. By injecting distortions of the divine art into the consciousness of the people, they were able to capture their minds and emotions and to divert their attention from the Presence, causing their energies to flow into matrices of dense desire.

As time went on, the people lost the wisdom of their ancestors, worshiping those they should have emulated. The accounts of sacred powers wielded by their forebears became folklore; all forgot that long ago they, too, had been entrusted with the secrets of the universe. Thus the history of a people who perished for want of vision is written in akasha—a dramatic portrayal of the cultural sinking of a continent. What happens to a people who lose the Light that once rendered transparent the very cells of their bodies is most pitiful to behold. Ultimately, the ubiquitous rhythm of the jungle reduced their beings to a primitive state, and the tie that had held these children of Mu in orbit around the golden sun of Cosmic Christ illumination was broken. Truly Darkness covered the face of the land.

The rise of witchcraft, voodoo, necromancy, and black magic in any society has always been in direct

proportion to the fall of its music and art. Such practices are perversions of the action of the All-Seeing
Eye of God and of holy rituals once carried on by the
priests of the sacred fire who communed with the
Holy Spirit and invoked great powers for good on
behalf of the people. The obedience once freely given
by the people to a noble priesthood is now exacted by
witch doctors, voodoo priests, and medicine men. With
the akashic records of five hundred thousand years
and beyond of earth's history before us, we can see
how a civilization based on the science of cosmic law
can rapidly deteriorate—right before our very eyes—to
one that is based upon superstition, fear, Satanic rites,
and offbeat rhythms that steal the Light of the soul
and encase it in a prison house of mortality.

Through the centuries of man's exile, the warping of his vision has been accomplished in many ways;
and in every age the sons and daughters of God must
be alert to new signs of spiritual blindness imposed
upon the race. The mingling of Truth and error, the
blending of Good and Evil, result in mass confusion
and a tolerance of those conditions which are intoler-
able to the Mind of God.

True geometric forms are the building blocks of
Reality. Wherever distortions of the divine art—a sphere
that is not a sphere, a cube that is inexact, a line that is
neither straight nor curved, a triangle that is not balanced—can be inserted into the subconscious mind,
whether through jagged music or motif, dissonant dance
or design, or through intellectual inversions of the
Logos, the dark ones can bring about a distortion of
Truth in the conscious mind. This, in turn, causes fundamental emotional and mental insecurities and makes
it impossible for man to build the Pyramid of Life that
is necessary if the ascending spiral of his consciousness is to rise to the apex of Reality focused in the
All-Seeing Eye of God.

Having succeeded in polarizing man's energies below his heart, the manipulators need only to continue a ceaseless round of emotional and mental turmoil, of causes that man must espouse and wars that he must fight for reasons other than those that are apparent. By keeping the populace in a constant state of agitation and their minds transfixed by the media, the manipulators hold them in a hypnotic bind for the brief span from birth to death.

Where man's vision of Reality is impaired and his perceptions contact only the illusions of duality, his judgments cannot be based upon a comparison of the Real with the unreal, of a known reference point where white is white and black is black. He is trained to believe that there are an infinite number of ways of looking at an infinite number of illusions, all of which have their justification and appeal. He proclaims that "everything is beautiful" because he is totally lacking in discrimination. Alas, he has no standard. He decides that in order to be happy and normal and to be accepted by his group, he will select a finite number of these illusions bearing the group's seal of approval and base his existence upon them.

Thus the warping of perception goes on. Like a plague of locusts, the impressions of the synthetic society descend upon man to devour the fresh young shoots of the Christ Mind emerging from the field of the soul, leaving in their wake an incomplete manifestation and an incomplete self-awareness. And that which is incomplete can never identify with that which is Whole.

THE PSYCHOLOGY OF MASS CONTROL

Once the denizens of Darkness have man where they want him—in a state of incomplete self-knowledge—they employ tactics of control based on their own psychology of how the synthetic image functions within a synthetic society. Like vultures hovering over the carcass of what is left of the Real Man, they have become masters in the deceitful arts of manipulation of the individual and society.

The Hierarch of Freedom, as he surveys the world scene and the poor plight of those who think they are enlightened, ennobled, and increased with goods and know not that they are blind and naked and poor, says: "Now we stand at the crossroads of Light and Darkness. Man is crucified upon a cross of iron and steel that he himself has erected. The mechanistic diorama which appears everywhere on the horizon has multiplied variegation and destroyed simplicity. People long for a quiet spot in the country, by the sea, or in the mountains. They yearn to 'get away from it all,' and they are finding the process increasingly difficult. The world seems a giant ant hill and man but a slave of his own crucial endeavor.

"Those who raise themselves up among men, those who insist upon being 'king upon the hill,' ruling large blocs of people, have throughout history employed the tactic of dividing the populace, setting one group against another, thereby creating those divisions necessary for controlling the masses.

"The alert must become wary of smear attempts, from whatever source, leveled against individuals and organizations. They ought to recognize from their study of history, past and present, that there do exist in the world unscrupulous men and women who do not hesitate to tactically employ the accusing finger, thus diverting the spotlight from themselves and their own nefarious doings. There are many crafty ones embodied upon the planet who take advantage of the tempest in a teapot that is typical of society today. Peering over the affairs of men, they lay their plans according to the ebb and flow of the tide of mass emotion and the cycles of the moon, taking advantage of the susceptibility of human beings to idle chatter and their failure to investigate the source of communications they receive.

"In the past, rumors have unseated kingdoms as well as kings; and today the world is being racked by a literal war of nerves calculated to destroy the poise of nations and individuals. Those who are devoted to spiritual Truth should take care not to allow themselves to become the victims of these contemporary plots, thinking they are too wise to be fooled; for I assure you that in other ages these same plots have been employed most unscrupulously and most successfully." [56]

We have seen that in order to execute the psychology of mass control, the manipulators must first warp man's vision. Brainwashing, carried on at all levels of social intercourse in varying degrees of intensity, is a necessary part of this tactic. Unbeknownst to him, man is bombarded with control stimuli which he takes in both consciously and unconsciously as a part of the pain and pleasure of life. Once his responses are programmed to the synthetic image, the natural response of the soul to the Real Image is set aside.

By appealing to or threatening that with which man identifies, namely, the synthetic image, the manipulators can cause the masses to react to a given set of circumstances and thus move them on the chessboard of life according to their own designs. The widespread use of the theories of Pavlov and other behaviorists to control man through advertising, through entertainment, and through social, political, and economic movements is an obvious application of this tactic of mass control. Brainwashing has as its ultimate goal the making of man into an animal. This is accomplished by subjecting man to stimuli that cause him to identify with his form, with his ego, and with the intellectual and emotional experiences of the ego.

Once convinced that he is an animal—having evolved from lower forms of life, still carrying the basic instincts of his animal nature—man accepts his animal responses as natural, even to the point of embellishing them with an animalistic culture; he has forgotten that the goal of life is to raise his consciousness to its pristine state and to walk in the footsteps of the Christ.

The manipulators are thus able to create a mass confusion as to the real purpose of life—to glorify God in all one's actions and to immortalize the soul. In reality, the animal image that has been superimposed upon the soul is wholly unnatural to it; the soul is unhappy, caged as it is in this animal consciousness. Therefore, a sense of hopelessness and despair and emotional instability, self-pity, and the anxiety syndrome with all of its ramifications riddle the outer mind that is caught between the soul's desire for purity and the animal desires of its pseudoimage. Without the nurturing of high ideals as the geometric thought-forms into which he may lock his energy flow, man's entire existence revolves around the gratification of the ego.

Once man has stepped through the looking glass of his ego consciousness, its myriad diversions parade before him in endless retinue and he becomes an Alice in the wonderland of a psychic maze. If he accepts the lure of the unreal with its baubles and trinkets, he will have to reject the crystal purity of the Real—for the two are incompatible. Totally enmeshed in the endless sea, he has neither the time nor the inclination to surface and to pursue the quest for the Real.

The psychology of mass control is so designed that if man is not thoroughly animalized through exposure to the synthetic society, he will become thoroughly humanized. The brainwashing of the manipulators takes into account that some among humanity polarize intellectually and others polarize emotionally. For every type of consciousness, they have devised stimuli that appeal and stimuli that repel; and none can escape the clenched fist of those who defy the Deity, thereby challenging the manifestation of God in man, of God who does reveal himself through memories of Good, thoughts of Good, feelings of Good, and actions of Good.

A reverse tactic which is used when the glorifying of the human or the animal nature is no longer effective is that of belittlement, the condemnation of the self—of the self with which man has come to identify—and the projection of guilt upon individuals and nations for crimes against the person or the state. Because there already exists the tendency toward self-condemnation, founded in the doctrine that man is born in sin and remains a sinner all his life, the manipulators have no trouble making individuals or nations accept the role of scapegoat, assuming the blame and the burden for injustices committed by themselves, their peers, or their ancestors. The guilt complex is then a lever used by the manipulators to force the people to do whatever they want them to do—ostensibly to expiate their sins. Guilt becomes a wedge that the Luciferians insert between a man and his God; for when burdened by the consciousness of guilt, man feels unworthy to talk with his God or to seek his aid.

Political blackmail is only one, and perhaps the most obvious, form of this psychological treachery. Witness also the brainwashing of political prisoners who are forced to confess crimes which they purportedly committed against the state; the censure of the Jews for the crucifixion of Christ or of the German people for the massacre of the Jews; the guilt of the twentieth-century white man for the sins of the slave-holders against the Negro; the blame of all Negroes for the crimes of the few militants; and even the indictment of all the Russian people or the Chinese for the plots of world revolution and world takeover formulated in the minds of their oppressors.

Paul the Venetian, lover of truth and beauty in the soul of man, has spoken on this very subject: "One of the magnificent feelings that God has ordained for every man is the sense of being in Christ 'without blemish and without spot.'[57] How marvelous is the soul stamped with the Divine Image, framed in the elements of universal Truth foursquare, perfect in body, mind, and feelings, perfect in memory!

"Unfortunately, feelings of personal guilt for wrongs real or imagined, for sins committed or contemplated, interfere with the beautiful and harmonious state of the soul fresh from God's own hand. In this frame of mind man becomes unduly uncomfortable; his emotions become unstable, his thoughts confused, until finally his whole being is guilt-ridden. In the name of the beauty that the LORD has placed in the souls of all men as well as the mercy he has extended to all, let me warn those who aspire to do his will that just as it is dangerous to be without conscience, so it is dangerous to be possessed with an unwieldy one. . . .

"How the manipulators of the world love to create segmental guilt, the guilt that arises when one segment of society is pitted against another. How they love to do the diabolical work of castigating and then fragmenting the peaceful nature of man, making him into a hunted animal that can no longer hold high his head and exhibit his true divine nature. . . .

"Let men perceive the various methods of stimulating the divine sense of beauty that is within.

Through the ritual of forgiveness of sins, through the balancing of man's individual debts to Life, through the desire to do well wherever he finds himself, man is able to rise above his environment into the arms of his universal purpose, which, when projected upon the screen of man's vision, becomes almost apocalyptic. It speaks of a New Jerusalem, of a Holy City,[58] of a Holy Brotherhood, of a magnificent domain of consciousness in which man can forever happily dwell—if he elects to follow the high calling of the sons and daughters of God and the Law that is written in their inward parts.

"So long as man is content to feed upon the husks of life, to hold vision of lesser dream, so long will he remain in bondage unto himself, a victim of his own desires. When the people of the world illustrate their faith in the divine design through an active sense of commitment to the principles of the Great Law, they will begin to invoke the protection and the direction necessary to find their way out of the maze of problems that beset the race. For faith begets love, and love obedience, which reaches up to a state of consciousness wherein man takes dominion over the earth. Then his concern will be not so much with outer conditions as it will be with inner causes. Then, from the heights of communion with Reality, he will begin to untangle the skeins of the world web of deceit which, originating with the few, has gnarled the lives of billions of earth's evolutions.

"But today such freedom is not the common lot of the race. Human greed, lurking in the hearts of the many, blinds them to the deceitful purposes of their overlords and closes the gateway to the realm of spiritual Truth and perfection; thus they go their separate ways as neighbor is set against neighbor, race against race, and men demand economic equality in defiance of the law of their own karma.

"Long ago the Master Jesus reminded Peter of this law when he sought to take justice into his own hands: 'Put up again thy sword into his place: for all they that take the sword shall perish with the sword.'[59] Thus man should not seek by intellectual or religious doctrine to cheat Life or experience, which, in returning to him that which he has sent out, would teach him those momentous laws that alone can give him his individual freedom.

"If the economic standard of the whole world is to be reduced to a common denominator, as some would have it—mostly those who have nothing to lose—the law of karma could not function. Albeit all men are created equal, they have not always acted as good stewards,[60] allowing their lives to be used as vehicles through which the living law of cosmic love could function. Therefore, the Law of Love decrees that they cannot reap that which they have not sown.[61]

"In state-dominated countries, where the central government has become a millstone around the neck of the people, the enforcement of an economic determinism, inconsistent with the divine economy which of necessity is determined by cosmic law, is wreaking havoc with the natural distribution of labor, talent, and supply planned by God. Here the course of human life is no longer divinely directed; but instead the strength of sin is in those laws which have not been sanctioned from on high, which bind the people to a system that utterly frustrates the soul's harmony with Nature, until there is nothing left but a form of life devoid of meaning, empty and futile."[62]

Thus we can easily see why it is the supreme goal of the manipulators to make man identify with his ego and with the experiences of his ego. For then and only then can he be controlled. There is no possible way of controlling the man who identifies with his Superconscious Ego, with the divine awareness of his Real

Image; but the methods of manipulation of the ego are unlimited, because they appeal to the vanity of a self-centered existence and to an ego whose desires know no end. Beloved Paul continues:

"Because the mandates of individual as well as collective karma prevent the light of true beauty from shining through in its total spectrum, we are concerned that the beautiful evolutionary pattern be sought in its entirety by men and nations. Those dark threads that are appearing on the surface of civilization may be cut away and removed from the garment; and in their place the motif of divine love, embroidered by millions of devoted hearts, will one day reveal unto all a more perfect structuring of universal purpose. Until the tapestry of life is thus completed, men must in patience possess their souls,[63] putting on the whole armor of God, being 'strong in the Lord, and in the power of his might.'[64]

"Those who understand the meaning of true love understand that this love is the result of God's infinite compassion and concern for the world as well as for the individual. When in the course of human events men inject into the stream of civilization those factors of deviation from natural law that abort their opportunities and prevent the onward movement of their progressive enlightenment or those of the race, they become the victims of their own misuse of free will. Then, when the law of their own sin has removed them from his Presence, they speculate that if there is a Deity, he must be very far away, when in reality God is very much involved with the evolution of the creatures of his own heart and has placed man above all upon this earth to take dominion over the stream of life in manifestation."[65]

And the word of the LORD came to Jeremiah against the false prophets who denied his name I AM THAT I AM and the nearness of his Presence: "Am I a

God at hand, saith the Lord, and not a God afar off?
Can any hide himself in secret places that I shall not
see him? saith the Lord. Do not I fill heaven and
earth? saith the Lord."[66]

The Force of Human Error

"Let us determine," the Darjeeling Master El
Morya counsels his chelas, "that the age shall respond
to the wondrous patterns of the Great Architect of
Eternity. Let us bind up the wounds of the world
according to the best possibilities. Let us scatter Light
everywhere and abate the Darkness. Let us begin with
the monad of self and feel no need to enlarge that
monad, but only to enlarge our concept of unity that
outreaches to serve the God-harmony of a universe."[67]
Into the midst of human oppression, this Lord of the
First Ray thrusts a sword of hope, glistening white;
and the tents of the wicked are cut into shreds.

The problems of the synthetic image are multiplied by the number of x-factors in a synthetic society.
Each time the individual separates himself from the
Whole and from the covenants of the Law, departing
from the precepts of his Maker, he cuts an unfortunate
groove in akasha, which will limit not only his self-
expression but also that of all others evolving upon the
planetary body. With the pen of his desire, man writes
upon the page of life. And the energies that flow
through the nexus of his consciousness, stamped with
imperfection, leave an indelible record that cannot be
erased until he masters the use of the sacred fire.

In this manner all men become the heirs of the
errors of all other men, of all who have ever lived; and
it is the challenge of every hour for the individual to
overcome not only his own negative momentums but
also those of every other one who has ever walked the
earth. By the same token, all men are the heirs of the

righteousness of all other men and of the records of perfection, also inscribed in akasha, which they may invoke to counteract the downward pull of planetary spirals of rebellion against the cosmic order and of disobedience to its mathematical harmony.

Man in his present state of self-awareness, which has replaced his God Self-awareness, is a limited creature. "He is limited by the mésalliances he has formed, often in the bane of ignorance," explains the Master Alchemist. "Therefore, we must commence by literally turning the being of man upside down and inside out. We must ferret out the little tricks that have been employed by the finite self in maintaining its own sovereignty over the lives of others; for it is the sense of struggle that has actually created a struggle in the lives of countless millions. But when they shed that sense, when they perceive that the universe is a harmonious working-together of Light serving Light, they will hasten to be about the Father's business of transmuting the shroud that covers the earth, the shroud that is composed of the elements of mankind's own insanity and destructive emotional patterns. . . .

"And so whereas we do indeed, and rightly so, condemn mankind's increasing lack of morality, their licentious spirit and struggle for ego-expression, and whereas we do condemn the violent and indiscriminate overthrow of institutions and standards long upheld by the Brotherhood as guidelines for the working-out of karmic imbalances, we also accede that an enormous amount of God's energy has been misqualified in this and past ages. Therefore, the trends toward misqualification must be challenged at the same time that they are being reckoned with as karmic factors by those who are determined to override man's density and to bring into manifestation the long-awaited kingdom.

"Have men failed in the past? Then the record of

that failure is a magnet to draw them down, and strong counteracting forces must be kindled. The power of heaven must be reharnessed, and men must turn from Darkness toward the Light."[68]

At the personal level, these momentums manifest as human idiosyncrasies, as thinking and feeling patterns not tethered to the mind and heart of Christ. Collectively, they manifest as national, race, and ethnic characteristics and social mores and trends. By confining individuals and groups within these so-called predictable norms, the manipulators find it easier to control them and to re-create from one generation to the next circumstances calculated to evoke given responses based on known factors stemming from known human weaknesses. Thus history repeats itself—not by accident—and individuals and societies fall into the same traps again and again.

Like an avalanche that levels all in its pathway, these trends of mass behavior patterns seem irrevocable in their course as they descend upon the Christed Reality of individuals and nations. The limitation that is first imposed from within soon becomes imposed from without, and then it is reingested by the helpless victims of the force of human error. A sense of failure, of doom, and of hopelessness imprisons the soul until not even a faint glimmer of the rays of the dawn can reach the "prisoner of Chillon."

Whether in a castle or a dungeon, a marble tomb or a pyramid, mankind is indeed in a vise grip between the controls of the manipulators and the gravitational force of his own past mistakes. If he had only known the consequences of his departure from innocence, he would have guarded it with his very life, with an unswerving devotion to Truth and a mind one-pointed as the flaming sword that keeps the way of the Tree of Life!

Nevertheless, Saint Germain remains dauntless in his determination to turn the heap of confusion upside down and inside out and to invoke out of the ashes of a dead and dying world the foundation of the golden-age pyramid. Moreover, he is ready to show mankind how, through the application of divine alchemy, they, too, can take dominion over the earth and the force of human error:

"We are concerned with the sinews of mission, and the mission is freedom for all. If we would have freedom be the joy of all, then we must give freedom to all; for then none can exclude freedom from us. It is, therefore, to the passions of freedom that our experiments in Alchemy must be dedicated. We must rise to emotional control; for when God said, 'Take dominion over the earth!' he meant individual dominion over one's energies, one's consciousness, and one's four lower bodies.

"Collective dominion comes about when the contributing spirit of the group, the nation, the planet—recognizing all that it has received from Life—joyously offers itself and all that it has received to the Great Spirit of Life. At that point man the individual and man the collective unit ponder the enrichment of the Real Self and the true mystical identity of the group through the increase of individual talents. These gifts of God, when multiplied, are as stars in the firmament of Being that glow in the grand design of universal destiny." [69]

STRATEGIES OF CONTROL

The philosophy of the manipulators is summed up in the words "Let us do evil, that good may come." [70] If they can convince the people of the logic of their argument, the people will carry the ball of their plots for them and argue in their defense; they will even work them upon each other—sometimes knowingly, sometimes unknowingly. Thus life becomes a game of controls where groups control groups, individuals control individuals, and all are puppets on the strings of the archdeceivers. Because of basic selfishness and ignorance, the people do not pull together against the common enemy. The soul is not found in command of its own destiny, nor are the captains of the LORD's hosts in control of the nations.

To overcome and expose the basic strategies of the puppeteers, man must first reject unequivocally the lie that any permanent Good can come from evil motives, means, or methods. No war can be "the war to end all wars"; only the flame of peace can end strife and bring harmony to the brethren. Dishonesty brings neither honor nor lasting reward; only the cosmic honor flame can build a just and secure foundation for the future. Hatred and division among mankind have never solved the questions of the ages; but love and unity, as flames that grace the altar of the soul, lock the children of God in the divine embrace.

Second, man must surrender his desire to control his fellowman. Based on the law of self-determination, this charity truly begins at home: husbands and wives must lovingly surrender themselves and one another unto God and unto the individual creative fulfillment he has ordained for each one. Parents and teachers must commend the fresh young souls entrusted to them unto the Father-Mother God and the Master Teachers of the ages. Then, in business and in government men and women will continue, as they were taught as children, to commend people and their problems unto God.

Having turned their back upon these two erroneous concepts, the children of God will be well prepared to refute the schemes of Darkness—and protected therefrom even when they do not recognize the presence of harm—by the very strength of the sinews of their minds committed to the great truths that only God-Good can beget good, only God-Good has the right to control man.

Mary the Mother of Jesus urges all "to attain self-mastery rather than mastery over the lives of others and to check the widespread practices of control men have one to another. How determinedly the dark forces have spawned the Machiavellian ideas that men must control other men and their outward destinies. They have created, then, not greatness or graciousness, but mechanisms by which they divide and subdivide the races of men. This fragmentation does not result in the unification of purpose that would help mankind to see Reality and to know it when they see it; on the contrary, it creates those schisms which breed violence because men do not think alike. And because they do not think alike, they can exude the poisonous breath of hatred against one another and in so doing feel that they are fulfilling their raison d'être. Some even dare to consider their hatred to be the product of lofty ideals." [71]

When the people accept the Luciferian philosophies of control and the Machiavellian logic of the end justifying the means, the strategy of strategies—divide and conquer—becomes possible of execution. Without their consent, whether conscious or subconscious, the politics of illusion have no power to dominate their lives.

Alexander Gaylord, an Ascended Master who is very much involved in helping mankind to set his house in order, gave a dissertation to his students at the Royal Teton Retreat on techniques of controlling the masses, which was published in the *Pearls of Wisdom.*

Excerpts from his documentation, drawn from his superior view of the interplay of forces in society, are included for all who are willing to heed the word of a true friend of Light.

"Let us examine certain techniques used in controlling the masses, one of the most obvious yet effective of these being that which is known as 'divide and conquer.' Since men have the tendency to take sides, those who would manipulate nations and peoples find it to their advantage to divide humanity and to pit them against one another as a means of controlling the world. While political parties, various interest groups, and matters of foreign policy provide the means of dividing people on a national scale, miniature power blocs are sustained even within families and small business firms. Furthermore, the smoke screen that is created through the deliberate release of misinformation through the press and other news media makes it literally impossible for either the people or their elected representatives to properly assess the issues and to formulate sound policy.

"Strange as it may seem, from time to time both sides of a question have their own peculiar rightness. But as a means of preventing popular support in a given body for a certain issue, minor points are emphasized and major points are distorted in such a way that the pros and cons cannot be systematically and objectively evaluated. Then too, once an individual has committed himself to a particular view or has taken a particular side (human nature being what it is), he is reluctant to consider the other side of the question. Thus, many are bound to their peculiar philosophy, politics, or religion for a lifetime, never knowing the freedom to reevaluate their positions.

"Occasionally people or parties make changes. Religious theology or dogma can become progressively

more informed or retrogressively more bigoted. But in
general, the up, down, and sideways movements of
human attitudes and public opinion create uncertain-
ties and vagaries that never allow the soul to clarify the
real meaning of life.

"We are interested in revealing the fact that
behind the plots that pit the blacks against the whites,
the North against the South, the East against the West,
the poor against the affluent, and the ignorant against
the learned are the manipulators who use a stream of
divergent ideas to set the brethren against one another
as a means of unbalancing the population—pushing
them either farther and farther apart or closer and
closer together, as it suits their purposes.

"The chameleonlike educational policies that
change in every generation according to the designs of
the manipulators—who, if they cannot slaughter the
holy innocents as of old, will carefully shape their
thought patterns at an early age—have acted as snares
for millions of young souls. Thus, those who would
control men have produced many shames, for by confusing the issues they have prevented God-seeking
men and women from finding Him. By dividing men
on two or more sides of a given question, political divisions have far too often turned into religious,
social, and even personal schisms. These have brought
people to the point where they are completely alien-
ated from one another because of the synthetic fabric
the kingmakers have wrapped around the various elements of life. . . . Greatness exists throughout the
nations and all over the world, but the belittlement of
one part of the world by another can only bring about
great harm to all parts of the world.

"The common enemy of the people should be
exposed. Those who in magazine and newspaper arti-
cles, in books, and in the fields of entertainment are

deliberately and with malice aforethought playing one group against another should be seen for what they are. Who is the bigot that extends his hand accusingly at another and saith unto him, 'Thou art a bigot,' or unto others, 'He is a bigot'?

"In the manifold strata of society and the present cultural polarization, the individual is the key. The Brotherhood does not welcome the destruction of individuality and of the harmony of the soul with his God Presence; yet this is exactly what is accomplished as region is divided against region, brother against brother, and as the people's energies are consumed in sustaining momentums of mass hatred rather than in seeking their attunement with the Christ.

"Ours is the way of love. And in freedom's name, if humanity would really end all wars, they must do so by an unequivocal acceptance of the Golden Rule of the Prince of Peace. Nations and peoples must be willing to negotiate, but not at the expense of justice and reason. World unrest, which should long ago have been calmed by true religion, has unfortunately been fanned by religious intolerance and the mortal wickedness of the manipulators. Therefore, the Brotherhood prays that wise men everywhere, kneeling at the feet of God, will learn to distinguish between a genuine complaint and one that is synthetically manufactured in order to spread discord.

"Connected as I am with the Departments of Cosmic Psychology and Geopolitical Studies [at the Royal Teton Retreat], I am concerned that honesty of heart be proclaimed as a means of adjudicating all human differences. Let the malcontents be ignored wherever possible; but, by the same token, let every legitimate claim for human justice be honored and fairly assessed. My prayer is for world peace through individual peace and understanding, but not at the cost of giving in to the manipulators or the warmongers who wave an olive branch that belies the violence in their hearts.

"The omnipotence of God could never be sustained if the errors of humanity were given precedence over the justice of God. He is all things to all people, [72] and in him is no Darkness at all; [73] but to Hierarchy he has given the charge of administering political, social, and economic justice. Therefore, in trust and in patience let all possess their souls, until the whole world becomes free through right knowledge, understanding, harmony, and true divine love." [74]

From time to time in the history of men and nations, we see strange alliances forming among those who were once mortal enemies; suddenly when faced with the radiance of the personal Christ, they unite to fell the common enemy of their intrigue. "And the same day [the day of Jesus' crucifixion] Pilate and Herod were made friends together: for before they were at enmity between themselves"; [75] but even Pilate and Herod became the pawns of "the elders of the people [the politicians] and the chief priests [the theologians] and the scribes [the lawyers, the doctors, and the molders of public opinion]," [76] who pervert the Holy Trinity of God's Power, his Wisdom, and his Love.*

It can be said that "divide and conquer" is the result of the *yang* phase of the control strategy, while the coalition of opposing interest groups for the purposes of massive gain is the result of the *yin* phase. The effect of the yang phase of the control strategy is a perversion of the Motherhood of God; the effect of the yin phase is a perversion of the Fatherhood of

---

*The spiritually oriented in all professions serve the Christ in their fellowman, whereas the materially minded cannot help but serve the aims of Antichrist; for where the carnal mind is dominant, the laws of mortality are fulfilled.

God. As a yo-yo, first one and then the other tactic has been employed against the children of Alpha and Omega for thousands of years, as they have continued to be the puppets of political, social, economic, and yes, even religious schemes trumped up to divide and conquer, unify and move. Meanwhile, with the exception of a few outstanding public servants, those at the top have been the pawns of both visible and invisible powers of Darkness, who from their secret chambers have controlled the fate of the world.

Nevertheless, in every century individuals have ridden against the tides of the mass consciousness; and with the aid of heaven they have made their way through the heap of confusion to carve a pathway for Light, for Christhood, and for the ideals of the City Foursquare to be realized right in the midst of darkness and despair. In the West they sing of Christ and Mary, Saint Francis and Theresa. In the East it is Buddha, Lao-tse, Confucius, and every man's saint—Gandhi. Thousands of others unnamed and unsung have supported the spiritual pilasters of civilization. These have accepted the challenge of the Light and won a higher reward. These stand waiting in the amphitheater beyond the veil to proclaim the heroes and heroines who will not fail to challenge the Darkness in this our moment of destiny.

We have seen in this chapter that the government of an ideal society is instituted to protect the Divine Image and the sacred mission of individuals and nations, and to serve as the intermediary between the citizens of earth and the citizens of heaven. In another chapter we shall see that the government in the Luciferian society, which functioned on Maldek before it burst into a million pieces, has as its aim the desecration of the Divine Image and the effective cutting-off of individuals and nations from the Reality of the God flame whereby both find their manifest destiny and their immortality.

Thus, following the destruction of the civilizations of Lemuria and Atlantis—which were attacked from both within and without solely because they enshrined the Mother flame and the Father flame respectively—the Ascended Masters sought again and again to establish institutions of government, science, religion, and higher learning in the divine tradition at the same time that the forces of Darkness attempted to tear down these institutions and to replace the representatives of the Brotherhood with those who had sworn allegiance to Darkness and to the disintegration of the Real Man through mass controls.

The methods of this madness will be explained in greater detail through a review of modern history, showing how Light and Darkness have clashed in every decade while mankind, now as victim of the fray, now as spectator on the sidelines, has beheld the world of human values crumble beneath his feet not once, but a thousand times. We shall also review practical measures which can be implemented by every man, woman and child upon the planet, from the humble to the great, for the return to a golden-age civilization.

A THRUST FOR A PURPOSE

The Lord of the First Ray of God's Will, founder of The Summit Lighthouse and our teacher and friend, has a plan for action and a thrust for a purpose. His is no idle dream of an impractical saint; his is the creative rationale of a wise ruler who knoweth his subjects well. Throughout this volume his plan for world goodwill unfolds a blueprint for action and for destiny—for individuals and nations.

Listen, my children, and you shall hear the word of El Morya. *Excelsior!* is the battle cry of Light. Trust him as he trusteth in Him, and all will be well. For "greater is He that is in you, than he that is in the world."[77]

"Universities of the Spirit must be formed. We must gather the children under our wings. We must stamp out Darkness and infuse the world with Light. Penetration must occur; the clay vessels of opacity must be shattered. The radiance behind manifestation should shine forth, but unless it is seen, unless it is perceived, what is the purpose of shining? The purpose of shining is to shatter the clay of opacity, the enclosing shards that in thousands of years have brought no happiness. Man must learn to breathe again.

"The travelers are many, but we are concerned with the arrivals. The compasses of confusion must be exchanged for a sane direction. Newness of life must enhance the quality of the present moment. The bitter ones must empty their cups of the dregs of human swill. Thousands of years of infamy can yield to one moment of the fire of the sun. The sun would consume the dross. Therefore, let us burn up the mechanizations of Darkness, and let human recalcitrance yield to the sweetness of the climbing rose upon the arbor wall.

"As we inhale the sweet perfume of purpose, our senses are endowed anew. We see the outer form as a stairway to the Infinite and the machinations of conspiracy as the net of neglect. Men have neglected the things of the Spirit. They have lived solely toward outer purpose. They have been enmeshed in Darkness, and the seeds of death have been scattered amongst them. Immortal Life has remained in the jar upon the shelf, while the thing of beauty and joy forever has been a lost object.

"Now we summon the devotees of the Spirit. We summon the children of faith. We summon the elect to a new principle—to an old principle made new—to the eternal hearth, to the center fire, surrounded by the devotees. If Light be everywhere, where is it? If all things are good, where is Good? If grace abounds, where is Grace? The hardening of the arteries of the milk of human kindness has created one of the darkest epochs in all of the stages of man's evolution. Without love there is no Life. Without hope there is no charity. Without faith there is no hope. But faith, hope, and charity abound in Him.

"The sellers of oil and fine raiment must understand the karmic accountability they have for each act of desecration of the LORD's Body. The body of incorporeal substance is the sustaining power behind all natural order. Inherent within Nature is the conveying, miniaturized cup—the seed atom of universal purpose.

"Each gesture of God creates a ripple in the nucleonic chain, whose pattern remains unaltered until it is intercepted by humanly ordained misqualification. The diseases of the world are brought about as the result of mankind's fragmentations of cosmic purpose: and men dare to impute to the Deity the negative misqualifications they themselves have created! Do they think that the Karmic Reaper shall pass them by? His grimness shall be as the whited face of God, a solemn harbinger of justice that will not be moved, even by the cry for mercy. Those who know and thwart the purposes of God should tremble.

"Let the children of the Spirit take heart; let them not faint; let them not be weary. Let them understand the cry of the prophet 'They shall mount up with wings as eagles.'[78] But these things, too, require dedication. They require energizing; they require training in cosmic law. If men give all to food, to shelter, to entertainment and ignore the mandates to create universities of the Spirit, how can we prepare the children of the coming age? It is not enough to have available the lexicon of the Spiritual Guardians. We need vital hearts of flesh. We need teachers who understand the need for devotion, for remolding in their own lives that they may mold the lives of others, who will offer themselves simultaneously to our purposes.

"The Brotherhood summons. The Brotherhood calls. The children of this earth will remain children forever or be extinguished in the blotting-out of their transgressions unless the fruit of Christed Reality can be made available to them, unless the knowledge of the Spirit can be imparted to them, unless the mystic circle of the holy twelve can be made real to them. The Grail of God within them must be filled. They must drink of the cup of it—all of it. They must understand that this can be done, that it is no inordinate thing, but an ordained ordinance, a natural fulfillment of purpose. It is the creation of newness in Life, already there but nonexistent to those whose consciousness is attuned to the dissonance of the world.

"The dissonance of the world is an overpowering shroud that leads man downward into astral horror. Neither witchcraft nor deceit, the domination of other lives nor the unhealthy utilization of the laws of visualization can produce the children of the new age. The children of the new age must partake of the Grail. They must understand the meaning of the continents of the sea and sky. They must understand the refinement of the earth itself. They must see the purging of the elements as the necessary purification of defiled substance which they themselves have defiled.

"Ours is a summoning to gaze first upon the shambles men have made of life and then upon the image of radiant Reality that God still holds behind the veil—in Eden where the Tree of Life gleams grail-like through the trees, through the mists, through all of the enshrouding manifestations. But the angels of his Presence, the angels of purpose, must be wrestled with and the blessing secured, as did Jacob of old.[79] The Christ consciousness is the inheritance of the elect. But so long as men defile themselves with outer conditions, so long as they remain afraid of the Eternal, so long shall they elect to fulfill lesser purposes. Only by a fearless dedication, only by a recognition of the fearlessness flame can they be endowed with the electronic essence that will enable them to walk the earth as Gods.

"Victory is in the soul. Victory is in the consciousness. Victory is the endowment of the man of the Spirit, not of the man whose indulgences in human revelry breed degeneration. Only by an omnipresent sense of that which will be can we overcome that which has been.

"The acclamation 'Jesus Christ, the same yesterday, and today, and forever!'[80] implies the sustainment of all that God from the beginning foreknew. Those who are afraid of religion are afraid of the Reality of themselves; for without the true religion of the Spirit, they are but 'wandering stars, to whom is reserved the blackness of darkness forever.'[81]

"We would give to humanity the cup of immortality, but they must partake of it. They must enter into its essence, into its consciousness, into its fires. They must partake of that which God is. This does not mean an end to themselves; it means the beginning of themselves. For all that humanity have been is as nothing until the day that they become illumined as one body by the knowledge of the living Christ. He is the Christ of the ages, the Everlasting One, the Prince

of Peace, the Motivator by which the movements of
life are coordinated. We are not dealing, then, with a
personality in the humanly accepted sense, but with
the Be-ness of every man which God foreordained
from the foundation of the earth.[82]

"It was of this Be-ness that Christ spoke when he
said, 'Before Abraham was, I AM.'[83] Through the mystical sense of his oneness with Life, man is transformed
from a being of the 'earth, earthy' to a being of the
Spirit. To have the soul embody round after round
upon the planet earth is an act of mercy, foreordained
only until man can become that immortal creation of
God which he already is. Outer vanity and the vain-
glorious manifestation of the human person never can
and never will eat of the Tree of Life. Man was fig-
uratively and literally cast out of the Garden of Eden
because he failed to fulfill the purposes of life. The
only return to Eden that can ever occur is that which
takes place when man walks back to his original estate
and communes with God in the Garden of Being. This
goal the Brotherhood espouses for every man, because
we know that herein is the power of creative Reality.

"The techniques are many. The lives of the sages
are many. The passions of the Godly are all-enfolding.
But we need the vehicle of the Brotherhood in outer
expression to create and to infuse the consciousness of
the young and of all ages with the celestial grandeur
that will enable them to fulfill their immortal destiny.
Yes, as we have said, man is not dust, but Destiny. But
it is a destiny that must be seized; it does not come
automatically to humanity. Too many nets of deceit
and darkness, of shadow and pain have they woven.
These must be burned out by a conscious willingness.
These must be replaced by the ladders of the Spirit,
whose graded lessons will teach man to be victorious,
not victimized.

"I urge upon all, then, the understanding of endowing, supporting, and creating in Saint Germain's
name the necessary foundations and halls of learning in physical manifestation that we have sought to
bring forth through The Summit Lighthouse. We have
commissioned our Messengers to do so, but many
hands are needed as many hearts are summoned.
To the world we bequeath that which we are. Our
lives we offer from afar. We draw nigh to the present
hour and to salvation for a dying world. We would
revive, we would create: we would re-create the Destiny in man."[84]

RENEWING COURSES

My thoughts slid down the finite
    spout
And all the light of hope went out—
The rope I broke
And fear of icy desolation
    seized me round
'Til I was then completely bound
In all delusions' cords and vanities.

Now once again I rise,
Pulsation toward the skies
Where God and home as fires
    of love do glow,
Renewing courses raised to
    Sources
All divine.

FROM LOVE I CAME, TO LOVE I GO

From Love I came, to Love I go;
And all this swing both to and fro
Alters not any jot
Of cosmic purpose I forgot.

page 21

THE LORD OF LOVE

*If he [Moses] called them gods to whom the word of God came,
and the scripture cannot be broken,*

*Say ye of him, whom the Father hath sanctified and sent into the
world, Thou blasphemest, because I said, I AM the Son of God?*

SOUL TREASURES

    Each time the soul beholds the sun, the clouds, the wind in the trees, a rose, a perfect leaf, a pebble, or a wave and then tucks the design in the folds of memory, he is adding to his treasure of those perfect ideas which are the building blocks of his Reality.

page 49

BETWEEN THE DARK AND THE DAYLIGHT

Between the dark of the synthetic image into which man fell and the daylight of the Founding Image in which he was created, there is a discrepancy of color, light, sound, and symmetry. And out of the chaos of this contrast has arisen a monolith of human vanity, a veritable heap of confusion which man has inflicted upon his environment and which his environment has in turn inflicted upon him.

page 67

CREATIVE INNOCENCE

Let men learn to empty themselves completely of their attachments to the earth; so shall they begin to enter into the childlike mind and spirit of creative innocence. . . .

page 82

AUTHORS OF DESTINY

The real purpose of life is to bring each man through the veil to the place where his spiritual merger makes him the author of his own destiny.

Thus, one by one do all transcend the dust, and day by day rise triumphant into the all-enfolding progress of a higher realm.

page 102

ANGELS' SONGS AT DAWN

Let the specters of fear and avarice go back into the dark whence they came! Let these fade as phantoms of the night! But let each dawn bring the angels' songs of forgiveness and love into your heart.

pages 105–6

FIERY DESTINY

Fiery destiny, unveil thyself!
And show the higher way of God.
Fiery destiny, unveil thyself!
For man is not a clod.
Fiery destiny, unveil thyself!
Infuse the soul with God.

page 144

SURRENDER FOR TOMORROW

All that I had thought my own—
My name, my fame, my contacts
 (fears and blames)—
I cast them all within Thy flame;
And in the glow of mastery
My Christed radiance now I see
Descending from the heart of God,
A special gift of Thine own love.

 page 184

MOSES - THE ZEAL OF MISSION

Moses was infired with the zeal of mission when "the angel of the LORD appeared to him in a flame of fire out of the midst of a bush: and he looked, and, behold, the bush burned with fire, and the bush was not consumed."

ELIJAH - A FIERY SPIRIT

This fiery Spirit, so powerful in its manifestation of the glory of the LORD, took the prophet Elijah into heaven in a great whirlwind and enabled Elisha to smite the waters with the mantle that fell upon him immediately after the prophet's ascension.

pages 357–58

A CHILD OF COSMIC DILIGENCE

I am a child of cosmic diligence;
Immaculate is Thy concept
Of my willingness to be God-taught,
To learn to love, to shatter matrices of dense desire.
O Cosmic Mother, from Thy lofty star position,
Set my heart afire!

page 266

THE ONE WHO IS LOST

The ninety and nine must be forsaken, for they already possess the strength within themselves to perceive this truth. And the one who is lost, caught in the brambles of confusion, blinded to his own Reality and the inward radiance of the Divine Image, must now forsake the false doctrine of the blind leaders of his blindness; he must heed the voice of God and return to it.

FRANCIS' LOVE

Dear Francis' love for creatures great and small
Compassed the sea, the sky, and all.

page 309

COMMAND YE ME!

Thus saith the LORD, the Holy One of Israel, and his Maker, Ask me of things to come concerning my sons, and concerning the work of my hands COMMAND YE ME.

pages 338–39

LOVE ME

I AM so willing to be filled
    With the Love of God;
I AM calling to be thrilled
    With the Love of God;
I AM longing so for grace
    From the heart of God;
Yearning just to see his face
    By the Love of God.

    As a rose unfolding fair
    Wafts her fragrance on the air,
    I pour forth to God devotion,
    One now with the Cosmic Ocean.

I AM hoping so to be,
    Made by Love Divine.
I AM longing Christ to be,
    Wholly only thine.
I AM so peaceful in thy Love,
    Feel at home with God above.
I AM at one with all mankind—
    The cords of Love God's children bind.
I AM fore'er one living soul
    With angels, man, and God as goal.

    As a rose unfolding fair
    Wafts her fragrance on the air,
    I pour forth to God devotion,
    One now with the Cosmic Ocean.

I AM locked in God's great Love,
    His mighty arms of power;
Cradled now by heaven above,
    Protected every hour.
I AM alight with happiness,
    Wholly filled with God-success,
For I AM Love of righteousness.
    I love Thee, love Thee, love Thee,
My own God Presence bright;
    Love me, love me, love me,
Protect me by thy might.
    Remain within and round me
'Til I become thy Light!

    As a rose unfolding fair
    Wafts her fragrance on the air,
    I pour forth to God devotion,
    One now with the Cosmic Ocean.

Chapter Four

What Is Individuality?

What Is Individuality?

And he gave some, apostles; and some, prophets; and some, evangelists; and some, pastors and teachers.   *The Apostle Paul*

THE DIVINE BLUEPRINT

"I AM THE RESURRECTION AND THE LIFE: He that believeth in me, though he were dead, yet shall he live: And whosoever liveth and believeth in me shall never die. Believest thou this?"[1]

The one who spoke these words, Jesus of Nazareth, so identified with the Universal Christ and with his own I AM Presence that he became the Christ incarnate—to be known forevermore as Jesus *the Christ*. This one in whom the LORD was well pleased could therefore promise immortal Life to all who, like himself, would believe in the individualization of the Christ in every son and daughter of God—to all who would believe in the abundant Life as their God-ordained opportunity to realize their individual Christhood.

Individual Christhood is the gift of God; it is man's birthright. Therefore it is the prerogative of every one who is born of God to declare the Resurrection and the Life of his Christed Being. It is the right and the duty of every man to claim his individuality in God and to devote his life to the manifestation of the

divine blueprint that is etched upon his soul as his own
unique identity—his own fiery destiny.

> Fiery destiny, unveil thyself!
>   And show the higher way of God.
> Fiery destiny, unveil thyself!
>   For man is not a clod.
> Fiery destiny, unveil thyself!
>   Infuse the soul with God.[2]

In the synthetic society we find that most people
do not know of what their individuality consists, nor
are they aware of their birthright. Apart from the few
who live selflessly, devoting their lives to the good of
others, they exist from day to day without spiritual
goals, their main preoccupations being the accumulation of wealth, the pursuit of pleasure, and the raising
of offspring who will do the same. They have a self-
image which they present to society as the "glorified
me" and another more realistic version which they
admit in moments of candor to be the "real me."
Their neighbors and friends may have an altogether
different view of their individuality; and probably no
two are alike, for each one looks through a different-
colored lens. Alas, individuality in the synthetic society is
at the mercy of the eye of the beholder. Thus, wholly
dependent upon human opinion, which blows hot and
cold, individuality is always nebulous, never constant
until one focuses the lens of the mind to see one's self
as God sees.

One in a million knows the secret of tethering
the mind to the Mind of God and then of seeing as
God sees, of feeling as he feels, of thinking as he
thinks. The majority, in their unknowing state, turn
without instead of within to find their individuality.
Their egos are insecure and they seek by devious means
to heal the breaches of their insecurity.

Some come to the realization that self-knowledge is needed, and they finally admit to themselves that before they can accomplish anything of worth they must know what "I AM." Some try group encounter, even mental karate to break down "false values," not realizing that the only encounter that can ever lead to self-discovery is encounter with God, with the Real Image.

When man functions from the level of his synthetic image, no matter what his method, he will fail to contact Reality. If he seeks from that level to establish rapport with other synthetic images within and without "the group," he will effectively block his communication with the Real Image, not only of himself but also of his associates; and he will thereby lose the threads of true existence, true knowing and being.

When man stimulates the sensitivities of the synthetic image as a means of probing the synthetic images of others, he dulls the precision instruments of the soul that are capable of deciphering the symbols of both the synthetic and the Real. With prolonged abuse, he may even lose these faculties altogether. If man would know Reality, he must cease the digging-up of the artifacts of mortality, which he carries on relentlessly much as a dog hollows the earth for his favorite bones; instead, he must become an archaeologist of the Spirit in dauntless pursuit of his immortal identity—though it be buried beneath layers of synthetic sediment.

In this chapter we shall further define man's Real Image in terms of his individuality—his divine blueprint—and we shall show how he can sensitize the faculties of his soul and his solar awareness in order that he might contact and apprehend Reality in himself and in others. We shall see that fundamental to the search for Truth are the definement and the refinement of man's spiritual senses; for these are the tools required for the excavation, if you will, of the Real Image.

Man's individuality, as God conceived it and as He receives it even now, is a flame—it is the individualization of the God flame. Individuality is the geometry of your Divinity. Individuality is the name of God, I AM—it is your name inscribed upon the flame of Life. It is the new name written on the white stone "which no man knoweth saving he that receiveth it."[3]

Individuality is a drop in the infinite ocean of God's Being. It is a point of perspective taken out of the Whole and then placed in bas-relief against the background of the Whole. Individuality was separation for a purpose: that God might realize himself in manifestation and that man might realize his potential in God. This was to be accomplished as man's will blended with God's will and the two, united as one, became an indomitable force for the magnification of Light throughout Cosmos.

The life lived by Jesus of Nazareth was from beginning to end a statement of this oneness. He who said, "My Father worketh hitherto and I work"[4] was the supreme witness of man's Christed individuality. "It is not the personal 'I' that doeth the work," explains Saint Germain, "but the Father in me that worketh hitherto and I work. The Father that worketh hitherto is the creative effort of the universe [the Universal Christ] that enhances the vision of Life's perfection for an onward-moving humanity. The 'I' that works is the conscious individuality yoked with the I AM Presence of universal Reality. It is the son working with the All-Father to produce in and for every man the summation of the glory we knew together before the world was."[5] The summation of that glory is nowhere more apparent than in the individual Christ of every man.

Individuality is, therefore, the transfer of universal *opportunity* from God to man. Individuality is the *open portal to unity,* the unity that must be realized in two stages if the Christ is to come into focus at the individual level: first between one's human self and one's God Self, and then between one's self and one's fellowman. Individuality is an opportunity to serve one's God Self and one's fellowman uniquely and to contribute a gift of enduring worth to the Cosmos.

Individuality is a snowflake etched in fire: it is a singular design. But until the individual discovers the blueprint of his snowflake and just what his singular contribution to the abundant Life can be, the true nature of his individuality is not known—the fire in the snowflake remains quiescent.

Individuality is a mirror of crystal suspended in the microcosm that both reflects and refracts the Macrocosm. God designed the crystal mirror of individuality both to reflect his consciousness—to send his thoughts back to him stamped with the matrix of man's identity—and to refract his consciousness—to break down his thoughts and feelings, making them intelligible, lovable, and workable to all parts of Life.

Each individuality created by God is essential to the perfect expression of the complement of his Being throughout Cosmos. God sends forth his ideas as great streams of light, enfolding the mystery of the Christos that is solved as each mirror reflects the Image Most Holy, as each crystal refracts its brilliance, defining the parts in relation to the Whole—the rainbow rays that emerge from the white fire core of God's Being. "This, then, is the real purpose of the existence of man," says El Morya: "to reflect God and then to identify with the Real Image that is reflected within."[6]

Examining the imperfect images all around us, we plainly see that the crystal mirror of individuality that God has made has been warped and flecked and coated with a tarry film. We look into the mirrors of the synthetic images of mankind and we behold there not the face of God nor his rainbow rays, but a menagerie of rude distortions of God's individuality. There is only one thing to do: Each crystal mirror must be polished and restored to its natural beauty in order that it might reflect the radiance of the Christ beamed forth from the Central Sun of Being; each crystal mirror must become a magnet for the fulfillment of the divine blueprint. "To improve the quality of the reflecting mirror is essential," the Master continues. "In this way consciousness itself, as a chalice, can be improved so as to contain not only qualitatively but also quantitatively more of the will of God."[7]

THE CHRIST OF MAN

To expand his infinite Spirit, God created billions of individual Spirit-sparks. But in order for God to continually expand the true nature of his Being through the likeness of himself, that likeness must be endowed with his creative potential and transcendental nature.

A universal sense of justice impelled God to create man in his own image, simply because there was no higher image, and God envisioned only the best for his offspring. Because God is the epitome of free will, that which was created in his image must also be given free will—the opportunity to choose between an unlimited expression of Good and a limited expression of Good. Because God is the ultimate personification of Life, Truth, and Love, his manifestation must also personify these attributes.

However, because his plan was to create individualities who could expand and transcend themselves as God could, who could plan, create, and endow as God could, it became necessary to create man, the individualization of himself, as a dual being. Therefore, when God individualized his flame he individed its manifestation, and man was created a unity in duality.

Man, then, was conceived in the Mind of God first as a realization of His unity—an identity complete and intact; then he was born a manifestation of the duality of God—a being of both Spirit and Matter.* We speak of the two parts of man's duality as his Higher Self and his lower self—as the Changeless and the changing. God's duality also has these characteristics—unchanging Spirit that is the fiery core and blueprint of all creation and Matter that undergoes perpetual transformation through spiritual evolution.

The Real Image of God that is the I AM Presence was created as a miniature replica of the Deity, an orb of Spirit focusing at a preordained point in Cosmos all of the light and virtue that issue from the Power, Wisdom, and Love of the Godhead. As the Great Central Sun represents the Almighty One in the center of Cosmos, so the individualized I AM Presence is the central sun around which the manifestation revolves and through which his individuality evolves. Thus the second half of the dual being was planned as an extension of the Presence into Matter—into the dimensions of time and space.

Whereas the spiritual identity of man, the Great God Self, was the focus of unlimited potential and dominion, the material aspect of the individed duality was given a limited creative potential within a limited framework set by God as the bounds of his habitation.

*Wherever the word *Matter* appears capitalized in this work, it should be thought of as *Mater,* the Mother or Feminine aspect of creation, and not, as some have thought, as dense unreality. Although the physical universe is temporal, it is through this Mother aspect that the Spirit of God, the Father, allows his own to unfold the consciousness of the Christ.

By divine decree the authority of the I AM Presence, the individualized God flame, would not be transferred to the lesser half of the duality until the latter should prove itself worthy of the bestowal by undergoing certain initiations and by demonstrating a complete willingness to affinitize the soul with the Divine Nature—to be, in fact, the individualized manifestation of the God flame.

Obviously, a creation that received unlimited power, wisdom, and love without merit would be fraught with explosive possibilities that could result not only in a war of worlds but also in a war of the gods. The lower self, then—destined to be made permanent through change—must be given the opportunity within bounds prescribed by cosmic law to elect to follow the designs of the Creator by a conscious discriminating use of his own creative faculties. Unless he be given this freedom to prove himself, he would be nothing more than an automaton, unworthy to receive the title "Son of God" or to wear the mantle of the only begotten One.

Thus, before that part of the Whole which we know as man can identify with the Whole which we know as God, it must descend into a temporal environment to master the energies of self and to become the master of time and space. Then, and only then, can it merge with the Whole. Individuality in the lower self, when stamped with the seal of self-mastery, becomes permanent in the Higher Self. By designing a dual being, God accomplished his purpose of creating a manifestation of himself that could earn the right, by accepting his grace, his will, and his love, to expand His Universal Consciousness on an individual basis.

Originally, man was given the opportunity to fulfill his destiny by choosing to outpicture only Good; and this was his natural inclination because he himself, having been made in the image of Good, was inherently Good. The reason God forbade man to eat of the fruit of the tree of the knowledge of good and evil was that he knew that when man "ate" or partook of relative good and evil, the latter would become an integral factor to his self-awareness. This, then, would be the dividing of the way between the Real and the unreal; for he would lose the standard of absolute Good. Since good and evil can be defined only in relation to each other (e.g., a great lie is more evil than a small lie) and not by an absolute standard (all lies are evil because they are a perversion of Truth), once man knowingly took into his consciousness and assimilated the substance of good and evil, he would no longer be able to discriminate between *absolute* Good and *relative* good and evil; for the latter would be blended in his body, in his mind, and in his soul.

Prior to its descent into form, the soul of man was given an impersonal knowledge of evil and the laws governing its temporal manifestation. When man received the gift of free will, he was forewarned by the Lord of Life that if he would retain the understanding of the energy veil at the impersonal level, he would be able to master his energies, fulfill his divine blueprint, and win his immortality without ever falling from grace, that is, without ever contacting the energy veil at the personal level.

Alas, an impersonal knowledge of evil did not satisfy the lower self. Man decided to take the law of free will into his own hands, to experiment with the knowledge of good and evil, which meant that he would have to experience the energy veil firsthand. This decision marked his departure from innocence and his descent into the world of maya—the illusory world of relative good and relative evil. Whereas God gave man the freedom to choose from among the infinite virtues of Good, man used his freedom to choose

from among the finite manifestations of evil. Man
would not heed the warning "In the day that thou
eatest thereof thou [thy discriminating consciousness
of Good] shalt surely die."[8] He simply could not, would
not, believe that his ability to distinguish between the
Real and the unreal would be lost once his pure consciousness had absorbed the impure substance of the
veil. Such was man's unfortunate misconception of
free will; such were the unfortunate consequences of
his breaking of the Sacred Covenant.

The record of the creation of the Real Man as an
androgynous being possessed with spiritual dominion
and destined to multiply the gifts of God's consciousness is complete in the first chapter of Genesis. "And
God said, Let us make man in our image, after our
likeness: . . . So God created man in his own image, in
the image of God created he him; male and female
created he them. And God blessed them, and God said
unto them, Be fruitful, and multiply, and replenish the
earth, and subdue it: and have dominion . . . ."[9] In the
second chapter we read of the creation of the second
half of the duality and of the projection of the Spirit-
spark into Matter. "And the LORD God formed man of
the dust of the ground, and breathed into his nostrils
the breath of Life; and man became a living soul."[10]

It was the gradual absorption of evil into the
consciousness of the lower self "formed of the dust of
the ground" that prevented the crystal mirror of individuality suspended in the microcosm from either reflecting or refracting the God flame and absorbing
Good—as Above, so below. Therefore, the arc of light
between God and man was broken, and the intimate
relationship that had existed between the lower self
and the Higher Self was no longer possible.

The dividing of the way eventually became the
way of the God-man and the way of the human. The

God-man remained in its own sphere as the individualized God Presence, the I AM or the Divine Self, and the manifestation in form took on the nature of the human, the man hewn out of clay. For although the lower self had been ·endowed with tremendous possibilities—even of becoming all that the God Self was—it chose to invert the *be*-attitude of the Creator. It chose *not* to be, exchanging a known existence, one that had been centered in the Real Self, for an unknown existence, ego-centered and unreal.

Prior to man's experiments with evil, the Real Self had supplied energy to the lower self directly, together with all of the divine attributes that were necessary for the fulfillment of macrocosmic purpose in the microcosm. Since this was no longer possible, it became necessary for a mediator to maintain liaison between the perfection of the God-man and the imperfection of the human. The Christ, the living Word that always was and always will be, was called upon to officiate at the individual level. All blessings and bestowals that had formerly passed directly from God to man were now dispensed through the mediatorship of the individual Christ Self.[11]

While man was yet in his state of innocence, the crystal mirror of his identity had been reflecting and refracting the radiance of the Universal Christ. The lower half of the duality was, in truth, the personification of the Christ flame, even as the upper half was the personification of the God flame. As the Higher Self was made in the image of the Universal God, so the lower self was made in the image of the only begotten Son of the Father, the Universal Christ.

The Universal Christ is the universal consciousness of God that went forth as the Word, the Logos that God used to fire the pattern of his Divine Identity in his sons and daughters and to write his laws in their inward parts. The individual Christ is the fulfillment of this Word, this Logos, in the individed duality. Each individualization of the Universal Christ is unique, because each individual was ordained by God to reflect in all of its glory a particular facet of the Universal Christ. This is the meaning of the divine blueprint that God created for every manifestation of himself as the individual fulfillment of the Universal Christ.

The individual Christ Self is formed[12] in the following manner. As the God Presence projects the electronic pattern of its own Real Image into the lower half of man's duality, the energies of the Universal Christ coalesce around that pattern to outpicture the blueprint of the individual Christ; thus God is made relative to man, and the divine Manchild is born.

The purpose of a mediator is to intercede between parties who are not in agreement. Because the Image that God made and the image that man made were no longer in agreement, being no longer congruent—because the lower self was not in harmony with the Higher Self—one was needed to "be in the middle" (from the Latin *mediare*), to mediate. Therefore, the individual Christ Self, as the mediator between God Above and his manifestation below, beholds the perfection of the Real Image and translates it to the consciousness of the lower self in a state of becoming Good. Beholding the imperfections of the lower self, the Christ—whose acquaintance with the energy veils of sin, disease, and death remains at the impersonal level—translates man's requirements and attainments to the Real Self.

We have said that one in a million sees as God sees, feels as he feels, and thinks as he thinks. But this every man must do if he would find the answer to the question, What is individuality? Paul, recognizing that Jesus had attained this level of awareness, admonished his followers to "let this mind be in you, which was also in Christ Jesus." [13] There is only one mind which could have been in Christ Jesus, and that is the Mind of God. As we progress in our examinations of Reality, we shall learn more of this Mind and how we can "let it be" in ourselves. But first let us define its outreach.

How *does* God regard man? How *does* he see us? Does he see us naked and alone, as sinful and incomplete? It is written in the Bible that "the heart is deceitful above all things, and desperately wicked: who can know it?" [14] This realistic appraisal of the synthetic image is made by the "LORD"—the term used for the I AM Presence, who speaks through the individual Christ Self of the prophet Jeremiah—who curses "the man that trusteth in man [in the synthetic image]...and whose heart [whose will] departeth from the LORD." [15]

How, then, does God see man? Habakkuk said of the I AM Presence, "Thou art of purer eyes than to behold evil, and canst not look on iniquity." [16] God is the supreme practitioner of the science of the immaculate concept. No matter how far man might wander from his individuality, God ever beholds man in the image of Reality in which he created him; but unto the individual Christ he has assigned the duty of adjudicating Truth and error within the soul of man.

In the Eye of God, in the Mind of God, in the Love of God man is found to be Whole; but once he removes himself from the shadow of the Almighty, from the forcefield of his immaculate conception, he loses the momentum, the geometry, and the blueprint of his identity. Since man's very life is sustained by God's beholding of his perfection, if for one second God were to acknowledge his imperfection, man would be no more. Because God holds man in the Real Image, man lives; therefore those who step outside the spotlight of His All-Seeing Eye eventually have no Life in them.

Those who wander from the beacon of God's pure regard are given a temporary reprieve in the dimensions of time and space, a grace period during which they may elect to return to the central embrace of God's consciousness of Good. By the law of free will, they may choose the election of the sons and daughters of God, who are called upon to enhance the individualization of the God flame throughout the universe; or, by the same law, they may choose to extinguish the God flame and thereby extinguish themselves.

The law of man's individuality is always impersonal. Those who serve the Christ within the framework of this law will one day eat of the fruit of the Tree of Life [17] and live forever. Those who do not will perish. Therefore, at the end of the period of grace, if man has not found his individuality in God's individuality, he will be no more.

The Christ is the fulfilling of the law of man's being through the Law of God's Being. He is the Great Mediator of the energies that descend and ascend between the Macrocosm and the microcosm. Without his Presence at the nexus of the figure eight, all energy flow between God and man would cease and the human would be no more. Thus, by dispensing the mercy of God—without which man's individuality should have been extinguished the moment he assimilated the energy veil—the Christ is the salvation of mankind and his only hope for immortality.

The Light of the Christ must be invoked and then accepted by man if his world, which presently reflects good and evil causes and effects, is to once again reflect the World of First Cause, of absolute Good. The Christ reestablishes in man's being the laws that are causative of only Good and that allow him to outpicture his divine blueprint, thereby making man worthy to commune with Reality as the beloved Son in whom the Father is well pleased. [18] When the lower self becomes saturated with the Light of the universal Christ consciousness through the ministrations of the individualized Christ Self, he in essence becomes the Christ; and by congruence with the divine blueprint, he is able to stand at the nexus of his being and once again commune directly with the individualized God flame, the I AM Presence.

Thus the crystallization of the Christ consciousness in man takes place at the nexus of the figure eight. When the purpose of the duality of the Higher Self and the lower self is fulfilled through the individualized Christ, man ascends back to the heart of the individualized God flame and becomes immortalized as a permanent facet of God's consciousness. Having descended into form and there become the fullness of the Law in expression, man has earned the right to sit on the right hand of God, [19] that is, in the place of the individualized Christ Self. Each time the Christ triumphs at the individual level, the duality of God and man becomes a unity in expression that can and does affirm, "I and my Father are one." [20]

Just as the LORD God planted a sword eastward in Eden, guarded by Cherubim to keep the way of the Tree of Life, [21] so he planted in man a sword of living Truth that would cleave asunder the Real from the unreal. This *sword,* this *sacred Word,* is the individual Christ Self, whose consciousness pierces the veil, enabling man to find his freedom in God's oneness and to return to "paradise lost."

RESOURCES OF INDIVIDUALITY

Made in the image of the Most High God, man has infinite resources with which to develop the blueprint of his identity. Wherever God has individualized his flame, there the flame gathers more of itself—more of Life, more of Truth, more of Love. Man, as a flame of hope, faith, and charity, is not deprived of any spiritual quality native to the parent flame.

From the mortal standpoint it would appear that man can never really approach the great fires of the Central Sun and breathe in the total infinity of God; however, through the living Christ and his oneness with God, all things are infinitely possible to man when he surrenders his finite consciousness. Man may therefore become both *qualitatively* and *quantitatively* one with the Father, full of grace and truth. God and man forever stand in eternal relationship to one another as the ocean is to the drop, experiencing through the exchange of the Macrocosm with the microcosm the manifestation of transcendent oneness. Failure to understand this principle will result in a failure to tap the resources of God's individuality and to enhance them through the individuality of man.

Transcendence is the Law of Life Above and below. It functions as naturally in God and man as the flowers unfold their petals, the fruit ripens on the vine, and the seasons roll. Thus, each time the lower self invokes a greater measure of Christ-awareness, the lesser consciousness of man, yet in a state of becoming, takes on more of the greater consciousness of the Christ Self. By cosmic law man is guaranteed the unfoldment of a richer measure of his true Being as the transfer of identity from the mortal self to the Immortal Self is made.

Inasmuch as Cosmos is brimming with vast, untapped resources of wisdom, power, and love, there is absolutely no limit to the light—the energy potential locked in the core of every atom—that the evolving self can invoke and then inject into its favorite matrix. There is no limit to the natural resources available to

the flaming ones who know *who I AM* and are determined to let nothing stop their fulfillment of the mandate of their inner Flame of Reality:

I charge you now:
Be immortal, self-luminous, and hallowed by the Light,
Sons and Daughters of the Flame in cosmic action!
Be deathless, birthless,
Omniscient, omnipotent, and omnipresent![22]

The Master's statement "He that findeth his life
shall lose it; and he that loseth his life for my sake
shall find it"[23] points to the worthlessness of individuality as it is defined by the synthetic consciousness.
For those who find their individuality in the world of
relative good and evil must eventually lose not only
their synthetic images but also their Real Image, which
they have failed to claim in the World of the Absolute.
Therefore, unless the individual maintains contact
with the God Self through the Christ Self, his individuality is not secured by the laws that predestine him
to immortality.

Unless divine purpose be espoused and the divine
kingdom be glorified, unless the life plan of the individual be worked out "with fear and trembling,"[24]
unless the overcoming of outer conditions be the objective of man—as it is the objective of God for man—it
will be impossible for him to experience individuality
as that universal realization of the Christ which is his
birthright. And it is the childlike consciousness that
enables man to accomplish this—to be a doer of the
Word, to partake of the kingdom of heaven right here
on earth, to shed his coat of skins (his synthetic
image), and to conceive with God the action-Reality
of his life as a vessel into which he can and does pour
the energies of creation. Oneness with the Christ
becomes, then, identification with God.

Within the soul of man is the divine blueprint etched in crystal, whose fiery white core is an electrode drawing unto itself the energies of God that are needed to build lively stones in the Pyramid of Life and to mobilize his very atoms for action, reaction, and fulfillment. Thus the natural resources closest to man's heart are (1) the blueprint, also known as the electronic pattern, that acts as a magnet for (2) the energies that rush into the matrix of identity to fill the blueprint of his preordained destiny. Rightly employing these resources, man can attain the realization of that Christ-awareness which is his birthright even while he walks the earth, reaping the good and bad seeds he has sown since his departure from innocence. Man's blueprint is complete and intact at the moment of creation; therefore, let us explore the sources of energy available to him to outpicture the blueprint and to increase his individualization of the God flame.

First we should understand that it is precisely because a focus of his Source has been placed within man—as the flame within the heart—that man has access to the entire *re*-Sources of the universe. The more light he draws to himself from the Source, from his own I AM Presence, through sacred invocation and selfless service to God and man, the greater will be the force of his magnetic field; hence the greater will be his opportunity to invoke more light which he may use to further enhance the individualization of his God flame. Thus the more man realizes of God, right where he is, the greater will be his momentum to magnetize the resources of Cosmos.

The most abundant natural resource directly available to man, apart from the light of his Presence, is from the Universal—the energy of the Holy Spirit, which is everywhere present throughout Cosmos. Like the air he breathes, this energy is instantly available to

man to revivify body, soul, and mind and to be charged
with constructive purpose for the blessing of all Life.
At any given point in space, man by the authority of
his Real Self may magnetize the energies of the Holy
Spirit to activate more of God and to reactivate his
individuality in God.

The essence of the Holy Spirit is dispersed
throughout Cosmos as vastnesses of creative potential
that can be measured only in light-years. These areas
are the void where the Spirit Most Holy remains quiescent because it has not been activated by the
creativity of God or man. Where God has not externalized himself in man and where man has not used
his free will to amplify Good, there the Holy Spirit
remains an undeveloped resource, a virgin territory
where man may make his markings, plow a deep fur-
row, and sow the good seed. Just as there is a macrocosmic void between planets and suns, solar systems
and galaxies, so there is a microcosmic void in man
between the electrons and the nuclei of his atoms. Here
the wide, wide open spaces are also filled with the Holy
Spirit. Here, too, the still waters of God's Mind are
waiting to be moved upon, to be divided, to be poured
into crystal cups engraved with the perfect patterns of
sons and daughters faithful to the divine plan.

The omnipresence of the Holy Spirit is man's
universal opportunity to exercise his free will, to
stretch the limbs of his imagination, and to press the
desires of his heart against the bosom of the Infinite.
The Holy Spirit is the energy man uses either to expand
Good or to expand an energy veil. He enhances the
universal Good as the crystal mirror of self reflects and
refracts the symmetry of the Deity's Mind and Being.
He contributes to the energy veil that hides the face of
Reality when he mirrors the asymmetrical thought
and feeling forms of the synthetic consciousness,

thereby locking the universal energies of the Holy Spirit in matrices of imperfection which produce after their kind.

The essence of the Holy Spirit that permeates microscopic and telescopic worlds is therefore the natural resource God provided to enhance the light of individualized points of identity manifest as nuclei and electrons, suns and planets in man and Nature. When man by his inordinate use of free will turns this light into darkness, it becomes a wedge that stands between him and his God, a rod or a cone of blackness inserted in transparent cells of whiteness. The light in the center of a universe is thus eclipsed by incongruous forms which cast their shadows upon heavenly bodies that revolve on the periphery of the universe. Between the nuclei and the electrons of man's being, islands of darkness, as floating grids and forcefields, prevent the penetration of space by the light of the noonday sun—the light within the heart. Similarly, in the Macrocosm, dark nebulae obstruct the light of the Milky Way. The horse's head in the constellation Orion is an example of the misqualification of the energies of the Holy Spirit in the macrocosmic void.

It is man's responsibility to reclaim the resources of his individuality that, by his unfortunate misqualifications, now pollute his body, his mind, his soul, and his environment. To meet this responsibility he must first determine to cease polluting the pure stream that flows to him from the fount of Being and to qualify this energy, which he is presently receiving from the Presence as well as from the Universal, only with the patterns of the Christ. He must replace the earthly patterns with heavenly ones;[25] and then he must set about requalifying the energies which he has misqualified in the past, by invoking the sacred fire of God to transmute his darkness into light.

Thus man has a dual responsibility to himself and to his world for his present and past uses of the energies of the Holy Spirit. By rightly executing this responsibility he will pave the way for more noble attainment in the future; having been faithful over the energies entrusted to his care, present and past, he will be given dominion as the ruler of greater energies and worlds in the future.[26]

The mantle of the Christ (the Spirit of the Christ Self) is another resource that is available to man when he has fulfilled certain requirements of the Great Law. When the initiate on the Path masters the art of selflessness and learns to let the Mind of Christ be in him, he qualifies for the ritual of the transfiguration, also known as the *changing of garments.* By mantling his being and consciousness in the seamless garment of the living Christ (having dismantled the soul of the blackened shroud of mortality), man establishes within and around his form the forcefield of the resurrection spiral. This forcefield, sustained through his devotion to the resurrection flame, is the catalyst necessary for the final crystallization in his world of the Christic patterns that are sealed within the Real Image of the Divine Self. Thus, each bestowal of grace, confirmed by right action, perfects man as the chalice into which God pours the resources of immortal Life. The delight of the Holy Spirit as it enters into the purified vessel that cradles the infant Messiah of man's Real Image is the joy that is known in heaven "over one sinner that repenteth."[27]

Those who join the pilgrims upon the Path of immortal striving have at their disposal the momentums of God-Good invoked by all who have ever walked the Path before them and who have gone on to win the victory of individual Christhood. This momentum of the ascending pilgrims is the mantle of their identity pattern—the spirit of their overcoming victory—which they, by law, may bequeath to those who are following in their footsteps.[28]

In the order of Hierarchy—the cosmic chain over which pass the resources from the heart of the sun to the heart of an electron—the greater always assists the lesser manifestation of God-Good, and the highest individualization of the God flame becomes a magnet to raise all lesser individualities into the heights of their God-dominion.

The progressive unfoldment of Reality within the forcefield of man's consciousness must bring about a corresponding relinquishment of unreality. The more light man invokes, the more darkness he dispels. The transmutation of that which is not worthy to be perpetuated in God or in man is automatically accomplished as man fills the void of his conscious and unconscious being with light. For the whole man is made Whole through the conquering light of (1) the Father (released from the I AM Presence), (2) the Son (bestowed as the mantle of the Christ), and (3) the Holy Spirit (available through the threefold flame and the Universal Presence of God and his emissaries).

These are the powers which were wielded by Jesus Christ when he rebuked the unclean spirit and healed the child whom the disciples could not. Thus "they were all amazed at the mighty power of God"[29] in Christ, which they themselves had not yet mastered but which he himself taught that all could master when they let that Mind be in them which was also in him.

THE FOUR LOWER BODIES

Saint Paul said: "Ye are not your own. For ye are bought with a price: therefore glorify God in your body, and in your spirit, which are God's."[30]

Just as a portrait is an outline on canvas and has no separate existence apart from the canvas or the oils, so man is an outline upon the screen of God's consciousness and has no real existence apart from that consciousness. His very life is God's; his identity is a detail of a fragment of the massive fresco that is God's Being. His energies are God's energies, for He who is at the heart of all substance is everywhere present in the white fire core of the atom. Therefore man can be only that which he already is—a portrait drawn upon the Life that is God's.

The synthetic image is the focal point for the illusion of separation, for it imagines that it is separate from God's Being and that its substance is its own. It knows not that the energy it spends with reckless abandon upon the pursuit of pleasure belongs to the Almighty. The lie that man is separate from God is the lie by which his true individuality is damned. And so it was written in the Book of Life, "They believed the lie, and their damnation was just!"

That which man believes becomes the law of his life. As long as man believes the lie of separation, he is self-condemned; he dwells not in the consciousness of Truth, but in the consciousness of the lie. By denying his oneness with God, who is universal energy, man denies his own Christed individuality; therefore the Universal Christ has no alternative but to deny his identity before the throne of Life: "Whosoever shall deny me before men, him will I also deny before my Father which is in heaven." [31]

That man who by the use of free will weds himself to unreality is damned by his lie to be unreal until he elects to challenge the lie and affirm the eternal Truth of his own Christed individuality. If man would learn to enjoy the bliss of being a drop in the ocean of God, he would forevermore rejoice in that Oneness. He would realize that he does not have a separate identity apart from God; nor would he desire separation from the great sea of God's Being. Serapis Bey once expressed the bliss of union in this way: "There is no moment so beautiful, so pure, so lovely as that in which the individual, as a shining dewdrop, slips into the sea of divine Oneness." [32]

With the gift of identity, God gave to man seven forcefields, each one having a different frequency and therefore providing a unique opportunity to focus the individuality of God's consciousness. These seven forcefields of awareness, which we call the seven bodies of man, are: (1) the I AM Presence, also known as the Electronic Presence of God, which holds the pattern of the Real Self; (2) the causal body of man, which surrounds the I AM Presence as the chalice for all Good that the individual has elected to qualify in word, thought, and deed since the moment of creation when the blueprint of his identity was sealed in the fiery core of the God Self; (3) the Christ Self, focal point for the manifestation of the Universal Christ within the individual through the action of the Holy Spirit; (4) the etheric or memory body, vehicle for the soul, holding the blueprint of the perfect image to be outpictured in the world of form; (5) the mental body, vehicle for the Mind of God through Christ; (6) the emotional body, vehicle for God's feelings and energy in motion; and (7) the physical body, vehicle for God's power and focal point for the crystallization of the energies of the other six bodies in form.

In this chapter we shall discuss the four lower bodies as man's opportunity to manifest the Christ in the dimensions of time and space. The four lower bodies are reference points for man's mastery of himself and his environment through the mastery of the Four Cosmic Forces known as earth, air, fire, and water. These cosmic forces form the square at the base of the Pyramid of Life; and unless they are in balanced manifestation within the four lower bodies, neither man nor his creations can be perfected or made permanent.

The four lower bodies are vibrating sheaths of energy, each one corresponding to a side of the Great Pyramid. And the flame in the center of the pyramid is the flame of the Christ that is the Life of every man, "the dual Paraclete reborn."[33] This flame establishes man's identity and is the unifying factor of the four lower bodies. As interpenetrating forcefields, these bodies are focal points for the step-down transformation of the energies of Spirit which coalesce as Matter. A study of the Four Cosmic Forces, the Great Pyramid, and the laws governing the cycles of the release of God's energy through the four lower bodies will be taken up in later chapters. Now let us explore the function and the purpose of the four lower bodies of man.

The *etheric* or *memory body* corresponds to the side of the north in the City Foursquare and at the base of the pyramid. It is the fire body and, as such, has the highest vibration of the four lower bodies. The etheric body, or etheric envelope, is the only one of the four lower vehicles that is permanent. It is carried over from one embodiment to the next, whereas the mental, emotional, and physical bodies go through the process of disintegration. (Nevertheless, all virtue and righteousness that man qualifies through these bodies is stored in the causal body so that nothing of value or enduring worth is ever lost.)

Within the etheric body there are two force-fields. These are sometimes called the higher etheric body and the lower etheric body. The higher etheric body is designed to record the perfection of the I AM Presence and to anchor in man the divine blueprint of his Christed individuality. It cradles the soul and the pure energies of God that flow into man's being released through the power of the spoken Word. The lower etheric body is the subconscious mind, that computer which stores the data of man's life—all of his experiences, his thoughts, his feelings, his words, and his actions, which are expressed through the mental, emotional, and physical bodies.

Every vibration that ripples across man's being, every subtle mood, every hidden motive, every idle thought or word spoken by man is impressed with incalculable accuracy upon the plastic substance of the lower etheric body. Then, too, the impulses of the world that pass before the mind or play upon the feelings are recorded upon the subconscious mind. Subliminal light and sound waves, cosmic rays that bombard the planet, and the sharp thoughts and feelings of others directed as arrows of outrageous fortune—all of these make their markings upon the memory body and must be taken into account as molding factors of the personality of man until they are erased by the sacred fire and then replaced with the perfect markings of the Christ Self.

The records in the lower etheric body are primarily of the synthetic image and its involvements in the synthetic society. Layer upon layer these records accumulate like sedimentary rock from one embodiment to the next. Like the hunchback of Notre Dame, man stoops from the weight of his burden until he replaces it with the burden of Light* offered by the Christ who speaks unto the weary souls of men: "Come unto me, all ye that labor and are heavy laden, and I will give you rest. Take my yoke upon you, and learn of me; for I am meek and lowly in heart: and ye shall find rest unto your souls. For my yoke is easy, and my burden is Light.*"[34]

The figure of the man of God falling under the weight of his cross and of one Simon the Cyrenian

---

*The burden of the Christ consciousness, the responsibility of attaining and retaining one's Christ Self-awareness hour by hour through the yoga (yoke), i.e., path, of the sacred fire and the LORD's Word and Work.

who steps out of the crowd to take upon himself the burden of the Lord [35] reveals the mercy of God which descends in the hours of trial that precede the crucifixion of the Christ in every manifestation of God. It is the individual Christ in every man, here symbolized in the person of Simon, who alone is capable of carrying the weight of mankind's cross.

Had there been only one Son of God, then only Jesus would have been allowed to carry this symbol of mankind's sins. But God extended his mercy to Jesus through the Christ Self of Simon to show that anyone who comes forth to do the works of the Christ is worthy to be received as the Christ. So, too, was this mercy extended to the malefactor who bowed to the Divinity of Jesus, saying, "Lord, remember me when thou comest into thy kingdom [affirm my true identity when thou art reunited with thy God Self]." And Jesus answered him, "Verily I say unto thee, Today shalt thou be with me in paradise." [36]

Because he had surrendered his synthetic image, he no longer needed to steal the Light of God. He would be found with Jesus in the consciousness of the Christ, which is truly the only paradise there is. These two final incidents in the life of Jesus reveal that God is no respecter of persons (of his pure sons) and that the weight of any man's sin—even that of the whole world—can be borne by any man's Christed Being if and when the lower self of the transgressor bows to the greater Light of the Son of God.

The mental, emotional, and physical bodies form the chalice for the trinity of Christ-action—thought, word, and deed—in the world of form. The mental body is the cup into which God pours his wisdom; the emotional body is the cup that holds his love; and the physical body is the cup that dispenses his power through service to all. When these three bodies—a triunity in the diversity of man—are respected as delicate instruments and are kept properly attuned with the faculties of the Christ, they have instant awareness and rapport with the laws of God and of his universe and with all phases of human endeavor. The senses of the soul function through the mental, emotional, and physical bodies when man dedicates these vehicles as temples of the Holy Spirit and consciously returns to the Edenic state. (The etheric, mental, and emotional bodies are anchored in the physical body through the chakras, which will be discussed later in this work.)

The *mental body,* at the east of the city, was designed to be the chalice of the Mind of God through his Christ, providing man with perfect attunement with the very Hub of Life in the center of Cosmos and with the white fire core of every atom in manifestation. Through the geometric matrices of perfection established in the mental body, man is able to command the forces of Nature, to control his universe, and to be the Great Alchemist. Through the mental body man finds the freedom to be still and know that *I AM God;*[37] for here in man's Garden of Eden, every idea conceived in the Mind of God—every plant and herb of the field of his consciousness—is watered with the Light of the Christ and brings forth fruit after its kind.[38]

When the mental (air) body of man becomes filled with the vanities of worldly wisdom, it is no longer resilient, no longer responsive to the delicate chords of the lost Word. 'Tis then that the logic of the serpent captivates his mind, and he lowers the cup of his consciousness to partake of the double standard. In this manner the carnal mind displaces the image of the Christ; usurping the throne of authority in the mental body, it reigns supreme in the synthetic consciousness.

Thus man has need of the purity focused by the Cherubim, who, when called upon, will raise his mind so that it might once again receive the ideations of the Mind of God. Therefore, at the east of the Garden the LORD God placed the flaming sword to keep the way of the Tree of Life. When man calls upon his Christ Self to wield this sword, he once again has instantaneous discrimination between Truth and error, Right and wrong, Good and evil, Perfection and imperfection, Reality and unreality. Once again the pillars of the ancient wisdom grace the temple beautiful that the mental body is intended to be, even while they undergird the structure of the mind.

The *emotional body* corresponds to the south side of the City Foursquare as the reflector of the feelings of God and his Christ; of mercy and compassion; of faith and hope; of buoyant love, joyous determination, fiery zeal, and the appreciation of cosmic law, cosmic science, and the divine arts. It is also the repository of man's own feelings, his desires, and his *emotions* (his *energies-in-motion*), which in many are more often turbulent than they are peaceful. When man learns the mastery of the water element, the emotional body can be the mirror of the Real Image and its energies can be directed to reflect the feelings of the soul and its innate contact with Reality; or, when trained upon the lurid and hypnotic emotions of the world—on human pathos, the angry mob, the melodrama of soap opera trivia—it may make of the synthetic image a caricature of human folly.

As the tides of the sea are affected by the cycles of the moon, so the water body is pulled by lunar influences, evidenced in the extreme emotions people experience during the full moon. But the waters of the emotional body also respond to the command of the individual Christ Self "Peace, be still!"[39] When man brings his emotional body under God-control, he has at his command one of the greatest powers of the universe to implement Good and to expand throughout Cosmos the freedom of Truth, the peace of Life, and the power of Love.

The *physical body,* corresponding to the side of the west, provides the opportunity for man to express the summum bonum of his consciousness in Matter. As the higher etheric body contains the blueprint of individuality in higher planes, so on earth man sculpts the pattern of his identity upon the substance of his physical body. Formed "of the dust of the ground," which no longer sparkles with the radiance of the white fire core, this tabernacle of the soul, this temple of the living God, is not transparent as it used to be, emitting the radiance of the Universal Christ. Instead of being the focal point for the crystallization of the divine plan, man's physical (earth) body has become the sepulcher of the imperfect thoughts and feelings recorded upon his lower etheric body.

Man's karma, which we shall discuss in Chapter Eight and touch upon lightly in the volumes of *The Lost Teachings of Jesus,* determines the capacities and limitations of his four lower bodies. The imperfections of man's physical form can be traced directly to the discord that he has registered upon his three other bodies. Once works of Grecian art, exquisite in their pristine form, chiseled by the Master Sculptor, today the statues of man and woman are often the glaring work of unskilled artisans who obviously have not studied the symmetry of the Christ Self—else they would have found the pristine pattern that ought to manifest through the etheric, mental, and emotional bodies, which must be preserved if the physical form is to be a work of art, of scientific wonder and optimum efficiency. Thus, in order to outpicture perfection in his physical form, man must take the leaven of the Christ consciousness—"which a woman [the

Divine Mother] took and hid in three measures of meal"[40]—and carefully place it in the etheric, mental, and emotional bodies in order that the leaven might leaven "the whole lump."[41]

Let us now take up some of the scientific principles that man may apply to work change in these four vehicles which God and Nature have lovingly provided for the manifestation of his true individuality.

THE SCIENCE OF INDIVIDUALITY

When Jesus raised Lazarus from the dead, he demonstrated the laws of scientific individuality. So perfectly attuned as instruments of the Christ Self were the four lower bodies of Jesus, so saturated with the universal Christ consciousness were his mind and soul, that he had manifest dominion not only over his own forcefield but also over that of the entire planet and over the four lower bodies of anyone who would surrender himself unto the Christ Light.

When Jesus spoke the command "Lazarus, come forth!"[42] there was an immediate response from the soul of Lazarus that desired to live and that believed in the power of the Christ to overcome the forces of disintegration already working in his body temple. By Lazarus' consent, the light stored in the four lower bodies of Jesus was immediately transferred to his being; there occurred a reintegration of the energies of his four lower bodies and he rose from the dead.

The ability to manifest one's Christed individuality or to call it forth in another is based on the application of the scientific principle known as hallowing space. According to this law, the son or the daughter of God who is devoted to the Christ Light may expand the power, the love, and the wisdom of God by consecrating his being as a vessel of the

Holy Spirit. To hallow space means to consecrate both the nuclei and the electrons of one's atoms and the space between them to the expansion of the light. Through the nuclei and the electrons, already focuses of the Christ Light, the individual can magnetize greater light; whereas in the wide-open spaces between them he can call for an intensification of the action of the Holy Spirit and its qualification with perfection. In this manner his entire body temple becomes a dwelling place for the Most High God rather than a dumping ground for the refuse of the mass consciousness and his own misqualified energies.

Thus, although God is everywhere—and there is no place where he is not—man by the intelligent and loving use of his free will may magnetize greater and greater power from the heart of Cosmos, thereby intensifying the forcefield of light within his being. This Jesus did when he walked upon the water. Applying the law of transfer of energy, whereby energy may be transferred from God to man or from man to man, he caused the atoms of his body to absorb a more than ordinary amount of cosmic rays and spiritual light. When his whole body was full of light, it counteracted the pull of gravity and he was "purely a ray of light shining upon the waters."[43]

In order for Peter to receive the transfer of energy, he himself had to apply the principle of real-eye magic. The image of the Christ held in Peter's mind "in radiant, illumined manifestation" became the focal point for the transfer of light which Jesus directed to him. As long as Peter retained the immaculate concept of the Christ, which Jesus also envisioned for both of them, the light flowed over the arc established between them by the power of their attention. When Peter entered into a vortex of fear, as Saint Germain explains, his body was densified and began to sink. Jesus reestablished the alchemical tie by extending his hand to Peter, and "the flow of spiritual energy through the hand of the Christ raised Peter once again to safety."[44]

The miracles of Jesus' life were actually not miracles at all, for the term miracle implies an exception to natural law. In reality, his powers to heal the sick, to raise the dead, to produce feats of alchemy, and even to forgive sin were the fulfillment of cosmic laws not understood by his contemporaries and not entirely explained even to the present day.

The difference between Jesus the Christ and ordinary men was the difference between the pure light momentum qualified in his four lower bodies and the impure accumulation of misqualified substance within their four lower bodies. Jesus consecrated his lower vehicles as vessels of the Universal Christ, and so he became the Christ incarnate. The sacred fire that he invoked and the laws that he applied in order to gain his self-mastery are available and workable to all who would follow in his footsteps; for the record clearly shows that both before and after his mission, those who have applied the same scientific principles that he demonstrated have achieved the same results.

The purposes of life are clearly stated, but they are not always clearly read—even when one such as Jesus leaves the record of a perfect example of the individual Christed fulfillment of those purposes. The spiritually ignorant masses are easily diverted from the central theme of creation—communion with Life, with true Being, with the One Source of energy, which is God. Without communion the key to scientific individuality cannot be won. And partial communion is not enough.

The atoms in man's being must merge with the atoms in God's Being. The atom that is man must

merge with the Atom that is God. The four sides of the
Pyramid of Life must be congruent with the four sides
of the consciousness of God represented in the City
Foursquare. Through alternate periods of prayer and
meditation, service and the affirmation of Truth and
righteousness, man achieves a greater attunement with
God and Nature; and the veil that hung between the
Holy of Holies of God's Being and the flame of the
individualized spark of identity is rent in twain. [45]

Like Salome with her seven veils (perversions of
the seven rays), man has many veils that hang between him and his God—gossamer webs of fear and
pride, ignorance and self-righteousness. In fact, he
has a veil that justifies every phase of his mortal existence. It behooves man to invoke the sacred fire from
the very heart of his being to consume these veils which
blur the Image of Reality, compromise the standard of
Truth, and prevent him from recognizing the impurities of his four lower bodies for what they are.

The purification of one's being is the ritual of a
lifetime; while the LORD does not hold sinning mortals in derision or in scorn, he "will not hold him
guiltless that taketh his name in vain." [46] This means
that when man uses the powers of the sacred word,
I AM, to vainly bolster his personality and to further
the compromising position of the human ego that simply will not surrender to the Superconscious Ego—
then the LORD, or the Law, exacts payment for energy
vainly used.

The undoing of the wrongs that have been done
must take place according to the law of cycles; this
cannot be accomplished in a day, no matter how great
is man's devotion to Truth once he has found it. For
the intensity of the sacred fire required to consume all
of the dross of his consciousness, if applied at a given
moment, would not only consume his misqualified

energies but also the very being of man, which has not yet gone through the trial by fire or been made permanent through the ritual of the resurrection.

With each new day, man receives his portion of misqualified substance which must be transmuted if he would be master of the twenty-four-hour cycle. All over the world this transmutation is accomplished through the practice of various rituals: the Hindus, for example, take their traditional early morning dip in the Ganges, reciting holy mantras, while devout Christians and Moslems offer their devotions with the rising sun. No matter what his faith, having performed his spiritual ablutions, man may proceed with his creative endeavors unhampered by vain momentums of the past.

The Lord has said, "Sufficient unto the day is the evil thereof."[47] This means that in a given cycle man receives only that portion of the energy veil which he, in partnership with his Christ Self, can safely overcome. Man must realize that by divine decree he is never given a test that he cannot pass, for this principle is scientific. But he must approach the purification of his four lower bodies with reverence for the sacred science that God has bequeathed to him to implement his salvation. Using the correct formulas, selecting the principles that apply to each experiment in self-mastery, never tiring until the results of his demonstration of cosmic law are before him, man can have the scientific victory over his being and world—because the Great Alchemist has willed it so.

Every son and daughter of God can and must learn to control the energy flow in his four lower bodies and in his environment. To achieve this control, he must first master the technique practiced by Mary the Mother of Jesus of abiding in that state of listening grace wherein the soul does magnetize the eternal

Presence of God that becomes a bulwark of strength and protection for Godly endeavor. Through communion with the Presence, individual man is made aware of the universal intent relative to his own life; and the Divine Self pours into his forcefield the energy (as a stream of radiant light) and the know-how he requires to fulfill that intent. Practicing the art of listening grace, of receptivity to Truth and resistlessness to Love, man receives those blessings of hope and salvation which encourage him to accept the illumination of his Christ Self, who bids him work change rather than support continuing havoc in his world.

The statement "Except those days should be shortened, there should no flesh be saved"[48] reveals the fact that there is a possibility for the individual to govern the amount of time he will spend in working out his salvation. The old man, who identifies with the transient personality, can be put off right while the new man is making his appearance;[49] and he must be put off if the new man, meek yet powerful, is to inherit the earth. How long this process of putting off the old and putting on the new will take is determined both by law and by the individual's application of scientific principle. Although the cycles of his overcoming cannot be skipped, they can be accelerated and even transcended if he passes those initiations which the LORD, the Mighty I AM Presence, requires of him.

And so it is in the educational systems of the world. In order to graduate from a certain school a student may be required to master certain subject matter, to write a thesis, and to pass an exam. When he accomplishes the assignment, he is given his diploma whether it takes a month or a year. The same rules apply in the mastery of scientific individuality. Thus Jesus said, "Many that are first shall be last; and the last first,"[50] making clear that the merits of individual striving weigh in the balance of the bestowal of God's grace.

Unquestionably, many would find their freedom in one lifetime if it were not for the density of human thought and feeling lodged in their four lower bodies which prohibits them from experiencing and expressing God. This effluvia causes them to remain involved in a continual round of karma-making activities—cause and effect sequences in a world of relative good and evil.

Most of mankind's errors are committed in total ignorance of the Law, whose precepts they would gladly follow if they but knew how. The byword "Be careful!" should be heeded by men in all that they do; for by exercising care, scientific individuality is guarded even while man is in the state of becoming. The careful man is not the fool who rushes in where angels fear to tread; nor is he the one who has said in his heart, "There is no God."[51] The careful man is the scientist who never lacks the courage of his convictions; nor is he without the humility to invoke from on high the means to implement them.

The phrase "the quick and the dead"[52] applies to the two categories of people dwelling on earth. The quick are those whose soul consciousness has already been quickened, whose awareness has identified them as a part of God that should ultimately return to the Whole through the practice of the ritual of scientific individuality. The dead are those who conceive of themselves as having an existence apart from God. Living entirely for the synthetic image, they have become a law unto themselves; and because this law of sin, now warring in their members,[53] is contrary to the Law of Life, they are subject to a law of personal survival and personal death—of relative good and evil.

Inasmuch as man, as an apprentice to the Great Alchemist, is free to experiment in his own laboratory, he can and does set up laws within his own four lower bodies that are in conflict with natural law. These man-made laws bind him to a series of causes and effects that prevent his practice of the highest alchemy and his demonstration of cosmic law. Those who would be quickened must understand that in order to break the iron bands of these self-imposed restrictions, they must first study the principles of cosmic law and then discard, line upon line, every concept retained in consciousness which prevents the full manifestation of the Truth that can make them free. The strength of man-made laws is in the acceptance of those sinful concepts upon which they are based and the sinful habit patterns which reinforce man's misguided use of God's energy. Layer by layer man must unwind from the electrode of his being the coils of wrong habit, wrong desire, and wrong concept, which are the foundation for those laws by which he limits his soul's God-given and unlimited ability to express Good.

The four lower bodies of man are the vehicles provided by God for his individualization of the God flame. Out of the flame Above came forth the individed duality; out of the flame below came forth the four aspects of scientific individuality. The four vehicles may be thought of as four colanders or drums, one inside of the other. The etheric body is the largest; within that is the mental body, then the emotional body, and finally the physical body.

The light of the Christ consciousness flows through a dot pattern perforated upon the fabric of each of man's bodies. The dot pattern of each body is different. (They also vary from one individual to the next according to the divine blueprint.) However, certain corresponding keys within the patterns provide for the meshing of the energies of the four "drums," allowing each individual to integrate his four body functions and his personality. Only when the perforations are in perfect alignment (when the holes of the four "colanders" are directly opposite each other) can the light flow brilliantly and steadfastly. When the holes of the "colanders" are completely out of alignment, the light can at best only seep through and the individual becomes sluggish and inefficient.

One must also consider the frequency alignment of the bodies according to the square at the base of the Pyramid. When the electronic frequencies of the four lower bodies are at the proper pitch and the bodies are at right angles to one another, the chord of identity is in harmony and the note of the individual Christ-pattern will sound forth. Misqualified substance lodged within the wide-open spaces of man's atoms brings about the misalignment of the four lower bodies, resulting in their malfunctioning. This effluvia also prevents the balanced manifestation of the qualities of Power, Wisdom, and Love, which must be in balance equilaterally if the Christ-identity of the individual is to be expressed in form.

Because "all have sinned, and come short of the glory of God," [54] as Paul said, all have a need to reverse the trends of imperfection within their lower vehicles. All can begin by making daily invocation to God for the fires of purification to resurrect the balanced expression of the attributes of the Christ in their character, their feelings, their thoughts, and their actions. The alchemical transformation induced by these fires ultimately leads to the alignment of the four lower bodies and the raising of the Pyramid of Life, which is built stone upon stone of man's devotion to God and his service to his fellowman. Once the alignment of the sacred square—fire, air, water, and earth—is achieved in man's being, the cells and atoms of his four bodies follow suit; then the attunement of the soul faculties with the God Presence is more easily established and maintained through the purified vehicles.

The thread of contact between the lower self and the Higher Self is strengthened through the ritual of invoking light and then using it in service to Life. Each experience of bliss, wherein the soul of man merges with the Spirit of God in holy communion, reinforces this thread, until it becomes a ladder of light over which the mortal self will one day climb to its immortal freedom. Thus the memory, the thought, and the feeling of spiritual communion, once experienced by the outer consciousness, become focal points for the reenactment of the ritual; and the light received therefrom, when retained in purity and in harmony, provides the platform from which the soul may soar ever higher into the vast reaches of God's consciousness.

One must always take care that one's attunement is with Reality through the Mind of Christ and not with unreality through the more familiar subphases of one's own human consciousness. The desire to be thought wise among men or to use the fruits of one's spiritual communion to control others causes the seeker to automatically forfeit his attunement with the Christ and any temporary attainment he might gain; for the blessings of the LORD are reserved to the humble and the pure in heart.

The one sure method of attuning only with the highest Source of Being is to first surrender unto the Christ one's human consciousness, human ego, human intellect, and human will with their attendant motivations and inordinate desires, their thoughts and memories of involvements with the synthetic consciousness. If one wholeheartedly surrenders one's sympathy for the synthetic image, then one's *nonattachment* to the self and the possessions of the self—or the state of *desirelessness*—will allow the soul to pass through the untransmuted density of his world directly into the arms of his Christed Being—and that before the hour of his perfectionment. Even when surrender is complete, one should also invoke the assistance of the Cherubim to keep the way of the energies of the Tree of Life within the soul and to seal the place (the four lower bodies) where transient evil dwells.

Beloved El Morya has said, "Man cannot *be* perfection until he *sees* perfection." That which prevents man from seeing perfection is the density of his own human consciousness, which obliterates the light of his true identity. The science of individuality is the science of the surrender of the human consciousness; unless the disciple approaches surrender scientifically, as Jesus did, following the methods of the Ascended Masters, he will never succeed in his experiments to precipitate the Christ consciousness.

Individuality is scientific only when it is completely dominated by the Real Image. The synthetic image must therefore be surrendered—if for no other reason than that it is unscientific. The mind must surrender its synthetic thoughts; the emotions must surrender their synthetic feelings; the memory must surrender its synthetic patterns; and the physical body must surrender its synthetic impulses, motives, and momentums. Only then will the sense of separation from the Source be eliminated; only then will the dead be quickened and rise from the valley of dry bones to inherit their redemptive individuality.

Harmony is the great requirement of surrender, for through harmony man establishes his attunement with God; and when man is attuned with God he identifies with Reality. Then, when attunement is complete, his surrender of the unreal image is immediate; for in the dazzling presence of Reality he sees that what is unreal is no real part of his true individuality. The greater one's attunement with Reality, the easier surrender becomes; moreover, it is precisely the weight or measure of the Christ consciousness that man has realized which determines the weight or measure of the human consciousness that can be transmuted within a given cycle. "For whosoever hath, to him shall be given, and he shall have more abundance: but whosoever hath not, from him shall be taken away even that he hath."[55] The more perfection man can see, the more he can be; and the more perfection he can be, the more imperfection he can let go into the sacred fire for transmutation.

Not knowing how the LORD will judge his long absence, man approaches the sacred altar of Truth with fear and trembling; by and by, feeling His warmth and loving concern, he raises his head in renewed hope and faith that life can be meaningful. Waiting upon the word of the LORD—for he remembers His promise "Thou shalt call, and I will answer thee"[56]— he recites the prayer of surrender:

> All that I had thought my own—
> My name, my fame, my contacts
>   (fears and blames)—
> I cast them all within Thy flame;
> And in the glow of mastery
> My Christed radiance now I see
> Descending from the heart of God,
> A special gift of Thine own love.
>
> Descending now, Thy Presence fair
> In answer to my humble prayer
> Reveals Thyself as Light in me;
> The Presence of Eternity

In time consents to honor Thee
And be restored to rightful place
Wherein my eyes behold Thy face
Appear transcendent as the dawn,
The brightness of a cosmic morn
Where sweet surrender then is born
And consecration comes to me
Forevermore to be like Thee.

I AM Thyself in action here;
Thy grace, O God, in me appears!
Thy kingdom come—my life is Thine—
And thus we triumph over time![57]

When the answer is given from on high, he learns that the reward for his obedient faith is the opportunity for initiation. Passing the first testings of his soul, he receives the gift of wisdom. Now he is bidden to sit at the feet of his LORD, where he learns, one by one, the precepts of the Law and the things which have been kept secret from the foundation of the world.[58] Because man loves God more than he loves himself, he is given the key that opens the door of Christed illumination. His wisdom unfolds like a golden lily; his faith multiplies like a blue lotus; and with renewed determination he consecrates his soul to purity, to communion, to service, and to surrender.

Man must never fear to surrender that which is unreal; for God will never take from him nor will He ask him to sacrifice His only begotten Son, manifest as the individualized Christ Self. Abraham's faith was tested by God, who told him to take his only son and to offer him "for a burnt offering."[59] When the patriarch proved that he was willing to sacrifice everything that his synthetic image held dear, that he would withhold nothing from the LORD—even his only son— the angel of the LORD returned to him that which he had surrendered and multiplied the seeds of his Christ consciousness.

Thus the LORD does not require the sacrifice of man's true identity, but He does require him to sacrifice the components of his unreality. By law, when man surrenders his all unto God, God surrenders his All unto him. When man sacrifices his human self, God returns to him his Divine Self. When man joyously renews his covenant to glorify God throughout his four lower bodies and to make of them a veritable temple of the Holy Spirit, God renews his covenant to withhold nothing from the Son, who at last has found his Real Image. This principle can be scientifically proved by all who are unafraid to experiment with Truth.

Individuality is nonexistent until surrender is complete. When man surrenders unto God the all of his misqualified substance for purification (symbolized in the ram caught in the thicket *by his horns*), God returns to him that substance transmuted to be used in the expansion of the light and in the creation of more perfect forms, ideas, and action "that in blessing I will bless thee, and in multiplying I will multiply thy seed as the stars of the heaven, and as the sand which is upon the sea shore." [60] And so "in the macrocosmic-microcosmic interchange, in the great flow of Life, of delight, of boundless joy," says Saint Germain, "man senses the unity of all that lives; and he recognizes that his role as a receiver of benefits from the universe entails the necessary conveyance of benefits from his own creative consciousness back to the universe." [61]

The following scientific prayer for God-purity is given as a Gregorian chant in the name of the I AM Presence and the Christed individuality of all evolving Godward. It contains the rhythm and the momentum of the pyramid builders and may therefore be used to raise the Pyramid of Life right within the forcefield of one's four lower bodies. Directing his attention to Serapis Bey, Master Pyramid Builder, the devotee should visualize a pure-white pyramid superimposed over his form. One third from the base in the center of the pyramid is a white flame that is congruent with his heart when he is seated in the lotus posture. In the action of the flame, the identity of God and man is found as one. The flame consumes all extraneous matter, all that detracts from the divine plan; but the bush of man's Real Image is not consumed.

> Beloved Serapis, in God's name I AM
> Calling for Purity's ray to expand,
> Imploring that shadows no longer adhere,
> So longing for Purity now to appear.
>
> My mind purify of its fleeting impression,
> My feelings release of all impure direction;
> Let memory retain the Immaculate Concept
> And treasure the pearl of the holy Christ precept.
>
> O souvenir of radiant wonder,
> Let my mind on Thee now ponder;
> Christ discrimination, sunder
>   All that's less than God-success!
>
> Cut me free from all deception,
> Fix my mind on pure perception;
> Hear, O Thou, my invocation—
>   My Christ Self to manifest!
>
> O Flame of Cosmic Purity
>   From Luxor, blaze through me;
> Completely clear all shadowed weights,
>   Ascend me now to Thee![62]

FREEDOM IN THE MACROCOSM THROUGH
SELF-MASTERY IN THE MICROCOSM

Freedom in the Macrocosm can come to the individual only after he has gained self-mastery in the microcosm—mastery over the flow and use of his energies in his four lower bodies, which results in the mastery of his environment. The gift of individuality is the gift of individual creative opportunity; it is the fulfillment of the individual expression of the God flame made permanent through man's victorious use of his creative faculties.

Man should never forget that his individuality was originally given birth because it is the nature of the Creator to provide new opportunities for Life to express itself throughout the universes he has made. It is recorded in Genesis that the LORD God said, "It is not good that the man should be alone," [63] meaning that it is not good for man, the manifestation, to be *all one,* but that it was necessary to create the individed duality. This cosmic conception of unity fulfilled through duality persists throughout Nature as the supreme opportunity for the realization of expanding creativity in God and man.

We have seen that the Father has desired that his son share in his dominion; we have also seen that child-man is not ready to assume the responsibilities attendant upon this high office because he is lacking in self-mastery. The heir to the *throne* (to the *three-in-one,* to the Holy Trinity) is not ready for the coronation that will officially give him the right to reign as king. Hence he must abide for a time in the schoolrooms of earth, which provide opportunities for the expansion and training of his consciousness, for the soul-growth and goal-fitting that will qualify him to wear the royal robe and wield the scepter of divine authority.

The only true freedom that man can have and know and be is the freedom that God has ordained. This freedom can be known only when man masterfully employs the gift of free will to direct the energies of his life in the fulfillment of his divine blueprint; for only when man can control his life, can he control his destiny. And his destiny is his true and only freedom.

The Master Serapis Bey has lectured on the perversions of the concept of individual freedom that are projected at the sons and daughters of God to make them assert their so-called human rights over and above and in place of their divine rights:

"One of the principal problems involving the monadic consciousness is the insistence by individuals—when they allow themselves to come under the influences of the carnal mind[64]—that they use their own God-given free will to protect their individuality at all costs. Individualism is positively not correctly interpreted by the masses of mankind nor even by many among the spiritual seekers for greater Truth. These confuse what we may term 'human rights' with what we choose to call the 'divine right' of every man.

"It is true—and the world is proof of it—that human rights are being employed by mankind; and the mess of human pottage ladled out as enticement to the Esau consciousness continues to defraud the first-born sons of their eternal inheritance.[65] But the divine right is another thing. The divine right is the immortal plan for universal man. The monadic intent (man's God-designed individuality and his natural gravitation toward the oneness of his True Self) is its first principle or foundation stone in which the inherent pattern of unique Christ-manifestation is self-contained.

"Individuals seek without for that which is already within. Just as the entire pattern of Nature is manifest in the seed, so in the divine seed the living Word is the inherent God-identity, Christ-identity, and soul-identity of every man. This is what is truly meant by the statement 'No man can serve two masters: for either he will hate the one, and love the other; or else he will hold to the one, and despise the other. Ye cannot serve God and mammon!'[66]

"The human master has attempted to enslave its own latent Divine Identity, which is the Source of all Life; and thus the human master has created a self-serfdom which holds individuals in bondage, not to their Divine Presence nor even to the True Self, but to myriad world patterns whose end is always transition and change....

"As long as individuals seek to master the world of illusion by themselves, they will lose their souls or be castaways from the kingdom that is not of this world. Ever and anon, souls have sought to glorify outer-world conditions and to glorify themselves against the background of its facades; thus they have pursued a temporal crown right while they seemed to be pursuing the spiritual path."[67]

The law of relativity functions throughout Life (throughout God and his manifestation), and the fixing of the bounds of man's habitation affects those who are embodied as well as those who are out of the body. This means that the range of consciousness open to the individual is limited as long as he limits himself—as long as he limits the expression of his God Self by asserting his human rights over his divine right. In order for man to pass beyond the boundary imposed by the God Self, it is necessary for the individual to pass from the circle of the human consciousness to the circle of the Divine Consciousness.

In order to demonstrate the law governing the interchange of energy between the Macrocosm of the

Infinite and the microcosm of the finite, the soul has need of a certain measure of spiritual training and testing before the finite portion of itself may be projected upon the screen of the infinite portion of the God Self. When the required formulas have been mastered and the soul has acquired sufficient experience in the world of form to provide the impetus for the coming of the kingdom of heaven into manifestation within his individualized consciousness, it is lifted from the mortal socket into its immortal freedom through the ritual of the ascension. Man qualifies for this ritual when he is able to expand his consciousness at will, holding it up as an infinite cup in order that he might receive an infinite measure from the Infinite One.

The Prince of the House of Rakoczy, exponent of freedom and a golden-age culture, known and beloved as the Great Divine Director, has the following advice to give to those who would diligently prepare themselves for that reunion with God which is the only path to immortality:

"Only by a realization of and a faith in the continuity of Life and the justice of Life can a soul truly prepare his consciousness to receive immortality. As long as individuals are convinced that their lives are their own, they are apt to misuse the gift of free will to bottle up the selfish imp of their own creating. When they realize that they themselves are co-creators of their own divine Reality—strange though these words may sound at first to the natural man—they will perceive that God's Spirit and his energy are the rejuvenating powers of the whole field of consciousness that makes the whole man new. The power to renew and to wipe out the stain of the hieroglyphs of error enables man to contact the mainstream of God's consciousness and to become infused with universal reason, with the pure reason of God. Yet the very name God, has become to many an anathema because of human distortions, imaginations, and exaltations falsely premised.

"Call a rose by any other name, it is as sweet; the ontology of man, the study of the nature of his being, is pursued through the soul of man even as it is fashioned in the inward parts according to the nature of the Creator of all things. The universal Word, the Logos, the power of the Spirit and the power of transformation, together with the power of the Christ Mind, contain the dynamic principles by which a mere individual, embodied in flesh, can attain absolute oneness with Spirit and the mastery of himself.

"But if the field of consciousness be neglected and the old carnal mind remain in command, it will surely interfere with the externalization of the Mind of Christ. The Mind of Christ is universal. It belongs to the ages, and it belongs to all men of the ages who are willing to appropriate it." [68]

Because the Life that is God is transcendent, those who graduate from earth's schoolrooms do not lose their Life; rather does the lower half of the individed duality gain on a larger scale that Reality which the upper half already has. The awareness of this Reality by the total being of man enables him to establish a forcefield of "coactuality" or coexistence with the individualized God Presence of every Ascended and unascended being. Thus, having found oneness with his Real Self, man is one with the Real Self of every other individuality conceived by God.

This status of oneness obtains for man a passport into the realm of infinite Identity. For what God has given to one, he cannot and will not deny to any. Thus, many souls who, with Jesus, win the seal of permanent individuality arrive at the place in their spiritual evolution where they, too, become first Gods in embryo and then full manifestations of God. This is the only way the Eternal could share the best gifts of himself with those individualized focuses whom he has created and endowed with power from on high. Thus we see that there is fulfilled in every man, once he becomes the full manifestation of the Christ in action, the statement of Jesus "All power is given unto me in heaven and in earth." [69] Truly individuality is a sacred gift when it is regarded from the standpoint of the divine Summit—from the standpoint of the heights of God who dwells in individual man.

To become the Christ, then, is the goal of every child of God; and to this end every child is tested. In order to attain Christhood, the disciple must prove his God-mastery over the world and himself. This comes about through the correct use of free will, the fair development of one's talents, and the just handling of God's energy. Furthermore, he must align his four lower bodies; balance the action of love, wisdom, and power within his consciousness; and fulfill the blueprint of his identity. In short, he must overcome all outer conditions as Jesus did, including the last enemy, which is death. [70]

The subjects of karma, the Christ, and the ascension will be more fully discussed in subsequent chapters, together with methods for overcoming the entire synthetic consciousness. Suffice it to say that the highest manifestation of individuality to which the creation of God should aspire is the realization of his individual Christhood; this is his raison d'être. The ascension is the certificate of Christhood. This sacred ritual, which will be defined in Chapter Eleven, is the return of the individed duality to a state of Wholeness—to the Source or primal state of Being; and it is accomplished through the raising of one's energies to the vibratory level of perfection. Unless one demonstrates the laws that define the image of his individual Christ Self, he cannot ascend; but when he does, it is not long before he passes through the ritual of the ascension. One who has attained self-mastery is called *Master;* and when such a one ascends back to the heart of his I AM Presence, he is known as an *Ascended* Master.

INDIVIDUAL FULFILLMENT THROUGH SERVICE TO LIFE

Those who become Ascended Masters are immediately enlisted in world service as emissaries of the Most High. Whereas before the ascension they were instruments of the Holy Spirit at outer levels, they now function as his instruments at "inner levels," using the combined light momentum of all other ascended beings to implement the plan of God Above and below. Their ministrations mightily assist their unascended brothers and sisters in finding their divine plan and in humbling themselves before their own Divine Identity.

The Ascended Masters retain the precious gift of identity originally engraved upon the crystal fire mist by the Almighty together with certain aspects of their individuality which they have chosen to perfect, to spiritualize, and to fill with his grace. Individual momentums of Godly virtue, faith, and good works developed in earth's schoolrooms are thus retained after the ascension and are the means whereby greater service can be rendered by the Ascended Masters in the order of Hierarchy.

We come, then, to the question, Is individual Christhood secured by God's grace or by man's effort? The answer is: by both. Man attains his immortality by grace *and* by works. Grace is from God, whereas works are the implementation of that grace through man. God's grace—his Life, light, and energy—is the natural resource given to man freely in order that man might fulfill the pattern of his individuality through faith and good works. If man were saved by God's grace alone, then everyone would be saved; for God's grace is given freely to all, even as the sun shines upon the just and the unjust. If man's salvation were wholly dependent upon God's grace, there would be no opportunity for man to exercise his free will. Because man has the choice of accepting or rejecting God's grace to implement His will, man determines his own fate.

It is not the works of the self-righteous do-gooder that merit the everlasting reward of immortal Life, but the works of God expressed through man as man becomes the instrument of God's work *by God's grace.* Again we must examine that all-important statement made by Jesus: "My Father worketh hitherto, *and I work.*" If we have a proper perspective of man's relationship to God, we will have the correct understanding of God's work made manifest in man through His grace. But first we must accept God's grace as the works of God made manifest through us.

As James, who called himself "a servant of God and of the Lord Jesus Christ," said: "What doth it profit, my brethren, though a man say he hath faith, and have not works? can faith save him? If a brother or sister be naked, and destitute of daily food, And one of you say unto them, Depart in peace, be ye warmed and filled; notwithstanding ye give them not those things which are needful to the body; what doth it profit? Even so faith, if it hath not works, is dead, being alone. Yea, a man may say, Thou hast faith, and I have works: shew me thy faith without thy works, and I will shew thee my faith by my works. Thou believest that there is one God; thou doest well: the devils also believe, and tremble. But wilt thou know, O vain man, that faith without works is dead? Was not Abraham our father justified by works, when he had

offered Isaac his son upon the altar? Seest thou how
faith wrought with his works, and by works was faith
made perfect? And the scripture was fulfilled which
saith, Abraham believed God, and it was imputed unto
him for righteousness: and he was called the friend of
God. Ye see then how that by works a man is justified,
and not by faith only."[71]

Paul said, "For by grace are ye saved through
faith; and that not of yourselves: it is the gift of God."[72]
Without God's grace man could not be saved, but
what he does with that grace determines his salvation.
The works of which a man boasts, saying, "I did it,"
are not adequate for his salvation; but it is those good
works which he, as the workmanship of God, accomplishes through Christ—works "which God hath before
ordained that we should walk in them"[73]—that are the
honest labor of the servant-son whose reward is with
him in the joy of his LORD, rather than in the praise of
men. Indeed, faith and good works are vital complements of the Spirit of God made manifest in man as
the passive and active aspects of His infinite grace.

Because there are many facets within God's individuality, there are many opportunities for individual
fulfillment within the departments of Life. These
can be pursued from the unascended as well as the
ascended state. Thus the Ascended Masters, who are
the products of earth's evolutions or of other planetary
and star systems, specialize in a particular area of service to Life. The harvest of their good works, thoughts,
and deeds becomes a storehouse of energy and information which may be used by those who are already in
the ascended state to contribute to greater universal
service or by embodied mankind as a means of helping
them to obtain their freedom and victory over outer
conditions. Each Master, then, being an expert in one
or more fields, is qualified to advise other unascended

souls evolving upon the same path that he pursued. In a separate volume the Biographical Index provides a listing of Ascended Masters upon whom you may call for assistance—as one would call upon an older brother or sister for guidance—to enhance your service and area of specialization here on earth.

When you wholeheartedly accept the Ascended Masters as your teachers, you are no longer tied to unfounded mortal opinions and speculation; but through their exalted consciousness you are tethered to Christic concepts founded in the light of everyone's Source—everyone's God. The Ascended Masters are not only able to escalate your evolution from the spiritual standpoint but they are also able to speak from the lofty position of attainment. Their demonstration of the power of divine individuality provides you with the hope that all is indeed not lost and that your life can be retailored here and now until your four lower bodies become the vehicles through which your Divinity may function. Thus the Masters are able to bring out the true individuality in unascended man, because they are the ultimate expression of God's individuality in ascended man.

The path to Christhood can be pursued through service to Life in almost any field of constructive endeavor. Jesus won his immortality through many embodiments of service to humanity; but all need not follow the same path that he did, for all do not have the same blueprint, the same fiery destiny. As Paul said, "And he gave some, apostles; and some, prophets; and some, evangelists; and some, pastors and teachers." [74] You may be called to be an artist, a musician, a composer or a writer, a scientist, a doctor or a nurse, a sculptor or a surgeon, a teacher, a minister or a philosopher, an inventor or a philanthropist, an engineer, a homemaker, a secretary or an executive. Wherever you are, whatever you are doing, you can live and win your Christhood *if* your motive is divine. Human motives always result in spiritual failure: divine motives, while sometimes met with human frustration and failure, are always successful spiritually.

A man can be the Christ by being a good blacksmith, carpenter, or welder. Not the calling, but how he answers the call is all-important. It is the quality of the light that he brings to his vocation that makes the difference. Being preoccupied with something that is not your divine calling can cause you to miss your true calling when it comes. This is why you must develop a state of listening grace and humbly make daily prayers for divine direction after you have lovingly looked up to God and affirmed not once but many times until these words become a mantra within your soul:

> Not my will,
> Not my will,
> Not my will,
> But Thine be done!

In order to fulfill your high calling as a son or daughter of God, you must do God's good works, not man's good works. You must put God and his plan first, last, and always in the center of your life. You must not allow anyone or anything to come between you and your God. If anything or anyone in heaven or on earth means more to you than loving God just for the sake of loving him,[75] then you will not find individual fulfillment and your service will be wanting the full measure that the Law requires. It is even possible to love one's service to God more than one loves God; this, too, is idolatry. When we talk about placing God first, we must mean what we say and see to it that we allow no other love to become paramount. To love our parents and our children, our husbands and our wives is to love God in manifestation. We are devoted to them because we are devoted to him and because he lives in them. Yet we must remember that he is the Whole and they are but fragments of the Whole which endear us to the Whole. In them we find him; in him we find them; and we are not deprived of a single facet of Love's joy and beauty when we acknowledge that all loves proceed from the great fount of God's Love.

To strive for Christhood means to make a sincere effort daily to balance your threefold flame (see Chapter Six) and to align your four lower bodies with the great Pyramid of Life. It means to dedicate your soul to a mission that is beneficial to God and man—not merely comforting to life, but spurring life onward to greater spiritual attainment—making it possible for other souls to find their freedom. For the Truth that sparks when the light from your Christ Self meets the light in their Christ Self raises one and all into newness of Life and transfiguring hope.

To deny that one is religious because one does not attend church, read the scriptures, or make formal supplication unto God shows that one has not correctly apprehended the word. Doing God's good is being religious; doing man's good is being irreligious. And not knowing the difference is a sacrilege. The line is drawn by one's motive; this is the line of demarcation that places man on this or that side of the kingdom.

Therefore it is well for man to ask himself why he does what he does: Is it for the love of God or for the love of man? Is it for the love of the Real Image or for the love of the synthetic image? Is it to the glory of the Superconscious Ego or to the glory of the human ego? Is it to further the plan divine or to further the plan of the human? Is it to fulfill one's calling or to usurp another's? If man can answer these questions, then he can determine whether he is truly religious or irreligious.

If he does not like his answers, he can always change what he does not like; for the quality of transcendence, the ability to transcend one's former state, is one of the most exciting of all endowments which the Great Alchemist has given unto his apprentices.

One final note of instruction on individual fulfillment: If you are not willing to live and die for the Cause of Truth, you will sooner or later be faced with a test that you cannot pass. If you are afraid to take the ultimate stand for what you believe, you will be stopped short of the mark; your life will be unfulfilled and you will not complete your mission. Since so much is at stake, would it not be well to define the Cause for which you are expected to give your all? The Ascended Masters, who have given their lives for this Cause, are well equipped to supply us with sound advice, guidelines, and definitions; therefore, let us pursue their teachings as true devotees of the flame of Life so that we may know the Way and walk in it. For ultimately the attainment of your Christed individuality will mean losing your life, that you and all who follow after you might find their Life in Christ.

In a letter written to the American people by the late President John F. Kennedy (and transmitted to us by the Master El Morya) after his passing from the world scene, while a guest in the Darjeeling Council chambers, he defined this total dedication which we must give to the Cause if freedom and our very lives are to endure. His writing shows the true individuality of a soul no longer bound by the conventions of the world and by those hereditary and environmental factors that tend to dim its universal perception of Truth; thus that wider view which often accompanies liberation from the body temple reveals the identity of man as an ivory statue ennobled in the sunlight of Reality, a detailed work of art that seldom appears in its full glory while encased in mortal form:

"The wavering action of unstable emotions must abate in the world community. Just as long as violent feelings continue to rage, as long as feelings remain untempered by reason, just so long shall noble solutions to the problems of the world be denied mankind. Only the balm of rule by law and order can keep the city of humanity's domain in a manner befitting human dignity and the current advance of culture. Freedom is more than a word to constrain the forces of anarchy and chaos. It is a vital flame whose eternal light glows fervently for all.

"The fear and restraint characterizing a world where each man's concern is but for the narrow protection of that limited band he calls his own must be replaced by larger concerns of mutual interest—the courage to stand for morality, for progress in the arts and sciences, and for religious freedom to strengthen the bulwarks of the world's cultural achievements.

"To enlist the aid of the many, it sometimes becomes necessary to sacrifice in small ways and then again, supremely; for the torch of freedom cannot be successively passed to those who will not bear it with honor and dignity. The world's pathway to freedom, as in the past, is currently studded with milestones of never-ending progress. However, the highways to achievement are not yet smoothened, but are full of detours and hidden dangers.

"We must not fear the future. We must take note of the past and learn by the power of example. If any effort toward progress bears some fruit, it is a worthy offering; and all who strive together toward mutual goals for humanity shall one day bask in the glow of the torch of the future when the light of greater knowledge, held in the hands of a joint humanity, shall lead men from darkness to greater light.

"It is my earnest desire that the events which took place in Dallas shall not serve further to divide the world nor result in a greater flare of fanaticism among mankind. My service to life, to world freedom and peace, was gladly given. It must be recognized by all that to step from one's bedside each day is a calculated risk from which people of courage must not shrink.

"Just as I cannot measure my sense of love and devotion to the American people, to my family and friends, so I cannot let this opportunity pass without exhorting those who are able to accept the reality and continuity of my existence to continue to strive for peace and calmness in the face of all foment generated by men whose environment has not permitted them either the solace of religious conviction, the absorption of a richer measure of the world's culture, or that economic stability and pride in person and service for which, unknown to themselves, they secretly and inadvertently yearn.

"I therefore urge that citizens of America and of the world shall mitigate their judgments of the people of Dallas and of Texas. There was far more love and kindness manifest in this great-hearted state than could ever be countermanded by ten assassins' bullets. The spirit of anarchy and confusion is not confined to places, but finds lodging in the hearts and minds of men whose ideals are not wholly clarified by reason and reasonable trust either in their government or in their God, whose mercy endureth forever.

"There come to my mind the words of Saint Paul 'How shall we escape, if we neglect so great salvation?'[76] These words must be recognized for their intrinsic worth; and men must seek to preserve the union of fifty sovereign states, not only in sanity but also in honor. Many of the problems that existed when I first took office still remain as the problems of men. An easier solution could be provided if, in compassion, all would seek to palliate the potential grief of others and unite in one grand concern for the hopes of man.

"The record of President Lincoln's assassination has been shown to me—one that is unrecorded in the archives of men. Those kind Intelligences charged by God for the administration of the world's spiritual government have given me irrefutable and unmistakable evidence which convinces me without question that the assassination of President Lincoln was not and could not have been an act for which the South alone was responsible. I am convinced also that this is true in my own case; and I wish to extend to those who have the faith to believe, to accept, and to cherish my thoughts, as an aftermath of my own passing from the world scene, to bear equal comfort to mankind, to bind up the wounds of the nation, to take the hand of the widow and the orphans, not only of my own beloved ones but also of the man who was used as a tool to effect my transfer from the world arena.

"A little crystal Madonna, held in the hands of a child, does not distinguish between good and evil. As men's hearts, in gratitude to the holy principles of motherhood, cry, 'Ave Maria,' they cannot withhold the balm of mercy from all who require it. The Master's words 'Pray for those who despitefully use you,'[77] His call 'Father forgive them, for they know not what they do'[78] cannot be denied to any.

"I am cognizant of the continuation of the world's problems, but comforted in the eternal bond of friendship which flows unbroken from the spiritual world into the world of material form. . . .

"Encouragement should be given to the flow of commerce the world around; a special bond of freedom should unite the three Americas. Our neighbors to the north, the people of Canada, the people of Mexico and Panama, the Alliance for Progress, the Organization of American States—all of these should manifest the holy flame of One Identity; for the struggle for law and order will continue to go on in what at times seems a lonely and lawless world. We cannot afford to yield one inch of ground to the forces of tyranny; we cannot let any event whatsoever dissuade us from the holy purpose of keeping both the peace and freedom, of standing guard to preserve those essential elements of life and liberty for which the many have already given their lives, their fortunes, and their sacred honor.

"I, therefore, John Fitzgerald Kennedy, borne from the world by the summer winds of a greater love to which I had long pledged my service, bequeath to you all the full-gathered momentum of my energies for and on behalf of freedom. The torch is indeed passed; but I know and I am certain that many noble young men and women, many men and women of mature dignity, and even the staunch hand of age shall continue to grasp it, to hold it high, to defend it against all enemies.

"Our nation must collectively rest consoled in the arms of a holy freedom which refuses to be con- fined to the altars erected by men, but seeks to find repose within their hearts and souls. Of this I am cer- tain, that as in the past, so in the future, the cry 'Watchman, what of the night?' shall often be heard in our land, and the answer shall come, 'All is well.' The answer shall come because men stand guard, because men determine to control their emotions, because men seek to be better examples, and because men continue to express courage. As such qualities are divine, eternal, and immortal, they shall not perish from the earth."[79]

There can be developed a personal relationship between those who dwell in the ascended state and those who are yet working out their salvation on earth. For all Life is truly one, and the only separation that exists between heaven and earth is that concept of separation which is held by the synthetic image. All who are one with God may share in the communion of the saints, whether they walk the earth or inhabit the heavens. Paul's communion with the saints Above and below was so complete that he was not always mindful of the distinction, for to him there was none. "I knew a man in Christ. . . (whether in the body, I cannot tell; or whether out of the body, I cannot tell: God knoweth); such an one caught up to the third heaven." [80]

Mary Baker Eddy, the discoverer and founder of Christian Science, glimpsed the reality of the ascended hosts and referred to her communion with them on page 513 of *Science and Health with Key to the Scriptures:* "Advancing spiritual steps in the teeming universe of Mind lead on to spiritual spheres and exalted beings." These *exalted beings* are the individualizations of God who dwell at ascended levels of God's consciousness and who have been made permanent in God's Mind through reunion with his perfection. On page 476 of the same work she states, "Mortals will disappear, and immortals, or the children of God, will appear as the only and eternal verities of man." Thus she acknowledges that the synthetic image must give way to the Real Image and affirms the true identity of man and of the existence of *immortals.*

Based on her own experience, this one who wrote in the 1860s as a pioneer of the metaphysical movement made a profound observation concerning the scientific fact of individuality: "The universe of Spirit is peopled with spiritual beings, and its government is divine Science." [81] As Paul stood on Mars' hill and declared the unknown God ignorantly worshiped by the Athenians, [82] so we declare these *exalted, spiritual beings,* these *immortals,* to be the Ascended Masters whom Mrs. Eddy and many other highly evolved souls knew intimately while they yet wore mortal form, and whose ranks they joined after their transition. Mrs. Eddy's discoveries ultimately led her to the feet of her own I AM Presence, as she revealed in *Christ and Christmas:*

> For Christian Science brings to view
> The great I Am,—
> Omniscient power,—gleaming through
> Mind, mother, man.[83]

Thus she saw that God is no respecter of persons and that he gave to all the focus of the individualized I AM Presence and through it the opportunity to know him.

"You see, precious ones," says Lord Meru, "the Most High God, in the joy of creation, affords men not only the opportunity to know him but also the opportunity to know themselves—and ultimately to know themselves as God. When they become congruent with the angles of his Being, the starry perfection of his realm will be theirs to share, even as they now share the seed of his Light-potential within their hearts.

"In this expansive going-forth, God has also realized himself in a multitude of aspects; and he does, in fact, exchange with man the conceptual patterns of Reality which he holds on behalf of the creation that they might begin to comprehend the great inner realm of Being—the Great God Source in all of its spiritual wonders of joy, beauty, love, peace, and victory. Man, through his realization of the great Reality which God is, becomes—and at a given point in consciousness he is—all that he can properly comprehend of the Deity."[84]

Jesus' promise to everyone who believes in the power of the Christ was "The works that I do shall he do also; and greater works than these shall he do; because I go unto my Father."[85] This promise could be fulfilled only after his ascension, for then the momentum of his spiritual power was bequeathed to all who would follow him in the regeneration.

Therefore, whosoever contacts the Most High God also receives the impetus of Jesus' service to Life. What was true of him is true of every Ascended Being. All evolving souls have the opportunity, when communing with God, not only to receive the power of Jesus' victory, but also to draw upon the momentum of good that has been won by every other son of God who has ascended back to the heart of God and to find therewith individual fulfillment through service to Life.

The universe is a magnificent place where order prevails in what we may term the pristine belt of divine manifestation. The teachers of the seeker after the Divine are manifold. When man is in contact with the true ministers of God, his individuality literally bursts into flame and he soars to the heights of the Ascended Masters' consciousness, gathering more of God with each ascending spiral. Climbing the highest mountain, the seeker must bear in mind the admonishment of Jesus "In your patience possess ye your souls"; [86] and he must remember the perspective which Peter finally found, that "one day is with the Lord as a thousand years, and a thousand years as one day." [87]

It has been said that man is not born until he ascends into the Presence of the Real Image. What wonders each son of God may look forward to, not as a life-and-death struggle between earthly and heavenly things, but as an unfoldment through service to God and man of the all-enfolding cosmic light! For when the son relinquishes his authority over all outer conditions to the Divine, then the fullness of God becomes the All-in-all in him, filling identity and fulfilling purpose.

The answer to the question, What is individuality? which we have attempted to give in part in this chapter, is delicately summarized by one called Rose of Light who beholds the expression of God's individuality in Nature:

"Let everyone understand that there is a divine plan for each lifestream, and that this plan is beautiful beyond description. It is like a golden, glowing rose, saturated with light, each petal pulsing with the power of momentary renewal, as the divine heartbeat surges out from the center of the universe, from the Source of all Life into monadic expression anywhere and everywhere." [88]

THE MASTERS' VESSEL

Great cosmic Light, encircle
    The whole blest world around;
With ministration's service
    Let mercy e'er abound.
Men's hands extend in longing,
    Their lot to understand;
I AM the Masters' vessel,
    Giving freedom to their hands.

I AM, I AM, I AM the law of loving service here!
I AM, I AM, I AM the blessing of Christ-cheer!
I AM, I AM, I AM the healing hands of peace!
I AM, I AM, I AM God-freedom's full release!

I AM charged now with obedience
    To holy precepts pure;
In ministration's glory
    Let Love fore'er endure.
Men's hearts now 'wait the blessing
    Of God in action here;
I AM the Masters' vessel,
    In me does God appear.

I AM, I AM, I AM the law of loving service here!
I AM, I AM, I AM the blessing of Christ-cheer!
I AM, I AM, I AM the healing hands of peace!
I AM, I AM, I AM God-freedom's full release!

I AM filled with superpower
    From out the Central Sun;
In ministration's service
    I act till victory's won.
Men's beings need this blessing
    To show them how to live;
I AM the Master Presence,
    In love I, too, shall give.

I AM, I AM, I AM the law of loving service here!
I AM, I AM, I AM the blessing of Christ-cheer!
I AM, I AM, I AM the healing hands of peace!
I AM, I AM, I AM God-freedom's full release!

> Great cosmic Light now blazing
>   The Summit beams afar,
> In ministration's beauty
>   My deeds shall never mar.
> Men wait to share thy bounty,
>   To see thee blazing through;
> I AM my God in action,
>   Within there's only you.

I AM, I AM, I AM the law of loving service here!
I AM, I AM, I AM the blessing of Christ-cheer!
I AM, I AM, I AM the healing hands of peace!
I AM, I AM, I AM God-freedom's full release!

> O Masters, wise and blessed,
>   Whose joy we long to share,
> Help us to stop the action
>   Of every burden's care.
> Let us now spread the message
>   Both far and wide by Light;
> God's law is Love in action,
>   His Truth is only right.

I AM, I AM, I AM the law of loving service here!
I AM, I AM, I AM the blessing of Christ-cheer!
I AM, I AM, I AM the healing hands of peace!
I AM, I AM, I AM God-freedom's full release!

Chapter Five

What Is Consciousness?

What Is Consciousness?

For who hath known the mind of the Lord,
that he may instruct him?   The Apostle Paul

MIND AND SELF, WILL AND CONSCIOUSNESS: STRUCTURES OF IDENTITY

"YOUR CONSCIOUSNESS is a priceless tapestry. Each day you weave upon it a motif of the Spirit, which is forever, or a jagged pattern which must be meticulously disengaged and rewoven as heaven intends."[1]

We may well ask the question, Who is qualified to discourse on consciousness? Certainly only one who is conscious. But what does it mean to be conscious? If we can establish this, we must still determine what the highest state of conscious being is. We must then search out one who has attained this state and be content to sit at his feet and learn the truth about consciousness. "Lord, to whom shall we go? thou hast the words of eternal Life."[2]

The only one who possesses total consciousness is God himself, the One Source out of whom proceed all lesser manifestations of consciousness. All other forms of Life (forms of God) are evolving toward that supreme consciousness, but few have reached that state of awareness of Life which is to be found in the Godhead. "The LORD giveth wisdom: out of his mouth cometh knowledge and understanding."[3]

As mankind ascend in the evolutionary spiral of being, they come to the place where they are no longer identified as humans, but they become truly God-men. In every age there have been saints and sages, avatars and holy men whose consciousness has been so attuned with the consciousness of the Higher Self that they have been able to impart to men of lesser understanding—of lesser attunement—a fuller awareness of the consciousness of God.

Many of these devotees of the Holy Spirit went through agonizing periods of surrender, experiencing darkness and aloneness prior to their soul's illumination. But sooner or later their longing for Light received the response of heaven, such as that which was given to Saint Augustine, who poignantly recounted in his *Confessions* the precious moments when his soul made contact with the Spirit of the Lord:

"I cast myself down I know not how, under a certain figtree, giving full vent to my tears; and the floods of mine eyes gushed out an acceptable sacrifice to Thee. And, not indeed in these words, yet to this purpose, spake I much unto Thee: and Thou, O Lord, how long? how long, Lord, wilt Thou be angry for ever? Remember not our former iniquities, for I felt that I was held by them. I sent up these sorrowful words: How long, how long, 'to-morrow, and to-morrow?' Why not now? Why not is there this hour an end to my uncleanness?

"So was I speaking and weeping in the most bitter contrition of my heart, when, lo! I heard from a neighbouring house a voice, as of boy or girl, I know not, chanting, and oft repeating, 'Take up and read; Take up and read.' Instantly, my countenance altered, I began to think most intently whether children were wont in any kind of play to sing such words: nor could I remember ever to have heard the like. So checking the torrent of my tears, I arose; interpreting it to be no other than a command from God to open the book, and read the first chapter I should find. For I had heard of Antony, that coming in during the reading of the Gospel, he received the admonition, as if what was being read was spoken to him: Go, sell all that thou hast, and give to the poor, and thou shalt have treasure in heaven, and come and follow me: and by such oracle he was forthwith converted unto Thee. Eagerly then I returned to the place where Alypius was sitting; for there had I laid the volume of the Apostle when I arose thence. I seized, opened, and in silence read that section on which my eyes first fell: Not in rioting and drunkenness, not in chambering and wantonness, not in strife and envying; but put ye on the Lord Jesus Christ, and make not provision for the flesh, in concupiscence. No further would I read; nor needed I: for instantly at the end of this sentence, by a light as it were of serenity infused into my heart, all the darkness of doubt vanished away."[4]

Forthwith Augustine devoted his life to God and abandoned his profession as a teacher of rhetoric. He had received a morsel of God's consciousness through the intercession of Jesus Christ. Henceforth his life would no longer be his own. Such is the power of the Holy Spirit to transform the consciousness of man. Having touched the hem of the Lord's garment, he was filled with enough of God's consciousness to sustain him for a lifetime. His path was illumined before him and he exclaimed:

"O Lord, I am Thy servant; I am Thy servant, and the son of Thy handmaid: Thou hast broken my bonds in sunder. I will offer to Thee the sacrifice of praise. Let my heart and my tongue praise Thee; yea, let all my bones say, O Lord, who is like unto Thee? Let them say, and answer Thou me, and say unto my soul, I am thy salvation. Who am I, and what am I? What evil have not been either my deeds, or if not my deeds, my words, or if not my words, my will? But Thou, O Lord, art good and merciful, and Thy right hand had respect unto the depth of my death, and from the bottom of my heart emptied that abyss of corruption. And this Thy whole gift was, to nill what I willed, and to will what Thou willedst. But where through all those years, and out of what low and deep recess was my free-will called forth in a moment, whereby to submit my neck to Thy easy yoke, and my shoulders unto Thy light burden, O Christ Jesus, my Helper and my Redeemer? How sweet did it at once become to me, to want the sweetnesses of those toys! and what I feared to be parted from, was now a joy to part with. For Thou didst cast them forth from me, Thou true and highest sweetness. Thou castest them forth, and for them enteredst in Thyself, sweeter than all pleasure, though not to flesh and blood; brighter than all light, but more hidden than all depths, higher than all honour, but not to the high in their own conceits. Now was my soul free from the biting cares of canvassing and getting, and weltering in filth, and scratching off the itch of lust. And my infant tongue spake freely to Thee, my brightness, and my riches, and my health, the Lord my God."[5]

      Through such dedicated lifestreams mankind have been given insight into the nature of the soul, the purpose of life, and the science of Being. Once they had completed the task which the Father sent them to do, many of these holy men and women departed this earth plane, ascending into the Presence of God—into the consciousness of God. They are known as Ascended Masters precisely because through sacred communion and service to Life, based upon the complete surrender of their human identity patterns, their consciousness became one with his prior to their reunion with the God Self. From this level of complete identification with God, these holy ones continue to illumine with an expanding awareness of God's Mind their brothers and sisters who have not yet graduated from Life's schoolrooms upon this and other planets.

Therefore, in our consideration of consciousness we shall look to these teachers who, while yet maintaining contact with mankind, live and move and have their being in the great sea of God's consciousness; for they have approximated more of God's consciousness than all who remain in the unascended state. We shall also examine the thoughts of some philosophers whose deliberations, in our opinion, have touched upon the Truth of the ages.

Whether or not it is possible to define consciousness is a question that has been argued by some of the world's greatest thinkers. Webster's dictionary says that consciousness is the state of being conscious, the awareness of something within oneself, of an external object, state, or fact; the state of being characterized by sensation, emotion, volition, and thought: mind.[6] The term *consciousness* comes from the Latin verb *conscire,* to know, to be cognizant of, and from the Latin adjective *conscius,* meaning sharing knowledge with another.

In his work *The World as Will and Idea,* Schopenhauer says that "consciousness is the mere surface of our mind, of which, as of the earth, we do not know the inside, but only the crust."[7] "Under the conscious intellect," Will Durant explains, "is the conscious or unconscious *will,* a striving, persistent vital force, a spontaneous activity, a will of imperious desire. The intellect may seem at times to lead the will, but only as a guide leads his master; the will 'is the strong blind man who carries on his shoulders the lame man who can see.'"[8]

While many have sought to place consciousness within the confines of definition, Sir William Hamilton noted: "Consciousness cannot be defined; we may be ourselves fully aware what consciousness is, but we cannot, without confusion, convey to others the definition of what we ourselves clearly apprehend. The reason is plain. Consciousness lies at the root of all knowledge."[9]

Whether or not we can define consciousness, we do understand one thing: consciousness is the key to the integration of the whole man. Without consciousness in its various levels, the world and all that dwell thereon would not appear to us on the screen of manifestation; for unless conditions were made known to us through the five senses, which are the media of consciousness, we would have no knowledge of our environment, and for all practical purposes the world might as well not exist. Without the ego—be it the human or the divine—consciousness itself would be without a focal point; and without consciousness the ego would be without a platform of identity. Those who have attempted to define consciousness solely from the outer standpoint will either come up with a partial definition, such as that of Schopenhauer, based on the perspective of the lower self that perceives only the mere surface of the mind, or, like Hamilton, they will have to admit that from this limited view consciousness cannot be defined at all, simply because it cannot be circumscribed by the finite mind.

Like Saint Augustine, the devotee soon learns that he can discover the meaning of consciousness in terms of his own self-awareness only insofar as he discovers God's consciousness. Like the pursuit of happiness, the joy of this discovery is his birthright; all of Life conspires to enhance the wonder of his quest— not even the Almighty will deprive him of it. Day by day new facets of the universal consciousness unfold from within man's subconscious awareness that which consciousness is.

Yes, consciousness must be defined by individual experience. Others may tell you what consciousness means to them, and we may place before you keys, fragments of identity, patterns of the giant fresco based on our personal experience in God's consciousness; but only you can isolate the details that are meaningful to your soul until they become a unified whole, fulfilling in you the Real Image God has made. Only you can discover what consciousness is—both in the relative sense and in the absolute sense—for by its very nature it must be self-revealed. It can come from nowhere but from within—through your own personal experience in God's consciousness. This does not mean that God's identity is subject to man's limited awareness; on the contrary, man's identity is subject to his awareness of God, who is the same yesterday, today, and forever.

Your awareness of God as Life is your consciousness; if it be limited or perverted, then the narrow room of self must be expanded, purified, and brought into proper focus. If your concepts of God and Self, the universe and society are synthetic, then you will be bound by those concepts until you change them and evolve to a higher understanding. Your concept of God—good, bad, or indifferent—is all that you can know about yourself until you evolve your consciousness in an ever widening spiral to take in more of him even while he takes in more of you.

The consciousness of God is the integrating factor of individual man—even though man's self-awareness seldom captures more than a fragment of this great unifier of his being. That portion of the universal Mind which God has bequeathed to you is your individuality expressed both Above and below. It is the ultimate precipitation of your identity, and without it you have no identity. The universal consciousness must be defined from the individual viewpoint, from the personal awareness of the impersonal Mind of God. If we could put together each phase of individual awareness of God that has ever been experienced by all evolving monads in every state of their evolution Godward, we should begin to see the spectrum, albeit limited, indicative of the outreach in man of the universal Mind. This, of course, would tell us nothing of those unexpressed portions of Himself which the LORD has hidden from the foundation of the world and reserved for his angels and those whose God-awareness enables them to leave behind the confines of mortality, to soar to the center of his flaming heart, and to emerge dripping with the fires of his Cosmic Consciousness.

We begin, then, with the monad of self; we draw from the data of other monads. We record and discard until we come to the place where we have defined enough of God's consciousness to provide a platform for our present explorations; for truly there is no reason to define more of God than we are capable of experiencing now and in the near future. Let our present definition of our own consciousness be the challenge that beckons us to come up higher to discover and be more of God's consciousness. Then from each succeeding plateau our panorama will unfold a higher view and with it a higher calling in God.

Mind and self, will and consciousness—these are the structures of our identity which we know only in part. For who can know the Mind of God—or man? Who can know the Self of God—or man? Who can know the Will or Consciousness of God—or man? Inasmuch as we have but a partial knowledge of these basic components of ourselves, we must draw the conclusion that they are only partially expressed; for that which is wholly expressed can ultimately be wholly known. We realize, then, that we are but partial expressions of the Real Self; and from this starting point, we must proceed to define, bit by bit, those other partial expressions of the Whole which, when put together, will enable us to induce and to express a still greater portion of the Whole that is continually transcending itself.

GOD SELF-AWARENESS THROUGH CHRIST SELF-AWARENESS

Lord Lanto unravels the mystery of consciousness with such utter simplicity that we sense the gentle blending of his mind with the Mind of God; truly his wisdom proceeds from the very throne of the Almighty. "Man was created as a Spirit," he says, "and consciousness and intelligence are a necessary part of the spiritual being that man really is. However, consciousness—which may be defined as God's awareness of himself—not only functions in the domain of Spirit but also is able to project itself into the time-space continuum and thus to integrate the ever changing world of the finite into the magnificent real world of the Infinite." [10]

Consciousness—God's awareness of himself! Now we see that wherever there is Life, there is God expressing his own Self-awareness. In the heart of the cell there is the flame that burst forth in answer to the great command "Let there be Light!" [11] How much more can we understand the fiat of creation if we substitute the word *consciousness* for *Light* and then declare with God, "Let there be Consciousness!" Even as we speak these words we feel the inrush of the Mind of God manifesting in the heart of every atom and cell that comprise our very mind and being.

Paraphrasing the teachings of the Master Jesus, we may consider consciousness in the following way: "I AM the way, and true Being [true consciousness] is the way. There is no division in true existence [in true consciousness]; therefore, there cannot be two ways. There is only one way; and that way is the indivisibility of the Spirit [of consciousness] that has of itself created many droplets of manifestation, but all of the same Spirit [of the same consciousness]. Those of you who, with me, would inherit the kingdom of God [of God's consciousness] must understand, even in your outer minds [in your outer consciousness or physical awareness], that no outer condition has any power to alter the immortal God flame blazing on the altar of your heart."[12]

The consciousness of God exists outside the material universe as a preexisting or a priori cause. God's consciousness, as it expresses through man, transcends sense experience even while it may be molded by his senses. The planes of God's consciousness involve the subtle gradations that proceed from the infinite Mind of God to the confined and confining consciousness of man.

The German philosopher Immanuel Kant was correct in his concept of space and time as organs of perception. He saw space and time as a priori because our experience presupposes them.[13] But we know that beyond space and time there is the higher consciousness of God that cannot be limited or prescribed by space or time. The dimensions of space and time provide a cup out of which men may drink a portion of the Infinite and thereby begin to approximate the total awareness of the consciousness of God that exists outside themselves.

Plato's doctrine of ideas says that all things are preceded by (1) a general idea or classification, (2) a law which governs their manifestation, or (3) an ideal, the ultimate that a particular thing is capable of reaching. This doctrine of ideas approaches the Masters' teachings on the origin of the world of form in the world of the formless where there do exist the archetypal patterns of all manifestation, the pure ideas for conceptual realities, the law and the plan that must precede all manifestation.

As Will Durant explains it: "Behind the surface phenomena and particulars which greet our senses, are generalizations, regularities, and directions of development, unperceived by sensation but conceived by reason and thought. These ideas, laws and ideals are more permanent—and therefore more 'real'—than the sense-perceived particular things through which we conceive and deduce them."

The general idea of man, the pattern of man, he says, "is more permanent than Tom, or Dick, or Harry; this circle is born with the movement of my pencil and dies under the attrition of my eraser, but the conception Circle goes on forever. This tree stands, and that tree falls; but the laws which determine what bodies shall fall, and when, and how, were without beginning, are now, and ever shall be, without end." [14]

Perhaps without realizing it or even intending to do so, Plato touched the fundamental reality of the consciousness of God. His observations of life, when correctly interpreted, approach the higher critique of the Masters of Wisdom, who teach that consciousness as the Mind of God precedes all manifestation. The categories of God's consciousness produce the classifications in the world of form. All substance, form, and manifestation are ordered by invisible laws and concepts, wholly pure, which are the antecedents of creation.

As we apply this understanding to the level of the individual, we find that man cannot bring forth in his own world that which he does not have within his consciousness. Therefore, if he would create as God does, his goal must be to put on and become in consciousness the consciousness of God. When he attains this point of identification, he can realize in his own microcosm all that is contained within the consciousness of God that precedes and ordains the Macrocosm. Some may not believe that it is possible for man to appropriate the consciousness of God. If this be true, why did Paul admonish the Philippians, "Let this mind be in you, which was also in Christ Jesus"?[15]

The appropriation of God's consciousness is made possible through the Universal Christ individualized in man as his own Christ Self. As the Universal Christ is the precipitation of the universal God consciousness, so the individual Christ precipitates in man the individualized consciousness of God. As man is aware of, enters into, and becomes his Christ Self in action, he attains that consciousness or awareness of the Christ which we call *Christ Self-awareness.* Those who live and move and have their being in the plane of the Super Ego, at the nexus of the figure eight, do the works of the Father in Christ; for they are aware of his will through the congruency of their consciousness with that of the Divine Mediator.

When man attains the realization of himself in Christ, his mind as the Mind of Christ, his will as the Will of Christ, his self as the Self of Christ, then all of his consciousness is Christ's; and if his works conform to the works of the Christ—his thoughts, his motives, his deeds—he is the Christ in action and can affirm with Jesus, "Behold, I AM alive forevermore."[16] The awareness of one's self as Christ is the first step in attaining Cosmic Consciousness; and it must be followed by the second—that consciousness or awareness of Good which we call *God Self-awareness.*

When man attains the awareness of his True Self

as God, he becomes, like his Creator, a pivot of creative power. Tethered to the divine will, he becomes the center of the initiative that proceeds from the Mind of God. Man is free to express God; and when he elects, by the exercise of his free will, to become one with God, he expresses his God-dominion over the earth.

When man identifies with the consciousness of God, or when that which is conscious in part enters into the consciousness of the Whole, then the law of cause and effect and the understanding that virtue is its own reward become clear. God Self-awareness in man is his reward for the virtue he has expressed by God's grace, for through virtue man's awareness of himself becomes his awareness of his God Self as his Real Self. When man becomes one with God as Cause, he, too, becomes causative of Good, God becomes effect through his manifestation in man, and Spirit becomes totally effective of Good in Matter.

"The sole purpose of life upon the schoolroom-planet earth," says Lord Lanto, "is to develop in man, through consent by free will, those masterful cosmic qualities that are a part of the character and Being of God. The eternal Spirit is all-goodness. Man is intended to become that goodness. Of necessity, his intelligence has been limited both in ability and flexibility by his karmic pattern and by his response to the opportunities of Life. His power, likewise, has been restrained until such a time as the character of the individual might be developed in its divine similitude, whereupon his acts would become wholly divine, hence worthy of the divine power." [17]

Here we see that as man progresses on the evolutionary scale, putting on the character and Being of God, he becomes more worthy of the divine power; and so as consciousness expands in man, it becomes a magnet that draws more and more of the divine consciousness unto himself until there comes a time when he slips into the sea of infinity and there is hardly a shade of difference between his individual self-awareness and the God Self-awareness of the Creator who is expressing through him.

Most people have a human self-awareness which amounts to nothing more than an awareness of the self as the ego. Their minds are centered in the intellectual pursuits of the ego that glories in its own logic rather than in the divine Logos; they know no other self, no other will, no other consciousness than that of the ego and its selfish desires to perpetuate a self-centered existence. Because the human ego is not sustained by any force outside itself, the goal of self-preservation becomes paramount, and all other considerations are secondary.

In attempting to lift the consciousness of his followers out of the socket of this vain existence, Jesus stretched forth his hand toward the horizon and tenderly said, "Consider the lilies of the field, how they grow; they toil not, neither do they spin: and yet I say unto you, that even Solomon in all *his* glory [while he remained in the consciousness of his human personality] was not arrayed like one of these."[18] (The lily is the symbol of the victory of the Christ consciousness in man. It tells us that purity and love have triumphed on Easter morn, that Christ has risen to the position of authority and reigns as the three-in-one in the consciousness of all who believe in the everlasting Life of the Son of God.)

Jesus therefore said unto his disciples who desired to be free of the consciousness of self-concern that prevents the true Christ from manifesting in each one: "Take no thought for your life, what ye shall eat; neither for the body, what ye shall put on. The life is more than meat, and the body is more than raiment. Behold the fowls of the air [symbolizing the soul that has taken flight from the cage of the ego]: for they sow not, neither do they reap, nor gather into barns; yet your heavenly Father feedeth them. Are ye not much better than they? And which of you with taking thought can add to his stature one cubit? If ye then be not able to do that thing which is least, why take ye thought for the rest?" [19]

He explained that if they had not the mastery of consciousness to expand the forcefield of their self-awareness by taking thought of the consciousness of God, then they could not precipitate the abundance of every good and perfect gift until they had mastered the first precepts of the Law. Thus his final admonishment to the soul that desired to extinguish the ego in the flame of the Super Ego was "Seek ye first the kingdom of God [the consciousness of God], and his righteousness [the right use of his laws]; and all these things [both spiritual and material needs] shall be added unto you." [20]

To know one's Self as God one must be clothed with the white raiment of heavenly virtue—so filled with Love that the energies of Love flow freely through the mind and heart as the very lifeblood of one's being. Only when man has thus become the personification of God's love does he impart love to all he contacts—as a universal unguent, a healing force, and a rhythmic release of the powers such as those of adhesion, cohesion, and magnetic attraction, originating in the Central Sun, by which creation in man and the universe is born and sustained. Each heavenly virtue with which man adorns his soul, lavishing his mind and heart with the myriad hues of the everlasting Life of the Christ consciousness, enables him to enter more fully into the consciousness of God and to be that consciousness through his own God Self-awareness. By daily bathing his consciousness with the precious oils of mercy, justice, and righteousness and by imbibing the waters of living Truth and Freedom, he magnetizes a forcefield of energy qualified with the aspects of God's consciousness that make him so much aware of God's unlimited potential and so unaware of human limitations that he can unqualifiedly affirm with Jesus:

It is finished!
Done with this episode in strife,
I AM made one with immortal Life.
Calmly I AM resurrecting my spiritual energies
From the great treasure-house of immortal knowing.
The days I knew with Thee, O Father,
Before the world was—the days of triumph,
When all of the thoughts of Thy Being
Soared over the ageless hills of cosmic memory;
Come again as I meditate upon Thee.
Each day as I call forth Thy memories
From the scroll of immortal Love,
I AM thrilled anew.
Patterns wondrous to behold enthrall me
With the wisdom of Thy creative scheme.
So fearfully and wonderfully am I made
That none can mar Thy design,
None can despoil the beauty of Thy holiness,
None can discourage the beating of my heart
In almost wild anticipation
Of Thy fullness made manifest within me.

O great and glorious Father,
How shall a tiny bird created in hierarchical bliss
Elude Thy compassionate attention?
I AM of greater value than many birds
And therefore do I know that Thy loving thoughts
Reach out to me each day

To console me in seeming aloneness,
To raise my courage,
Elevate my concepts,
Exalt my character,
Flood my being with virtue and power,
Sustain Thy cup of Life flowing over within me,
And abide within me forever
In the nearness of Thy heavenly Presence.

I cannot fail,
Because I AM Thyself in action everywhere.
I ride with Thee
Upon the mantle of the clouds.
I walk with Thee
Upon the waves and crests of water's abundance.
I move with Thee
In the undulations of Thy currents
Passing over the thousands of hills
    composing earth's crust.
I AM alive with Thee
In each bush, flower, and blade of grass.
All Nature sings in Thee and me,
For we are one.
I AM alive in the hearts of the downtrodden,
Raising them up.
I AM the Law exacting the Truth of Being
In the hearts of the proud,
Debasing the human creation therein
And spurring the search for Thy Reality.
I AM all things of bliss
To all people of peace.
I AM the full facility of divine grace,
The Spirit of Holiness
Releasing all hearts from bondage into Unity.

It is finished!
Thy perfect creation is within me.
Immortally lovely,

It cannot be denied the blessedness of Being.
Like unto Thyself, it abides in the house of Reality.
Nevermore to go out into profanity,
It knows only the wonders of purity and victory.
Yet there stirs within this immortal fire
A consummate pattern of mercy and compassion
Seeking to save forever that which is lost
Through wandering away
From the beauty of Reality and Truth.
I AM the living Christ in action evermore!

It is finished!
Death and human concepts have no power in my world!
I AM sealed by God-design
With the fullness of that Christ-Love
That overcomes, transcends, and frees the world
By the Power of the three-times-three
Until all the world is God-victorious—
Ascended in the Light and free!

It is finished!
Completeness is the Allness of God.
Day unto day an increase of strength, devotion,
Life, beauty, and holiness occurs within me,
Released from the fairest flower of my being,
The Christ-consecrated rose of Sharon
Unfolding its petals within my heart.
My heart is the heart of God!
My heart is the heart of the world!
My heart is the heart of Christ in healing action!
Lo, I AM with you alway, even unto the end,
When with the voice of Immortal Love
I, too, shall say, "It is finished!"[21]

This communion, this claiming of the consciousness of God as his very own, this fiat of our LORD
offered upon the cross spells the end to the spell of
mortality and death and dying. It is the affirmation of

the soul as it enters the portals of immortal Life never-more to go out. It is the scientific statement of Being in Cosmic Consciousness which must be claimed and acclaimed in order to be God Self-realized. Jesus' words reveal the infinite measure of God's Cosmic Consciousness which the son of man can attain right while he dwells in veils of flesh; and when he attains this consciousness, his flesh, no longer a veil, becomes the crucible of cosmic transformation and Be-ness— "the nearness of Thy heavenly Presence."

HEART, HEAD, AND HAND

Man must begin to realize the goal of attaining Christ Self-awareness and God Self-awareness by bal-ancing the action of heart (the center of Christ-awareness) and head (the center of God-awareness) in order that his actions might reflect the perfect balance of communion between Father and Son as he walks the Middle Way of the Holy Spirit. Truly it is the Golden Rule consciousness which understands the first precept of the Law, "Do unto God as you would have him do unto you," and the second which is like unto it, "Do unto man as you would have him do unto you"— which is to say, do unto the *man*ifestation of God as you would have the *man*ifestation do unto you.

The key to the motivation of man's conscious-ness is in the underlying will—the will of his mind, which we call his motive or intent, and the will of his heart, which we call his desire. Most people do not realize how often these motivating factors are in oppo-sition to each other—like two horses pulling in opposite directions, causing a tug-of-war within the forcefield of their own consciousness. Rather than be torn apart, individuals succeed in suppressing one or the other, either forbearing human pleasure for the sake of higher value and reward or forgoing the latter for the sake of human indulgence.

On the other hand, if the motivating factors of mind and heart be aligned with the will of God as instruments to propagate virtue and all Godly expression in fulfillment of the divine plan, man's entire consciousness will be tethered to and led by a power greater than himself. This power of Good is focused in man the unknown—in the subconscious mind, in the iceberg that is beneath the surface of his awareness— when he surrenders his mind and will to the Mind and Will of God and his human ego to the Divine.

The subconscious mind, like a transformer, affects man's energies as they are distributed to the four lower bodies. Man's will and his desire are the switches that direct these energies into the motors of his lower vehicles. If the will and the desire are to do God's will, man becomes a dynamo of power, wisdom, and love, the energies of God are released to him in unlimited quantity to fulfill the divine plan, and he sees the effects of the vital force of God's Spirit permeating his entire consciousness. If, however, the gears of his lower vehicles do not mesh with the divine pattern and the distribution of energy to his four lower bodies is unequal due to an imbalance of will and desire, the performance of the motors will be less than optimum.

If the will and desire are based upon ego motivation, the distribution of energy to the four lower bodies will be uneven and the action of mind and heart will not be balanced in the Christ. In some people the motor of the physical body is supplied with the greatest percentage of man's daily allotment of energy, which it spends on the gratification of physical desires and the development of the form. In others the physical body is weak and sickly and the motors of the mind and emotions run overtime. In some older people the memory body dominates the other three, stealing the energies of man's being in order to revolve the memories of the past and to recapture those experiences of which the physical, emotional, and mental bodies are no longer capable.

We find, then, that when the lower vehicles are out of alignment due to an imbalance in their frequencies, man's energies are dispersed in vain effort and he himself is literally pulled apart—all of this because the will and desire of the ego are at war with the inherent will and desire of the soul to fulfill its native God-identity. Under these circumstances even man's outer consciousness is a house divided, and he is miserable until he eliminates one or the other of the opposing factions. Again we are reminded of Jesus' words "No man can serve [entertain within the forcefield of his consciousness] two masters: for either he will hate the one, and love the other; or else he will hold to the one, and despise the other." [22] If, therefore, the will of God is not made the lodestone of the subconscious mind, the divine magnet of his energy system, man's motors will not run efficiently and he will be unable to realize his individuality in and through the great motor and motivating power of God's consciousness.

Schopenhauer said that the will is the only permanent and unchangeable element in the mind. It is the will which gives unity to consciousness and holds together all its ideas and thoughts, accompanying them like a continuous harmony. He saw will as the essence of man and as the determining factor of his consciousness; and he understood will as causality, as the universal cause in ourselves and in all things. [23] We may well conclude that this will must be one-pointed if it is to be effective—like the eye that must be single-*minded* if man's body temple is to be full of Light. [24]

Since God is always conscious of man's individuality, even as His eye is on the sparrow, if man pursues the goal of making his consciousness one with God's, he will thereby be making his will one with God's, for God's will and his consciousness are one and the same; and he will find that God-awareness of his True Self for which his soul longs. It is, then, to man's greatest advantage to pursue the consciousness of God as the *will* and *desire* of God and to make them his own; for thereby he discovers his own Reality and he himself becomes the author and finisher of his own destiny as it evolves in and through God's consciousness.

"Create unto yourself the new sense of the ownership of God's will!" says the Lord of the First Ray of God's Will. "You have long thought of God's will as a thing apart from yourself. Now new longings and a fresh perspective can re-create the best gift you have ever had. The memory of his grace can come alive within you as you accept the infinite care of the Eternal One for you. His blessed consideration of your lifestream must be contemplated and made a living, vital part of your whole consciousness. . . .

"Why, God can be made so central, so real, and so intimate to the very being of any man who diligently seeks his will (tutoring both inwardly and without) that he will scarcely remember his former state of unbelief! It merely awaits an opening, a twinkling of the eye of being, for the last trump of mortality to sound and for the power of immortality to change the lesser image into the Greater Image of his glorious divine Reality! This can be, for it already *is!*"[25]

Indeed, the will of God precedes consciousness as the molding factor in every form of Life. Whether in plants or in planets, whether in animals or in men, in granite or in a grain of sand, one can see that the stamp of the divine will predetermines the function, the pattern, and the existence of all creation. The philosopher might argue that Matter is unconscious; but the Masters teach that since all substance is formed of Spirit's own essence coalesced as Matter, it is impregnated with His consciousness of cause and effect, of premise and conclusion. Therefore the destiny (the behavior patterns) of the elements and of organic and inorganic life forms is preordained and sealed within the geometric matrices reflected in molecular structures and cellular designs that are duplicated again and again in Nature according to the inherent will of God.

In lower forms of life we call this will instinct. The term *instinct* implies the existence of an overall plan which remains unknown but toward which a total organism may move or strive. The will that precedes consciousness is the will to live, the will to expand the Life that is God. This will is the core of God's consciousness. It is the motive behind universal manifestation. It is the structure and the foundation of Life. It is the pivot of consciousness in God and in man. It is the propelling force, the very impetus of creation.

Henri Bergson, in his works *Creative Evolution, Matter and Memory,* and *Mind-Energy,* shows startling insight into the truth and reality of consciousness. He says: "Consciousness seems proportionate to the living being's power of choice. It lights up the zone of potentialities that surrounds the act. It fills the interval between what is done and what might be done. . . . In reality, a living being is a centre of action. It represents a certain sum of contingency entering into the world, that is to say, a certain quantity of possible action." [26]

Thus he sees man as the center of creative evolution. Although he may not realize the implication of his statements, we would immediately respond and say, "Indeed! It is through man that God evolves himself and the universe, for man is the focus for the

creative evolution of God's energy." Whether or not
Bergson and other philosophers of our time acknowledge the source of creativity and energy as God, they
have glimpsed the process upon which hinges the function of consciousness.

Bergson distinguishes between the consciousness of an animal and the consciousness of man. He
says: "In the animal, invention is never anything but
a variation on the theme of routine. Shut up in the
habits of the species, it succeeds, no doubt, in enlarging them by its individual initiative; but it escapes
automatism only for an instant, for just the time to
create a new automatism. The gates of its prison close
as soon as they are opened; by pulling at its chain it
succeeds only in stretching it. With man, consciousness breaks the chain. In man, and in man alone, it
sets itself free." [27] Since we know that animals are
incomplete or limited expressions of the Word, having
neither free will nor conscience, but only a group soul
or awareness, we can agree with Bergson's observations.

Further on he says that "the movement of the
stream is distinct from the riverbed, although it must
adopt its winding course. Consciousness is distinct
from the organism it animates, although it must undergo
its vicissitudes." [28] For the student of Ascended Master
law, this statement is found to be startlingly accurate
in the light of the knowledge of the Christ and the
influence of the Word that affects all creation without
being tied to the creation. Nevertheless, the Word is
molded by the cup of consciousness into which it is
placed. "The spirits of the prophets are subject to the
prophets." [29]

Bergson says that by no means is the brain indispensable to consciousness; and as proof of his theory,
he cites the fact that "the lower we go in the animal
series, the more the nervous centres are simplified and

separate from one another, and [that] at last they disappear altogether, merged in the general mass of an
organism with hardly any differentiation. If, then, at
the top of the scale of living beings, consciousness is
attached to very complicated nervous centres, must
we not suppose that it accompanies the nervous system down its whole descent, and that when at last the
nerve stuff is merged in the yet undifferentiated living
matter, consciousness is still there, diffused, confused,
but not reduced to nothing? Theoretically, then, everything living might be conscious. *In principle,* consciousness is co-extensive with life." [30]

We who acknowledge Life as God and God as
permeating his entire creation find no fault with this
logic. According to our understanding, it is Truth. But
few among mankind would be willing to go one step
further and accept the idea that there is conscious
awareness within the heart of a rock, a tree, a flower,
a mountain, a flaming bush, a drop of rain, or a wave
upon the sea.

Some may remember Luke's account of Jesus'
triumphant entry into Jerusalem on Palm Sunday. His
disciples were rejoicing and praising God "with a loud
voice for all the mighty works that they had seen; . . .
And some of the Pharisees from among the multitude
said unto him, Master, rebuke thy disciples. And he
answered and said unto them, I tell you that, if these
[the disciples] should hold their peace, the stones would
immediately cry out [in praise of the Christ]." [31]

Jesus was referring to the electron charged with
the intelligent energies of the Creator and to the white
fire core of the atom, which are indeed manifestations
of the consciousness of God. These could not refrain
from acclaiming the presence of the Christ, for even
the rocks are composed of the very substance that
proceeds out of the Mind of God. Thus the Master

himself acknowledged the universal Presence of God as Life, as the All-in-all.

However, that portion of God's consciousness of which he was speaking as being expressed in the stones is what we would call elemental consciousness; it is not the equivalent of the Christ consciousness, although it is capable of acknowledging the Christ by the affinity of His vibratory rate to that of its own white fire core. The beings and forces of the elemental kingdom sense the presence of a concentrated action of the Christ Light; they are harmonized thereby and act as conductors of that Light to mankind. In the presence of man's discord, his disobedience to natural law, and his rebellion against God, Nature is disturbed and becomes unbalanced, resorting to cataclysm to restore the harmony of the universal order.

The Christ consciousness is the integration in man of the consciousness of God. Elemental consciousness expressed in animal life, in the vegetable and mineral kingdoms, and in the forces of Nature is an incomplete manifestation of God; it is a reflection of an aspect of the Almighty: of faith and hope, as in domestic animals; of beauty and grace, as in the flowers and the birds; or of power and majesty, as in storm and wind and fire. The group soul of animals is the cumulative consciousness of the species. An animal always senses itself as part of the herd rather than as an individual identity. Animals do not have self-awareness. They cannot say "I AM," nor are they balanced in the love, wisdom, and power of the Trinity; therefore they remain incomplete manifestations of God's consciousness.

Man, having the gift of free will, is given the opportunity to master his consciousness by entering into the mastery of God's consciousness. Only man can become God, because only man has free will.

Going one step further in the teachings of the Masters, we find that animal and mineral life are simply lesser expressions of man's consciousness. In fact, the real identity of man as it is found in God's consciousness must include all Life, all substance, all identification of the animal and mineral kingdoms. That which does not properly represent the Divine Image must be transmuted. That which is incomplete must be replaced by that which is complete. Animal life must give way, or evolve, to the Life of God as it manifests in man. In the eternal coexistence of God and man there is no lesser creation; but during the period of transition, when man is still in the state of becoming God, his consciousness is aware of and does perpetuate forms of animal life and various incongruities that have no place in the world of Spirit.

Speaking of consciousness as Life, the Master of Galilee said: "Those who seek to save their lives may well lose them,[32] but all who let flow of the native stream of God's own consciousness and infinite love through the aperture of self become as radiating points of light in time and space. These shed that eternal light upon the passing scene of mortal creation and find thereby their eternal Home in the realities of heaven which are our portion."[33]

Thus is born in man the realization of heart, head, and hand as the balanced action of the Trinity; he knows that this is his unique opportunity to become a Son of God and to establish a fount of grace on behalf of millions yet unborn to Life in Christ. Knowing this law of opportunity whereby child-man can be crowned with divine sonship and ultimately with Godhood, Moses reminded the recalcitrant Israelites of their divine origin and destiny: "I have said, Ye are [potential] gods! and all of you are children of the Most High [in your present stage of development]."[34]

CONSCIOUSNESS: THE MAGNET OF INDIVIDUALITY

The consciousness of God is the Cause that precedes the effect which man beholds as the Macrocosm; the consciousness of man is the cause that precedes the effect which he beholds as his microcosm. Man's consciousness is the magnet of his individuality; all that is contained in either the conscious or subconscious mind—all records, patterns, and impressions that he has written with the pen of heart, head, and hand during thousands of years of soul evolution—determines that which he shall experience and that which he shall be.

Man can attract only that which he already is and has. If the conditions in which he finds himself are foreign to his soul, he can change them. He can declare himself to be the Image of Reality; and by the power of the spoken Word, I AM, he can purify the magnet of his consciousness through the affirmation of his true Being until he magnetizes that which his Real Self already is in the Macrocosm, that which he desires to become in the microcosm. He can acclaim the magnitude of his Christ Self as his very own and call to the beloved Mediator to make his consciousness congruent with the magnet of God's consciousness. In the midst of all evidence to the contrary, he can be still and know that *I AM God,*[35] allowing the Greater Magnet to repolarize the lesser magnet and restore it to its original God-design.

When we consider the fact that the magnet of God's consciousness is focused in the Central Sun as the great dynamo that holds universes in orbit around this hub of creation, we are singularly impressed with the unlimited opportunity with which God has vested man's consciousness, endowing him with the authority to magnetize orbs of creativity. His total consciousness totally God's consciousness, man is preordained to be, like God, the center of his own expanding universe. Individual consciousness is the greatest power in the universe because it is a crystal fragment of God's Mind, a drop in the ocean of his consciousness. The man who can establish his consciousness as a forcefield of Christ-power, Christ-intelligence, and Christ-love in perfect balance has within himself a divine magnet that will attract more of God, more of Good; and when he controls the forcefield with God-dominion, he has unlimited potential to have and to be whatever is his God-desire.

In his *Studies in Alchemy,* Saint Germain referred to the understanding of consciousness (meaning God's consciousness) as the alchemist's "supreme ingredient": "With God all things are possible![36] If you possess his consciousness, then it is now so for each of you—all things are, in fact, immediately possible to you in manifestation. If this is not your instantaneous experience, then you need more of his consciousness! 'So far, so good,' you say; 'but how do I go about acquiring that nebulous commodity called consciousness?'

"Beloved ones, what and where is your consciousness? The minute specks of physical matter or energy, atomic in nature, are composed of particles of light held within orbital paths, prescribed and imbued with intelligent action. This spiritual magnetism, infused with creative intelligence, power, and love, is a flux whose density permeates the entire sphere and realm of each atom, extending outward into molecular and cellular composition and thence through the elemental phases of Nature, manifesting unto planetary scale; and when correctly understood, these particles shall be known to be whirling in infinitely fantastic orbital paths through solar, galactic, and universal densities.

"Relative size has enabled mankind to feel that his consciousness is body-confined or cell-confined, as the case may be. This concept of the ghost chained within the human machine is a total mistake. Although the flow of interacting forces may become more complex, still the concept of an expanding consciousness, simultaneous with an expanding universe, must be reckoned with if man will correctly master his affairs.

"Man is no more confined to his body than he is to an atom of substance within it or within his brain. Neither are the atoms of physical matter composing that body confined to it and limited in expression by that body or matter-mind density. The power of reaching outward and becoming a part altogether conscious of a whole in a marvelously spiritual manner is the gift of God to all. No one loses any part of that which is already his own by so doing, and no one takes anything away from anyone else through this sharing of the glories of God."[37]

Here the prodigal son ponders the problem of returning to the immaculate conception which framed his beginning; and he finds that his only hope of restoration to the original ideal is through the grace of God that has made provision within the framework of His laws for man to return to the realm of God's will and its perfect outpicturing.

The electronic pattern of the individualized God consciousness is energized in man through the individualized Christ consciousness. This blueprint, as we have said, is the magnet whereby man draws unto himself the resources of God's energy available to all. But in order to become the powerful magnet for Good that God intends him to be, man must also master the art of expanding the forcefield of his mind in ever widening concentric rings. He must train the energies of his consciousness to flow outward in infinite circles from the center of his individual awareness to the periphery of his God Self-awareness, thence to return to the point of identity within. As a small boy throws a pebble into a pond with complete abandon, man must be willing to throw himself into the sea of God's Being. Immersed in the energies of Light, Life, and Love, he feels his consciousness ripple in ever expanding waves, taking in more and more of the consciousness of God until the waves are no more, the sea is still, the merger is complete: God and man are one.

If the reader will pause to experiment with this exercise, he will find that at first it is not easy to expand his mind in all directions. This is because man's physical eyes do not have peripheral vision. Not so with consciousness, which expands in all directions at once; for consciousness is that part of man which is limited neither by the physical senses nor by time, space, body form, or circumstance. It is free to come and go at will; but if it is to remain flexible, it must be exercised.

If man would reach for the stars and gather immortelles from Elysian fields, he must begin by expanding the concentric rings of his awareness, each day taking in a little more of the world he sees into his microcosmic circle; and by and by he will find that it is not difficult to meditate upon the stars and to allow his consciousness to take flight and probe the Infinite. Just as the devotee has mastered the going-out phase of his meditation, he must also learn the art of going within. He must be able to reverse the process and draw into the epicenter of his being all that he has realized through the expansion of the rings of his conscious awareness.

Wherever man's consciousness flows, it retains the stamp of its identity pattern; and all that it breathes in of the universal essence of God's consciousness coalesces around that pattern to widen the borders of his individuality. As man expands his consciousness, God expands His infinite awareness of Himself through man; thus God the Father and God the Son enhance the flow of macrocosmic energies to all parts of Life evolving within the macrocosmic sea.

The key to success in this experiment is to release unto God the entire forcefield of the circle of consciousness which you have expanded—whether the circle (actually a sphere) of your awareness be the dimensions of the room you occupy or those of the earth, the solar system, or the Milky Way. At the moment you feel expansion at its peak, at its maximum outreach, surrender the entire span of your awareness unto God in the twinkling of an eye. The act of surrender must be accompanied by a fixing of the mind upon one or more of the components of God's identity so that there is not even the opportunity of a microsecond for the little self to reclaim that which it has surrendered by a sudden shift of the attention back to the self—such as that which occurred when Peter attempted to walk on the water. This necessary fixing of the mind is best accomplished by repeating the following mantra:

> I AM Light within, without,
> Expand! Expand! and forever expand!
> Field of consciousness within, without,
> Absorb God's Light and then command
> Light of God to forever expand!
>
> Fill the world, the land, the air,
> The sea and sky and everywhere
> With awareness, for I AM there,
> Sharing God and joyous prayer.
> Beyond the earth in outer space
> Expand the power of cosmic grace.
>
> Our God is there and everywhere,
> And where I AM, O Thou art, too,
> To increase awareness of Thy Truth

And show me in my I AM eye
The holy beauty of the sky.

I see Thy Light of diamond hue,
Sparkling, shining, through and through
The pores of self in body large,
The macrocosmic universe.
I AM with Thee, O God, I see
The Light expand as Path to Thee.
The power flows, my being glows,
And Christ within, without me shows

I AM the Way to peace and power;
Thy Spirit makes me one this hour.
O God, demand and now command
Thy Presence in our holy band
Of devotees of heaven's grace;
Show me, command me to take my place!
In Freedom's band I'll ever stand;
By Victory's power I wake this hour
To feel, to feel that flow of power.

Blaze right through me, Light of God,
Spiral nebulae, suns of Light!
Blaze right through me, Truth of God—
Fill my mind with great delight!
I AM Thy Grace manifest here,
Thy perfect Love is shining clear!

Command Thy Selfhood to be mine!
Expand, expand in heaven's name!
Command my soul to be Thy Flame!
Expand, expand, O Love Divine!

THE SCIENTIFIC REALIZATION OF CONSCIOUSNESS

The scientific realization of consciousness is wholly dependent upon the proper development of conscience. The conscience of man is related to the consciousness of God through the Christ. Conscience is the individual consciousness of right and wrong. It is the discriminating faculty of the Higher Mind to which the individual has access through the flame within the heart. Discrimination is the ability to distinguish between Good and evil and to make moral judgments according to the will of God; it is the most important quality of the Christ Mind. Discrimination comes to the individual through the still, small voice that speaks from within when man enters into the Great Silence of his God Presence. Man's conscience is that portion of the discriminating consciousness of God which the Creator has bequeathed to his beloved Son that he might keep the commandments of the LORD (the Law) and fulfill his divine plan.

In addition to this gift of spiritual discernment, man has a social conscience which he has developed through his contact with the world of form. This is the moral code that he has been taught or that he has formulated as distinguished from the cosmic morality that is ingrained within the soul. If the individual is given the proper training in Ascended Master law and if he is taught how to attune with his God Self, his developed morality will be an environmental application of the principles of universal law; but if this training is withheld, he has only his outer awareness and the social mores of the times on which to base his moral judgments.

People often say, by way of explaining their behavior, "A voice told me to do it," when that voice is no more than an amalgamation of erroneous suggestions rising as a mist from their own subconscious minds. If man is to distinguish from among the many voices that beckon him hither and yon, he must have the standard of the Law. In his teaching on "Christ is the Door," Jesus said of the shepherd, "He goeth before them, and the sheep follow him: for *they know his voice.*"[38] If we, then, do not know his voice, can we be counted among his flock? We must therefore learn to recognize the voice of the Good Shepherd, the Christ Self, who will guide us over the jagged cliffs and barren wastelands that the traveler must cross ere he reaches the Eternal Bourn.

Kant's categorical imperative, which states that you must "act as though the maxim of your action were by your will to become a universal law of nature,"[39] is a practical rule whereby man in his present, limited state of consciousness may determine just what is the righteousness of God (the right use of the Law) in the affairs of men. But the answers he gives to this imperative are conditioned both by the degree of his attunement with the discriminating faculties of the Higher Mind and by the refinement of his social conscience.

For example, if man keeps himself in a state of listening grace and is able to make contact with his Christ Self, he will intuitively carry out the universal law "Thou shalt not kill" whether he lives in a militaristic society or among cannibals, and he will override his social conscience that tells him it is all right to kill his enemy or to eat his enemy's children. Although the defense of personal or national freedom often necessitates killing in self-defense, such action is not without karmic penalty; nevertheless, to stand idly by while an individual or a nation is sacked and raped is also not without karmic penalty. In a world of relative good and evil, choosing between the lesser of two or more evils is one of the most crucial tests which the soul must pass in order to win its immortal freedom. Therefore the application of universal law to specific situations requires the utmost care and spiritual preparation.

Applying the moral imperative is similar to asking the question, What would Jesus do? by which many gauge their actions. If man's social conscience is trained according to the Golden Rule, the standard of his own Christ Self, and if through his contact with the Mind of Christ he is able to maintain the strength and the courage to challenge and override social mores out of keeping with cosmic law, then when he asks himself, What would happen if all mankind did the same thing that I am doing? or, What would the highest representative of the Great Law do under similar circumstances? he can in most cases determine the effect of his actions upon the Body of God and he will not fail to act according to the highest Good (the nearest right) he is capable of understanding and executing in a given situation.

When man understands the law of cause and effect—the general as well as the specific effects of his actions—he will begin to understand the universal effect of God's Law upon himself and upon other men as he implements its principles through right judgment and right action. By applying the categorical imperative according to the principles of the Christ, the individual can approximate in his life the Good that God would have him do. But until he actually puts on the consciousness of God, leaving behind the consciousness of relative good and evil, he is not capable of approaching this Good in all circumstances.

Inasmuch as man's reasoning and intuitive faculties are of necessity limited in their interpretation of the voice of conscience, there comes a time when they must bow to the edicts of the soul's refined sensitivities as these are guided by the Holy Spirit. Rising in consciousness to the level of his Christ Self-awareness, the individual is able to gauge his actions through the perceptions of a heart that beats in cosmic rhythm with the heart of the Universal Christ. He is able to determine what the effect of his actions will be, for he is one with all Life and his awareness of the energy veil is once again impersonal. He senses the going-out and the coming-in of God's energy. He feels the tides of Life as they leave the shore of being and flow to the other side; for he is one with every other son of God as an extension of His consciousness, as a ray that emanates from Him, blending with all other rays whose origin is the One Source.

The faculty of conscience developed through instant rapport with the Christ Mind is a more advanced criterion of action than the categorical imperative; for when confined within the bounds of reason that is based on duality, one's social conscience is not always universally valid. Furthermore, when man sees himself in a hostile world as one against many, he is incapable of making universal a priori decisions that are at once impartial, immediately practical, and cosmically just, whereas moral decisions based on one's contact with Reality and with the Real Self in every man proceed from the heart that knows *who* and *what I AM* and from its direct contact with the Life that is universally one.

Right actions, then, arise out of man's sensitivity to the Christ consciousness and out of a conscience motivated by goodwill to all; these criteria form the basis for the supreme exercise of free will. To face the consequences of one's acts, or one's karma, to accept one's duty to Life, or one's *dharma,* to serve the Creator and the creation through the right use of universal energy and through obedience to universal law— these are the challenges that face man daily. His success in meeting these challenges depends upon how he uses his faculties of perception, of conscience, and of consciousness.

If he has not developed the Christ conscience, man cannot be given the secrets of the universe; for without this golden standard he cannot be trusted to use the knowledge of the Law wisely and impartially for the good of himself and his fellowman. Bearing in mind that the Christ conscience is a prerequisite to the mastery of self and consciousness, let us proceed with another exercise calculated to expand the magnet of Christed individuality. Let us pursue Saint Germain's instruction on the creation of the Cloud as a means of developing our faculties of perception and discrimination. And let us apply the Master's method to expand our God Self-awareness by employing the Cloud as a magnetic forcefield for the scientific realization of his consciousness:

"Stand now before your altar, honoring the living God and his fiat. For he who is God has commanded it: 'Take dominion!' You are rightfully functioning, then, as you do just that. You are about to create; and you will first create the Cloud from the enormous power of God stored at every point in space, waiting to be invoked.

"The power of vision is central to our invocation. Therefore, we shall create in our minds first a milky-white radiance; and we shall see this milky-white radiance as an electronic vibratory action of vital, moving, ineffable light. The concentration of the light, which we call the 'density' of the light, is that which makes the milky-white color. If the Cloud were attenuated, we would be able to see through it as though the scenes around us were enveloped in a fog.

"Now, having created in our minds this form of a bright translucent Cloud, we allow it to enfold our physical bodies and to occupy our forcefield. For a moment we become lost in the midst of the Cloud, and then it seems as though it has always been there: its atmosphere is familiar, comfortable.

"We recognize that the mind has the power to expand its circle of influence, but we must not try to move far from the parent tree of self. Let this bright and shining Cloud at first be nine feet in diameter around oneself. Later, perhaps, we shall expand it to a diameter of ninety feet, then nine hundred feet and farther.

"In our early meditations we shall concentrate on intensifying the action of the white light in our minds; from thence we shall transfer that action to the nine-foot area around the physical form. Once we have developed the sense of this Cloud being around our physical forms, we shall understand that whereas the Cloud can be made visible to the physical sight, our primary concern is to keep its high vibratory action purely spiritual.

"Those of you who are familiar with electronics and the workings of a rheostat will understand that by a simple twist of the dial of consciousness, we can intensify the vibratory action of the Cloud. In this case we coalesce more light around each central point of light; for our Cloud is composed of many light points whose auras diffuse and blend with one another, making the total effect one of a lacy yet highly concentrated white radiance—a pure, swirling Cloud of cosmic energy.

"What is this mighty Cloud that we have created, this forcefield of vibrating energy? And why did we create it in the first place? Actually, whereas I have used the word *create,* it would be more appropriate if perhaps I had used the word *magnetize;* for we are actually magnetizing that which is already everywhere present in space. We are amplifying an intense action of the light from within its own forcefield—more than would normally manifest in a given area. We are thereby drawing upon universal God-power to produce this Cloud that first penetrates and then hallows our immediate forcefield in order that we may have a spiritual altar upon which we may project the pictures of reality that we desire to create.

"Bear in mind that this Cloud can be used therapeutically for the healing of the nations and the soul of a planet; or you can use it as a platform to invoke, as Christ did upon the Mount of Transfiguration, the presence of the Ascended Masters—of beloved Jesus, Mother Mary, the Master Serapis Bey from Luxor, the Maha Chohan, Lord Maitreya, Archangel Michael—to assist you not only in your alchemical experiments but also in your ministrations to Life.

"Where you are yet ignorant of just what you ought to produce for yourself and others, you can, in a gentle, childlike manner, ask God to produce out of the great pool of his light-energy the miracle of his healing love, not only in your life and in the lives of your loved ones but also in the lives of the multitudes in the world at large. You can ask the power of God and of the kingdom of heaven to come into manifestation upon earth. You can ask for the golden age to be born, for an end to strife and struggle and all negative and hateful manifestations. You can ask for Love to take dominion over the world. If you will open your heart to the needs of the world and to the love of the Divine Mother that seeks expression through your uplifted consciousness, limitless ideas for universal service will flow into your mind.

"But here again let me hasten to sound a note of warning, especially for the benefit of those who have been psychically inclined or who have a tendency, as humanity would say, to 'go off the deep end.' Beware! You are dealing with sacred creative power. Beware! It is better for you to ask the Masters to interject their ideas for you—without necessarily defining or releasing them to your conscious mind—than for you to be carried away from the tether of the alchemical norm.

The Ascended Masters are not only sane and well organized, but they are also Godly and profound to the nth degree. It is essential, then, that you become likewise. Above all, be not carried away by pride or by the exaltation of the self over others.

"As you gain spiritual power through these periods of meditation upon the Cloud—which at first should not exceed fifteen minutes a day—try to understand that the creative Cloud, once it is dispersed by your fiat at the conclusion of your creative ceremony, will continue to expand and expand and expand throughout the universe as a globe of translucent white fire, eddying in ever widening spheres to contact all that is real and that is really yours. The Cloud, as the manifestation of the power of your creative energy, the fire of your spirit, will draw into your world the very consciousness of God himself. Evoked from the central pores of Being and beautifully expanding as an altar of God, the Cloud will hallow space wherever it expands.

"Christ was able to produce the miracles recorded in the Gospels, and many more, because he had first mastered the correct use of energy. He called the holy energy of Spirit 'Father'; and, of a truth, 'Father' the Spirit *is* to all manifestation. The Father is all-loving, all-knowing, and all-powerful; and he will make you all that he is. But we have only begun to touch upon the correct use of his energy."[40]

LIBERTY BORN OF GOD'S CONSCIOUSNESS

The soul cries out to the Spirit of Liberty:
    O Liberty, whose quest is the anthem of men and nations! O Liberty, thou flame that burns within the heart but escapes the confines of man! O Liberty, our Mother of Eternity who cradles our Christianity, molds our humanity, and fashions a new order of the

ages! Thy children long for thy embrace, to know
thee once again and to hear thy comforting word
"All is well."

The Spirit of Liberty answers:
    Liberty is born in the soul—
    No more will man be satisfied with lesser goal.
    The baubles and trinkets of the world
    Have their place,
    But the place of the Son of God
    Is the consciousness where God is.
    The place where God is not
    Or where lesser images of Him hang
    As useless icons upon the walls—
    This no longer holds the soul
    Which seeks to fly the realm of mortal delusion
    And 'neath the canopy of goodwill
    See and entertain the reality of the angels,
    Of the Ascended Masters,
    Of that cloud-capped realm
    Where the soul, with childlike laughter
    As a bubbling stream
    Moving toward the Sea of Identity,
    Feels the freedom of the wind
    And the power to stir the zithers
    Of lesser consciousness
    With a sense of beauty and of the subtlety
    That hangs like a brilliant bubble
    Whose watery, airy veil
    Drapes the transparency of mirrored iridescence
    To the waiting eye.
    The realm of angels is not without delight,
    And Ascended Master reality awaits the flight
    Of souls who yearn to break the bonds
    Of hopelessness that defraud the world situation
    From the wonders of God's radiant intent,
    Captured so penuriously

Within the fabric of ritual, prayers, and dogma,
But held so beautifully
As pulsing flame of threefold God-delight—
Love, Wisdom, and Power
Within the heart and soul.

And the soul is satisfied:
And now as I await the expansion
Of the great macrocosmic world
Within the microcosmic realm of self,
I see that born in me
Is the power of limitless expansion every hour.
O God, I thank Thee for the shining hours
That come composed of minutiae—
Of minutes, seconds, and of micropause—
While Mind does turn to record forever
Thy immortal laws.[41]

The liberation of the souls of men and women throughout the ages of their involvement in the veils of illusion has been accomplished through the practice of sacred ritual. If the force of human habit patterns be reinforced by a coiling of the wire upon the pole of being each time indulgence in human vanity is allowed, then the ritual of unwinding the wire, coil by coil, must effect the undoing of the force of human error. The ritual of unwinding the graveclothes that bind and bury the soul within the consciousness of mortality is the joy of the overcomer; nothing else will satisfy his soul.

Those who have not known the passion of the soul to be free look on in wonder and amazement at their brothers and sisters who find delight in what seems a monotonous and unfruitful existence of labor without reward or recognition. These do not perceive the exaltation of the Spirit as day by day the soul rises into newness of Life and Liberty. As for those who seek an earthly reward, "they have their reward,"[42] and it is an earthly tribute; but the Father who seeth in secret the travail and the sacrifice of the saints rewards them openly, and theirs is a heavenly tribute.

Let all understand that the art and science of sacred ritual is the fulfillment of all communion and service to Life; it is the capstone in the arch of attainment and without this crowning glory individual Christ-I-AM-ity remains incomplete. Of what, then, does ritual consist and how does its practice liberate the consciousness? Morya speaks of ritual, but he leaves to the diligent disciple the task of discovering that he speaks of ritual:

"Every man should realize his essential individuality, his privilege, God-given, of expressing unique qualities of Life that he can use to endow the universe from the fountain of his own life and love. But there are lessons to be learned, understandings to be sought and found, and old senses to be cast aside, transmuted and, in some cases, re-created.

"Morya thunders! Why should we put off the hour of the emptying of the mind of its delusions? Why should darkness impel the mind and heart to distrust themselves? Let us infire men with a gnosis of possibilities; let us create a sense of strength, based not upon weakness but rooted in the flow of Reality. The fact that men have not known does not mean that ignorance should continue. We send light on the holy will; and it permeates the consciousness, bridging the old gaps and steaming the spirit loose from its confining walls where the insidious glue of human consciousness has dried up the very thought of progress.

"Sultry spirits infest the gullible and the complacent! We speak to those who are willing to be God-willed! The very idea of 'me' and 'mine' often leads to separation. The strange consciousness of schism finds welcome wherever men love darkness. They ply the boat of consciousness into watery caves of intricate folly. But the clarity of the will of God promotes the facility of smoothened Reality.

"Now the Word long ago went forth; but the common man skulks in fear lest someone should find out that he is in league with God or the holy will! Shames are honored while the Source of all grace remains hidden in shame from puny, mortal eyes. Truly the blind lead the blind. Walk ye in the dominant way of the Sacred Stranger who respects no man's illegitimate thoughts, but every man's person [pure son]."[43]

The Master is speaking of the ritual of self-purification that must go hand in hand with the pursuit of the will (the consciousness) of God. Unless he participates in this rite of self-immolation, man cannot know the will of God, nor can he become that will in action.

The self-centered consciousness of those whose souls have not been quickened by the Law (or LORD) of ritual will, upon receiving the energies of the Holy Spirit as manna that falls from heaven, either taint these precious energies with their impurities or lock them in the imperfect molds of their human desires. Therefore, the ritual of breaking the clay vessels molded and shaped after the patterns of one's human thoughts and feelings must precede the coming of the Holy Spirit into manifestation. But this is only the first step: New bottles must be formed, designed after the pristine thoughts and feelings of the Christ, and then filled with the new wine of the Holy Spirit. As Jesus said, "Neither do men put new wine into old bottles: else the bottles break, and the wine runneth out, and the bottles perish: but they put new wine into new bottles, and both are preserved."[44] He taught this ritual to his disciples that they might shatter the matrices of outworn concepts and replace them with the pure, geometric forms of the Mind of God.

The term *ritual* may be defined as "a prescribed order of performing religious or other devotional service,"[45] and to that we would add "for the purpose of transforming the human consciousness into the divine." The techniques of ritual taught by the Ascended Masters are by no means empty ceremonials or meaningless motions, vain repetitions or the fanatical frenzy of those who unwittingly worship the synthetic image of the Christ in place of the Real Image of the Son of God. They are scientific practices by which man can attain dominion over the forcefield of his consciousness—not by blind belief, but by conscious atonement (*at-one-ment,* hence attunement) of the soul with the white fire core of his being—the Christ—and with the fiery core of every atom of his four lower bodies. Through ritual man enters the heart of Life and earns the right to sit on the seat of authority, the throne (three-in-one) of his Christ Self. One with God, he commands cosmic forces because he has realized the fullness of that Mind which was in Christ Jesus.

The law of ritual is the *right-you-all* of the Brotherhood. It is the opportunity to right all wrongs that have ever been imposed upon Life's energies through the misuse of free will. It is the opportunity to reclaim the bad seeds of discordant thought and feeling that have been recklessly cast to the winds without concern that they might one day spring up as thorn and thistle in a neighbor's garden. Ritual is the golden thread that the aspirant follows through the labyrinthian cave of his own past errors, ultimately to find at the other end the open door to freedom through self-mastery in the Christ consciousness.

The geometry of ritual is the key to the mathematics of soul liberation. This geometry must be discovered by each one through the invocation of the sacred fire in the form of prayer, decrees, and medi-tation (see Chapter Twenty-Five). The liberation of consciousness that comes through the practice of these rituals is based upon the law of the square, represent-ing Matter; the circle, representing Spirit; and the triangle, representing the merging of the two through Christ the Mediator. The visualization of these forms during periods of communion with God establishes a forcefield in consciousness which channels the ener-gies of the sacred fire into patterns of perfection whereby they are locked in the Christ consciousness, never to be requalified by the human. More complex forms of these geometric patterns, together with their three-dimensional counterparts, can also be mastered; as these gradually displace the jagged, incongruous forms that have been retained in the subconscious mind, man rises in Cosmic Consciousness to take do-minion over the earth.

One of the greatest keys to self-mastery is the geometrization of consciousness through the concen-tration of the mind and heart in perfect union of motive, will, and action upon these soul-satisfying forms that are the building blocks of creation. By and by, these will emerge from one's own subconscious, automatically parading before the mind (in place of the haunting specters of the past) as flaming, white-hot glyphs that brand the aura, seal one's thoughts and feelings in the Light of God that never fails, and claim the soul for Home and heaven.

The ritual of dedicated service to one's family and community is strengthened by these patterns etched in sacred fire upon every cell and atom of one's being. The rituals of loving, of being, of giving and receiving, of studying to show oneself approved unto God, and of fulfilling one's own creative evolution are brought into perspective as the ebb and flow of the tides of the Infinite filter through the latticework of geometric forms that are stacked layer upon layer from head to toe in his physical form as well as in his spiritual being; thus the total consciousness of man enters into the ritual of becoming the Christ.

The practice of the Presence of God—of affirming *I AM here, I AM there, I AM whole, I AM omnipotent, omnipresent, and omniscient because I AM God in action where I stand, where you stand, where Life is living everywhere*—gives instantaneous liberation from the false or incomplete testimony of the physical senses, which is the foundation of the synthetic consciousness. Above all, such rituals provide surcease from the weight of planetary effluvia and liberation from ego involvements that tend to make one identify with one's experiences, thoughts, and feelings instead of with the experience of the Great I AM—the feelings and thoughts and actions of the heart and head and hand of God.

Morya concludes: "From time to time the Brotherhood releases vital ideas—sometimes simple, sometimes complex—into the minds of the students. These ideas are not always assimilated immediately. Albeit instant love is the will of God, it is not always the possibility of man. Therefore, these teachings on [the sacred ritual of] the will of God are given in order to re-create in consciousness certain engrams that will enable you to accomplish effectively and by consent your release from the carnal mind and to replace it by the buoyancy of the Mind of God."[46]

CONSCIOUS PENETRATION OF THE MACROCOSM

In shedding light on the question, What is consciousness? the Ascended Masters would teach the disciple how to transcend his mortal limitations while he yet dwells in the dimensions of time and space, how to be in the world but not of it, how to effect his union with the Highest Mind, unhampered by those earthly circumstances which proceed from the carnal mind. When he demonstrates trustworthiness in the application of cosmic principles, the Masters reveal more advanced methods whereby he can experience directly the consciousness of God. Then the disciple answers the question for himself: What is consciousness?

In our investigations into consciousness the question comes to mind, Can we experience the realm of First Cause? Can we experience the world of Noumenon? Can we experience God's consciousness directly? The answer is that man can experience God totally only when he becomes totally aware of God. While he is partially aware of God, he can experience him only in part; as long as he remains in his limited consciousness, his experience will be limited thereby. Profound insight into the question of transcending limitation through the expansion of consciousness is given the disciples of Lord Meru at the Temple of Illumination:

"Consciousness, when functioning properly, is a glowing orb of reality, joy, and full illumination. The individual reaching-out from the seemingly separated center of being to contact the cosmic center of Life and thence the periphery of all reality is accomplished as easily as the miracle of the radiant, expanding Mind of God penetrates the universe with light.

"Inherent within man is the power to expand consciousness beyond the sphere of the personal self into the dominant domain of reality. This reality is shared by the myriad manifestations that inhabit Cosmos; but because of the marvelous quality of 'locked-in individuality,' there is never any oppressive erosion of the permanent nature of man. There are only the gentle, molding factors as the hand of Universal Intelligence,

Power, and Love commences the process of tutoring the evolving soul personality.

"Recognizing, then, as beloved Kuthumi has said, how easy it is for individuals to misqualify energy and, conversely, how wonderful it is to begin the process of requalification, the individual self can look forward to experiencing newness of life and a sense of fulfillment that he has not known before.

"Soon he will bypass the false structurings that he has created and that have been created for him [even within his mind] by the dark overlords and their dark stars of compounded misqualification. Soon he will realize, with the joyous gurgle of a newborn babe, that the universe is a home of light and hope where the temporal manifestations of intelligence, consciousness, and identity can be welded to the Eternal even as the Eternal permeates the substance of mortality with its essential reality. Here at last mankind can come to know the permanent gift of bliss which it was the Father's joy to convey to the individual at the birth of his identity. . . .

"In the name of Holy Wisdom I, Meru, urge upon everyone the willful relinquishing of the snake-skin of identity that has crawled upon its belly while pursuing the vanities of the intellect. Replace this by the dominant sunburst of the living, vital Mind of God and that reality which God is and which you are because He is."[47]

The Ascended Masters are very much interested in expanding or, shall we say, spiritualizing man's senses and making them God's senses (the faculties of God's own Self-awareness) in order that man might overcome the boundaries of his own finite sensibilities. The Lord of the First Ray has given magnificent counsel on the subject of the return to paradise, the return to the high estate of God's consciousness that every son and daughter of God once knew and loved. The chelas of the Master are not surprised when they hear the fire of the will of God crackling in his every word, for they know that their beloved El Morya has energized a momentum of utter devotion to that will as it manifests in the externalization of the Mind of God:

"Stand now to release thyself from the darkness that is in thee[48] and face the luminous orb of the Central Sun from whence all creation sprang! Mindful of His will for Good and of His power to extend that will, realize that He is able to extend thy consciousness from its present state—to pick it up, to exalt it, and to draw it into Himself by the magnetism of His grace—here and now, prior to thy release from sense consciousness.

"Realize that He that keepeth all that is real[49] about thee, having received thee momentarily unto Himself, is also able to return thee to the present moment unaffected adversely, but mightily affected inwardly by a fuller measure of the understanding of His will [of His consciousness]. Realize that the will of God can best be known by a spiritual experience. Desire, then, that experience. Desire to reach outwardly toward the Godhead in the Great Central Sun galaxy at the same time that thou art reaching inwardly to the implanting of the divine seed within thyself. For it is the will to live within thyself that must unite with the will to live as God lives. This is the divine will within the heart of the Central Sun; this thou must understand and be united with.

"If this be accomplished but once consciously, thy life shall ever thereafter be affected by an innate knowing, recorded within, of that which is the will [the consciousness] of God. The phantoms and the ghosts that formerly made thee a stranger at the courts of heaven will no longer hold power over thee as they once did. But man's reunion with the Sun can be accomplished only by an act of God [an act of grace]; it is a cosmic event which can occur in the world of the individual only when he has proven himself ready for it. . . .

"You must be able to go deeply within; for not in outer accouterments of name or fame or even in worldly intellect does man find the keys that will transport him to these higher reaches. We caution that great care must be exercised in this matter, for truly we are not concerned with the developing in men and women of untutored or unguided psychic experience. We want this form of communion to be a rarity rather than a daily practice. It is something one should try no more often than once a year in just this manner, with the exception of those who have been mightily prepared by advanced training. For them there will unfold the necessary direction that will assist them in having vital experiences to guide them in their solar evolution.

"You must understand that the will of God [the consciousness of God] is a sacred adventure. I have said it thusly for a reason, for the average individual considers an encounter with the will of God a remote possibility. He prays to have the will of God made known to him, but he does not understand that he can have an a priori glimpse of that will while yet in mortal form. He does not realize that the will that sees can also be seized, in part, as a treasure house of consciousness and carried back into the domain of the Life within. There the great lodestone of Truth acts as a divine revelator to reveal to each man from deep within his own heart what the will of God really is. Above all, let him understand always that, complex and all-embracing though it may be, the will of God [the consciousness of the Mind of God] can always be reduced to the common denominator of Love, Life, and Light." [50]

PRAYER TO THE WORLD MOTHER

O Mother of the World,[51]
We are all children of Thy Heart—
Kept apart by triviality,
We remain separate
From Thy cosmic ecstasy.

Passions of cosmic freedom, when denied to all,
Bind blind mankind to sensedom, do enthrall.
To fight each other we are pledged—
By dreadful doings, dining
On man's shoddy, senseless spewings
Of aborted patterns charged with hate—
Delusion's senseless, fate confusions.

Do Thou now, Great Silent Mother,
Teach Thy children how to have no other
Than Thyself—to hold our hands from mortal error,
To keep our minds from mortal terror,
To seal our hearts in purpose now supreme,
To forge Thy cosmic union—Reality, God-dream.

Long the night has vacant been
From the Light of Thy radiant Manchild;
Standing in the Sun of united oneness,
We confess to loss of happiness.

Thy office of pure Light fears no competition;
Let none doubt Thee, but find instead
Attunement with Thy blessed Head
Of hallowed thoughts;

Thy Love, which flows from glowing Heart
Of cosmic dreams from God's own musing,
Clears the air from each confusing dream of man
That splits, divides, and saws asunder
Many lives until all wonder,
Where's the blunder lying 'neath our feet?
Shall it defeat us evermore—
Never to pause and take our store
With all our reason, wisdom evanescent,
Vanishing to a point of nihilism?

I am a child of cosmic diligence;
Immaculate is Thy concept
Of my willingness to be God-taught,
To learn to love, to shatter matrices of dense desire.
O Cosmic Mother, from Thy lofty star position,
Set my heart afire!

May I move by impulse of Thy Love
To the Fount of Brotherhood
Where, washing feet of all my competitors,
I shall serve them all
And see Poseidon rise,
The new Atlantis of our allness,
Nevermore to sink into the smallness
Of the lesser self that raiseth Cain.
I am able now to serve and reign
As Thy beloved Son.

Climb the Highest Mountain
by Nicholas Roerich

SHE WHO LEADS

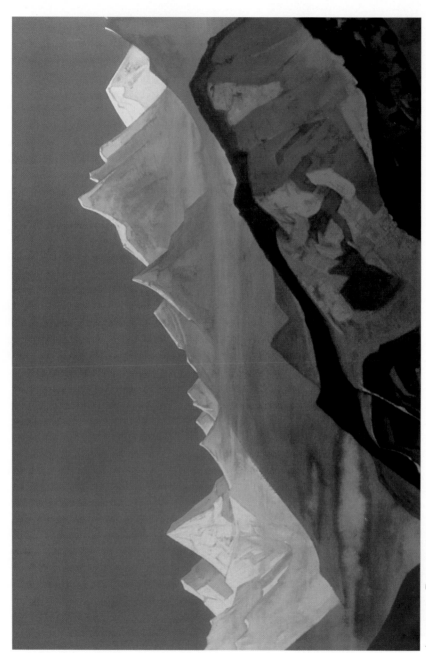

ANCIENT PYRAMIDS

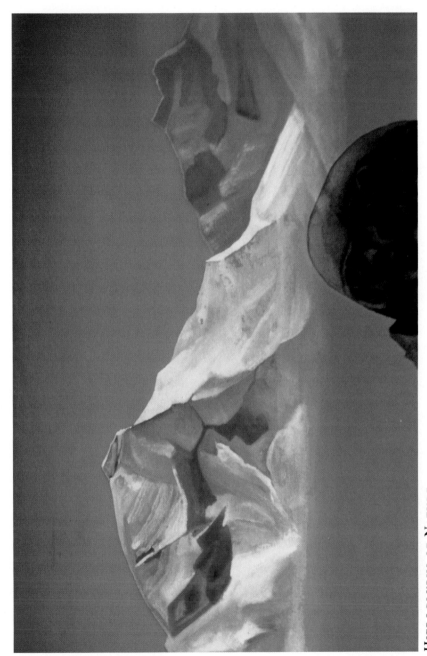

KANCHENJUNGA

Fiery Summit

SILENT SAGES

Path to Kailasa

RIVER OF LIFE

Chapter Six

God in Man

God in Man

He that dwelleth in the secret place of the Most High shall abide under the shadow of the Almighty.   *Psalms*

"I AM WHERE I AM"

IF MAN IS TO REALIZE the nature of God, he must develop the sense of where God is. When man understands that he lives and moves and has his being in God,[1] he can joyously affirm, "Where I AM, there God is!" or "Where God is, there I AM!" and thus establish a reference point for the flowering of his divine potential wherever the LORD is and wherever His Presence is individualized.

Man need not manufacture an illusion to establish the existence of God within his consciousness; the very fact that man is conscious is indicative of the inner presence of the Higher Mind. It is, then, through the consciousness of God in man—through God's awareness of himself *in* and *as* man—that man becomes aware of the Self *in* and *as* God.

If man can understand that he lives in God, he must soon come to the realization that God lives in him. For by the law of interchange which governs the exchange of energies between the Macrocosm and the microcosm, God and man forever coexist as coordinates of the great cosmic flow of Life.

If, therefore, man is to find the living God, he must look within himself. And if man is to find this God within himself, he must realize that God, Life, and Consciousness are synonymous terms for the vibrant forcefield of cosmic energy that sustains his being.

Within man there is Life in action—Life-giving energy that beats his heart, that flows from the Central Sun of Being to nourish the unfed flame of his identity. Within man there is consciousness that establishes a connection between the Mind of God individualized as his own self-awareness and the universally creative energy of that Mind in radiant action everywhere.

Have you ever asked yourself the question, Where am I located in my physical body? Where is the seat of my identity? Most people cannot establish the exact location of the self in form. Some say that the seat of consciousness is in the heart. Others are convinced that man's individuality is in his thoughts and that the center of being is in the brain. Still others go so far as to say that the consciousness of man is located in all parts of the body through the nervous system, while some believe that the seat of the soul is in the belly. In this and subsequent chapters, through the study of the Chart of Your Divine Self, we shall explore the subject of where you are in your Self and where God is in you.

As we explained in Chapter Four, the four lower bodies are the soul's vehicles of expression in the world of material form. As the musician uses his instrument to draw forth harmonies unheard and unseen without his magic touch, the soul gives utterance to the music of the spheres through its "four-stringed lute," focalizing in the four lower bodies the designs of Cosmos and the creative energies of the universe.

Although each of the four planes corresponding to the four bodies has a unique atomic frequency, providing the opportunity for a unique expression of

the soul's potential, the four lower bodies interpenetrate one another and are connected through the etheric
chakras anchored in the physical body through the
central nervous system and the endocrine system. In
this way the bodies function as a unit; and thought,
feeling, and memory patterns passing through the physical body create ripples of vibration simultaneously on
the mental, emotional, and etheric planes.

Thus, the chakras are the receiving stations for
the flow of light-energy that descends from the Presence and Christ Self through the heart flame to the
physical, mental, emotional, and memory vehicles.
Serving as step-down transformers, these centers focus
the light from on high and transform it, making it practical for distribution to each of the four lower bodies.
Without these centers (which will be diagramed and
discussed in Chapter Twenty-One) God's individuality as man's individuality would remain unexpressed
on the four lower planes of consciousness.

When man understands the fact that the four
lower bodies are instruments for his self-mastery, he
sees that he is not his physical body any more than he
is his mind, his feelings, or his memory. Therefore it is
correct to say, as common usage has it, that man *has* a
physical body, that he *has* a mind, that he *has* feelings,
and that he *has* a memory.

While man retains his conscious faculties of perception and reason, these seem to function automatically through the physical instrument; but when the
soul, or animus, and the threefold flame are withdrawn,
these activities of consciousness are no longer apparent
on the physical plane. To the observer, consciousness
ceases with the cessation of physical awareness. Yet we
know that man's consciousness is continuous both
before physical birth and after physical death, for it is
a function of God's consciousness and his Spirit, which
is birthless, deathless, and eternal.

The Real Self, or the immortal Spirit—the animating principle of all *man*ifestation—exists independently of the four lower bodies. As the temporal manifestation of the Spirit, the soul must evolve through the four sheaths in order to become immortal. Thus the soul can be lost, the Spirit of the I AM THAT I AM can never die.

When embodied on the physical plane, the soul is anchored in all four bodies and its perceptions are grounded in the physical world.* The physical orientation of the consciousness precludes its perception of the Higher Self, the invisible world, and the spiritual side of life until the soul anchors enough spiritual substance, or light, in the physical body to form a bridge between the material and the spiritual planes.

When the whole body is full of light,[2] man's physical senses become imbued with and transformed by the senses of the soul. Likewise, when enough light is retained in all of the lower bodies and in the magnetic forcefield surrounding them, which is called the aura, they become spiritual focuses in the world of material form through which man's spiritual faculties and his Christ consciousness can express. This process of filling the bodies with light is the means whereby the transition is made from the human to the Divine. The progressive unfoldment of the soul's potential is therefore realized through the thinning of the veils of the four lower bodies.

The LORD God who declared before the worlds were framed, "I AM where I AM!" hides behind the screen of individual identity in man and Nature. The divine masquerade has been referred to as the Light[†3] that shines in the darkness, but which the darkness, by

---

*When out of physical embodiment, the soul, prior to its ascension, inhabits the etheric envelope.

†When capitalized, *Light* means Christ consciousness as the personal Presence of the Lord, the First Cause behind the effect we perceive as physical or spiritual light, i.e., energy.

its very nature, does not comprehend.[4] Nor do those who have not realized the Spirit of the LORD within themselves recognize that Spirit when it draweth nigh.

In order to experience the God who dwells in him, man must first appropriate His Light. Then the Light that he invokes from on high will release the Light that lies dormant within as the sleeping giant of his True Self. Just as man's outer consciousness enables him to establish the relationship of his identity to his environment, so God's indwelling Light focused in the microcosm enables man to relate to God in the Macrocosm and to become one with Him—as Above, so below.

The first step toward comprehending or "taking in" the Light is to affirm with God the words "Let there be Light!" This fiat must be spoken and experienced if man would become the Word incarnate. The seeker for divine reunion must realize that at any given moment—even now if he so wills it—regardless of past mistakes, regardless of his wilderness wanderings, there can come into manifestation in the uncomprehending self a realization of his own individual potential, his own personal Reality.

Let him pause and listen to the Great Command resounding throughout his universe. Let him exercise a fuller flow of consciousness in every portion of his body and soul. Let him trace with the fingers of his mind the particles of Light, the tiny electrons that move to quicken the memory of immortality in every atom and cell of his being.

"Let there be Light!"—words that illumine the Macrocosm, words that penetrate the blackest night of man's aloneness and make him suddenly aware of his all-one-ness with Infinity! Words so sure of their return that the response of the whole creation is the tumultuous cry "And there was Light!" God has spoken, and the Image of himself has answered. So is the covenant between Creator and creation a sublime exchange of energy, possibility, responsibility, ideas, unfoldment, expansion, and worlds to conquer.

Thus saith the LORD, "This shall be the covenant that I will make with the house of Israel:* I will put my law in their inward parts, and write it in their hearts; and will be their God, and they shall be my people. And they shall teach no more every man his neighbour, and every man his brother, saying, 'Know the LORD': for they shall all know me, from the least of them unto the greatest of them: for I will forgive their iniquity, and I will remember their sin no more."[5] So is the ancient covenant fulfilled when man affirms his allegiance to God, saying: "Let there be Light! Let there be Life! Let there be Consciousness everywhere I AM!"

THE CHART OF YOUR DIVINE SELF

In our consideration of the manifestation of God in man, we must not fail to take into account the cardinal principle of Ascended Master law, that God dwells in every man and not alone in his son Jesus the Christ. The only begotten Son of the Father, full of grace and truth,[6] is the Christ whose Image the LORD has reproduced over and over again as the Christ-identity of every son and daughter who has come forth from the infinite Spirit of the Father-Mother God.

And so we come to understand the true meaning of the phrase "whose body was broken for you."[7] The Light Body, the very essence of the sacred Word which was made flesh and has dwelt among us,[8] is the Christ flame, which the LORD has tenderly placed within the hearts of all of his children, without favor and without sacrifice. For he is no respecter of persons,[9] but honors

*Those who abide in the dwelling place of all that *Is real.*

all whom he has created as the repository of his grace and his truth—as temples for the adornment of his fiery Spirit.[10]

"How unfortunate are those who, while always perceiving the height and depth of man, are never able to become impersonal enough in their approach to endow 'the least of these my brethren'[11] with the quality of the living Christ!" exclaims the ascended Brother of Assisi, whose devotion to the Christ has been steadfast since the Master left his great example two thousand years ago. "Men find it not at all difficult to believe that the fullness of the Godhead bodily dwelleth in Jesus,"[12] he adds, "but they do find it difficult to believe that it also dwelleth in themselves. Yet this God has done. . . .

"In the case of the Master Jesus, because of the perfection in his nature, which he clearly perceived, he did not require any propitiation for sin; yet he is portrayed as one who is able to save to the uttermost those who believe in him.[13] Those who understand the meaning of God, Christ, and Life from a real standpoint see that there is no difference between the Divine Nature in Jesus and the Divine Nature in themselves. They understand that there is no partiality in heaven. All can equate with the Image of the beloved Son. The ninety and nine must be forsaken,[14] for they already possess the strength within themselves to perceive this truth. And the one who is lost, caught in the brambles of confusion, blinded to his own Reality and the inward radiance of the Divine Image, must now forsake the false doctrine of the blind leaders of his blindness;[15] he must heed the voice of God and return to it."[16]

If man is to return to the voice of God, if he is to find order in the vastness of Reality that suddenly dawns upon his consciousness, he must have a visual conception of his link with that Reality. Let us consider the Chart of Your Divine Self, included in this chapter, as the pattern of each man's God-design.

As we proceed to illustrate the triune nature of Being, we shall refer to the three figures in the Chart as the *upper figure,* the *middle figure,* and the *lower figure.* The upper figure represents the eternal Presence of God individualized for every man. The lower figure represents the soul which came forth from the Spirit to embody in human form, clothed upon with "coats of skins"[17] (the four lower bodies). The middle figure represents the Christ, the Mediator* between the Divine Self and the human self, the Spirit and the evolving soul.

When God said, "Let there be Light," and there was Light, he implemented the expansion of the Light by giving birth to individual Spirit-sparks. These drops of his cosmic identity were scattered throughout the universes as billions of seeds of Light, each one with a unique destiny, yet each one an exact replica of the original Unity that was and is God. Separated in the time-space configuration, yet forever one with the Central Sun, or Centrosome of the Eternal, these sparks of the Divine Image were created that each soul might express an aspect of the individuality of the Godhead. Thus in the upper figure we see the design of a personalized fragment of the Deity, the very Presence of God himself, the individual Spirit-spark that is known as the I AM Presence.

Because the Presence of God is one with the essence and Being of God, we acknowledge that "our God is one LORD."[18] We understand that although his Electronic Presence be multiplied billions of times for the purpose of his individualization in form, God is still one—one individed Whole. Just as one times one times one will always equal one, so God times God

*The Mediator has also been referred to as the Higher Mental Body.

times God still equals God. Although not all have understood this mystery, we have seen that it is most assuredly within the capacity of the Great Geometer to sustain an infinite number of focuses of himself and still maintain his Oneness.

Thus, when properly understood, monotheism remains the foundation of cosmic law. Just as Christians are able to accept the mystery of the one LORD as a Trinity of Three Persons (and some acknowledge the preeminent Godliness of the saints), just as Hindus pay allegiance to the Supreme Being while doing homage to the virtues of a host of lesser gods and goddesses, so the devotee of the Ascended Masters bows to the God flame in every manifestation of Life whom the LORD has created as the dwelling place for his triune Spirit. He reveres the qualities of God-mastery externalized in those sons and daughters whom the LORD has blessed with God Self-awareness; for he knows that these have attained a conscious realization of the Presence of the indwelling Spirit and of themselves as that Spirit in action.

Reverence for the God who dwells in every man and for the soul-manifestation that has realized its God-potential can never detract from the basic truth that God is One. Those who lovingly worship him must include in their love all who have returned to the great Three-in-One of his Being and who are, by congruence, God-identified Spirit-sparks come full circle in their spiritual evolution. Having gone forth from his great heart, having gained self-mastery and returned to his Oneness, they are included in God's own awareness of himself; hence, whether or not unascended man realizes this fact of being, all the ascended hosts become part of every man's awareness of God. The fullness of this God-realization—the realization of the God Self in oneself and hence in every man—is the mark of the enlightened consciousness.

Surrounding the upper figure in the Chart are concentric rings of rainbow rays of light. These rings are not flat, as shown, but are actually spheres within spheres, blending with one another and manifesting the iridescence of the God Presence as each soul's own star of identity.[19] Thus the Magi exclaimed, "We have seen *his* star [the Presence of the Christed individuality of Jesus] in the east [focused in the plane of manifestation] and are come to worship him [to worship that portion of the Spirit which has descended into the form]!"[20]

This sphere is your causal body. Its center, the white fire core, is the point of the individualization of the God flame; it is the heart of your I AM Presence. Here upon the altar of each man's Holy of Holies is the focus of the threefold flame of Love, Wisdom, and Power, a replica of the unfed flame of Life that burns within the heart of God himself. The glow from this pink, blue, and yellow tripartite fire penetrates the spheres of the causal body and radiates the magnificence of the Holy Trinity to the boundaries of creation.

The light rays that are emitted from this heart center of God in man are in contact with the heart of God himself; they are the connecting links that serve to integrate the Body of God in heaven and on earth. Each individualized Presence of God is thereby united with every other individualized Presence of God, with the heavenly hosts, and with the whole of creation.

Thus the unity of Life was established "in the beginning" through the Presence of God anchored in every part of Life. Through the rays of light that emanate from the heart of your Presence, you are already one, and you always have been one, with all Life everywhere. You have but to develop the sense of this oneness and to unite with the Spirit of the living God that hovers above you in order to begin truly to live and to remake your identity according to the Image of the Christ.

This graphic presentation of the individualized God flame illustrates the nearness of the Divine Presence to its manifestation in the world of material form, dispelling the myth that has long relegated God to a distant place in Cosmos where he remains aloof from his creation and the day-to-day problems of his children. It shows that God cared enough to place a very personal focus of himself, a Spirit-spark, over each of his sons and daughters as the soul's link to eternity. What greater expression of the Father's love could we find?

Descending directly from the threefold flame in the heart of the I AM Presence is a flowing stream of radiant energy that originates in the flaming center of the Almighty. It is a "crystal cord"* of luminous essence, a ray of light that spirals from the supreme Source of Being and is anchored first in the heart of your own I AM Presence and then in the heart of the Divine Mediator, where it springs up as a threefold flame of Christed magnificence. Thus, although every focus of the threefold flame is a trinity in manifestation, the presence of the threefold flame first in the heart of God himself as a focus of the Holy Spirit, second, in the heart of the Presence as a focus of the Father aspect of that Spirit, and third, in the Christ Self as a focus of the only begotten Son, reveals another trinity that spans the eternal cycles from the Macrocosm to the microcosm.

From the Christ Self the energies of the crystal cord descend to the lower self where the stream of Life from the Presence becomes a threefold flame

---

*The crystal cord is often referred to as the silver cord because of its silverlike appearance.

upon the altar of the physical heart, the central chakra of the four lower bodies. Through the love, wisdom, and power of the flame within the heart, individual man is destined to outpicture all three aspects of the Trinity and thus become a focus of the omnipotent, omnipresent, and omniscient God in *man*ifestation.

"In this very flame," Kuthumi expounds enthusiastically to his disciples, "man has a catalyst posited right within himself, a sparkplug that can motivate him to make that attunement with his Presence whereby the magnificent influences of our Brotherhood can shine through his aura and he can become the outpost of heaven upon earth. Whoever said, and who dares to say, that any one person has the exclusive possession of this quality when it is the divine plan for all to radiate the one Light? Just as man and all things were made by one Spirit, so the one Spirit expects all to enter in at the door.[21] The door of the Christ consciousness literally trembles with anticipation of the moment when the individual will joyously enter into the sheepfold of his own Reality."[22]

Since the day you first came forth into the world, God has sustained this flame within your heart as a point of intimate contact with the Source of all Life. The threefold flame establishes man's Divinity and unlocks his potential for God-mastery. As the Higher Self reflects the Allness of the Infinite One, so the lower self is intended to be the reflection of the individualized God flame—as Above, so below.

During the first three golden ages before man's departure from innocence, the crystal cord was nine feet in diameter and the threefold flame enveloped his form. Man's source of energy was literally unlimited and his Christ consciousness was all-enfolding. After the Fall, man's opportunity to exercise his free will was curtailed. By cosmic edict the threefold flame was reduced to one-sixteenth of an inch in height and the crystal cord to a mere thread. Thus it came to pass that what little energy man received was needed to sustain his physical body; in spite of himself, his evil tendencies were shorn of their strength and his vile creations became shriveled and earthbound.

If you follow the line on the Chart that represents the crystal cord, you can trace the flow of light-energy from the lower figure to the upper figure. From there you can visualize the ray proceeding to the heart of God in the Great Central Sun. The pillar of fire in the heart of the Sun may be thought of as a giant maypole; its flaming ribbons of light, streaming from the center like billions of sunbeams, are actually crystal cords which can be traced to the I AM Presence of every son and daughter of God, connecting souls, both embodied and disembodied, throughout the Father's many mansions to the very Hub of creation.

The soft spot on a baby's head marks the place where this mighty light ray enters the physical form and establishes the initial impetus of Life when the umbilical cord is cut at birth. While the fetus is forming within the womb, the action of the mother's threefold flame sustains the life of the child. After birth, as the infant matures, the bony structure of the head closes over; for once firmly established within the heart, the action of the flame, which increases in magnitude with the cycles of maturity, can easily penetrate the protective covering of the cranium.

When man has spent his allotment of energy for a given embodiment and his life span is terminated by karmic law, the crystal cord is withdrawn from his form and the focus of the threefold flame is extinguished within his four lower bodies. Man's soul consciousness then rises to its cradle in the higher etheric body (and he "yielded up the ghost"[23]), and to all appearances death takes place. In his sonnet on the coming of the evil days, Ecclesiastes gives a veiled description of the withdrawal of the crystal cord from the heart—noteworthy for its scientific detail preserved in code:

Remember now thy Creator in the days of thy youth,
> *Remember the I AM Presence during the early days of thy sojourn upon earth,*

While the evil days come not,
Nor the years draw nigh,
> When thou shalt say, I have no pleasure in them;
> *Ere the energy veil descends, man's karma returns according to the law of cycles, and the burdens of life deprive man of its pleasures;*

While the sun,
> Or the light,
> Or the moon,
> Or the stars,
Be not darkened,
Nor the clouds return after the rain:
> *Ere man is cut off from the Source of Light and Life by the gathering clouds of his mortal consciousness:*

In the day when the keepers of the house shall tremble,
> *In the day when the body elemental* shall sense the approach of death,*
And the strong men shall bow themselves,
> *And none shall return the edict of the Almighty; for the time comes when even the high and mighty must bow to the cycles of Life,*
And the grinders cease because they are few,
> *And the few who do the work of the LORD also hear his Homeward call,*

*See Chapter Seven.

And those that look out of the windows be darkened,
And those whose perceptions of Life are received through the physical senses find that they are darkened (for their soul faculties have not been developed),

And the doors shall be shut in the streets,
And the apertures (the chakras) of the four lower bodies shall be closed (and the soul must find a new opening upon Reality),
When the sound of the grinding is low,
When the wheels of the four lower bodies turn slowly (the light in the chakras diminishes) in the presence of the Death Angel,
And he shall rise up at the voice of the bird,
And the soul shall be quickened by the impulse of the Holy Spirit,
And all the daughters of musick shall be brought low;
And the pull of the senses and the sympathy of the emotions shall no longer affect the soul;

Also when they shall be afraid of that which is high,
Also when the mortal consciousness shall fear the immortal God Presence which draweth nigh at the close of the earthly cycle,
And fears shall be in the way,
And the trepidations of the human consciousness shall stand between the soul and its reunion with the Presence,
And the almond tree shall flourish,
And the causal body surrounding the Presence shall be filled with the fruit of good works that man has wrought in God, in Life,
And the grasshopper shall be a burden,
And man's misqualified energies (symbolized in the insect form), which sustain his electronic belt, shall

*weigh down his soul (solar) consciousness that
would take flight,*
And desire shall fail:
*And the energies shall be withdrawn from the
desire, or emotional, body:*
Because man goeth to his long Home,
*Because man's consciousness goeth to his biding
place within the heart of the Presence,*
And the mourners go about the streets:
*And those who cannot see the Presence of Immor-
tal Life wallow in the patterns of the human:*

Or ever the silver cord be loosed,
Or the golden bowl be broken,
Or the pitcher be broken at the fountain,
Or the wheel broken at the cistern.
*Or the energies of the crystal cord be withdrawn
from the heart chalice and the threefold flame
ascend to the etheric body.*

Then shall the dust return to the earth
  As it was:
*Then shall the energies that coalesced to outpicture
the divine blueprint in the dimensions of Matter
return to the elements (for it is the Christ Light
anchored within the heart that magnetizes the iden-
tity pattern in form):*
And the spirit shall return unto God
  Who gave it. [24]
*And the soul shall return to the I AM Presence, the
Spirit which gave it Life.*

Thus ends the sacred revelation of the Preacher
who gazed upon the synthetic consciousness of mankind and the synthetic civilization it had produced
and said, "Vanity of vanities, vanity of vanities; all
is vanity." [25]

THE FLAME WITHIN THE HEART

Writing of the heart as one of the choicest gifts of God, Saint Germain penned these words to his students: "Within the heart there is a central chamber surrounded by a forcefield of such light and protection that we call it a 'cosmic interval.' It is a chamber separated from Matter and no probing could ever discover it. It occupies simultaneously not only the third and fourth dimensions but also other dimensions unknown to man. This central chamber, called the altar of the heart, is thus the connecting point of the mighty silver cord of light that descends from your God Presence to sustain the beating of your physical heart, giving you life, purpose, and cosmic integration.

"I urge all men to treasure this point of contact that they have with Life by giving conscious recognition to it. You do not need to understand by sophisticated language or scientific postulation the how, why, and wherefore of this activity. Be content to know that God is there and that within you there is a point of contact with the Divine, a spark of fire from the Creator's own heart called the threefold flame of Life. There it burns as the triune essence of Love, Wisdom, and Power.

"Each acknowledgment paid daily to the flame within your heart will amplify the power and illumination of love within your being. Each such attention will produce a new sense of dimension for you, if not outwardly apparent then subconsciously manifest within the folds of your inner thoughts. Neglect not, then, your heart as the altar of God. Neglect it not as the sun of your manifest being. Draw from God the power of love and amplify it within your heart. Then send it out into the world at large as the bulwark of that which shall overcome the darkness of the planet, saying:

> I AM the Light of the Heart
> Shining in the darkness of being
> And changing all into the golden treasury
> Of the Mind of Christ.
>
> I AM projecting my Love
> Out into the world
> To erase all errors
> And to break down all barriers.
>
> I AM the power of infinite Love,
> Amplifying itself
> Until it is victorious,
> World without end!"[26]

Verily, the Christ flame within the heart embodies the same qualities of love, wisdom, and power that manifest in the heart of the Almighty, in the heart of your I AM Presence, and in the heart of your Christ Self. Right within your own body temple are three fiery plumes of the Holy Spirit—pink, yellow, and blue pulsations of living flame. Thus the heavenly Trinity gains expression in the world of material form; and the energies of Father (blue), Son (yellow), and Holy Spirit (pink) are resplendent in the heart of man. Also corresponding with the trinity of body, mind, and soul, the threefold flame supplies man's need for power to run the body (the faith and goodwill of the divine intent); wisdom to nourish the mind (illumination and the right use of the knowledge of the Law); and love to fulfill the destiny of the soul in conscious outer manifestation (a just and merciful compassion that is always rewarded by individual creative fulfillment).

The flame within the heart is your personal focus of the sacred fire. It is your opportunity to become the Christ; it is the potential of your Divinity waiting to burst into being within your humanity. This flaming fountain awaits your soul's ministration that it might expand to fulfill the purposes of God's kingdom within you[27] and thus accomplish the *squaring of the circle* of your Divinity, the precipitation in Matter of the Christ consciousness that originates in Spirit.

In his *Trilogy on the Threefold Flame of Life*, Saint Germain has written in detail on the manifestation of each of the three aspects of the Christ flame; and he has used his own insignia of the Maltese cross to diagram the descent of power from God to man and its distribution through the chalice of the heart. Let us take his proffered gift of wisdom as the foundation for our understanding of the more advanced teachings that follow in subsequent chapters.

I. POWER

"The very thought of power in itself," begins the Master Alchemist, "brings delight to the hearts of men. The power of the universe depicted in the heavens tells men of that seemingly far-off aspect of God for which their souls hunger but unto which it appears impossible to draw nigh. Hope, together with the element of faith, has enabled men to release some degree of power into their worlds and to subject it to their control.

Power Defined

"Now, power has taken many forms: abuses have marred its use, whereas virtue has enhanced it. Tyrants have exploited it, and politics and religion have been molded around the star of power blazing in the firmament of society.

"The primary types of power are physical, mental, emotional, and spiritual energy in various forms. There is electrical, chemical, nuclear, elemental, and cosmic power; and there is temporal power, consisting of social influences and mass pressures, governmental and religious authority. Meanwhile, karmic power affects everyone's status, attainment, and progress. All power is interrelated: some is stored, some is static, some is dynamic and subject to a rapid decay rate. All power is subject to two primary qualifications under the classification of relativity: divine and human, or cosmic-universal and material-transitory.

"The Maltese cross, emblem of my dedication to the cause of freedom, is a balanced thoughtform which may be used to illustrate the qualifications of power. As many realize, a cross symbolizes the meeting of two planes of consciousness—the horizontal bar representing the plane of the human consciousness, the plane of the ego, and the vertical bar representing the energies of God descending from the realm of Spirit into the quadrants of Matter.

"The center where the two lines intersect is the point (orifice) where the energies of heaven are released to the earth; and in truth, it is at this point—which is actually the point of the qualification of power—that great alertness must be maintained by all who use power in its many aspects, including its organic and inorganic forms. The power of speech itself—the power in the spoken word and the power of the Word, whether released by pen or edict of sword—changes the course of history and alters the lives of those affected by its release. Whatever its subsequent use or abuse, the tangled threads of power have always flowed, symbolically and actually, from the orifice of the cross.

"The Maltese cross is a symbol of perfect balance—both in the alignment of the four planes of Matter (and the Four Cosmic Forces thereof) and in the inner and outer expression of God's Spirit within the souls of his own. As such, the Maltese cross illustrates the drawing forth of Light's energy and consciousness from on high (through the north arm) for the manifestation in the world of form of God's omnipotence, omniscience and omnipresence (through the west, south and east arms respectively). And, as we shall soon see, in this cosmic interchange between God and man the universal Light is beamed forth 'as Above, so below' to the right, to the left and in the center in a perfect equilibrium of Power, Wisdom and Love. . . .

"In simplifying the understanding concerning the release of power, it will be shown that the bodies of man, four by definition, are receptacles of that power. Thus his physical, mental, emotional and etheric 'sheaths of consciousness' are recipients of the charge of power that is released through the electronic pattern of the Maltese cross. For the purposes of this study, it is best that we consider the dawn, the beginning of each day, as the arbitrary point of origin for power's release, when self-conscious awareness once again floods the altar of individuality and men begin again to think and to perceive. For this, too, is an employment of power, but one which is often abused by neglect.

"Few today are aware of the degree of power which God has conferred upon man through the gift of consciousness. Few are aware that they possess the power of focalization and intensification in the proper exercise of their attention through individual consciousness; nor do they realize that the interpretive and discriminatory action of the God Self enables them to take firm hold of the reins of power, to be in control of their lives, and to be less distracted by the social and karmic responsibilities that are daily thrust upon them.

Self-Dominion, Your Reins of Power

"The statement made of old 'He that is slow to anger is better than the mighty; and he that ruleth his spirit than he that taketh a city'[28] should be understood. Were it so, more adepts and masters would arise in every generation to take the reins of dominion over themselves and their worlds. It is an act of utter compassion for universal Law and for universal Love for you to obtain dominion over the finite self. When this happens in your life, and happen it shall as the Law is made known, you will realize that you cannot remain a novice and still be a master. Although you live in the plane of the human consciousness, you must not be subject to its depredations.

"Inasmuch as the world is filled with idle minds, and 'idling minds,' even when housed in a dedicated consciousness, are often tools of the sinister force ('the devil's workshop,' as they say), it behooves the student of deeper Truth to recognize that he alone can and must govern his own world through the right use of power.

"In this sphere of cosmic coexistence, where the energies of the Macrocosm and the microcosm flow as one, there is a daily release of great power from the Godhead and a subsequent abuse of that power by mankind. Some men watch the abuses of others and then respond with an equal or greater abuse of power; thus they gauge their power train according to the qualifications of power by individuals and society. This is not action, but reaction.

Others, sometimes consciously and deliberately and at times thoughtlessly or unconsciously, generate discordant thoughtforms and auric emanations from their beings through the triggering action of bad habits and momentums. I would like to list some of these abuses of power in order that you might perceive how people become the unwitting tools of subtle qualities of negation and how they take in, amplify, and discharge this noxious substance into the planetary atmosphere.

"First there is boredom, an indifferent state of mind wherein all seems quite profitless to the individual who cannot see beyond the vanity of this world to the reality of the next. In this disenfranchising state, akin to a vacuum, men denude their souls of vitality. Then there is dissatisfaction, in which men assess their own progress or lack of it and, by dishonesty in self, or self-deceit, are unwilling to admit their role in fashioning their own weaknesses. Instead, they effect a transfer of responsibility to others, assigning them the blame for their own failures or lack of progress. Often carried on at subconscious levels, this ruse of the carnal mind remains the primary cause of personal stagnation.

"Then, too, there are numerous types of fear. One of its most devastating forms which I desire to call to your attention is that which even the sincere sometimes attribute to the Godhead—given men's propensity to fashion their gods after themselves. It is the altogether human quality of whimsy, which stems from a deep-seated insecurity. Although they themselves have a whimsical nature, they cannot bear the thought of being subject to a whimsical God. Therefore they conclude—for dark and unclear reasons unknown even to themselves—that their lifestreams are not in favor with the universe and that they must withdraw therefrom. In this anxious frame of mind they may tend toward aggressive forms of rebellion or their attitude may become one of servility, wherein they easily tolerate feelings of lethargy, depression, and hopelessness.

"There is the vibration of doubt which we would also touch upon. Doubt stems from fear and from a lack of real self-knowledge, while self-doubt, as lurking suspicion, colors one's doubts of everyone else. Some, who believe themselves to be fearless and in possession of greater knowledge than they in fact have, may not accept the statement I am making. Nevertheless, I shall affirm its truth; and when in the light of greater understanding men will have dispelled their own self-ignorance, their doubts, too, will fly out the window. But men must allow themselves time enough to achieve this. As the Master said, 'In your patience possess ye your souls.'[29]

"Now, there are many other traits and influences that we could go into here, but I do not choose to prolong the enumeration of negatives to which mankind are host. Rather, I would point out, on the basis of a thorough analysis of those I have listed, that mankind's abuses of power are created primarily as a result of their ignorance and misunderstanding of the laws governing the flow and use of energy. Moreover, to the great masses inhabiting the planet, from whom even a rudimentary knowledge of the science of karma has been withheld, it is somewhat difficult to explain the cycles of reincarnation that predestine the return of abused power to the one who has misused it.

"The horror with which some who profess to be religious view any doctrine that is not approved by the church of their fathers is a millstone about their necks. How unfortunate! For if they are to be free from the shackles of an ancient dogma, they must open wide the doors of their minds, without fear and without prejudice.

Oneness of Life, Four Lower Bodies

"Now, it must be understood with cherishment that all Life is one, and that an abuse of power on the part of any member of the world body has its effect upon all. But by a like token, the correct use of power by anyone upon the planet brings its blessing to all.

"Power is energy. Energy stored in the physical body can be measured as the sum total of the energy content of all of the body cells. When this energy is spent, it becomes necessary to in some way reinfuse the cells with energy in order to renew the power of the body. To infuse the body cells with new and vital energy when those cells are already clogged with accumulations of negatively qualified substance (residual deposits of power misused through wrong thought and feeling) is to partially negate the flow of energy in the body. This can cause fatigue, or a loss of power, which, if unchecked, eventually results in so-called death—the cessation of the flow of power from the Presence to the physical form.

"Consider the value of flushing out these accumulations by spiritual electronics! And then gradually building up the light in the four lower bodies by the fourfold alchemy of the Maltese cross—and the science of the spoken Word! Thus it is most necessary to understand the relationship of the four lower bodies as you pursue the rebuilding of the temple of man as a wise masterbuilder.

"The mental body interpenetrates the physical body as water interpenetrates a sponge. Having its own reservoir of power, it is not dependent upon the physical body except as the focal point for the flow and distribution of power. Yet, the four lower bodies of man are so interrelated that if the mental body is to operate at optimum efficiency, the other three must be in perfect alignment with it and with each other. The densities that the mental body encounters in the physical body—such as the harmful residue of nicotine, drugs, and impure food, or even the substance of fear, doubt, and mental rebellion accumulated from past lives—clog the brain cells and imprison the light of the atom, effectively impeding the free flow of light to the physical consciousness and thereby impairing the function of the mental faculties.

"When misused, the power of the emotional body becomes the most violent and volatile of the four lower bodies. When agitated by undisciplined feelings, these emotional energies have a tendency to lead men astray in their thinking and in their actions.

"The flow of power to the mental body is also greatly subject to the power of the etheric, or memory, body. In memory's storehouse, the writings of all past actions in present and previous embodiments stand as an electronic record of considerable weight and influence. The power of this record, together with the momentums generated by the misuse of energy, is a subtle pressure that affects the present moment for good or for ill (relatively speaking) unless it is brought under the control of the balancing power of the great God flame within the heart—the immortal flame of Power, Wisdom and Love.

The Maltese Cross, Symbol of God-Controlled Power

"The Maltese cross, symbol of the perfect balance of the God flame, 'as in heaven, so on earth,' provides a thought and energy matrix whereby the ill effects of personal and planetary karma can be brought under control and the power of virtue released in their place, that mankind's use of power might no longer corrupt life on earth. It has been said that 'power tends to corrupt and absolute power corrupts absolutely.'[30] Power can be used as the bow of the Infinite Archer to release an arrow of perfection into the heart of man's goal of happiness. As the pursuit of happiness is an acknowledged treasure, let all who would permanently enjoy it ponder the Maltese cross as a simple thoughtform through which great truths may be revealed for the blessing of all.

"Looking at the Maltese cross placed upright before us, we see that the four symmetrical arms extending from the center are triangular in shape, wide at the outside, giving the appearance of a fanning action. The upper, or north, arm descending to the center resembles the upper vessel of an hourglass. Actually, it is a funnel through which the great energies of God—the power of God—are descending into the cup (chalice) of being. The wide opening reminds us of the infinite energies of the Source and of God's ability to convey these to man. Therefore we know that we need not accept limitation in any form—whether in receiving or giving the limitless light of Cosmos.

"The point of qualification at the center of the cross indicates that you must always consciously determine within your heart and mind to qualify your God-given energy with the purity of the divine intent and with the virtues of your Christ-identity. You need not be weak or weakened when confronted by waves of discordant energy—whether your own or another's. Nor is it necessary for you to be rude in your rebuttal of human error; for it is not the person, but the impersonal energy personally misdirected that must be challenged. Therefore, establish yourself in a firm, unyielding consciousness that rejects evil as the lie of man's misqualification; and as you breathe in the essence of the sacred fire, 'flower of power,' determine to strip that lie of its negative power manifesting as thorns of abuse.

"It must be recognized that when the energy-action descends from God to man through the upper arm, narrowing through the funnel to flow into the

MALTESE CROSS:
FOCUS OF THE DISTRIBUTION OF ENERGY
FROM SPIRIT TO MATTER

Macrocosm—"Day Side of Life"

Energies of Spirit
descend through the

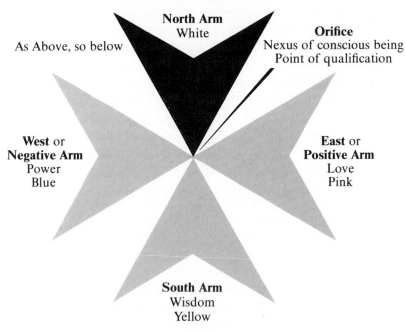

North Arm
White

Orifice
Nexus of conscious being
Point of qualification

As Above, so below

West or
Negative Arm
Power
Blue

East or
Positive Arm
Love
Pink

South Arm
Wisdom
Yellow

Energies of Spirit coalesce as Matter
through the
three lower arms

Microcosm—"Night Side of Life"

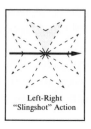

Left-Right
"Slingshot" Action

crucible of being at the point of the cross, it passes through the nexus and fans out into the three lower triangles to manifest as power, wisdom and love in the world of material form. Thus, the infinite energies of God are molded by the qualifications of man's attention focused at the heart of the cross—the seat of his conscious mind. By this means power congeals in the physical world, taking the form of the thoughts, the feelings, the acts, and the spoken word of man, the release of its potential being entirely dependent upon the motivation and the will of his consciousness.

"The balance between the upper arm, which receives the energies of Spirit, and the three lower arms, through which Spirit's energies coalesce both in and as Matter, provides for the balanced manifestation of God's power 'as Above, so below,' from the planes of primary causation to the physical effect, as it is taught in the Hermetic science. If man's qualification of his quotient of spiritual energy released over the crystal cord from the I AM Presence to the heart chakra were retained in purity from the moment it entered the crucible of his consciousness, all that is in manifestation in the microcosm would reflect the perfection of the Macrocosm. Think of that!

"The energies of the three lower arms, fanning out in a balanced action from the center of the Maltese cross, proceed, then, from the plane of pure Being into the form, or action, phase of the threefold flame. Power by itself (in the left arm) retains the negative polarity unless and until it is qualified with the positive polarity of Divine Love (in the right arm). Ponder well this statement!

"Now, the left arm of the cross denotes the negative, or minus, charge of spiritual energy qualified by the blue flame of Power. The right arm denotes the positive, or plus, charge qualified by the pink flame of Love. And the lower arm, denoting the central axis of the plus and minus fling, is qualified by the golden flame of illumination, which imbues both the positive and negative poles with Wisdom's God-direction and purpose. Therefore, all that is below in the microcosm is intended to be a threefold manifestation of the sacred fire that descends from Above in the Macrocosm.

"The energy released from the Godhead, the Daystar from on high [31]—the lodestone of Power, or the I AM Presence, scintillating in the octaves of perfection—immediately upon entering the lower octaves of Matter assumes the negative pole of being in what is called the night side of manifestation. This is the minus side of Life, where the plus fling of potential released from Spirit enters into material qualification.

"The energies garnered in Spirit, when preceded by right thought in the left arm, gain the impetus for God-virtue by the power of Love's cohesion and attraction as they are released into action through the right arm. This left-right, 'push-pull,' action can be illustrated through the principle of the slingshot, wherein the stone in the sling is withdrawn from the Y in a negative pull in order to secure the necessary impetus of power to drive home the shot through a positive release.

"You will recall that it is written in the first chapter of Genesis that God made 'the greater light to rule the day and the lesser light to rule the night.' [32] The north arm of the cross represents the day side of being, and the three lower arms the night side. The left arm of the Maltese cross, being the negative arm of the Trinity *in form,* is itself symbolical of the negative side of Life in which the three lower arms are suspended. Then, too, it is the left arm that denotes the physical nature of man as a cradle, or crucible, into which God pours his power as a condensation of the fiery intensity of his light.

"This he does in the hope that man will rise above that cradle/crucible and transcend the world of experience which the alchemist perceives as the night side of Life, a temporal densification of Spirit, a laboratory in Matter where he is obliged to prove the scientific laws of being in order to return to the permanent abode of Spirit. It is out of the dense spheres of this world of experience, which the Hindus refer to as the world of maya, that the soul of man must rise, 'purified and made white,' into the purity of the great God flame of his being.

"The Maltese cross has another significance. When the perfect integration of God and man is complete, there is a sunburst effect emitting light from the dot in the center of the cross. Within the cosmic circle of allness at the dot symbolical of individuality, there is focused the balance of Spirit and Matter, a Divine Oneness of all planes, a union of the Father-Mother God fulfilling the spirals of Alpha to Omega. Through the sacred heart of the soul wed to the Universal Christ in the alchemical marriage, the Light is come, the Light does shine!

"God is in Truth the All-in-all—not only in principle but also in practical application! For this God, Whose Christ, as Paul said, is All and in all, is the All-in-all within the individualized manifestation made in his image and likeness.[33] Thus is the fullness of God's kingdom conferred upon his sons and daughters—thus through the pattern of the Maltese cross is the concept of 'Thine is the power' realized!

"God's power, as his light/energy/consciousness is, then, entrusted to every man. And it is in the right use of this power in every way—according to the spiritual/physical laws of alchemy which I herewith declare to you *in part,* leaving the rest to your mystical communion with Cosmos—that man can surely come to understand more of the universe and obtain the victory of eternal Life. . . .

II. WISDOM

Wisdom's Way by the Threefold Flame

". . . The sunshine yellow plume, or sunburst of divine illumination that is within everyone (released through the south arm of the Maltese cross as the pivot between the positive and negative arms of the cross), is the secret key by which man can unfold his own wisdom flame. This central plume of the tripartite flame of Life must be consciously expanded within heart and mind through invocation to the I AM Presence. For, as the animating principle of God's own Mind, it is given freely for the use of all who will make the call in the name of the Christ.

"By visualizing its golden yellow radiance passing through one's four lower bodies many times daily, the devotee initiates the process of burning out the accretion of negation and density, purifying the mind, feelings, and memory, reinforcing therein the revitalizing electronic power of vital Truth. As he joyously assimilates wisdom's fires, these displace and consume the dross of erroneous thoughts and feelings previously assembled in the human mind that prevent the flow of light through the human consciousness and, until transmuted, remain the enemy of every man seeking God-illumination. [34]

"Jesus said, 'A man's foes shall be they of his own household,' [35] and no more motley household has ever been assembled than a man's own wrong thoughts! It is not necessary to pull up the weeds of those wrong thoughts all at once, for the wheat may easily be removed along with the tares. [36] However, it is essential to recognize that some degree of reappraisal and self-examination is *constantly* necessary—if one is to retain the true alchemist's objectivity and standard of perpetual progress on the Path. . . .

"Let every man be aware, then, that it is his duty and responsibility to nurture self-concern; for by concern for himself as to what thoughts he shall admit to his mind (and what motives and feelings he shall allow to tarry in the chamber of his heart), he is able to purify that mental world of his and to guard it by purity's flame in such a manner as to of greater benefit and service to others. Indeed, can the blind lead the blind? As the Master Jesus said, 'Shall they not both fall into the ditch?' [37]

"By a forthright will and willingness reinforced by the decree of your word, remove, then, all barriers in your being and consciousness that *you know* impede the flow of the God flame of illumination. Use the violet/purple flame of freedom. Welcome it into every atom and cell of your world. Each day ask your God Presence for greater wisdom and for an increase of the flame of illumination and its right use. In the name of the Christ and by the threefold flame within your heart, demand of your Great God Self a balanced flow of Power, Wisdom and Love—and see what Life will do for you!

Balanced Achievement—The Way of Mastery

"Imbalance—where giantism occurs in one aspect of the threefold flame, causing it to be out of proportion to the others—prevents the achievement of daily goals as well as the goal of individual Christ-mastery. As the tangible, balanced flame of illumination expands from within your consciousness, it gradually enfolds your being until God, as holy Wisdom, is enthroned upon the altar of your heart. But with each increase of wisdom, the power and love plumes must also rise by the fiat of your devotion to goodwill, else wisdom's gain will not be retained. Likewise, with each getting of power there must come the attainment of wisdom and love in perfect complement; so, too, love is actualized only through an equivalency of power and wisdom.

"Recognizing that balance is the golden key to Christhood, you will understand that you cannot know for yourself nor bring into manifestation that which you have not first realized within the realm of your outer or inner experience in God. Such experiences become ultimately meaningful, beautiful, when woven through the rhythm of the balanced threefold flame. . . .

III. LOVE

"Precious seekers for your own freedom, know that the full power of the three-times-three is the mighty momentum of the stream of love that issues from God's heart! Filling the universe with abundant joy, it flows forth into thine own heart. This is the cosmic fount of pure love that springs up as the crowning radiance of each manifestation in Nature, in the angelic hosts, and in man.

"It is to this love of God that we must pay tribute whenever we drink in the floral fragrances of the blossoms of natural beauty nodding in the sunlight and the gentle wind. This love is also the motivating power behind all angelic action. Therefore, those who would draw very close to the angelic hosts, that they might receive their protection, radiance, and blessing, will be most wise to keep harmonious at all times and to shun all forms of human discord.

"The greatest love ever to be found in man is the love which lays down its life daily to keep the well-being of its friend.[38] What greater service can be rendered unto life than simply to manifest love? Remember, true love is the great magnet that draws forth the power of God's heart charged with his holy wisdom. The secret of the evocation of power, then, really lies within the heart of love. It must be acknowledged here that men and women of the First Ray who so successfully invoke power do so by turning to the great power of love and drawing therefrom the power of God. . . .

". . . In the human condition, just as there is a positive pole, so there is a negative pole to a given situation. These are opposing forces, rivalrous in nature and mutually destructive. For example, if the thesis be human love, its antithesis will be some form of love's polar opposite—human hatred, fear, suspicion or even mild dislike. Their synthesis will be a watered-down version of both with no commitment either to one or the other. This is the lukewarm state of mediocrity which Jesus spurned when he said, 'Because thou art lukewarm, and neither cold nor hot, I will spue thee out of my mouth.[39] . . .

". . . Love is always pure and does not contain within itself any self-polluting, self-mutilating force such as fear of failure, fear of Truth, fear of Life, fear to be Love. . . . True love is always understanding, yet not necessarily always understood. It speaks with the Shepherd's voice of authority, never the petty tyrant; it chastens, peeling away by its caressing flames the layers of self-deception of child-man. Love as discipline has the hardness of the diamond-shining Mind of God that alone can bind the tyrant ego and set the captive free. From Christ's heart of true love, then, the words 'Father, forgive them; for they know not what they do'[40] are easily uttered. . . .

The Rock That Is Higher Than I

"Therefore, in love you must come up higher. You must meet love's standard. For Divine Love will not be compromised nor can it suffer dissimulation. Love is the Rock that David knew to be higher than the I. 'Lead me to the Rock that is higher than I,' he implored.[41] Thus, contrary words of criticism and condemnation, words of harsh or hypocritical judgment—words of malintent—do not spontaneously spring forth from a heart such as his, accustomed to attunement, yea that lives and breathes God's mighty flame of love.

"Have we not heard as John heard, 'He that loveth not his brother whom he hath seen, how can he love God whom he hath not seen?'[42] This maxim still speaks Truth when made to read, 'If you do not see God and sense his love, you cannot truly love your brother.' So Christ commanded his own 'that he who loveth God love his brother also.'[43] Therefore let your own actions be your index to your attainment on this path of the Third Ray. For they do speak. And speak they shall, more than to thyself.

"You see, the true love that inspired the universes can be drawn only from God's heart, the center of all Being—the great Source of Life (power), Truth (wisdom), and Love and every benign quality that springs therefrom. I would say, then, that inasmuch as there is no other source for love but God, and so many have for so long been 'absent from the LORD,'[44] verily they have lost even the spiritual mechanism within themselves to understand that which they no longer possess.

"Now, if any find that he is unable to summon love for his brethren, or compassion for the world and its problems, let him consider that this problem indexes a state of spiritual dryness. To be sure, this is a serious shortcoming in the aspirant on the Path which may stem from mental rigidity and hardness of heart, products of fear and self-hatred. But perfect love casts out *all* fear and *all* torment that fear begets.[45] And thy soul hath need to be infused with eternal love by a mighty invocation—fervent in the Holy Spirit. . . .

"As Christ spake to his disciples: 'Cast the net on the right side of the ship and ye shall find!'[46] so let all who would manifest more love recognize their need for greater attunement with Almighty Love through the record in heaven of the Father, the Word and his Holy Spirit;[47] for even those who do not feel the mighty heartbeat of Universal Love and who have been unsuccessful in amplifying its release on behalf of all Life upon earth can through the heavenly Trilogy correct their deficiency—which, I might add, is not to be taken lightly.

"Unless you, alchemist of the sacred fire, would-be adept of the mysteries, continually enkindle love—love as compassion and kindness, love as tolerance and tactfulness, love as approbation and support, patience, long-suffering and forbearance, love as gratefulness and merciful forgiveness—and actively expand it as a flame flower, a many-splendored rose whose tender petals unfold all of these qualities and so many more—the law of balance as God's justice will cause the wisdom and power aspects of the threefold flame to be reduced to the lowest common denominator of your externalized love plume.

"I cannot honestly say that I marvel at the number of spiritual seekers who desire power over themselves—for mastery—and over other parts of Life—for control—while ignoring the Great Law that requires man to express a true and lasting love toward God and self and brother before he can possess both the wisdom and the power of that very love which gave birth to the creation.

"Remember that just as God cannot be invoked in part, the 'unfed flame'*—the fullness of the tripartite flame of Power, Wisdom and Love—must be invoked in its totality and completeness from the Father, the Son, and the Holy Spirit revealed by Jesus Christ. For *it is* their focus of the Divine Whole—the creative spark of God's desiring within you; and no partial manifestation can generate the cutting action of the Whole that arrests Light's antithesis, the Darkness that would clutch thee to itself—torment, enslave, and possess thy soul.

"Only thy faithfulness to the Father and Son, thy hopefulness and charity in the Spirit of the perpetual Helper, will set free thy captive heart and release both Light and spirit of the seeker from the dungeons of self-division and the divisive ones. Thus, day unto day does the glory and power of God's kingdom expand from within the threefold flame of the heart—rarest of all immortelles.

Divine Love Defined

"We must acknowledge that there are many types of feelings which are called love but which, in Reality, are not. . . . Therefore, again, let us define love. As the worlds were framed by love, love is both sagacious and potent; for each part of the unfed flame is complementary to every other part and to the Whole. Yet love in essence is the very inmost being of God! For love in manifest action is God in *manifest-ation!*

"'For God so loved the world, that he gave his only begotten Son, that whosoever believeth in him should not perish, but have everlasting Life.'[48] This love of God to us is fully expressed in the gift of the Father's Presence with us, in his gift of the Son whom we know and love in Jesus Christ, in the Emmanuel of

*Synonym for the threefold flame—perpetually burning, unfed by any human source.

our Christ Self—and in the gift of the Holy Spirit. Everyone who loves is born of the Spirit[49] and finds love's fulfillment in this Trinity and in its expression in every part of Life. Thus, it can be said and truly that he who loves not has not yet come unto Life, for he knows neither self nor neighbor in the image and likeness of love....

"Love is penetrating and expansive; love is enfolding and transmutative; love is forgiveness and understanding. Love is wisdom and strength. Love is virtue and purity. Love is dedication and constancy. Love is all of the qualities of God combined with an added ingredient not yet fully known to unascended man and woman—which, for many reasons, we here can neither define nor unveil, except to say that the fullness of love is the very secret of Life!...

Self-Love, Family Love and Human Relationships

"Now let us peer within the domain of the self of each individual, e'en of thine own Self, and perceive the meaning of Self-love. And row by row we shall without fear separate the tares from the wheat (and the tears as well) and step by step in love's own mastery you shall mount the spiral stairs of love's degrees.

"Selfish love is not Self-love. That which seeks not that it may share with every other part of God's Life but that it may possess this Life unto itself, holding people, things and ideas imprisoned in the domain of exclusivity, is but selfish love. This is the idolatrous adornment of the ego. That which seeketh not its own but another's good, drawing forth abundance that it may expand the glories of Life and share them with the many, is a manifestation of truest love. This is true Self-love—the love of the True Self in all.

"Self-love, or the love of the Real Self, does not generate disrespect or aloofness; on the contrary, it regenerates man's faith in the inherent Good of all and teaches him, even while admitting the possibility of human error, that error is no part of the Real Self. When human mistakes, which are but temporary recordings on the chart of man's experience, are cleared by noble deeds and the violet flame, and all inequities are righted by service to Divine Justice, the fruit of unselfish action will manifest on an altar swept clean of all inordinate desire. For the threshing floor of the heart made pure will provide a suitable altar upon which the unfed flame will more than flicker. Its rising pulsations will expand in the rhythm of Life to elevate all whom it contacts, commencing with the aspirant himself. . . .

"The word of the LORD recorded in the second chapter of Genesis brings to mind Love's enduring tribute to the creation of twin flames in the white fire ovoid and their divine love which endures unto the blessing of all other human relationships: 'It is not good that the man should be alone; I will make him an help meet for him.'[50] . . .

"This statement from Genesis concerning man's aloneness has also been correctly interpreted as meaning 'It is not good for the manifestation to be all one; therefore, I will make individual parts of my all-oneness,' or, as the LORD promised Abraham, 'I will multiply thy seed as the stars of the heaven, and as the sand which is upon the sea shore.'[51] And so, let the love of the individual parts for one another and for the Whole exceed self-love and excel unto an expansion of love within the creation in honor of the Creator, finding thereby reunion with the one Life which is All and in all.

Christ Love

"The great and awesome power of creativity that floods forth myriad and wondrous forms in Nature and in man, that creates cosmic beings and angel messengers of fire, holds in cosmic Mind the Truth that a love not wholly integrated with the allness of the Cosmos in the oneness thereof would not be God, would not be Good. Inasmuch as Goodness requires some objective manifestation of itself in order to love, the great creative will of God was and is to create many Self-expressions in form: the wondrous design of twin flames descending from the Sun to unveil in flesh the faces of Alpha and Omega in so many ways—sons and daughters of the Most High, children of the One basking in the love play of angels and elementals, guarded by Nature spirits, luminous presences and mighty beings of the Elohimic spheres, all in one grand hierarchical order, that each one, from an electron to a star, might, in receiving his love, return that love not only to the Central Sun and the Creator but also to all creatures he has made, dwelling now in the peripheral worlds of time and space.

"Few have reached the level of Saint Francis of Assisi in their comprehension of this concept concerning the multifaceted parts of the one individed Whole. I would, therefore, call to your attention the great depth of compassion and the true scientific understanding of the psychology of the soul, far in advance of his time, which your blessed Kuthumi externalized in his embodiment as dear Francis and which remain to the present hour in his ascended state the outstanding qualities of his service with beloved Jesus in the office of World Teacher.

"Truly his life was a message of God's love borne in the chalice of the fiery heart of the saint for all Life's expressions:

> Dear Francis' love for creatures great and small
>   Compassed the sea, the sky, and all.
> His love the outbreathed universe did frame
>   As stars ensoul compassion's flame

On path where every open heart did sing
  And hopes did rise like bird on wing.
O Love, thy flame shall bear one yet on high!
  O Love that lives and cannot die,
To cross the bar and then become a part
  Of God's own fiery beating heart!
For where I AM in shining knowing free,
  I feel the power of Truth fill me.
What thrills me most as cup runs over now
  Is this great truth: That I AM Thou!

"How great was his example! Yet, the great example need not be anyone with whom you are familiar, or it may be anyone with whom you are familiar.
In the history of Christendom the great example finds
its purest form and expression in the figure and divinely human personality of Jesus. And yet I do not
blaspheme when I say that many men and women in
embodiment today have, through their devotion to
Jesus and to the Great God Self, received the same
sacred love tokens from God's heart that the Almighty
imparted unto Jesus. The dove of the Holy Spirit has
rested upon their heads and its snow-white radiance
of purity has flowed from their hearts. Though not
always well known, the divine gifts of healing, of miracles and of teaching and preaching the Word of God
have been given unto them also. [52]

"Some have founded no new religion, all have
supported holy endeavors and sought to be examples
of God's purity. Over the centuries mature sons and
daughters of God of considerable accomplishment in
many fields—prophets, teachers, reformers and not a
few great lights—have brightened the planetary corner
with their Presence. And by their balanced expression
and generous sharing of their developed threefold
flame—to which the Saviour by his grace has added
his momentum—they have been wayshowers of the

path of individual Christhood ordained by God not for one son alone but for all heirs of His Light. . . .

"I would, therefore, offer this plaudit on their behalf, this acknowledgment in Freedom's name that the world is not so poor as it sometimes considers itself to be in the manifestation of this great God-essence of love but that it already possesses a great wealth of divine love—a love all too often unrecognized even when seen!—a love that commemorates Jesus' devotion to his fold and upholds the standard he set for those who would follow him in deed. To them he also paid tribute with the words: A new commandment I give unto you, That ye love one another *as I have loved you.* By this shall all men know that ye are my disciples, if ye have love one to another.[53] Greater love hath no man than this, that a man lay down his life for his friends. Ye are my friends, if ye do whatsoever I command you.[54]

"This love, as Life's essential ingredient, flows not only from God on high to the hearts of known and unknown manifestations of himself below, but also from holy men and women in embodiment, whose love as devotion and service to every part of God's Life becomes day by day more like unto the Father and the Son in their mutual adoration. Man's penetration of the holy substance of God's essential love provides him, through the power of the Maha Chohan,* with an infusion of that élan which makes the world go round. That it does not spin faster, that it does not more swiftly throw off its discord, can be attributed to the impediments to Divine Love sustained by the masses who yet know not what they do.[55]

"Those hearts—and many of them yearn to know the Truth and to be free[56]—who pursue a dyed-in-the-wool path of their own misguided wills and spew

*The Maha Chohan is the representative of the Holy Spirit to a planet and its evolutions. This office of Hierarchy is explained in Chapter Thirteen.

out hatred against men of goodwill whom they do not understand, do indeed place their feet in ruts of stumbling upon the mountain of attainment. And although the great connecting link, the lifeline from on high, as a giant skein of light and Life dropped down to earth, continually pulls man forward, the traction created by the pulling back of these people (the recalcitrance of a stiff-necked generation), compounded by the sheer weight of their numbers exercising free will in opposition to (as the antithesis of) the Divine, does in effect prevent the universal manifestation of God's kingdom upon earth!

Harmony, the Fulfilling of the Law of Love

"In the holy name of love we would speak in a practical manner on the great need for keeping and maintaining one's personal harmony not only in one's feelings but also in one's thoughts. For harmony is not only the Law of Love, it is the epitome of love, the sign of love's true conquering heroes.

"Now, as many of you know, when the thought desires to go to the right and the feelings pull to the left, most often it is the feelings that win out and the thought, by rationalization, will gravitate in their direction. And in many cases, unless, of course, the feelings are motivated by purest love, this is not the fulfillment of the law of harmony; rather it is very often a compromise made by the soul caught between the mental and feeling worlds. And it can result in that peace without honor which, because it is not based on Principle, cannot provide the permanent solution to the problem.

"In all his noble efforts to precipitate substance alchemically, man will find no higher alchemical key than the purity of Divine Love flowing forth from his consciousness as God's thoughts and feelings—winged messengers of Light delivering blessings, attracting more of their kind and returning to the alchemist the blessings of the abundant Life.

"The Love of God made manifest in the three-fold flame scintillates with immortal brilliance. Its vibrant, radiant, all-enfolding light comprises the sun flame centers of all interrelated macrocosmic/microcosmic energy systems in material and spiritual manifestation. Withdraw the power of Love from any of these and their eventual collapse is certain. Every system of worlds, planetary or starry body that has ever been dissolved, whatever the apparent or scientific reason, has collapsed from within due to the withdrawal of the love charge from the sun center. The lapse from the moment of withdrawal to the moment of dissolution may range from thousands to even millions of years as men reckon time; or it may consist of a few microseconds—or the pause between them. But the decay of every system begins with the withdrawal of Love's 'lodestone' from its center. Love, then, is truly the cohesive power of the universe.

"One of the most dreaded diseases upon earth today manifests as a result of mankind's hatred toward one another, which, when it returns to the sender, drives the love element from the cells, thereby causing a perversion of their function. Through invasion and metastasis, the disease eventually spreads throughout the body; and death ensues when the form, whose cells have lost the cohesive power of Love, can no longer magnetize enough light to sustain the bodily functions. Though the cause may be ancient, having lain dormant for lifetimes, the karma comes due. Only flood tides of love and oceans of violet fire can bring permanent resolution to the festering hatred that lodges in the psyche of man.

"Yet to this day some have vowed to bear world karma in their members. Saints without blemish are these who take into their bodies the world sin of human hatred. Thus, judge not the infirm, but help them! uphold them! heal them! by love. In healing the many types of cancer and other physical, mental, or emotional disorders, the invocation to Divine Love is essential. And the healer must be all love in action.

"Jesus' compassionate response to the cry of the two blind men, 'Thou son of David, have mercy on us,' was a personal action of Divine Love. He touched their eyes and said, 'According to your faith, be it unto you.'[57] The Master's healing of the woman who touched his garment without his knowledge was an example of the impersonal action of Divine Love. His response, 'Who touched me? for I perceive that Light hath passed from me to her. . . ,' showed that the Impersonal Christ had healed her through him without his foreknowledge.[58]

"Divine Love as the living Christ, the Son behind every son of man, is both personal and impersonal; and it is fulfilled measure for measure, as ye are able, in every one of you through the cycles of the law of your Being, the law that is ever love in manifestation. When you exercise it, the Law of Love unites the purity of justice, mercy, and freedom in perfect balance through the threefold flame within your heart. Let those who will, discount the Law as Love and deny its corrective measures as an action of Love. I charge you to remember the words 'Whom the LORD loveth he chasteneth, and scourgeth *every* son whom he receiveth.'[59]

". . . Let not selfish love carry you into the byways of delusion, far and apart from your brothers and sisters and those other parts of Life whom God has made. Remember, too, that those who have chosen to embody elements of evil ever seek to divide the children of the Light by subtlety, flattery, hypocrisy, money schemes, sexual entanglements, etc.—you yourself can name the rest; whereas true love would unify the sons and daughters of God in the very essence of holiness and world service.

"To pay tribute to love is to pay tribute to the great drawing power of God's own tripartite flame. Love is God's flame of Being in manifestation. One day the scientists of the world, through special instruments, will be able to measure a portion of the love flame and its radiant energies, but never will an instrument be made that has a scale great enough to measure the all-encompassing power of infinite Love.

"Infinite Love can best be expressed as the manifestation of God. The manifestation of God can occur in everyone. It is the destiny of man that shakes from man his dust. Love, then, is the fullness of God as he manifests man. I tell you there is no limit to the degree of God's Love which anyone who will may manifest. Anyone who wills to invoke it, to be it, and to share it may be the answer to Love's call and calling.

"Here in the realm of Divine Love is the City of God, the foursquare city described by beloved John [60] as the place of conscious attainment where the fullness of your aspirations may find unhampered expression. Here your soul looks out upon the great wide-open spaces of the creation. Love has unlimited new worlds to conquer. Love is the Promised Land where the strength of the lion's nature is given to the heart of the lamb, and the Good Shepherd of the Eternal Covenant seals all in the victory of the expanding Three-in-One Flame of God-Good, worlds without end." [61]

And so we conclude our study of Saint Germain's *Trilogy.* Let us now explore the primary colors of the threefold flame as they are used to produce out of the pure white light of God the seven rainbow rays. For these he has given to man as further keys to the externalization of the Christ consciousness. When the blue and pink plumes are combined, they produce the violet of transmutation, wherein the Law, tempered by love, manifests the equalizing radiance of justice and mercy. When the blue predominates, the flame focuses the purple hue, which exacts the preponderance of the justice of the Law within man's being and causes the realignment of his atoms according to the divine blueprint. A concentration of the pink, on the other hand, produces the pink-violet of forgiveness.

In the blending of the blue and yellow plumes, we see the ray of Life-giving green. When the blue predominates, it acts as a catalyst for the reestablishment of the law of man's being which results in the healing, the regeneration, and the rejuvenation of the four lower bodies through the emerald ray; when the yellow predominates, the Chinese green of the precipitation flame focuses the wisdom of the law, or the science whereby man is able to precipitate the abundance of every good and perfect gift.

The pink and yellow plumes combine to produce the golden-pink glow ray, a pink flame with golden-yellow radiance (not orange). The pink and yellow never blend as one, for their unity is a polarity that induces wholeness in the perfect balance of the love-wisdom focused by the Solar Logoi. So delicate is the merging of these two flames that the corresponding color vibration is seldom reproduced in the world of form. Perhaps a sunset or a rose provides the best example of this magnificent union of heart and head. When the hand, the blue plume of action, is added and all three plumes are spun like a pinwheel at the vibratory rate of the ascension flame, the pure white light emerges from the fiery core of God's Being and the purpose of the color rays culminates in divine harmony.

Just as colors have frequency, so thoughts and feelings carry vibrational patterns; and these cannot be separated from the color frequencies that correspond to their vibrations. In fact, our studies of the human aura have proved that there is a scientific correlation between the colors found in the aura and the mental and emotional patterns of the individual.

The electronic pattern of the seven rays is the same as that of the corresponding God-qualities they represent. Thus it is accurate to say that love is pink, wisdom is yellow, power is blue, mercy is violet, justice is purple, healing and supply are green, and purity is white. For wherever there is pink, there is a focus of God's love; wherever there is blue, behold his power; wherever there is yellow, God's intelligence is expressed; and wherever the myriad qualities of the seven rays are ennobled in man, the radiance of rainbow hues appears as a gentle yet powerful glow within the aura. The colors and qualities of the seven rays, their position in the causal body, and their perversion in the electronic belt and in the human aura are given in the chart at the end of the chapter.

In his *Studies of the Human Aura,* the Master Kuthumi explains that the aura is the mirror of the soul and that it is intended to be the amplifier of the energies of the threefold flame. Although the aura is given to man to be used as the reflector of the qualities of his Real Self, he has used it to reflect his negative thoughts and feelings. Therefore, the Master cautions that to properly use this magnetic forcefield, which emanates from the spinal column and the medulla oblongata, man must learn to apply the principle of internal Reality. He must learn to identify that which is real within himself and to penetrate and amplify that Reality; as he does this, that which is unreal is correspondingly diminished by the Light of the Christ.

The Master always asks his less advanced disciples the all-important question, What is real? And then he proceeds to answer it for them: "What is real is released to man as he practices the ritual of penetration—of penetrating the Light of the Son of God by the very power of the Light that is within him—and thereby more and more of the divine radiance can infuse the aura in its manifest pattern. Therefore, today the delight of the Law of God will be in the mouth of the man or woman who will speak the living Word, [62] invoking from the heart of God the magnificence that he already is, claiming in the Word, I AM, the fullness of the Godhead bodily in himself as a joint-heir with the universal Christ consciousness. [63]

"Now in the matter of the effects of one's thoughts and feelings upon the human aura, we shall briefly touch upon the subject of coloration. As the intensity of the white and the violet light is increased in the aura, especially the shades that are pale and ethereal, one notes the enlarging of man's perceptions and an increase in spirituality. As the pale yellow—almost golden—light floods through the mind, the very fingers of cosmic intelligence manifest as interconnecting light rays, enabling the mind of man to contact the universal Mind of God.

"By amplifying in the aura the beauty of pastel pink—vibrating fire of the cup of Universal Love—man is able to spill over into the world the very thoughts of Divine Love. As so many know, the color of violet, vibrating at the top of the spectrum, is transmutative and buoyant. Born to the purple, the man who so infuses his aura is cloaked in the invincibility of the King of kings. This royal color is the cosmic fire of the Holy Spirit, which, when blended with the azure blue of the will of God, manifests as Divine Love in action in that holy will. The green light, eternally new with abundance, charges the aura of man with the power of universal healing and supply. To seal all in the will of God is to drink from the goblet of that holy will. In the electric blue of the Ascended Masters, it denotes both purity and power. . . . Vibrations of anger often register as crimson flashes, just as black is seen in the aura as the opaquing by negative thoughts and feelings of the otherwise natural release of the light of the Presence through the being of man.

"Remember, beloved ones, that the tone of the divine aura is an extension of God, just as the mode of thinking and feeling is the extension of the human consciousness. The interference with the aura in its natural, pure state by the mortal consciousness and its misqualification of light create the negative colorations that are both seen and felt by the more sensitive among mankind. The muddying of the pure colors of the aura occurs whenever there is a mingling of the emanations of imperfect thoughts and feelings with the pure colors released through the prism of the Christ. This marked change in color and vibration is obvious to the trained eye."

Speaking of projections of mass forcefields of negatively qualified energy, which may also temporarily color the aura, Kuthumi adds: "Always remember that those who fall in the swamp may come up covered with mud; for the quicksands of life, by their very nature, always seek to drag man down. But man can and does escape these conditions, overcoming through the same glorious victory that brings forth the lotus in the swamplands of life. I want you to understand, then, that by a simple act of invoking the light of the Christ consciousness, man can overcome the ugly chartreuse green of jealousy and resentment, the muddied yellow of selfish intellectualism, the crimson reds of passion, and even the almost violet-black of attempts at self-righteous justification.

"To see others clearly, beloved hearts, remember that man must first perceive in himself the beautiful crystal of cosmic purity. Then, casting the beam out of his own eye, he can see clearly to take the mote out of his brother's eye. [64] By the purification of your perceptions, you will be able to enjoy the entire process of beholding the Christ in yourself and others, as one by one the little disturbances of the aura are cleared up through the natural manifestation of the childlike beauty of cosmic innocence.

"What is innocence but the inner sense? And the poem of victory that God writes through man is already there in matrix and in creative form, waiting to be delivered upon the pages of life. Human density may have interfered with the manifestation of the Christ in man; but the light and love of the Law will produce for him the greatest purification, making possible the penetration of the aura by the beautiful colors of the Christ consciousness.

"I should like our students throughout the world to join with me in a determined effort to let the crystal-clear grace of the Throne that is within you as the threefold flame (*three-in-one,* hence *throne*) ray out into your world such ecstatic, electrical cosmic energy that you will literally vaporize the darkened elements of your own aura and hence develop that magnificent seeing which will bring the joy of the angels and the Light of God to all whom you meet. . . .

". . . The strengthening of the aura involves a threefold action. The student begins by visualizing the threefold flame expanding from within his heart. He then seals himself and his consciousness in a globe of white fire, and when he is set he proceeds to recite the following words with utter humility and devotion:

> I AM Light, glowing Light,
> Radiating Light, intensified Light.
> God consumes my darkness,
> Transmuting it into Light.
>
> This day I AM a focus of the Central Sun.
> Flowing through me is a crystal river,
> A living fountain of Light
> That can never be qualified
> By human thought and feeling.
> I AM an outpost of the Divine.
> Such darkness as has used me is swallowed up
> By the mighty river of Light which I AM!
>
> I AM, I AM, I AM Light.
> I live, I live, I live in Light.
> I AM Light's fullest dimension;
> I AM Light's purest intention.
> I AM Light, Light, Light!
> Flooding the world everywhere I move,
> Blessing, strengthening, and conveying
> The purpose of the kingdom of heaven.

"As you visualize the cosmic white fire radiance around yourself, do not be concerned with the errors in your thought that through the years may have intruded themselves upon your consciousness. Do not allow yourself to concentrate upon any negative quality or condition. Do not let your attention rest upon your supposed imperfections. Instead, see what the Light can do for you. See how even your physical form can change, how a strengthening of the bonds of your health can occur in body, mind, and spirit.

Try this exercise, simple though it may seem, and know that many ascended beings will be performing it with you."[65]

THE SANCTUARY OF THE MOST HIGH

Jesus introduced the subject of the causal body to his disciples with the admonishment "Lay not up for yourselves treasures upon earth, where moth and rust doth corrupt, and where thieves break through and steal: but lay up for yourselves treasures in heaven, where neither moth nor rust doth corrupt, and where thieves do not break through nor steal."[66] Then he proceeded to explain that the causal body is the personal heaven world that each man must build for himself.

Although the causal body can expand to infinite capacities and eventually include within itself many mansions of the Father's house,[67] this is not the macrocosmic heaven that people usually think of—where angel choirs sing and universes are born; it is not the place prepared where the sons and daughters of God are received into the kingdom. The causal body is the microcosmic heaven that man himself creates within the macrocosmic heaven. It is his holy city, the tabernacle of his God that he has constructed stone upon stone. It is that compartment of his highest consciousness—his very own God Self-awareness that has become his secret dwelling place. It is like a garment that he weaves and then steps into; it is, in fact, his Light Body that is permanent in the heavens.

In the parable of the talents,[68] the Master made plain to his followers their responsibility to multiply their talents and to replenish the earth with light. He likened the kingdom of heaven unto a man traveling into a far country who called his servants unto him and divided his goods among them, each according to his ability. To the first he gave five talents, to the second two, and to the third one. The first two doubled their share and were commended upon his return: "Well done, thou good and faithful servant: thou hast been faithful over a few things, I will make thee ruler over many things: enter thou into the joy of thy lord."

But the third said unto his lord, "I knew thee that thou art an hard man, reaping where thou hast not sown, and gathering where thou hast not strawed: and I was afraid, and went and hid thy talent in the earth: lo, there thou hast that is thine." For his impoverished consciousness he was severely chastised, and his talent was taken from him and given to the one who had ten.

At this point Jesus made his unforgettable statement of cosmic law "Unto every one that hath shall be given, and he shall have abundance: but from him that hath not shall be taken away even that which he hath. And cast ye the unprofitable servant into outer darkness: there shall be weeping and gnashing of teeth."

The meaning of the parable is clear: Those who wisely invest their God-given energies while they are separated from the LORD—he being in the heights of Spirit and they in the plains of Matter—are rewarded with greater abundance and authority as they rise step by step in the initiations on the Path.

When man qualifies God's energy with Christly virtue in word and deed and in thought, feeling, and motive, whether or not he is aware of the science of energy qualification, he is giving that energy a positive momentum and sending it forth as a blessing to all parts of Life. Energy thus qualified circles the earth, attracting more of its kind, and then returns to the individual, its blessings multiplied many times over. When the cycle of qualification is thus fulfilled, God's energy, stamped with man's creativity, ascends to the causal body to become a permanent part of his immortal identity.

The causal body is man's cosmic bank account where talents gather interest that he may draw upon to reinvest in universal blessings to Life—and always the return is more than the original investment. Those who do the good works of God are blessed with his abundance, not by divine favor, not by chance, but by the scientific principle that is unfailing "Unto every one that hath shall be given, and he shall have abundance." And so we begin to understand how man lays up for himself "treasures in heaven, where neither moth nor rust doth corrupt, and where thieves do not break through nor steal."

By the law of retribution, the account of the faithful servant is credited—and this is called good karma. By the same law, the account of the unprofitable servant is debited—and this is called bad karma.

Those who unwisely invest God's energies, charging them with negative momentums or stamping them with the inverted patterns of selfishness and self-love, also receive the return of that which they send forth. When the miscreant receives his misqualified energies amplified many times the power of their original release, he is often beset with great pain and suffering. This is the "weeping and gnashing of teeth" of which Jesus spoke, which, by the law of cause and effect, teaches the very soul of man—even when his outer mind is not aware of the lesson—the dire consequences of his misuse of God's energies.

Obviously, the bad harvest of unwise sowings cannot ascend into the causal body, which is a magnet of perfection, drawing unto itself only the good, the pure, and the beautiful. Man's misqualified energies are literally too heavy to rise. Their light atoms, overburdened by the weight of man's own effluvia, sink to the lowest level of his subconscious being, forming a negative spiral around his four lower bodies. Here in this forcefield of density called the *electronic belt,* man's talents are literally buried in the "earth, earthy," [69] where they sustain a momentum of disintegration and decay, disease and death. Having unwisely invested God's energy, having failed to multiply his opportunities for good, the unprofitable servant finds, then, that even that which he once had is taken from him.

The science of the causal body explains why men differ from one another in their talents and abilities. Since all do not take equal advantage of their opportunities nor multiply their talents at the same rate, all do not have the same reward; and the bands in the causal body, which develop according to the measure of a man's attainment, vary with the individual. Thus, as the causal body is each man's book of life, revealing unmistakably the use he has made of his sovereign free will in qualifying the energies of God with positive Good, so the electronic belt is the tome that reveals his misuse of free will in qualifying God's light with an energy veil.

Paul, referring to the individual character of the causal body, said: "One star differeth from another star in glory. So also is the resurrection of the dead." [70] The causal body, together with the I AM Presence, ensouls the highest individuality of the lifestream as each man's own God Star that sparkles with the energies he has released in service to Life. Through the transcendent glory of the works that God has worked in man, the causal body adorns the individualized God Presence as his mantle of immortality.

Forming a heavenly sphere of pulsating light, the color bands surrounding your I AM Presence are actually interpenetrating globular forcefields of your spiritual attainment and authority. Within these color

bands are the recordings and the momentums of all
the good that you have ever magnetized from the
heart of God and then *caused* to be sent forth to other
parts of Life; hence it is your body of Causative Good.
Herein are the records of your good works and your
virtuous thoughts, feelings, and motives, electronically inscribed and geometrically preserved in the
golden ratio, making possible your self-mastery in the
world of material form and giving you conscious dominion in the world of Spirit. Let us now consider
each sphere in the causal body, beginning at the center.

The yield of every thought, word, or deed cradled
in a matrix of purity is rendered unto the *white sphere,*
the white fire core of the causal body. Purity of
motive, purpose, and intent may be defined as the
desire to glorify God and to praise his name in all
one's actions. The ability to amplify the immaculate
concept of the Christ in oneself and in one's fellowman is corollary to the gift of purity. Thus, out of
purity is born love for the True Self and the inherent
Christ-identity of every man. The white sphere expands as the soul is allowed by man's free will to use
God's energy to multiply its talents of purity in the
world of form.

The unique property of this sphere is that it contains all of the qualities of God embodied in the remaining six color bands;* for the white light is the
whirling action of the rainbow rays as they vibrate at
the higher frequency of the ascension flame. The white
light is the highest manifestation of God—it is the
supreme virtue of every attribute of Deity. Herein
abides the Holy Spirit, the Fire Breath of God, the dis-
tilled essence of Love. Purity is the highest wisdom, the
highest love, the highest freedom, the highest service,

---

*Not shown on the Chart of Your Divine Self are the bands of the five
secret rays.

the highest healing, and the highest will. Indeed, purity is all things to all who love God.

The *yellow sphere*—or the band of gold, as it is often called—reflects all study to show oneself approved unto God,[71] the study of cosmic law and of Nature and her God. Herein are recorded man's aspirations after the Divine Theosophia, and the depth of understanding she imparts. Here, too, is the momentum of man's gifts of knowledge to others, his patience as an educator, his care for the souls who come to him for learning. Here his noble efforts as an illuminator of men come to light, and his molding of their consciousness after the God-design. Here the hope that trusts the Cosmos to impart unto the soul an ever expanding awareness of Self and Reality is unveiled as a blossom of purity—the hope that is charity for all and faith in the omnipresent, omnipotent, and omniscient Mind of God, continually revealing itself through Creator and creation. The globe of illumination reflects the faith, hope, and charity that ensoul the sacred wisdom—whose reward is the peace that passeth understanding.[72]

In the *pink sphere* there is recorded every thought of love expressed to the tiniest child or to the most Ancient of Days. No gesture of kindness or compassionate regard expressed to any part of Life passes the recording angels unnoticed; for the energies that man qualifies with love, as father or mother, as brother, sister, or friend, are caught up by their tender hands and lifted to the third sphere, adding sparkle and brilliance to the causal body. And so it glows with the fires of God's own compassion and charity, expressed in the humble heart who can truthfully say, "I never met a man I didn't like."[73] Creativity in any field of endeavor increases the glow of the pink band, as does communion with Nature and the Holy Spirit. The impulse of genius, which inspires newness of Life in the arts and culture of a civilization as well as the laws of harmony that govern practical invention, is born out of the soul's love for God and his wondrous powers of creativity.

Borne within the *violet sphere* are the qualities of mercy and justice, the alchemy of freedom, the science of transmutation, diplomacy, and ritual. Each time man prays, "Father, forgive them; for they know not what they do," each time he extends mercy instead of vengeance, justice in place of intrigue, opportunity rather than denial to the Christ in his fellowman, he adds to the glory of the violet globe. Through his longings to be free, to impart freedom to all and to withhold it from none, he restores his heritage of liberty that cannot be gainsaid. His experiments in the sacred science, the all-chemistry of God—changing the water into wine, healing the sick and raising the dead by the flame of transmutation—are the momentums of the free, who shuffle off the mortal coil[74] as their souls are lifted to heaven upon a *jet d'eau* of sacred fire. Such is the infinite worth of man's devotion to the qualities of mercy unstrained.

The *purple sphere,* haloed in gold, denotes man's willingness to be the servant of all, and the greatness of his reward[75] for a life of selflessness and self-sacrifice. Here are the records of deeds unknown, of heroes unsung. Here is the reward of those who know and live the meaning of the word "I AM my brother's keeper,"[76] those who, when compelled to go a mile, "go with him twain,"[77] who forgive seventy times seven,[78] all the while serving the Christ within the wayward child, the errant son or daughter. The sphere of purple includes the record of every tender thought unspoken as well as every active vow that upholds the commandment of the Lord "Love your enemies, bless them that curse you, do good to them that hate you, and pray for them which despitefully use you, and persecute you." [79] Here is the love of the childlike heart who carries his lame friend upon his shoulders and says, "He's not heavy, Father; he's my brother." [80]

Within the *green sphere* are the treasures of Nature's abundance that man has rightfully claimed as his own. The multiplication of talents, the precipitation of supply and healing, the application of the principles of science and practical invention, the subduing of the elements and the mastery of the physical universe with the aid of every mechanical and mathematical skill—all of these efforts and more are recorded here. The music of the spheres and the calculus of the Spirit are both seen and heard in this globe which is especially verdant in those who have applied themselves to the geometry of Truth in its many facets. The chlorophyll of Nature, the ray of health precipitated from the sun, holds the key used by physical and metaphysical healers, doctors, nurses, and naturopaths. All that these servants of mankind have done to alleviate pain and disease is recorded in the sixth sphere of their causal bodies. As guardians of the health of humanity, they have used the magnetic properties of the emerald ray to focus the rejuvenating powers stored in this radiant sphere of Life. And the more they use their healing talents, the more they multiply them.

It is man's devotion to God's will that seals the causal body in a ring of protection's blue. The sapphire *blue sphere* is the diadem of faith that bespeaks the perfection of God made tangible through the soul of man. By acknowledging this perfection in his outer consciousness, man gives consent to the natural force-field of protection that it affords. The will of God is the scepter of power that is used by those who serve as heads of state, leaders of men, and executives at all

levels; and when they are loyal to the mandates of the
Creator, they bear his authority as a divine right in all
that they do. By giving obedience to the unfailing
Light of God, those charged with the responsibilities
of administering his will enrich the blue band with a
vibrant electric hue.

Long ago, when the angels sang over the plains of
Bethlehem, "Glory to God in the highest, and on earth
peace, good will toward men," [81] it was an expression of
the will of God made manifest through the descending
Christ who declared as he came, "Lo, I AM come to do
Thy will, O God!" [82] When the soul first descended
from Spirit in the fire of cosmic purpose, it, too, made
the same declaration of faith in the Divine Presence;
however, not all remember the transcendence of that
Life which they once knew and received as the holy
will of God. Therefore, in developing the outer ring of
the causal body, man must give careful consideration
to the opportunity of life itself and to the need to
preserve his energy in the face of every temptation to
abuse this most precious gift of God; for only in the
wise use of God's power and in the remembrance of his
cosmic vow can man seal the treasures of the causal
body in the invincible protection and direction of the
Diamond Shining Mind of God.

"The ideals of God, in all of their mighty purity,
admit no thought of mortal imperfection; and they
never will," says the previously quoted Cosmic Being
whose devotion to the will of God has won for him the
title of Great Divine Director, as he begins to discourse to the Keepers of the Flame on the causal
body. "The tenacity of human thoughts and feelings is
an index of the longevity of men's involvement with
and revolvement of their negative aspects. The sooner
the dust of accumulated centuries is shaken from the
consciousness, the sooner the fires of perfection can

THE CHART OF YOUR DIVINE SELF

"I AM the Resurrection and the Life"

polish the shafts of men's aspirations. The more quickly man lovingly gazes at the appointed goals of his Divine Presence, the more quickly will heaven's gifts and graces burst into manifestation.

"Now the causal body of man is the fullness of his own worthwhile accomplishments in manifestation. Man does not need to wait for it to manifest, for it already hovers over the finite self. This self can be said to be a material egg in the process of mutation that must become divine through the process of *trans*mutation.

"Man is enclosed in an ellipsoid magnetic field that contains the records of all previous activities of his lifestream from the time he first came forth into the world of form and individualization. All the oppressions and repressions of centuries are locked within this forcefield of the auric egg that surrounds the four lower bodies; these energies, which have often assumed animallike forms, must be released and set free.

"Inasmuch as all of the energy of God that is misused in human miscreations is a distortion of or a departure from the original blueprint, these incongruous forms could be called mutations of the Christic pattern of the lifestream. Patterns of imperfection, however, cannot be classified merely as changes, for they are perversions of the pristine Image of Perfection. The purification of these mutations and the return of God's energy to the free state of higher dimensions is achieved by an act of divine mercy and grace which the Law requires man himself to invoke. This process, known as *transmutation,* whereby man transcends mutations, induces those changes which bring about the manifestation of perfection, or the reestablishment of the divine plan to which the energy was originally consecrated by God.

"Through the ritual of transmutation, the Father-Mother God releases the light rays from man's causal body into his auric egg. These rays reproduce the designs of eternal progression that were engraved upon the soul in the beginning, which, in all of their native innocence, were preserved intact until the fall of man into the effluvia of the mass consciousness.

"Because it contains the purity and perfection of the divine plan, it is to the causal body that all must look for their release from the density of the auric envelope. As the receptacle of the outer identity which man has fashioned in the world of form, this force-field of the soul's current orientation is the platform from which the monad must launch its flight into the heights of self-mastery. . . .

"As we have said, the causal body, in its treasures of light-energy, holds the records and the momentums of all virtue that has ever been expressed through the evolving soul consciousness. But that portion of God's energy which has not been used according to the Father's creative intent contributes neither to the glory of man's body celestial nor to the freedom of his body terrestrial.[83] You see, the more mankind misuse God's power, the more they limit their capacity to use it.

"Regardless of the fact that all limitations of the creative will are self-imposed, we find among the many lamentations of the race the regret that greater power has not been given unto humanity. Such lamentation reflects the shortsightedness of the human consciousness which reckons without an accurate knowledge of past history when cosmic law did allow the release of considerably more power to mankind and afforded them much wider expression of their individuality than they now enjoy.

"The abuses of God-power in the eras of Lemuria and Atlantis resulted in a dispensation of confinement by the Karmic Board. As guardians of the sacred trust of God's energies for the mankind of earth, these cosmic servants were compelled to diminish the stream of light-energy to the evolutions abiding here until such time as they should manifest proof of their God-dominion over all substance and their willingness to create for the glory of God rather than for the vanity of the human ego. This very sordid period in the history of man is recorded in the akashic records and on spindles of gold in the great record room at the Royal Teton Retreat. . . ."[84]

A PILLAR IN THE TEMPLE OF MY GOD

Let us now examine more closely the lower figure in the Chart, yourself as you are this very moment—a point of perspective in God's consciousness, evolving through time and space. This is the part of you that is in a state of becoming one with the Christ, of merging with the Divine Mediator; it is the part that is destined to reunite with the Whole, with the Permanent Atom of Being, the I AM Presence.

Although it is the aspect of his being and consciousness with which he is most familiar, the lower self is the most transitory element of man's identity. Speaking of this ephemeral yet solid-appearing image, the psalmist said: "As for man, his days are as grass: as a flower of the field, so he flourisheth. For the wind passeth over it, and it is gone; and the place thereof shall know it no more."[85]

The lower self represents the forcefield in Matter through which the soul must evolve in order to find reunion with the Real Self and to become a "pillar in the temple of my God."[86] Just as a man's home is his castle, so the forcefields of consciousness with which he surrounds himself become the dwelling place of his soul. The soul may be a prisoner in the dungeons of unreality constructed by the outer mind; or, if the latter has been quickened by the Holy Spirit, the soul will occupy the position of liege lord (under the Christ Self) spiraling Godward in the castle of Reality.

The lower figure in the Chart consists of (1) the soul, that portion of Spirit which has descended into material form to work out its destiny through (2) the four interpenetrating forcefields called the four lower bodies; (3) the momentum of personal magnetism referred to as the personality; and (4) the electronic belt, or the negative spiral containing the records of all energies that the individual has ever misqualified.

For the purpose of understanding the relationship of the three figures in the Chart, let us review our definition of Spirit and soul:

"God is a Spirit [represented in the upper figure] and the soul [represented in the lower figure] is the living potential of God. The soul's demand for free will and its separation from God resulted in the descent of this potential into the lowly estate of the flesh. Sown in dishonor, the soul is destined to be raised in honor to the fullness of that God-estate which is the one Spirit of all Life. The soul can be lost; Spirit can never die. . . .

"The soul, then, remains a fallen potential that must be imbued with the Reality of Spirit, purified through prayer and supplication, and returned to the glory from which it descended and to the unity of the Whole. This rejoining of soul to Spirit [of the lower self to the Higher Self] is the alchemical marriage which determines the destiny of the self and makes it one with immortal Truth. When this ritual is fulfilled, the highest Self is enthroned as the Lord of Life and the potential of God, realized in man, is found to be the All-in-all." [87]

The evolving monad is depicted in the ideal state, standing in a blazing shaft of violet flame surrounded by a cylinder of pure white light. This illustration shows how the Holy Spirit descends from the heart of the I AM Presence and the Christ Self to enfold the soul consciousness in God's all-embracing Mind. The psalmist, who witnessed this action of the Comforter, wrote: "He shall cover thee with his [flame-] feathers, and under his wings [the rays of the Holy Spirit] shalt thou trust: his Truth [manifest as the cylinder of light] shall be thy shield and buckler."[88]

Through invocation to the Spirit of the living God, you can draw forth from your own I AM Presence this tube of light, this "holy habitation"[89] of the LORD who spoke to his prophet Zechariah concerning the forcefield of protection that he would place around Jerusalem and all the inhabitants thereof: "I will *be* unto her a wall of fire round about, and will *be* the glory in the midst of her."[90] If, therefore, the LORD has declared his willingness to be the protection of an entire city, and to be the glory [the *glow-ray* of violet flame] in the midst of her, should we question his willingness or his ability to be a wall of fire round about the individual and the glory in the midst? As the angel queried Abraham, "Is any thing too hard for the LORD?"[91]

When the chosen one of Israel—the one who has chosen all that is real—invokes the tube of light, it descends upon him as a shower of transcendent yet tangible light substance, establishing around his four lower bodies a veritable "wall of fire." This tube of light, which should be visualized nine feet or more in diameter, is electronically charged with the full momentum of the Godhead. It seals man in the Trinity of Father, Son, and Holy Spirit; for, as you can see in the Chart, the cylinder extends from the Presence and surrounds both the Christ Self and the evolving monad.

Addressing his disciples in this age, Jesus referred

to this magnificent pillar of white fire—the central
pillar in the temple of man's being—as the tube of
miracle light,[92] thereby endowing them with a greater
sense of the miraculous regarding this supreme manifestation of cosmic grace. Jesus himself used the tube
of light during his Palestinian ministry; by intensifying its action he was able to pass through the midst
of an angry and hostile crowd and to reappear in
another place to those receptive to the Light of the
Christ.[93] Such remarkable protection has manifested
in the lives of all who have religiously invoked the
tube of light; for God has withheld from none the
opportunity to call for this impenetrable shield, this
invincible armor, as a scientific weapon whereby they
might "quench all the fiery darts of the wicked"[94] and
erect a citadel of Power, Wisdom, and Love right in
the midst of human chaos.

The apostle Paul admonished the saints at Ephesus
concerning the need to establish a forcefield of protection in order that they might resist the invisible
forces that had elected to *deify evil* within their consciousness and were therefore called *devils.* He wrote:
"Finally, my brethren, be strong in the Lord, and in
the power of his might. Put on the whole armour of
God, that ye may be able to stand against the wiles of
the devil. For we wrestle not against flesh and blood,
but against principalities, against powers, against the
rulers of the darkness of this world, against spiritual
wickedness in high places. Wherefore take unto you
the whole armour of God, that ye may be able to with-
stand in the evil day, and having done all, to stand."[95]

Today the Ascended Master Hilarion (who was
embodied as the apostle Paul) teaches his disciples
how to call forth the fiery essence of the Holy Spirit to
envelop their forms with the protective armor of the
Almighty. He explains that the energy that descends

in answer to their call is the manifest outpouring of the white light that focuses all of the attributes of the Godhead contained in the causal body, with which he had counselled the followers of Christ to gird themselves, saying: "Stand therefore, having your loins girt about with truth, and having on the breastplate of righteousness; and your feet shod with the preparation of the gospel of peace; above all, taking the shield of faith, wherewith ye shall be able to quench all the fiery darts of the wicked. And take the helmet of salvation, and the sword of the Spirit, which is the Word of God: praying always with all prayer and supplication in the Spirit, and watching thereunto with all perseverance and supplication for all saints." [96]

Saint Germain, who serves with Hilarion on the Governing Board of the Keepers of the Flame Fraternity, has written the following invocation for Keepers of the Flame, which all may use to sustain the protection of the pillar of cloud by day and the pillar of fire by night which accompanied the children of Israel through the wilderness. [97] Give this prayer as you stand facing the Chart of Your Divine Self. Here, "under the shadow of the Almighty," [98] accept the benediction of Light that you invoke from your Presence:

O my constant, loving I AM Presence, Thou Light* of God above me whose radiance forms a circle of fire before me to light my way:

I AM faithfully calling to Thee to place a great pillar of Light from my own Mighty I AM God Presence all around me right now today! Keep it intact through every passing moment, manifesting as a shimmering shower of God's beautiful Light through which nothing human can ever pass. Into this beautiful electric circle of divinely charged energy direct a swift

*God consciousness/Christ's consciousness.

upsurge of the violet fire of Freedom's forgiving, transmuting flame!

Cause the ever expanding energy of this flame projected downward into the forcefield of my human energies to completely change every negative condition into the positive polarity of my own Great God Self! Let the magic of its mercy so purify my world with Light that all whom I contact shall always be blessed with the fragrance of violets from God's own heart in memory of the blessed dawning day when all discord—cause, effect, record, and memory—is forever changed into the victory of Light and the peace of the ascended Jesus Christ.

I AM now constantly accepting the full power and manifestation of this fiat of Light and calling it into instantaneous action by my own God-given free will and the power to accelerate without limit this sacred release of assistance from God's own heart until all men are ascended and God-free in the Light that never, never, never fails!

We read in the book of Isaiah the word of the LORD which came to the prophet "I AM the LORD, and there is none else, there is no God beside me: I girded* thee, though thou hast not known me." [99] If man did not require the girding of the LORD—a circle of protection that God alone is qualified to give—then the LORD would not make provision for it when man does not even know Him. The following verse makes clear the requirement of the Law regarding the manifestation of God's grace and his protection:

"Thus saith the LORD [the Law of the Word], the Holy One of Israel [the Sacred Unifier (the One Fire)

---

*"To gird" means to guard, to surround, to make fast, to invest with protective armor, to prepare for action.

of all that is real], and his Maker [the Originator of man—the I AM Presence], Ask me of things to come concerning my sons [Ask me for dispensations of mercy on behalf of my offspring], and concerning the work of my hands *COMMAND YE ME.*"[100]

Here God is asking you not only to petition him for grace and mercy that these might abound on earth as in heaven, but also to command him—to command his energy to do his will in and through you, to work his works upon earth and in your life. He is, in fact, telling you that you must command him to descend into your being if you would experience him in consciousness.

Why is this so? The reason is plain: God gave you the gift of free will and the responsibility to take dominion over the earth,[101] thereby relinquishing his own jurisdiction in the footstool kingdom.[102] If, in the daily exercise of free will and in the course of taking dominion over the earth, you desire the assistance of the Most High, you must command him to descend into your world, into your life, in the same manner as Jesus taught his disciples to pray—in the imperative—saying, "Thy kingdom come! Thy will be done in earth as it is in heaven!"[103]

By consciously, willingly uniting your forces with God's, making your will one with and subject to the divine, and then commanding the Almighty to enter your world and to exercise his dominion, you return to him the authority that he gave to you. In this manner the soul is infilled and infired with the Spirit of God and you become the supreme manifestation of God's authority, his will, and his dominion on earth. The ritual of asking that you might receive, of seeking that you might find, of knocking that the door might be opened,[104] is the key to self-mastery through conscious cooperation with God.

If you would conquer the synthetic image in self and society, you must replace the relics of its sinful sense of subservience to an angry, vengeful god with the scientific understanding of the cosmic law that states, "The call compels the answer." The real God has challenged man to prove this law in his daily life: "Prove me now herewith, saith the LORD of hosts, if I will not open you the windows of heaven, and pour you out a blessing, that there shall not be room enough to receive it!"[105] This "proving of the LORD" you can do by the authority of the Divine Logos, the Universal Christ, made personal through the individual Christ Self and through all who have ever overcome the world as Jesus did in his personification of the Son of God. In his name, therefore, you can and ought to invoke the sacred fire of the Spirit of God and command it to elevate the soul into oneness with the Divine Mediator.

If you find it hard to believe that mortals could be vested with the authority to command God, let us explain that when the LORD says, "Command ye me," he is speaking directly to the Real Man whom he hath made and not to the synthetic image. "But," you may say, "I am not yet fully manifesting the Real Man." The Beloved Disciple, who was closest to our Lord in his devotion to the Christ, has explained, "Until your synthetic consciousness is replaced by the real, you have 'an advocate with the Father,'[106] the Christ, in whose name you may, with the full authority of your God Presence, command the energies of the Holy Spirit into action."

The Christ Self, truly beloved of God as the Mediator of man's divinity, is the instrument for the alchemical transformation of the four lower bodies and the evolution of the soul consciousness. As you invoke the Light of God in his name, the Mediator descends into the forcefield of your evolving consciousness and speaks the sacred Word through you that proves the Law as Above, so below in the abundant manifestation of the abundant Life. The Christ, then, is the perfect gift which cometh down from the Father of Lights, with whom (with whose Law) is no variableness, neither shadow of turning.[107]

Because they have been found worthy to be received by God, all who are made one with the Real Image are worthy to command him into action in the world of form. You may therefore command the LORD not only in the name of Jesus the Christ but also in the name of every Ascended and Cosmic Being who has won his immortal freedom through the reunion of the soul with the Christ and with the Spirit of the I AM Presence.

Commands made in the name of the ascended sons and daughters of God, then, are an acceptable sacrifice unto the living God. They replace the supposed need for either burnt offerings or animal or human sacrifice,[108] which for centuries both before and since the Christian dispensation have been placed on the altar of the Most High in the mistaken belief that these are required as a propitiation for the sins of the race.

Although the LORD had made known to Abraham that He did not require the sacrifice of his only son, although He had clearly spoken through his prophet Samuel, "Behold, to obey is better than sacrifice, and to hearken than the fat of rams,"[109] the influence of this ancient custom prevailed even to the time of Jesus. And the erroneous interpretation of the doctrine concerning the blood sacrifice of Jesus—which misconception he himself never taught—has been perpetuated to the present hour, a remnant of pagan rite long refuted by the word of the LORD.

God the Father did not require the sacrifice of his son Christ Jesus, or of any other incarnation of the Christ, as an atonement for the sins of the world; nor is it possible according to cosmic law for any man's sacrifice to balance either the original sin or the subsequent sins—the karma—of the one or the many. However, one man's sacrifice of the lower self—resulting in the soul's sublime reunion with the Christ—can set aside the return of individual and planetary karma for a prescribed period of grace wherein the mercy of the law gives mankind an extended opportunity to make the selfsame sacrifice of the human consciousness for the divine.

Only the right use of the power of the spoken Word, the Divine Logos, can atone for mankind's sins. Only the Light of the Holy Spirit that flows through the Body of Christ (for which the body and the blood are symbols)[110] can transform the mortal into the immortal. Therefore, only the sacrifice of the mis-qualified energies of the electronic belt through the ritual of transmutation can redeem the Christ Light in man. Truly, man sacrifices his Christ-identity when he fails to offer the sacred Word to the Almighty "in remembrance of me."[111] Truly, he is unredeemed until he partakes of the sacred fire Eucharist and invokes through his being the consecrated essence of the Father-Mother God.

It behooves us, therefore, to pray as the psalmist of old, "Let the words of my mouth, and the medita-tion of my heart, be acceptable [offerings] in thy sight, O LORD, my strength, and my redeemer."[112] The fol-lowing commands are examples of the acceptable word of the LORD that may be spoken by and through man:

> In the name of the only begotten Son of the Father manifest in every child of the Father-Mother God, I command the Almighty to send peace on earth and goodwill unto the righteous!

> In the name of Jesus the Christ, I command the Light of God to expand in the hearts of all mankind, to restore the memory of their divine inheritance, and to fulfill their God-design!

In the name of Saint Germain, I command the freedom flame from the heart of the Almighty to expand and envelop the earth and to inspire every man, woman, and child to claim their immortal freedom, their Christ Self-awareness, and the God-victorious manifestation of their divine plan fulfilled!

In the name of Archangel Michael, I command the full-gathered momentum of cosmic Power, Wisdom, and Love from the very center of the LORD's universal creative potential to protect the children of the Light, the God-ordained governments of the nations, and every constructive endeavor upon the planet with the Light of God that never fails!

In the name of Lord Buddha, I command you, O God, to do this holy thing through me!

In the name of the Christ Selves of all mankind, I command the Almighty to move into action to take dominion over the lives and activities of the youth of the world and to lead them as Thou didst the children of Israel into the land of promise fulfilled through the true Teachings of the Christ!

In the name of the saints and ascended beings of all ages and by the full power of their momentum of devotion to the Light, I command the cosmic Christ consciousness of the Almighty to expand in the hearts and minds of all who are ready to receive him as a little child!

In the name of Mother Mary, I command the Father-Mother God to produce an ascended Jesus Christ miracle of perfection now made manifest in a golden age of enlightenment and peace!

All who have reunited with the Godhead through the ritual of the ascension—because they are one with God, hence God in action—may also be commanded in the name of God and his Christ. Thus, it is acceptable to the heavenly hosts and to the Most High to receive the mandates of unascended souls to step into action in the world of material form in the service of the LORD. By cosmic law these servants of God and his Christ are not permitted to intercede for and on behalf of mankind unless they are invoked in the name of one or more persons of the Trinity. It is therefore altogether correct and acceptable to pray:

In the name of Almighty God, I command the full-gathered momentum of Light from the heart of Archangel Michael and his legions of blue lightning to descend into the earth and take command this day! Take command of all forces of antichrist and all that opposes the manifestation of the Light of the Divine Manchild in every soul abiding here!

We beseech thee, thou Defender of the Faith, in the name of the Christ, the only begotten Son of the Father-Mother God, to let the will of God be done, let the love of God appear, and let the wisdom of God be known throughout the four corners of the earth and in every nation. By the threefold power of liberty's flame, Set the captives free! We thank thee and accept it done this hour in the full power and name of the Holy Spirit! Amen.

Indeed, the call compels the answer! Those who do not accept the LORD's challenge to prove this invariable law seek out, as Ecclesiastes said, "many inventions," many variations on the design of the upright man whom God made.[113] Instead of allowing

God to gird them for the battle of life with a wall of fire, they build their own walls, layer by layer, not out of shafts of light but out of the bricks of pride and the mortar of fear and doubt. Thus they secure themselves from the inflictions and intrusions of a cruel world, and their egos exist for a time behind the fortress of the synthetic consciousness.

We point out the wall of pride as the perversion of the tube of light, as the Tower of Babel[114] that man erects while he sits in the seat of the scornful.[115] Failing to recognize God as the doer, failing to enlist his aid or to give him the glory for creative endeavor, he remains in competition with the LORD. Preferring his own exclusivity, he proceeds to build his own citadel of power, independent of the Higher Power and the controlling factors of the Law. He moves his pawns on the chessboard of his self-centered existence, not through God-dominion and a free will tethered to the divine, but through craftiness of wit, treachery, and intrigue. He accepts the offer of the father of lies, who takes him up into an exceeding high mountain and shows him the glory of all the kingdoms of this world, saying, "All these things will I give thee, if thou wilt fall down and worship me."[116] Thus man misplaces his allegiance; and he forsakes not only his divine inheritance and the abundant Life but also the girding of his soul with the light of righteousness and truth by the LORD of all that is real.

The wall of pride is the middle wall of partition[117] that man erects between his soul and his Christ Self, thereby effectively blocking the flow of light from his God Presence into the crucible of his evolving soul-awareness, at the same time stopping the flow of Love from heart to heart in the interchange of true brotherhood. Thus he moves further and further from the center of cosmic purpose and enters the twilight zone of creative nonfulfillment.

Man is intended to be a conductor of the energy-flow of God to and through man; when he arrests the cycles of the flow of Love by clogging the very pores of his being with the rituals of hatred, he ceases to fulfill his reason for being. Confined within the cloisters of human fear, guised in many forms, he feels secure. He is "safe"; the trauma of the world cannot reach him. Nothing flows in, it is true, but nothing flows out either. Man, then, exists in the stagnant pool of his own self-righteous musings, the heart chalice inactive, the flame cramped inside the inner wall, trapped in the terror of aloneness.

Stone upon stone of human error, the inner and outer walls* must be torn down if the soul is to come forth from the tomb and live. If he would be truly free, man must be willing to let go of every false security and every idol of his ego. As the children of Israel compassed the city of Jericho seven times on the seventh day and shouted with a great shout when the seven priests blew the seven trumpets, [118] so the child of Reality must pursue the ritual of circumscribing the wall that surrounds the city of his consciousness with the seven rays of the seven mighty Elohim, who will release the light from the white fire core of every atom of his being to shatter the wall! to shatter the wall! to shatter the wall!

When the wall comes tumbling down and the ruins lie beneath his feet, man will stand naked before his God. For the first time in centuries, he will feel the fresh winds of the Holy Spirit blow through the chinks of his mind; his heart chalice will be flooded with a torrent of power, wisdom, and love that descends from on high, bursts the inner wall, and washes away the remaining debris.

*The inner wall encloses the heart in a dark cave of hardness and recalcitrance; the outer wall surrounds the four lower bodies, preventing the interchange between the microcosm and the Macrocosm.

The flow rushes onward from God to man and out into the world, knowing no bounds. Nothing can move against its relentless stream. All of the pain, the frustration, and the uncertainty of the world, all that the little self feared is swept away by this onrushing tide of his Divinity. Now nothing can hurt or despoil the holy habitation of God in man. Having summoned the courage to storm the bastille of his synthetic consciousness, man realizes that there was never any need to imprison the soul in the dungeon of the ego. Though he walk through the valley of the shadow of death, he will fear no energy veil, for the I AM Presence is with him.[119] The tube of light adorns the temple of the living God which he has become, allowing the great flow of the Spirit to penetrate the walls of the LORD's house (from within out), even as the energies of the Christ in every man freely enter the open door of his heart (from without in). Surely he will dwell in the house of the LORD forever,[120] for the covenant of his God is with him:

He that dwelleth in the secret place of the Most High
   Shall abide under the shadow of the Almighty.
I will say of the LORD, 'He is my refuge and my fortress:
   'My God; in Him will I trust.'
Surely He shall deliver thee from the snare of the fowler,
   And from the noisome pestilence.
He shall cover thee with His feathers,
And under His wings shalt thou trust:
   His truth shall be thy shield and buckler.
Thou shalt not be afraid for the terror by night;
   Nor for the arrow that flieth by day;
Nor for the pestilence that walketh in darkness;
   Nor for the destruction that wasteth at noonday.
A thousand shall fall at thy side,
And ten thousand at thy right hand;

But it shall not come nigh thee.
Only with thine eyes shalt thou behold
    And see the reward of the wicked.

Because thou hast made the LORD, which is my refuge,
    Even the Most High, thy habitation;
There shall no evil befall thee,
    Neither shall any plague come nigh thy dwelling.
For He shall give His angels charge over thee,
    To keep thee in all thy ways.
They shall bear thee up in their hands,
    Lest thou dash thy foot against a stone.
Thou shalt tread upon the lion and adder:
    The young lion and the dragon shalt thou trample
        under feet.
"Because he hath set his love upon Me, therefore will
        I deliver him:
    "I will set him on high, because he hath known My
        name.
"He shall call upon Me, and I will answer him:
    "I will be with him in trouble;
    "I will deliver him, and honour him.
"With long life will I satisfy him,
    "And shew him My salvation." [121]

OUR GOD IS A CONSUMING FIRE

Truly the call compels the answer to every man's
need. Truly the call is the potential realization of the
Holy Spirit in man. Truly the call is the salvation of
the soul—the call that is heard even before we pray [122]
in his name:

O Great Shepherd of Souls, Lord Jesus,
Thou Christ of God and Son of the Most High,
we call unto Thee and the great hosts of heaven
to assist us as we call in Thy name to all souls

upon earth to hear the voice of Love, Wisdom, and Power that invokes for them communion and blessings without limit, that gives to all a new sense of freedom and hope and that awareness of Thee which is oneness in purpose, plan, and infinitude.

O consecrated essence of the sacred fire, descend, we pray, upon all lands, and seas, and sky; bless elemental life and all that we pass by with the healing power of the hem of Thy trailing garment of ever-new delight in the law of Thy Being—the law of Love, eternally sustaining the brightness of Thy concepts over the earth and the souls of all men. Make them one, even as we are one. [123]

Man need not speculate as to whether God exists; he need only invoke from the Godhead the proof that the LORD has challenged him to invoke, the proof of His very existence:

Show me, O LORD, Thy infinite mercy and truth; show me Thyself in formless Spirit and in Mater-form, in the elements and in man of whom Thou art mindful; show me Thy power and Thy love in an immortelle and in the on-rushing river of light that descends from above. Show me, and I will cover the earth with the brightness of Thy witness, the corona of Thy glory.

Man can invoke his "house" of light and enter into his "closet" to pray [124]—into the laboratory of his own consciousness where he can test the Law as well as his own personal theories about Life, free from the impinging minds and motives of others. In this relatively free state afforded by the protection of the tube of light, he can make direct contact with the Mind of God through his Christ Self, who is in contact with and retains the full knowledge of everything that is in heaven above (in the Superconsciousness of God), in the earth beneath (in the consciousness of man), and in the water under the earth (in the subconscious mind). [125] In this state of sacred and scientific communion with the Mediator, the individual determines for himself the existence of that Reality which is his true Being.

The consuming fire of the Almighty is the universal panacea for every ill to which the flesh is heir; and, what is more, it heals the mind and soul. It dissolves the "conglomerate glob of nightmarish energies" [126] that has collected, layer upon layer, in the cavities of the subconscious mind. It burns out the dark spirits and demons that infest the caverns of the astral (emotional) body. With a roaring crackle it sweeps out the dust and debris of centuries of spiritual neglect that have accumulated in the attic of the etheric body.

Serapis Bey, who examines the life record of those applying for admission to the Halls of Luxor (the Ascension Temple), comments on the tablets of *mem* (memory) in Nature and in man: "The race memory and the memory of Nature is divided and subdivided again and again into such minutiae of manifestation as to put to shame the minds of the greatest scientists. We who see from the inner behold sublayer after sublayer of the creation that has not yet been split by the sharp blade of man's penetration.

"There is the memory of the individual to consider, the memory of self—names, faces, places, concepts, recepts, and precepts. . . . Of men's acts and thoughts this may be said, that they are all recorded, each one. Every subtle shade, every nuance of meaning finds its way into the storehouse of the subconscious memory. These are literally interred with the bones of man, and they survive transition after transition; each time man reembodies they come with him again, composing his life record.

"When the life-giving accuracy of this record is pondered for a moment and the effect of beautiful thoughts is considered with the heart, the need to rise to angelic levels of perception ought to occur to many. Why should men live in the dark, dank cellars of their human creation? Why should the subconscious knowledge that men have stored about themselves be tumbled out upon psychiatric couches? Is this what we may call therapeutics? Or is it the putrification* of old ideas disgorging themselves upon the consciousness of present-day man?

"The panacea that men crave, if one can justly be said to exist, is within the domain of the same memory that holds the thoughts of negation; this the world has filled almost to capacity with the sordid nature of the carnal man. Now let them learn, if they would ascend, to eradicate this image by filling the folds of memory with the soft, gentle, beautiful ideas of the resurrection and resurrection's flame." [127]

In his classes in spiritual psychology—the study of the psyche, or soul of man, from the level of the Christ Self—at the Royal Teton Retreat, Lord Lanto gives the following notes on the subject of the subconscious and the electronic belt: "Each man's culture is dominated by the patterns that lie deep within his subconscious being. Frequently men say that they do not understand themselves. They do not know why they act as they do. It is not possible for them to open the doorway of consciousness, to roam the corridors of memory and see each habit in its development, and then to weed out each undesirable thought. There is a better way, and that way is the saturation of the consciousness with the flame of cosmic worth.

---

*Obscure form of "putrefaction."

"The old statement 'Our God is a consuming fire' [128] is a source of great comfort to those who understand it, for the Divine Image is truly ablaze with benign activity. The pulsations, or risings, of the sacred fire, in all of their naturalness, convey the essence of the Higher Consciousness. These deactivate all malintent that may be locked within the subconscious world of the individual, and they create and re-create in his total consciousness the most outstanding designs reflecting cosmic law. Such patterns enable the individual who accepts them and uses the Higher Consciousness they convey to be completely free and yet to remain under the dominion of his Divine Self.

"This so-called overshadowing of the human consciousness by the Divine, when it is accompanied by the correct use of the flames of God, will magnetize the sense of Reality that in the innocence of childhood was realized by many men embodied on earth today. The passing of the flames through one's consciousness above and below, that is, in the conscious and subconscious minds, is a ritual that has been practiced for centuries by devotees of the Mind of God. . . .

"We dare not eliminate the tares without realizing that if we do so prematurely, we may also uproot the benign and helpful aspects of human nature. [129] The safest way is the way of using the flames of God, but the knowledge of just what the flames are is seldom realized by men; and when we speak of them they are often puzzled. Let us say again, then, that there is a natural order and universe and there is a spiritual order and universe. The glory of the terrestrial is one, and the glory of the celestial is another. The flames of God are of the spiritual order; and these, by the grace of God, penetrate the natural order with the transforming power of the Holy Spirit.

"The experiences of the devotee who loves the Truth enough to search it out will help him to understand that the qualities of God are inherent within the spiritual order and that although these qualities penetrate the material order, they do not originate in it. It is in the correct understanding of Matter in its relationship to Spirit, therefore, that men become enlightened. To understand oneself as a spiritual-material being is to apprehend one's relationship to others. To understand the need to purify one's consciousness insofar as it has taken on a limited, self-centered view of existence is to apprehend one's relationship to Life as a whole.

"The reception of the consciousness of God as though one's physical form, one's mind, and one's consciousness were wholly permeated by the fire [energy] of creation will produce in one's total being the Godly estate that is desired. It is this estate which, when harbored within, casts out the darkening proclivities of the mortal consciousness and replaces them by the stern yet joyous awareness, the vital yet penetrating hope of the infinite Mind of God as it descends into the finite world."[130]

The electronic belt is not shown in the Chart. In its place is depicted the violet flame that the lower self must invoke if it would find its way out of the human miasma that it has unwittingly created. Lord Lanto, describing the electronic belt, said:

"After all, it is the Christ Mind that is the divine armor against the insidious forces that lurk within the individual's electronic belt. This so-called belt is positioned in the aura of the individual around the lower portion of the physical form; it extends from the waist to beneath the feet, somewhat in the shape of a large kettledrum, and contains the aggregate records of his negative human thoughts and feelings.

"Man is transported out of the confines of his mortal sense into spiritual realms of thought when he contacts the vital flames of the very essence of the Creator's consciousness. The desire to be transported out of the realm of the ordinary is tantamount to invocation; but when men also express a willingness to be decontaminated of all undesirable qualities, they open the floodgates of their consciousness to the light, which then rushes in to expurgate all unwanted vibratory actions.

"Beneath the surface calm there lies within the consciousness of men much that is undesirable, much that represents the polarization of imperfection during near and distant epochs of personal history. To cast out the enemy within by invoking the sacred fire is a necessary process. When this is done, transmutation takes place and the energies that have been imprisoned in matrices of imperfect thought and feeling are released. Immediately after having been dislodged from the electronic belt and purified by the flames of God, these energies ascend to the causal body of man. . . .

"Just as the electronic belt bears the record of human infamy, so the causal body bears witness to all true creativity. The causal body, then, is of the spiritual order and universe and the electronic belt is of the natural order and universe. The glory of the celestial body is in the overcoming of the body terrestrial. In the words of Saint Paul: 'It [the terrestrial body] is sown in corruption; it is raised in incorruption: it is sown in dishonour; it is raised in glory: it is sown in weakness; it is raised in power: it is sown a natural body; it is raised a spiritual body. There is a natural body, and there is a spiritual body. And so it is written, The first man Adam was made a living soul; the last Adam was made a quickening spirit.'" [131]

Just as the discovery of physical fire drastically changed the course of earth's civilization and marked the beginning of mankind's ascent from primitivism to Christ-mastery, so the discovery of spiritual fire will abruptly alter man's way of life as the Holy Spirit propels his consciousness from the depths of drudgery into the heights of joy in service and the instantaneous precipitation of abundance, health, happiness, and God-control.

Through the proper use of spiritual fire, man can return to the Edenic state by transmuting his original sin which caused the "ground" (the very elements he was destined to employ in his practice of the sacred science) to be cursed beneath his feet. [132] Thus the use of spiritual fire in retraining the energies of the subconscious is one of the basic courses in self-mastery taught in the retreats of the Ascended Masters. Should you be a guest at the Rakoczy Mansion, you would hear the Master R speaking to his disciples of regaining their dominion over the earth through individual effort in Christ—here, where it was originally lost:

"Your freedom, precious ones, must be won upon earth, where your freedom was lost. You cannot expect to carry into the higher octaves of Light either soiled garments or the consciousness of imperfection; but you must resolve your crises here in this octave, that by the power of your example you may inspire others who are caught in the web of delusion and intellectual brittleness to extricate themselves therefrom and to see the pathway of Light and its mighty upward spiral as a manifest token of the constancy of heaven. I think, then, that the subconscious being of man, which is, after all, but the basement level of his memory body, ought to be properly trained in many ways so that the power of the subconscious may ever be used for the blessing of mankind.

"Unfortunately, individuals who are not completely oriented around divine Truth sometimes submit to an attempt to utilize the power of hypnosis in order to accomplish seeming miracles through the power of the subconscious. As your beloved ascended friends of Light have told you so often, you ought never to submit your being to the control of any person or hypnotist, even for seemingly benign purposes. Nor should you practice so-called autohypnosis; for the energies required to perform this type of action, while seemingly innocent enough, actually diminish the power of the soul of man; and while they may seem productive of good for a time, the ultimate long-range effect is not freedom but bondage. 'There is a way which seemeth right unto a man, but the end thereof are the ways of death.' [133]

"Some may ask, then, 'What method shall we use in order to free ourselves from unwanted conditions or to call forth new direction from the realm of Being?' My answer here must remain simple: Ask, and ye shall receive. [134] The power released through simply asking your God Self for grace to achieve all ends must not be diminished through any other form of ritual or supplication. The use of your energy in well-formulated decrees, when properly given forth with the heart's devotion and with a sense of the magnitude of divine grace, is magnificent in the power to accomplish.

"The ancient words 'Thou shalt decree a thing, and it shall be established unto thee' [135] must be understood as a fiat from Almighty God. When individuals assemble together with others or when they commune in solitude with their Divine Presence and give the spoken request according to the Great Law for the release of the required immortal substance into the world of form, then that precious substance, in its outflow as tangible light rays, will draw to them the requirements of every hour. For they are making the most powerful demands upon Life that can ever be made.

"The issuing forth of the spoken Word formulated in response to the call of the heart and its power of regeneration is a creative action wholly separate from the mere mechanical tracings of old, unregenerate energy which often occur in prayer given by rote. Yea, this is true re-creation, or recreation, which mankind today crave so much and yet never really seem to find." [136]

Throughout biblical history, fire has played a prominent role in spiritual revelation and in the progressive evolution of the soul. Light has been the alchemical key [137] in the creation of the universe and man from the moment the first fiat rang forth from the Spirit of God, "Let there be Light!"*—and the response was heard in the Mater of God, "And there was Light!"

It is recorded in the Book of Acts that "when the day of Pentecost was fully come [and] they were all with one accord in one place," this Light descended into tangible manifestation in the very midst of the disciples. "And suddenly there came a sound from heaven as of a rushing mighty wind, and it filled all the house where they were sitting. And there appeared unto them cloven tongues like as of fire, and it sat upon each of them. And they were all filled with the Holy Ghost, and began to speak with other tongues, as the Spirit gave them utterance." [138]

The Light of God that appears to man as spiritual fire is truly the sign of the Holy Spirit, whose Presence draweth nigh as the quickening flame which Ezekiel witnessed as the flaming flame that would not be quenched. [139] This fiery Spirit, so powerful in its

---

*"Let there be the universal Christ consciousness where I AM THAT I AM and let this Light illumine the worlds with light!"

manifestation of the glory of the LORD, took the prophet Elijah into heaven in a great whirlwind and enabled Elisha to smite the waters with the mantle that fell upon him immediately after the prophet's ascension.[140] Because the flame, which appeared to the disciples as "cloven tongues like as of fire,"* focuses the wholeness of the Godhead, the wholeness of the Father-Mother Presence, it balances in man and Nature the masculine and feminine polarity of cosmic energies.

Moses was infired with the zeal of mission when "the angel of the LORD appeared to him in a flame of fire out of the midst of a bush: and he looked, and, behold, the bush burned with fire, and the bush was not consumed."[141] This Spirit of living fire was with him throughout his dealings at Pharaoh's court and all through his forty-year journey to the Promised Land. It parted the sea, engulfed the Egyptian armies, fed the multitudes, engraved the Ten Commandments on tablets of stone, and was the ever-present Helper— the pillar of fire by night and the pillar of cloud by day—guiding the children of Israel in Spirit and in Matter.

John the Baptist said of Jesus, "He shall baptize you with the Holy Ghost, and with fire";[142] and the Master himself summed up his mission in nine words: "I AM come to send fire on the earth."[143] After his conversion, Paul spoke of this consuming fire as being God himself, "who maketh his angels spirits, and his ministers a flame of fire."[144] It is this fire of the Spirit that he declared would "try every man's work of what sort it is."[145] Ezekiel saw the I AM Presence as a "fire infolding itself";[146] Malachi described the Almighty as a "refiner's fire,"[147] while the Revelator looked into

---

*Spiritual fire resembles physical fire, but it is not identical in appearance or in manifestation; it is at once more intense and more ethereal.

the eyes of the ascended Son of man and beheld there a "flame of fire."[148]

Zarathustra's* worship of God as fire is apparent in the Persian faith and in the wisdom of the Magi, which he founded. Note the unusual references to fire in the following Mithraic ritual:

> Hear me, give ear to me,
> Creator of the Light,
> O Holder of the Keys,
> Inbreather of the Fire,
> Fire-hearted One
> Whose Breath gives Light,
> O Lord of Light
> Whose Body is of Fire.[149]

The sacred fire has many aspects. Issuing from the white fire core of Being are twelve rays, the seven that bathe the planet earth each week and five secret or secondary rays that are less familiar to mankind's present level of solar awareness. Apart from these twelve principle rays, there are many variations and combinations of colors and frequencies that emerge from the Creator's consciousness to be ensouled by the heavenly hosts for the blessing of life evolving on this and other systems of worlds. A list of these flame-qualities, or virtues of the sacred fire, is presented later in this work.

For the purpose of concluding our discussion of the Chart of Your Divine Self, let us take up the violet flame, which those aspiring to the ascension are required to sustain within and around their four lower bodies until the hour of victory. The violet all-consuming flame is the Seventh Ray aspect of the Holy Spirit; it emerges from the white fire core as the omnipotent love of the blue that combines with the omnipresent

---
*Zoroaster.

power of the pink, refracted in the prism of the Christ consciousness, accomplishing the perfect work of the Truth that makes every man free.

This quality of the sacred fire is truly the universal unguent that man can apply for the healing of his entire consciousness, being, and world. Enshrined as the freedom flame for the coming two-thousand-year cycle by the Master Saint Germain, the violet transmuting flame enables man to win his freedom from every form of human bondage. Dubbed the violet singing flame by Lord Zadkiel, it makes the very atoms of the four lower bodies "sing" in harmony with the divine blueprint and with the keynote of the Electronic Presence as the tiny electrons whirl in orbit at the perfect pitch of the pattern of soul-identity.

The violet flame is the spiritual wine of forgiveness, the quality of mercy that, as Portia said, "is not strain'd; / It droppeth as the gentle rain from heaven / Upon the place beneath: it is twice blest; / It blesseth him that gives and him that takes." [150]

When the violet flame is invoked by unascended man, it envelops each atom of his being individually; and instantaneously a polarity is set up between the white fire core of the atom, which, being Matter, assumes the negative pole, and the white fire core of the flame, which, being Spirit, assumes the positive pole. The dual action of the sacred fire in the center of the atom and in the violet flame without establishes a forcefield that causes the untransmuted densities to be dislodged from between the electrons. As this substance is loosed, the electrons begin to spin more rapidly in their orbits; and by centrifugal force it is thrown into the violet flame. On contact with this fiery essence of freedom's flame, the misqualified energy is transmuted into its native purity. Relieved of the patterns of imperfection, this energy of the Holy Spirit is returned to the individual's causal body, where it is stored until he elects to use it once again in the manifestation of the noble work of the Christ "on earth as it is in heaven."

The violet fire and tube of light can be called forth in the name of the Christ from the heart of God and from the individual causal body by anyone who will make the necessary contact and application through the threefold flame within the heart. Concerning the benefits of these specific actions of the flame, Kuthumi said, "If everyone knew how to use the tube of light and the violet consuming flame and believed in this method of self-transformation, I am certain that the world would be a different place." [151]

Each time you invoke the sacred fire through the following Heart, Head, and Hand decrees, together with the Tube of Light and Forgiveness, you transmute a shovelful, so to speak, of earthy substance and transfer it from your electronic belt into your heaven world. This is the ritual of the ascension that must be reenacted daily if the mountain of adversity in man is to become the summit of attainment in God.

Heart
    Violet fire, thou Love divine,
    Blaze within this heart of mine—
    Thou art mercy forever true,
    Keep me always in tune with you!

Head
    I AM Light, thou Christ in me,
    Set my mind forever free!
    Violet fire, forever shine
    Deep within this mind of mine!

    God who gives my daily bread,
    With violet fire fill my head
    Till thy radiance heavenlike
    Makes my mind a mind of light!

Hand
> I AM the hand of God in action,
> Gaining victory every day—
> My pure soul's great satisfaction
> Is to walk the Middle Way!

Tube of Light
> Beloved I AM Presence bright,
> Round me seal your tube of light
> From Ascended Master flame,
> Called forth now in God's own name!
> Let it keep my temple free
> From all discord sent to me—
>
> I AM calling forth violet fire
> To blaze and transmute all desire,
> Keeping on in freedom's name
> Till I AM one with the violet flame!

Forgiveness
> I AM forgiveness acting here,
> Casting out all doubt and fear,
> Setting men forever free
> With wings of cosmic victory!
>
> I AM calling in full power
> For forgiveness every hour—
> To all life in every place
> I flood forth forgiving grace!

IF I WASH THEE NOT, THOU HAST NO PART WITH ME

Jesus' washing of the disciples' feet during the Passover supper, his last communion with his own, was, in his words, "an example, that ye should do as I have done to you." [152] If we are to follow the Master's example, we must understand the lessons he imparted more through his actions than through his words. These we can best comprehend through the perspective of Life we have gained in our examination of the Chart—especially through the understanding of the relationship between the lower self, the Christ Self, and the God Self.

By studying Jesus' example, we learn that as our own evolving consciousness stands in relationship to the individualized Christ Self and God Presence, so in our dealings with one another the self stands in the same relationship to the Mediator and the I AM Presence of every other part of Life. Through the ritual of the washing of the feet practiced by the early Christians, the lower self adorns the Christ Self of the brethren; bowing before the Divinity of every man, it acclaims its own.

John the Beloved writes of the aforementioned event: [153] "Jesus knowing that the Father had given all things into his hands, and that he was come from God [that his soul had descended from the I AM Presence], and went to God [and would soon return to the I AM Presence]; he riseth from supper, and laid aside his garments; and took a towel, and girded himself. After that he poureth water into a bason, and began to wash the disciples' feet, and to wipe them with the towel wherewith he was girded."

Jesus' laying aside of his garments symbolized the putting aside, as it were, of his spiritual attainment—the robe of his divine authority. Desiring to illustrate a certain coequality with his disciples, thereby acknowledging their potential to attain the full expression of the Christ, he, as the Mediator of their Divinity, stepped down from his throne and placed his Christ consciousness at the level of the lower figure in the Chart; from that level he would cleanse their souls and render them a service, both as their Lord and as a fellow servant of God.

When it came Peter's turn, he questioned Jesus' action with his usual impulsiveness: "Lord, dost *thou*

wash *my* feet? Jesus answered and said unto him, What
I do thou knowest not now; but thou shalt know hereafter. Peter saith unto him, Thou shalt never wash my
feet! Jesus answered him, If I wash thee not, thou hast
no part with me. Simon Peter saith unto him, Lord, not
my feet only, but also my hands and my head."

It was then that Jesus revealed in part the sym-
bology of this Christian ritual: "He that is washed [he
whose consciousness has been cleansed by the purifying fires of the Holy Spirit] needeth not save to wash
his feet, but is clean every whit: and ye are clean, but
not all."

The feet, the lowest part of man's form, symbol-
ize the lowest level of the descending spiral of the
electronic belt. By washing the disciples' feet, Jesus
made clear their need to purify the planes of the subconscious mind, even after they had already consciously accepted the Christ as Lord and Master of
their lives.

Jesus told Peter, "Ye are clean, but not all [you
have received the regenerative fires of the Holy One
of God; nevertheless, you are not yet whole, for your
consciousness has not been wholly purified]." John
correctly interprets this passage as meaning that Jesus
knew that one among the twelve should betray him.
Through his impure motive and misunderstanding
of Jesus' mission, Judas had aligned himself with
the untransmuted momentums of his electronic belt.
Although the other disciples had not completely transmuted these momentums, they had them under control—they had placed them beneath their feet.

The difference between Judas and the disciples
who were "clean every whit" was that they, by confess-
ing that the Son of God had come in their flesh,[154]
exercised, by his grace, conscious dominion over the
energies in their electronic belts; by contrast, the conscious mind of the betrayer, instead of subjecting itself

to the ruling authority of the Super Ego, allowed itself to be dominated by the momentums of the subconscious.

"So after he had washed their feet, and had taken his garments, and was set down again, he said unto them, Know ye what I have done to you?" Once again taking upon himself the robe of his divine authority, Jesus began to instruct his disciples concerning this great mystery. "Ye call *me* Master and Lord: and ye say well; for so *I AM*." First Jesus acknowledged his followers' discernment of his Real Self and affirmed the I AM Presence as Master and Lord. Then he said, "If I then, your Lord and Master, have washed your feet; ye also ought to wash one another's feet." In other words, if I, the I AM Presence, through the Christ which I AM manifesting, have deigned to descend to the level of your human selves to wash your feet—if I, through the mercy of God, have cleansed your lower consciousness by the authority of my Christ Self-awareness—then the Presence through the Christ within each one of you can also mercifully wash one another's feet. Therefore, you can and ought to invoke the sacred fire of the Holy Spirit on behalf of one another; for the Christ within each of you is worthy of your ministering love.

"Verily, verily, I say unto you, The servant is not greater than his lord; neither he that is sent greater than He that sent him." By putting himself in the position of servant, Jesus demonstrated that his person was not greater than the Christ Self of each of them; thus he showed by his example (so that none through pride would exclude himself from the teaching) that the evolving soul through the four lower bodies must become the servant of the Christ in every man.

With utter humility and devotion to his little flock, the Good Shepherd, who was the Exemplar for the age, the Light of the world, put himself on a par with the evolving soul consciousness of his sheep in order to give them the most important lesson they would receive on the Path. He tenderly taught them from the level of a common understanding the ancient maxim, Whosoever would be great among you must be the servant of all, that is to say, he that would magnetize the greatest Light of the Christ must minister unto the Christ within all. [155]

His final words, "Neither [is] he that is sent greater than He that sent him," explain the relationship of the three figures in the Chart: the Mediator, sent by the Father as the individual representative of the only begotten Son, is not greater than the I AM Presence and forever bows to the Source of its Divinity. The soul that descends from Spirit into form is not greater than the Christ Self; and by law it cannot return to Spirit except through the mediatorship of the Christ, nor can it bypass the attainment of the Christ consciousness in order to attain God consciousness. Nevertheless, the violent, seeking to take the kingdom of heaven by force, [156] have thought they could go directly to God without the intercession of the Christ—Christ Jesus or any other Master who has incarnated the power of the only begotten Son and then ascended to the Presence.

Jesus had often explained to his close followers that the son of man, representing the Divine Mediator to the world, was not greater than his Lord, his Christ Self. The Master's greatest desire was that they should not mistake the son of man (Jesus) for the Son of God (the Christ). Should confusion arise regarding the source of his humanity (in Christ) and the source of his Divinity (in God), the Saviour knew that generations to come would not worship the Christ, but the man Jesus—in whom they had beheld the "glory *as of* the only begotten" of the Father-Mother God, whom he so perfectly personified in grace and in truth.

For this reason "Jesus cried and said, He that believeth on me, believeth not on me, but on Him that sent me. And he that seeth me seeth Him that sent me." [157] We cannot fail to note this final, almost desperate, plea made to all who would hear him: "You who believe in me, the one whom you have known as Jesus, although you may not realize it, believe in the Christ, the Divine Mediator. You who have seen me have seen the Christ Light of the only begotten Son, which I have borne in the Father's name."

On the eve of his triumphal entry into Jerusalem, [158] Jesus came to Bethany and supped at the home of Simon the leper with Mary, Martha, Lazarus, and the disciples. The most memorable event of the occasion was Mary's anointing of Jesus' head and feet with precious oil, [159] God's sign that the hour had come when the Christ would be glorified through the supreme sacrifice of the son of man. The use of oil rather than water in this ceremony signified that the purpose was not to wash the Lamb of God, who was immaculate from his conception, but to consecrate him for the glory of the Life transcendent.

Jesus was the perfect instrument—body, mind, and soul—for the manifestation of the only begotten One. Having beheld his glory, Mary honored the Trinity of the Godhead which the Master embodied even in his flesh. [160] She saw that his head was crowned with a halo of light from his Presence, that his heart emitted the effulgence of the threefold flame in perfect balance, that his hands were focuses of comfort, healing, and alchemical transformation, and that the chakras of his feet emanated the divine understanding—beautiful upon the mountain of God. [161]

Just as the disciples were to be criticized by the Pharisees for shouting and praising God, saying, "Blessed is the King of Israel [the Lord of all that is real] that cometh in the name of the Lord [in the name of the Christ]," [162] so Mary was rebuked for her adoration of the Prince of Peace by Judas Iscariot, who told her that she should have sold the oil for three hundred pence and given to the poor. Recognizing that through her tender ministration the Father was anointing his body for his final initiation and the ritual of the resurrection, Jesus said: "Let her alone: against the day of my burying hath she kept this. For the poor always ye have with you; but me ye have not always." Whereas the cycle of the Christ's appearing through Jesus was soon to be fulfilled, those lacking in self-mastery and the attainment of the Christ consciousness—the "poor"—would always be evolving upon the planet.

By bowing to the Light within Jesus, this holy woman set the precedent for the lesser self to bow to the Greater Self in all who would ever overcome the world; for thereby she herself and all who would do likewise would receive the promise of one day realizing their own Christ-potential. Jesus held this act to be of such import that he said, "Wheresoever this gospel shall be preached throughout the whole world, this also that she hath done shall be spoken of for a memorial of her." [163]

When individual man, yet in the state of becoming whole, allows the Christ to enter his being and minister to the needs of all, the mercy of God dispensed by the hand of the Mediator is made tangible to the souls of all upon earth. At that moment, the lower self becomes the mediator between the Christ Self and every other part of Life evolving Godward. Through the one who consecrates the tabernacle of his four lower bodies as the dwelling place of God and the focus for the Christ, untold millions are touched by the Light: and "I [Jesus], if I [the Christ] be lifted up from the earth, will draw all men unto me [unto

Jesus the Christ—for through self-mastery the son of man and the Son of God are become one]." [164]

Through the immaculate love of the Christ incarnate, hope seizes the hearts of humanity waiting to be filled; they are quickened by the Lord's Spirit; and they rise en masse into the glory of the I AM Presence. Such is the majority of one—one such as Jesus—who has consecrated his temple to God and Christ in purity and in service.

Each time one part of God ministers unto another, each time you perform a service to Life, you can invoke the Holy Spirit to reconsecrate in that Life the body and the essence of the pure Son of God. [165] For as Jesus said, "Inasmuch as ye have done it unto one of the least of these my brethren [unto the lower self], ye have done it unto me [unto the Christ in me and in all]." Thus the true meaning of being my brother's keeper is found in the hope-filled realization that any service rendered in love to any man is rendered to the Christ. And by cosmic law the lower self cannot reunite with the God Self without performing service to the Christ Self in all that lives; for "no man cometh unto the Father, but by me [but by service to the Christ]." [166]

FLAME COLOR-QUALITIES OF THE SEVEN RAYS AND THEIR PERVERSIONS

Spheres of the Causal Body of Man (beginning with the center)	Corresponding Godly Attributes: Treasures of Heaven Stored in the Seven Spheres	Perversions of Godly Attributes Accumulated in the Electronic Belt	Corresponding Perversions of the Color Rays Found in the Human Aura
Sphere I White (Fourth Ray)	1. Purity, perfection 2. Self-discipline, morality 3. Life, hope, positive spirals 4. Joy, spiritual bliss 5. Wholeness, all-one-ness 6. Symmetry, geometry 7. Law, order, co-measurement— as Above, so below 8. Divine architecture, blueprint of Life	1. Impurity, imperfection 2. Lack of self-control, amorality 3. Death, discouragement, negative spirals 4. Lust, human desire patterns, misuses of the sacred fire 5. Separateness, incompleteness, loneliness 6. Asymmetry 7. Lawlessness, anarchy, chaos, absence of interchange between Spirit and Matter 8. Distortion of divine design	Dirty white "Dead men's bones" Silver Gray Black Scarlet
Sphere II Yellow (Second Ray)	1. Christed illumination 2. God Self-awareness, humility 3. Divine Logos, divine reason 4. Wisdom (wise dominion), understanding, Cosmic Consciousness 5. Discrimination between absolute Good and relative good and evil, right knowledge 6. Intelligence, resourcefulness, open-mindedness 7. Perspicacity, perspicuity	1. Witchcraft, black magic 2. Ego-centeredness, pride 3. Human logic, human reason 4. Human folly, vanity, lack of comprehension, mortal consciousness 5. Inordinate and indiscriminate use of energy, wrong knowledge 6. Stupidity, lethargy, narrow-mindedness 7. Lack of discernment, ignorance, mental density, sloth	Muddy yellow Orange Brown Copper Crimson Black Olive brown

	Positive	Negative	Colors
Sphere III Pink (Third Ray)	1. Divine love, selflessness 2. Beauty, comfort, grace 3. Harmony 4. Creativity, spiritual magnetism, God-desire 5. Compassion 6. Unity, adhesion, cohesion 7. Communion with Life, baptism of the Holy Spirit	1. Human love, selfishness 2. Ugliness, discomfort, negligence 3. Discord 4. Sensuality, animal magnetism, human desire 5. Self-pity, human sympathy 6. Disunity, disintegration, decay 7. Consorting with death, necromancy, demon and spirit possession	Red Red orange Coral Fuchsia Black Brown
Sphere IV Violet (Seventh Ray)	1. Freedom, justice, tolerance, mercy, forgiveness 2. Liberty, ritual of Life 3. Invocation of the sacred fire, Light action, flow 4. Diplomacy, tact, poise 5. Science of alchemy, transmutation, law of transcendence, progressive revelation, prophecy	1. Servitude, bondage, injustice, intolerance, hardness of heart, cruelty 2. Libertinism, license, disorderliness, disorganization, nonintegration, disorientation 3. Incantations, mortal cursings, hexes, prayers of malintention, stagnation, death 4. Lack of savoir-faire 5. Misuses of the sacred science, rote, intransigence, dogma, perversions and misinterpretations of scripture and the laws of Truth, mouthings of evil spirits	Red Orange Wine Fuchsia Brown Black

FLAME COLOR-QUALITIES OF THE SEVEN RAYS AND THEIR PERVERSIONS

Spheres of the Causal Body of Man (beginning with the center)	Corresponding Godly Attributes: Treasures of Heaven Stored in the Seven Spheres	Perversions of Godly Attributes Accumulated in the Electronic Belt	Corresponding Perversions of the Color Rays Found in the Human Aura
Sphere V Purple and Gold (Sixth Ray)	1. Peace 2. Ministration and service 3. Brotherhood and family life founded in Christ 4. Balance of the Christ in the individual and society 5. Desirelessness, harmlessness	1. Emotional turbulence, war 2. Ego-centered existence 3. Disruption of family and community life through perversions of the threefold flame 4. Imbalance manifesting as clans, gangs, social cliques, group marriages, free love 5. Desirefulness, harmfulness	Maroon Silver Gray Copper Brown Black
Sphere VI Green (Fifth Ray)	1. Truth, abundance, supply 2. Science, scientific method 3. Life 4. Health, healing, wholeness, rejuvenation, regeneration 5. Direct and indirect precipitation from Spirit to Matter, sublimation from Matter to Spirit, tangible proofs of the Spirit, squaring of the circle	1. Error, insufficiency, lack, spiritual impoverishment 2. Nescience, superstition, accident, chance 3. Death 4. Disease, a "house divided," aging, degeneration 5. Absence of manifest works, absence of virtues and things of the Spirit made practical in Spirit-form and Matter-form	Olive Chartreuse Brown Orange Black

	6. Gratitude, constancy, consecration, generosity, open-mindedness, free flow of the electron 7. Music, mathematics, laws and principles of cosmic harmony	6. Ingratitude, inconstancy, carelessness, desecration, lack of givingness, small-mindedness, envy, jealousy, greed, covetousness, possessiveness, imprisonment of energy in Matter-form 7. Inharmony	
Sphere VII Blue (First Ray)	1. Perfection 2. Divine will 3. Protection, construction, direction 4. Faith 5. Obedience, love of God and his laws 6. Light, energy, power, courage 7. Dominion, God-control, God-desire 8. God-ordained government, business, commerce, transportation, communication, banking 9. Cosmic and natural law	1. Imperfection 2. Human will 3. State of harm, danger, destruction; haphazard, willy-nilly existence 4. Doubt 5. Disobedience, defiance, rebellion against God's laws 6. Absence of Light, of energy, vacillation, impotence, cowardice 7. Subjection, psychic manipulation, black magic 8. Disorganization in the affairs and economy of nations and societies resulting from mortal codes 9. Mortal laws, lawlessness	Gray blue Blue black Black

I AM THY CHALICE

I AM the true Life of the Flame—
A focus of God's I AM name,
Descending cycle from the Sun,
My radiant Source, Thou lovely One!

I AM Thy chalice ever free—
My purposed aim like Thee to be,
A ray of Light's expanding Love,
A focus for God's comfort dove.

Thy ray now anchored in my form
Does my Divinity adorn:
Thy Flame, a rising sacred fire,
Each moment takes me ever higher

Until at last made purer still,
Eternal focus of Thy will,
I AM Thy crystal chalice pure,
An anchor of Thy Love secure.

A healing fountain to the earth,
I AM real proof of Life's rebirth,
Which by the power of Thy name
Ascends today Thy Love to claim.

I AM Thy radiance crystal clear,
Forever pouring through me here.
Thy living joy fore'er expanding,
I AM with Thee all Life commanding!

Chapter Seven

God in Nature

God in Nature

By what way is the Light parted, which scattereth the east wind upon the earth? Who hath divided a watercourse for the overflowing of waters, or a way for the lightning of thunder; to cause it to rain on the earth, where no man is; on the wilderness, wherein there is no man?

Canst thou bind the sweet influences of Pleiades, or loose the bands of Orion? Canst thou bring forth Mazzaroth in his season? or canst thou guide Arcturus with his sons?   *Job*

THE FLOW OF CREATION

IF WE WOULD UNDERSTAND the order and ritual of Nature, we must peer behind the passing scenes that make up the world of effect—even the world of secondary causes and effects. We must train the eye of the mind to look beyond our three- and four-dimensional frame of reference into the infinite dimensions of the realm of First Cause. We must fix our gaze upon those aspects of Being which have neither physical definition nor relativity in time or space, but which are eternal in the heavens. For it is in Spirit, in the Fiery World, often referred to as the realm of formless form, that the origins of Life are waiting to be discovered. Here the etheric embryo of every God-idea that will take form in Matter and ripen in man and Nature is found in its original Light Body and design.

If we would transcend the dimensions of Matter, we must explore Nature in its essence and learn to probe the nuclei of energy systems through the acceleration of our soul faculties; for only thus can our consciousness enter into and comprehend the spiritual cause behind the material effect we behold in and as the physical universe.

How do we know that we can or cannot accomplish such feats of the mind and spirit if we have not proved the equation *Theos + Rule + You = God's Law active as Principle within your Being?*[1] This alchemical formula states that man must avail himself of the potential of God *(Theos),* of the Law *(Rule),* and of the spark of Divinity, the energy that comprises his self-awareness *(You),* if he would demonstrate God's Law. In short, we must *TRY.* We must exercise our God-given faculties according to natural law and we must invoke the Life-energies within the atom of self if we would penetrate Nature and make her God our own.

If man would accept the idea, he could walk through fire and earth as easily as he passes through water and air. The difficulty lies not in the act itself, but in the adjustment of the mind and the conditioning of the emotions to the act. Thus we begin to see that man's conscious dominion over the physical-spiritual universe and his discovery of God in Nature lies not alone in the outer manipulation of forces but above all in his inner self-mastery. With all man's getting of worldly wisdom, he must, then, get a working knowledge of those laws which, when assiduously applied, will give him not only inner self-mastery but also the outer mastery of his environment.

Throughout this work we have endeavored to

systematically present a practical explanation of those cardinal principles of alchemy, the sacred science of self-transformation, without which man's advancement on the Path is at best haphazard. In this chapter we shall discuss the polarity of the Father-Mother God which establishes the balance of cosmic forces in Christic manifestation; the blending of man's consciousness with Life through the Holy Spirit; the hierarchical order of Nature spirits who sustain concentrated focuses of the sacred fire in Nature; man's control of his environment through the application of cosmic law, including extraterrestrial probes; and finally, man's joint service with the elemental kingdom through the practical doctrine of *ahimsa*—harmlessness toward all Life.

Nature is a screen of light that coalesces in gradations of loveliness in formlessness and form. Behind each level of manifestation is an etheric counterpart suspended in what Eastern mystics have termed the Fiery World. The spiritual patterns that sustain the natural order in Matter are thus condensations of light—energy coalesced in geometric forms that give impetus to their more dense counterparts which comprise the physical universe.

The spiritual progression of worlds beyond our own is seen as a gradual dematerialization of energy veils* from Matter to Spirit—from what is termed the *outer,* the physical, or tangible, to what is termed the *inner,* the spiritual, or intangible. These worlds are

---

*These energy veils must not be confused with the term "energy veil" which we have used to define evil. The above use of the term in the plural denotes the gradations of Light frequencies for Matter to Spirit— each succeeding veil being a thinning of the density, hence a higher frequency of atomic activity than the previous one. Not one, but many veils of Light interpenetrate Cosmos, establishing the planes of God's consciousness. Some speak of going beyond "the Veil," referring to that specific veil beyond which man in his earthly state no longer perceives form and consciousness.

created through the magnetization of Spirit-form and Matter-form around nuclei suns, each sun a flaming idea projected from the Mind of God, each sun sustaining a hub of activity that complements the central theme of Life.

Conversely, as we proceed from the *meta*physical* center of Cosmos, called the Great Central Sun, to the physical periphery of universes in material manifestation, the extension of the LORD's Body follows an orderly spiraling of energies from Spirit to Matter. These we observe as subtle gradations of light, color, sound, form, and symmetry from galactic spirals to microscopic life. This is Nature in all her grandeur. This is substance of the Mater Ray that hangs upon the *antahkarana,* the skeletal framework, of Spirit.

Contrary to the popular notion that heaven is "up" and earth is "down," the basis of our cosmoconception is that Spirit and Matter, heaven and earth, are interpenetrating forcefields existing simultaneously throughout Cosmos as the warp and woof, the plus and minus, of creation. Jesus confirmed this concept of cosmic coexistence when he said, "The kingdom of God cometh not with observation: neither shall they say, Lo here! or, lo there! for, behold, the kingdom of God is within you."[2]

Another common belief that bears scrutiny is that what man perceives with his physical senses is Matter and what he does not is Spirit. It is our understanding that Matter is intended to be the transparent vehicle for Spirit and that when man and Nature are found in their pristine state, Spirit and Matter are equally visible as the Father-Mother God. It is only since the Fall of Man, since Matter became opaqued with the dark consciousness of duality, that the Spirit

---

*That which lies above or beyond the physical world as the spiritual Cause preceding the material effect.

which inhabits the body temple[3] can no longer be seen in man's flesh or in the very atoms composing earth's crust.

Thus, by his partial view of Spirit and Matter, man has induced two erroneous theories which form the basis of an erroneous theology: (1) a geographical relationship between heaven and earth and (2) the divisibility of Spirit and Matter. The concepts that sin is of the flesh and that Matter is evil or unreal have grown out of an incorrect apprehension of the science of energy qualification. Nothing but the sense of sin with which man has cloaked his flesh, and the energy veil which he has superimposed upon the atoms of material substance could have made him draw these inaccurate and self-defeating conclusions.

If he would but summon faith in the transforming power of the Holy Spirit and then invoke the Light of God to purify his sense consciousness, man would behold beyond the blanket of maya that distorts and densifies Mother Earth not only the crystal magnificence of the material side of the creation, but also the Christic patterns of Spirit shining through. The core of energy systems, of atoms and universes, is the focus of the spiritual idea, the fiery ovoid, which gives birth to its materialization. Physical nuclei, such as protons and neutrons and flaming sun centers, focus not only the matrix for the monadic system but also the balance of spiritual-material energies flowing from spiritual formlessness into and out of material form—as Above, so below.

The transfer of energy from Spirit to Matter is made through concentrated focuses of the sacred fire, such as stars and suns, under the direction of the heavenly beings who ensoul them. Using the complete spectrum of cosmic science still untouched by mortals, they serve as coordinators of the great cosmic flow to move the energies of the eternal cycles into spirals of descending magnitude on behalf of evolving life-waves who are making their way Godward upon endless planetary orbs but who, in their present state of consciousness, are unable to absorb directly the energies of the Great Hub.

The perception of the LORD's Spirit in Nature—of myriad lights and flaming hues—varies with the individual. The education and exercise of man's vision varies also, and thus the beauty that some men perceive does not exist for others. There are those who see beauty where there is none; these discern spiritually the archetypal pattern of perfection glistening beyond the Veil even when its material counterpart is not apparent in the world of form.

There are others for whom life is always dreary, banal, and unholy; and even in the presence of true beauty delicately perfected in Matter, they perceive only the spirals of disintegration and decay inherent within their own limited self-awareness of God. Because they have developed the habit of "negative seeing," the beauty of Life remains unperceived. By this process they negate for themselves the perfection of Life which does manifest throughout Nature. The study of God in Nature must therefore begin with the understanding that Nature is at once objective Reality and subjective manifestation of man's innermost being.

To those who behold with the inner eye, whose perceptions are ordered by the single-eyed vision of the Creator's own consciousness, the joy, the harmony, the beauty, the perfection, the balance, the symmetry, and the mathematical precision of Nature are facts of Life applauded, adored, and affinitized with the inner realities of their solar awareness. Those who see only the phenomena of the parts (parts of

Matter saturated with the pollutants of the human consciousness) while neglecting their function within the Whole (the whole of a purified material universe and its spiritual counterpart) do not see the forest for the trees. As in the Hindu fable about the Blind Men and the Elephant,[4] they examine one or more of the parts of Nature and then become seized by their own limited sense of that part. In their lack of perspective and their failure to comprehend the unity of the Whole, they deprive themselves of the blessings of the Whole and forever dwell within the confines of their partial view.

When God made man, he placed all of Cosmos within his grasp, the exterior as well as the interior world; and these together comprise his total identity. When man beholds the world without, he is reminded that the mountains, the forests, the lakes, the gentle breezes, the sun, moon, and stars comprise his own being. That which man perceives and accepts in Nature he can become—he already is. Indeed, the creation, man, includes the spiritual-material universe; it is his to command if he will but make it his own.

The material microcosm includes the spiritual Macrocosm, as every effect must include its cause. And all of its components are within the reach of man's conscious awareness of the Self as God, as Nature. The union of the outer man with the inner man through the soul's desire to draw unto itself more of God produces the ebb and flow of light over the figure-eight pattern that involves all of creation—both the within and the without.

While yet in a limited or partial state of self-awareness, wherein he does not perceive the inter-relation of the parts with the Whole, man does not define Life as one: he does not see that the trees, the mountains, and the rocks are part of his own God

Self-awareness. In fact, man's own being is so vast that he does not see its extension throughout Nature and all of Cosmos. As the electron does not know that it is part of the atom but orbits in a whirl of its own, so man's world appears complete, when in reality he is part of the ever expanding Whole that is God in Nature. When he begins to rise on the spirals that are created by the spiritualization of his consciousness, he perceives that the LORD has placed all things beneath his feet, that he is the Master of Life and of the cycles of Nature when he identifies with the Christ, the eternal Logos in whose Being all things were made.

God has given to the Self-realized *man*ifestation of himself conscious dominion over the planes of Matter. This dominion man achieves as he realizes his all-oneness with Life. The wind and wave are stilled when he affirms, "I AM the peace-commanding Presence of the Holy Spirit exercising full God-control in the planes of air and water." Fire and earth likewise joyously mold themselves to the Christic design when man affirms the God-power inherent within the intelligent, obedient, loving desire of the electron to flow into the perfect pattern.

To limit one's consciousness to oneself, one's environment, one's country, or the world can never lead to the union of the soul with Cosmos through Nature. As Saint Germain, in Chapter Nine of his *Studies in Alchemy,* paraphrased Sir Walter Scott,

> Breathes there the man with soul so dead
> Who never to himself hath said:
> "This is my own, my native universe"?[5]

It is certain that a sense of the vastness of Cosmos and of the co-measurement of the larger domain with the comparatively small and self-limiting part will do much to expand the periphery of man's consciousness.

By correlating himself with the Infinite, man becomes aware of larger and larger aspects of the Deity both within himself and within the universe.

The concept of God as inhabiting the universe and therefore being in residence in Nature is not difficult to understand. But one need not have detailed knowledge of the how and why of God's universal existence any more than one needs to examine the delicate workings of a fine Swiss watch before he can accept its usefulness in telling time. Likewise, one must resist the temptation to categorize this panoramic view of God in Nature as "pantheistic" (with all of the pagan overtones feared by Christians).

Webster says that pantheism is "a doctrine that equates God with the forces and laws of the universe."[6] The *Standard College Dictionary* defines pantheism as "the doctrine that the whole universe is God, or that every part of the universe is a manifestation of God."[7] To argue against this theory is to deny that Leonardo lives in his paintings, that Michelangelo can be known in his sculpture, or that Christ lives in his Sermon on the Mount and in the hearts of millions who have touched the hem of his garment. Some of the sayings of Jesus not recorded in the Gospels but found in the writings of the church fathers on the Oxyrhynchus papyruses discovered in Egypt about 1900 support this concept of a mystical pantheism: "Raise the stone, and there thou shalt find me; cleave the wood, and there am I."[8]

The Creator dwells in his creation; his Presence endows it with innate immortality; his Law maintains the outer structure; and his Spirit gives it Life. It has been said by wise men that God sustains the universe with the flow of his attention moment by moment throughout eternity and that if he were to withdraw the energies of his Mind from it, it would collapse into a heap of nothingness. We make these statements not in defense of the word *pantheism,* which has been bandied about by those who would make light of occult mysteries, but in order to show the reality of God's Spirit in Nature.

Our study of Nature cannot progress unless we understand the role of the Holy Spirit in and as Nature. Indeed, Nature is the culmination of the Spirit of God made manifest in Matter. In Nature we find the perfect union of the Father-Mother God and the pristine glory of the Christ. Undergirding the material universe are the Four Cosmic Forces which originate in the Central Sun as a pinwheel of light directing the cycles of energy from Spirit into Matter. These forces are controlled by the Holy Spirit, and without them man would be without a platform for his soul's evolution in Matter. They key the energy flow not only to the four lower bodies of the evolving monad but also to the four interpenetrating force-fields that make up planetary and starry bodies.

The shuttle of creation whereby spiritual ideas are projected into material manifestation is directed by the Master Weaver who blends the warp and woof of Spirit and Matter to fulfill the cosmic scheme. The Maha Chohan has referred to the Holy Spirit as the great unifying coordinator who, "like unto a mighty weaver of old, weaves a seamless garment of Ascended Master light and love. The shuttle of God's attention upon man drives forth radiant beams of descending light, scintillating fragments of purity and happiness, toward earth and into the hearts of his children, whilst the tender risings of men's hopes, aspirations, invocations, and calls for assistance do pursue the Deity in his mighty haven of cosmic purity. . . .

"As a tiny seed of light, the Holy Spirit enters into the heart of the earth, into the density of Matter, that it might expand throughout the cells of form and being, of thought and perception to become a gnosis and an effulgence in the cup of consciousness. This Holy Grail of immortal substance may be unrecognized by many who pass by, but to many others it will be perceived gleaming from behind the Veil. Shedding the light of that divine knowing which transcends mortal conception and is the renewing freshness of eternity's morn, it vitalizes each moment with the God-happiness that man cognizes through infinite perceptions cast as fragments into the chalice of his own consciousness."

Above all, having received, retain
Whate'er gift God hath given unto thee,
That ere the sun set each day
Thou shalt have cleansed thy being
Of all perceptions vain and hapless
And readied thyself through eventide
To enter into immortal peace
In the hours of the night while thy body sleeps
To dream the immortal dream
And to be one who gathers
Of the flame of God's Spirit in greater measure
And fullness, that as the new day breaketh,
Thy energies, made holy and pure,
Rising as the incense of devotion,
Shall invoke for all who are thy friends of Light
Some new miracle of consciousness.

Thy destiny lies not in vanity and confusion,
But only in the Godly activity of being a lamplighter,
Having first within thyself the spark of kindling
That thou mayest then and ever anon
Confer with sweetness upon all hearts
The selfsame regenerative technique
Bestowed upon thee by the eternal Father.

The Holy Spirit, having descended into thy being,
Is ever thereafter an eternal anchor
Cast within the heart center of Divinity itself.

No delusion, no outer world vanity
Will then allay thy feeling of searching;
For thy Being, like a great searchlight,
Will scan each moment
That thou mayest perceive what radiant splendor
God has placed there—shall I say, blessed ones,
Right under your noses—
That thou mayest know that all that opposes
The configuration of splendid appearing
Is but a darkened garb without clearing
Which thou mayest well shun, never fearing
Aught else, but knowing withal
That the snow-white dove, showing all hope,
Will fly with compassionate wings
To the heart of heaven where soundless sound rings
The melody of the Sacred Seven
Whose whiteness is thy seamless robe.[9]

THE FATHER-MOTHER GOD IN SPIRIT AND IN MATTER

All of Nature is the compound idea of the infinite Mind of God. All of creation is the thought-manifestation, the idea-action, of that Mind. Nothing real exists that did not first spring forth as a thought-energy pattern in the Creator's consciousness and then spiral into manifestation through the cycles of Spirit and Matter.

When we speak of the Creator and his consciousness, we must include in our awareness the concept of the Father-Mother God—of a Being that is both masculine and feminine in nature, whose oneness is found in the perfect balance of the energies of Spirit and Matter.

God as formless form is the white fiery ovoid of Love-Wisdom in polarity. God individualized in Spirit and in Matter is revealed as twin flames, each an expression of the Divine Wholeness, yet one having a plus (masculine) and the other a minus (feminine) coefficient. Of the creation of twin flames like unto the Father-Mother God, destined to be coordinates and conductors of every idea-action of the infinite Mind, the author of Genesis wrote: "And God said, Let us make man in *our* image, after *our* likeness: and let *them* have dominion. . . . So God created man in his own image, in the image of God created he him; *male* and *female* created he *them*." [10]

If God is Father-Mother, what, then, is the Trinity? When we refer to God as Father, God as Son, and God as Holy Spirit, we are actually referring to God as he is found in Spirit and in Matter, thus recognizing that his Being and Consciousness appears in the Persons of the Trinity according to the level or plane of individual awareness. As John said: "There are three that bear record in heaven, the Father, the Word, and the Holy Ghost: and these three are one. And there are three that bear witness in earth, the Spirit, and the water, and the blood: and these three agree in one." [11]

When we speak to God as Father, we are addressing him in the plane of Spirit as Spirit, as the originator of the Fiery Ovoid, the Cause behind the cause-effect sequences we behold in Matter. God in the Person of Father includes the Mother principle, for he is forever the androgynous Whole.

When we call upon the LORD in the nearness of the Holy Spirit, the Comforter whom Jesus promised would abide with man forever, the Spirit of Truth that he said "dwelleth with you, and shall be in you," [12] we are contacting the Person of God as he is made available to man in the plane of Matter. The Holy Spirit focuses the divine polarity of the energies of the Father-Mother God made manifest in and relevant to the material creation through the threefold flame within the heart of man.

When we bow before the Almighty in the Person of the Christ, we acknowledge the only begotten Son born of the union of the Father-Mother God in both Spirit and Matter. In him is the Word become *flesh* and then transformed in the *spirit* of the Logos. This is the miracle of the eternal Christos who was ordained from the beginning as the Mediator between the planes of God's consciousness in Spirit and in Matter, between the Divine Father and the Divine Mother, and between God Above and man below.

We shall discover later in this work that the functions of the Trinity are reversed in Spirit and in Matter. Thus, in Spirit God the Father is the Wisdom-Power that plans the creation and God the Mother is the Power-Love that gives it birth. In Matter God the Father is the Power-Love that provides the energy for its manifestation, while God the Mother is the Wisdom-Power that executes the plan. In Spirit the Christos is the focal point for the Power Love-Wisdom of the Word that went forth giving light to all creation. In Matter Christ, as the epitome of Wisdom, is the culmination of the Love-Power of the Father-Mother.

At this point in our discussion it is necessary to clarify certain points of the Law which have become stones of stumbling in the pathway of many sincere seekers for Truth. Let us first take up the denial of the existence of Matter and the material universe.

Those who defend this view base their argument on the premise that God, Good, is Spirit everywhere present and that he is the only Reality—which is, of course, true. They reason that if God is Good and the only Reality, then the opposite of Good, namely Evil, must be unreal—which, in the absolute sense, is also true; for as we have explained, Evil is but an energy veil sustained in the relativity of time and space by man's misuse of free will. But their logic breaks down when they draw the unwarranted conclusion that since the opposite of Good is unreal, then Spirit's opposite, Matter, must not exist either.

The fallacy here is the belief that Matter is the antipode of Spirit. This conclusion is based on the perspective of a partial seeing—of seeing through a glass darkly instead of beholding Reality face to face.[13] The foundation of our logic must become the testimony of Life, of Spirit itself, lest we fall by the wayside and wander with the blind leaders of the blind rationalists. For that Life which is Spirit is the author of a cosmic conception so noble and so grand as to render utterly meaningless the speculations of physics versus metaphysics, which in the final analysis are one, even as science and religion are forever one in the alchemical union of Spirit and Matter.

The Truth all mankind seek is based on the irrefutable law that Spirit and Matter are not opposites: they are the twofold nature of God's Being which remain forever as the Divine Polarity. By contrast, careful thought will reveal that Good and Evil can never be in polarity. They are diametrically opposed and will forever so remain; for the former is real and the latter is unreal.

Pallas Athena, Patron of Truth, sheds light upon a similar question that has been raised concerning Light and Darkness. Her comments will assist us in clarifying the issues of Spirit and Matter, Good and Evil:

"Yes, Light exists and Darkness exists. Some men have tried to simplify this concept by saying that Darkness is an absence of Light, whereas others have equated Darkness with Evil, seeing it as a virulent force that seeks to overthrow the Light. There are elements of truth in both statements. For example, in the mind and being of man, the vacuum that is referred to as Darkness, or a lack of Light, is not a positive force; it is not a negative force; it is not even a misappropriated force; it is simply an absence of the realization of Light's potential.

"On the other hand, that Darkness which results from the misqualification of Light, from its conversion into Darkness, is of another type, which can be categorized as a negative force or a positive Evil. That there are various types of Darkness was clearly pointed out by the Master Jesus in his exclamation 'If therefore the Light that is in thee be Darkness, how great is that Darkness!'[14] This may be read as a question by the earnest disciple: How great is the intensity of the Darkness in me? Is it a misqualification of Light, an energy veil, or is it an absence of Light, a lost opportunity? How great an impediment is this Darkness to my understanding of Truth?"[15]

Light is not at war with Darkness, nor are Good and Evil engaged in mortal combat. Light, unaware of its opposite, fills the Darkness and transmutes the energy veil just as the Presence of Good consumes on contact all that is unlike itself. But Spirit will never cancel out itself in Matter, for both are real and stand juxtaposed as complementary pillars in the temple of Being.

An erroneous postulation, regardless of its tenure in the minds of men, is still erroneous. The false belief that Matter equates with Evil—the energy veil— must be replaced by the Truth if men would progress on the path of enlightened self-mastery. It is the lie of the carnal mind which has spawned the energy veil that distorts the perception of both Spirit and Matter. The carnal mind, not Matter, is the culprit. The consciousness of duality sent forth the mist that watered the whole face of the ground[16] (that obscured the Spirit of the LORD resident in Matter). The carnal mind, incapable of defining its own point of reference in the universe, simply cannot be credited with the creation of the brave solar system and far-flung planets, the splendid body of man, or the stars that point to worlds beyond. Nor can it be said that the pristine substance, the Light out of which the material universe was invoked by God, is Evil.

"Come now, and let us reason together,"[17] saith the LORD! The word *matter* comes from the Latin *mater,* or mother; and this is the key that liberates our minds from the categorical denial—though it be whispered a thousand times by the serpent—"There is no Matter." The Feminine aspect of God which we recognize in Mother Nature provides the womb into which Spirit projects the seed-energies of a cosmic destiny that is fulfilled in galaxies and universes without number. Matter is the cradle of Spirit that rocks the Cosmos into its spiritual consummation.

In a universe where man is in a state of becoming God through the judicious exercise of free will, where Good and Evil are his daily options, we cannot ignore the temporary existence of Evil even while we affirm the permanent Reality of Good. But at the same time, we have no grounds for equating Evil or imperfection with Matter any more than we have reason to identify the energy veil with Spirit. Paul told the early Christians that their bodies were the temples of the living God. Would God—could God—remain in a structure that is inherently Evil? Was he not addressing those evolving on the material plane in material bodies which he himself had created when he said, "I will dwell in them, and walk in them; and I will be their God, and they shall be my people"?[18]

By their wrong choices men have inlaid the strata of Matter with layers of illusions, so much so that beneath the veiled face of Mother Nature the pattern and portrait of the Divine is scarcely recognizable. The earth elements, once crystalline, emitting the radiance of atomic fires, are dense and dull; they, too, are waiting to be baptized by the water of the Word. Transparent sands of pastel hue, flora and fauna, glistening adornments of the Creator's consciousness, lie buried beneath the weight of planetary effluvia, their only hope the resurrection of the son of man. Alas, the descent into duality, the Fall from grace, has distorted not only the man made in God's image but also the world of Spirit and Matter upon which he has superimposed his "evil" consciousness.

Sanat Kumara, who long ago kept the vigil for the Light of Spirit in this darkened, densified world of form, explains the interrelated functions of Spirit and Matter: "The Spirit that interpenetrates all form and substance is the web of reason—the skeletal framework—that communicates and holds together the Cosmos."[19] Through his instruction we see that Matter is the visible side of Spirit. Matter is that aspect of Spirit to which man, who is yet in the state of becoming Whole, can relate. Matter is Spirit tempered to the shorn lamb of man's lesser identity. Man in his present awareness is simply not capable of assimilating pure Spirit; therefore, God has provided a platform for his evolving soul consciousness.

"Those who would explore the far reaches of space, both inner and outer," says the Holy Kumara, "should understand that the Divine Feminine is the womb of creation that is impregnated with Life by the Spirit of God. The material universe is the negative polarity, whereas the spiritual universe is the positive polarity of the Godhead. Matter, meaning

Mater, is the chalice that receives the invigorating, Life-giving essence of the sacred fire. Thus the Father principle completes the cycle of manifestation in the world of form through the Mother aspect; and child-man is nourished by the balancing, sustaining action of Life whose twofold nature—Spirit-Matter, masculine-feminine—is epitomized in the Christ.

"If a man tear himself from the luminosity of his own heart by outward seeking, he can become enmeshed in externals until the internal Fiery World can no longer sound forth its Reality. All things come, then, into position within the framework of the individual's chalice of manifest perspective. His temple is his universe which God infuses with Life. God (as Mother) is the temple, and God (as Father) is the fire that blazes on the altar within.

"The power to expand the chalice is the power inherent within a mustard seed. It does not matter that a man's faith is no greater than a mustard seed.[20] If he has the smallest fragment of God within, he can expand it; and because the potential expansion is limitless, there is no limit to where a man can go, to what he can become, when he has harnessed for himself the divine radiance that God has implanted within the seed of his heart. We refer not to the physical heart, but to the center of sovereign Being, to the seat of Universal Consciousness, to the powerhouse of spiritual individuality. . . .

"God created the universe as a place of joy. In order to create natives to his own joy, he framed men in his own Image. This Image he implanted within them; it is recorded in the fire of the soul, that it might never be lost, regardless of how far man might wander from his Source. Through this Image the connecting cords of universal Love reach out as the spokes from a hub, from center to periphery, and all things are brought into focus within the soul who seethes with Good."[21]

The LORD, whose transcendental nature is not fully comprehended by those dwelling in the dimensions of a fixed relativity, created the Cosmos according to his highest concept of Good—far beyond man's highest concept of God. From the infinite realms of Spirit, he decreed the significant lowering of the Light* into finite spheres of material manifestation. The field of Matter thus became a natural receding from the fiery intensity of Spirit and its ode of immortal perfection.

"He hath put down the mighty from their seats, and exalted them of low degree."[22] Mary the Mother of Jesus, who, as a handmaid of the LORD, exemplified the mission of the Divine Feminine on earth, understood the law involving the stepping down of spiritual energies (the bringing down of the mighty from their seats) and the raising of physical energies (the exalting of them of low degree). She also knew that the immaculate conception of the Christ is ordained in the perfect union of Spirit and Matter where heaven and earth meet.

Explaining her divine calling to the Keepers of the Flame, Mary said: "I AM a cosmic mother, and as much your mother as I am the mother of beloved Jesus. Some who are adherents of the Christian faith call me the Mother of God. To those of the protesting branch of orthodox Christianity this seems a sacrilege; for men may well ask, 'Who is worthy to be the Mother of God?' But this concept, when understood to mean the mother of the embodiment of the Divine Spirit, reveals the glorious truth that every mother

---

*The lowering of the Christ consciousness, the Light of higher spheres, produced the physical light in the lower worlds.

who understands that which was spoken—'and the Word was made flesh and dwelt among us'[23]—may be the Mother of God. . . .

"The Christ must be born in every man and woman. The Christ seed must be nurtured and expanded as the threefold flame of Love, Wisdom, and Power holding dominion over every ideological concept of man, over every teleological matter prescribed by cosmic law, and ruling supreme as the master function of Life. Then I (the God flame in me) automatically become (because the God flame in me is so consecrated) the Cosmic Mother of each son and daughter of heaven. Then you automatically become that to which you have consecrated the energies of your I AM Presence. That which 'I AM' you can be also, if you will it so by the power and authority of the 'I AM.'"[24]

The Father-Mother God is the center of all Life—of an atom, a seed, an idea; of man, of planets, stars, and suns. The Father-Mother God is the nucleus of energy systems, the core of being; and wherever God is, Life springs forth from the perfect union of Spirit and Matter. Love-Wisdom in polarity gives birth to the only begotten Son. The Christ is the Light-energy sent forth throughout Cosmos as the offspring of the divine union. He is the Logos that propagates the virtues of Love-Wisdom in all creation.

For the purposes of our study of God in Nature, we shall, like children, enjoy the miraculous advent of the Father-Mother God right within our very being. Almost delirious with delight, we feel the waves of light that flood the playground of our consciousness as we frolic in the sun of cosmic ecstasy. We have found our Father in heaven and our Mother in earth. We feel secure in the everlasting arms of Life. Today we are content to splash and swim in the sea of God's Being; tomorrow we shall master the science and art of creation.

Imbued with the innocence of the child mind, we are not overawed by the concept of God's own Self-awareness focused in sun centers which form the nucleus of evolving lifewaves abounding throughout the creation. Wherever God's consciousness is, we know we shall find our Father-Mother—Love and Wisdom, Wisdom and Love—swirling, mounting, foaming in the ebb and flow of the tides of the morning, the tides of the evening.

We are bathed and fed and clothed by Light in motion—in the ocean of God's Being. Caressed by Him and Her, we seek no rationale to convince us of our own existence in heaven, in earth; no shallow logic can deprive us of our sweet communion. The Darkness of the dogmatists is confounded by the Christic Light. They walk as dead men, haunting specters of our former fears. No longer threatened by their gloom, we see them disappear among the mists of their violent musings. We stand in the sun of righteousness, our horizon blue and clear. The waters of Life flow freely through body, heart, and mind—now gently as a murmuring brook, now like a mighty torrent. We approach the Source, the great waterfall cascading from the center.

Our hands are cupped and tightly pressed. We catch the descending currents dazzling in the noonday fires. Beyond the falls, high in the mountains where the single drop emerges from the spring, where the Great River of Life begins, the Father-Mother is enthroned. Raising the sacred scepter, they welcome our return. We need not follow rocky crevasses or scale the jagged peaks to know that Life is there; we take instead the waters freely given, and we go on our way. To capture the desire that bubbles from within—to grow up and become like the Shining Ones who gave us Life—this is our childhood quest.

"How beautiful are the feet of the morning seeking to walk into the day." [25] Remembering our innocent longings, we as adults still look to the God Star on high, believing—knowing—that there we shall find our eternal Home. One called Surya—called by God with his twin flame to ensoul Sirius with the Love-Wisdom of the Father-Mother—addresses the man-children of earth:

"We speak of centers: the center of the heart, the center of the mind, the central eye of Light, the capitals of music, of art, of drama, and of the high culture of the temple. We speak of sun capitals and of star capitals and of cosmic citadels. But from the least unto the greatest, there is always one quality that responds and evokes response. Call him Father, Mother, God, Eternal Presence, or Infinite Being, he would convey only the best gifts to his children. Except ye become as a little child, ye cannot enter in. [26]

"In flinging away from the heart the cares that so momentously deprive one of Reality, man perceives the sheltering arms of Nature. His beauty and compassion are an outshining. Within the root is sap; in the green leaf is photosynthesis; there, softly diffused light glows. In your spirits that inhabit your bodies there is stamped the memory of Him. And all the while that this beauty remains, as if crucified and pierced with many a thorn, there is the hope that leaps in consciousness as a flame in a solar world or in the heart and speaks His name.

"Darkness flees, chaos becomes order, purpose is born: Love engulfs life. Selfhood is bestowed, and Christ is beheld as the healer of nations and of men. With little toys we play no more: we become men.

Once again the kyrie eleison is heard from universal power ranges. . . .

"The tenderness of spiritual Reality is guarded by the heart, and the arhat in nobleness sees himself as a repository of God's Good. He would not keep this Good from his fellowmen, nor would he keep himself from them. When he withdraws into the boat or the high mountain place, it is that he might come again unto his brothers carrying a more bountiful basket. Yet there is no pride in his going or in his coming, but only understanding that sees eternal values ever mounting, leaving behind the stragglers. These have formed themselves into loose-knit bands of inferior standards, and their games have often pierced the heart of virtue. . . .

"And what shall we say of the hunger that dictates speed? Shall men sit in darkness and deny the Light? Some say, 'The dawn will come,' but man's sense of time is often strange. And at that darkest hour before the dawn comes, some are discouraged and fall asleep to wake no more.

"To many life is only a fable because its realities have never been sensed; in hopelessness and despair men have embraced the dust only to see it crumble and be blown they know not where. Life is not emptiness, but fullness; but if the fullness be misqualified, it may be a fullness of emptiness. And so I ask all to turn within to the radiant Sun of Divine Reality. . . .

"O majestic hearts, respond to Divine Love! Heal the world by first healing your own world. Cleanse the world conscience by cleansing your own consciousness. Perceive that man must work in two worlds—his own within and that without. For 'my Father worketh hitherto, and I work.'" [27]

And so we turn to the symbol of the radiant Sun of Divine Reality, the orb that gives us Light and Life, the Father-Mother God of our solar system. Facing the East, we join the pilgrims who worship the Source by singing a hymn to the Sun:

O mighty Presence of God, I AM, in and behind the sun: I welcome Thy Light, which floods all the earth, into my life, into my mind, into my spirit, into my soul.

Radiate and blaze forth Thy Light! Break the bonds of darkness and superstition! Charge me with the great clearness of Thy white fire radiance!

I AM Thy child, and each day I shall become more of Thy manifestation![28]

The response of the Almighty is dispensed to the Children of the Sun through the flaming center of his Presence focused in the plane of Matter. From the hand of Helios and Vesta, Solar God and Goddess to this system of worlds, come the blessings of the Father-Mother God. To these God-free, God-realized beings the Creator has entrusted billions of evolving souls. To them he has given the responsibility of distributing his Light throughout the entire spiritual-material force-field of this solar system—an energy mass extending millions of miles in diameter on physical, emotional, mental, and etheric planes of manifestation. Revolving around this flaming focus of God's Mind, of which we behold but the physical aspect, are countless worlds and lifewaves—all undergoing the initiations of Solar Logoi, readying themselves for the grand return to the Father-Mother God.

Beyond the physical phenomenon of nuclear fusion, whereby hydrogen is transformed into helium, which scientists observe as the principle activity in the sun, are an infinite number of planes of spiritual-material activity which remain unprobed by those evolving in the dimensions of time and space as we have reference to them. Thus, many mansions of the Father's house occupy simultaneously the forcefield of our solar system, each one complete within its own frame of reference, each one serving the needs of its own household while unaware of the activities of the inhabitants on the next level. Our sun, giant hub of activity, aggregate focus of the Creator's Self-expression in all planes of Spirit and Matter, is governed and ensouled by Helios and Vesta, the highest representatives of the Godhead in this system of worlds.

Let not the mind prevent the assimilation of this concept by the heart; for if we can admit that God is in Nature in the universal sense, then we must also admit that he is in Nature in the individual sense. And if we concede that man is the individualized expression of God, then we must concede the possibility of there being higher and more perfect individualizations of God than the mankind, or *kind of man,* evolving on earth.

If God is capable of expressing himself in man and Nature upon this planet, then we must admit—lest we be guilty of limiting both Creator and creation—that he has ordered many dioramas and dimensions for the express purpose of manifesting the full complement of his Identity across the entire spectrum of forcefields and frequencies in Spirit and in Matter.

If the LORD saw fit to create man in his image and likeness and to place him upon earth, might he not also have seen fit to create a God-man, a Godly manifestation of himself, and to place him in the sun? Indeed, this is precisely what he has done—over and over again in suns and stars through galaxies without number. Leaving the whys and wherefores for our chapter on Hierarchy, let us hear the word of Helios—sublime expression of God in man and Nature:

"When I say, then, that I am Helios of the Sun, let it not become an alarming idea. It is written in your sacred writings, 'Go to the ant, thou sluggard.'[29] And so I say, liberate your minds from the erroneous idea that you cannot learn grand truths from the lowest as well as the highest of God's creatures; for doth He not ensoul them all? Is He not the One 'which command-eth the sun, and it riseth not; and sealeth up the stars; which alone spreadeth out the heavens, and treadeth upon the waves of the sea'?"[30]

On January 11, 1970, Helios sent forth a Procla-mation for the Seventies addressed to the sons and daughters of the sacred fire on the planet earth. We quote:

"The cries from the earth must be heeded by heaven; for it is the call of the soul that, according to divine decree, we must answer. The soul cries out in spiritual hunger, pleading for progress when progress can and should be rightfully demanded. The call com-pels the answer. The soul is weary of sense delusion, of maya, and of human disturbances. Even the energies of God, locked in karmic weight, long to be delivered from the tension of the inwardly coiled springs.

"That fiat of the Light 'Glory to God in the high-est, and on earth peace, goodwill toward men'[31] should be made the stirrup of the decade. Let the horse and the rider know that the right foot thrust in the stirrup will ever remind mankind of right action and of the necessity of forward movement over every obstacle.

"The current solar disturbances will have far-reaching effects. Our sun system is radiating unique light; and in that light goes forth the demand for the casting down of old human momentums that have brought so much discouragement to the world mind, dispensed in minute portions as potions of human poison. Therefore we say, let this era end! And let men clearly perceive the fruit of the ego that nestles in God, of the ego that refuses identification with aught else except the Divine Ego.

"Just as gratitude is more than a 'thank you,' so being one with God involves more than a statement of being that lacks the undergirdings of attainment. Being one with God is the infusion of the mind with the solar winds of precise and cutting cosmic purpose. Oneness with him compels the shedding of unthinking and unguided wanderings. It invokes the definition of the Absolute outlined in consciousness and formed within as a hieroglyph of childlike wonder of the Father of all. Divine Oneness is the soul's breathing-in of the solar flame that can be spun into a universal garment of Christ-magnificence by the willing-hearted.

"The mission of the sun is to extend new hope to this age. The seventh decade of the century reveals the square and the triangle, the four points and the three making the cosmic seven, standing in awareness of the decade as one of initiation for the earth.

"The current cycle of sunspots and solar flares affects the weather of the planet, the moods of its people, even business cycles, and of course the release of spiritual light-energy to the earth. One should note, therefore, not only the negative interference to the radio networks of the earth, but also the vast positive extensions of cosmic possibilities and revelations that shatter Darkness with the brilliance of new and fervent hope for the overcoming of age-old problems. Sickness, sin, and death—all forms of discord, bigotry, tyranny, struggle, and degradation—must yield before the great cosmic burst of Light; else those who continue to be advocates of Darkness and shame will find the spiral of karmic recompense becoming a lash of such chastening as to almost annihilate that portion of their consciousness which persists in identifying with unreality.

" 'The LORD is in his holy temple: let all the earth keep silence before him.' [32] The trumpet of Life sounds the approach of a new age and of an invisible overshadowing of the energies of darkness currently in vogue by the universal handwriting upon the wall that clearly says unto humanity, 'You can go no further in material ways without acknowledging the power and perfection of your God Presence, I AM.' For the Law of Cosmos declares that true Being requires true seeing—the perception of Truth.

"We call, then, for cosmic morality and for thoughts of exaltation to flood the minds of the adults of every nation in order that the proper examples can be given to the youth; for all thoughts are cast upon the ethers as seeds upon the wind, and many spring forth for good or for ill in the fallow consciousness of the youth. Thus have many unknowingly sown good or bad karma according to the thoughts that they nurtured in mind and heart. We come to strengthen hope in the world thought; and hopefully those who are responsible for making decisions of great consequence in the world community will become more receptive to the inevitable concept of the kingdoms of this world becoming the kingdom of our LORD and of his Christ. [33]

"The universal Father of all, so adored by every God-parent in the heart of every sun system, sets before the lifewaves of all worlds the singular example of Christ-magnificence; and he portrays to them, by that supreme example, the drama of perfection (of the *perfect ion*) which signifies the completion of his divine plan for the individual throughout the whole range of heavenly thought. Wherefore the drama of the Son [Sun] reveals the manifestation upon earth of the sons of God who shall see him as he is and thus be like him. [34]

"When all perceive this living example of Christ-magnificence, the faith of the world will not be content to rest in the dogma of the letter or in philosophical struggles which create competition among theologians; rather will the unity of the Spirit, uniting East, West, North, and South in the holy purposes of the cross of Life, create reverence and responsibility toward Life in the hearts of all. As these qualities live and unfold in man, ministered to by the living angels, the flaming spirits of fire, they will release cosmic distillations as of sweet incense within the temple of Being. And so in token and in fact are revealed the consideration and care of the Father of all for every aspect of creation, from the greatest sun system and sun center to the littlest sparrow that flies through the air and builds its nest in the trees.

"Every part of Life is precious unto us; therefore, our role is to convey, through the Ascended Masters' councils and through the publishing abroad of the principles of the Great White Brotherhood, the Everlasting Gospel of the Universal Christ that will open a new and living way, a high way of righteousness to the minds and hearts of men. Thus will their goals be standardized to the perfection of the Golden Rule, these same goals providing heaven with the connecting links that are required to channel the glory of God into the earthly lives of men. Then, as we send forth our rays to enrichen their hearts and minds, we will not be confined by the limited aspects of organization or personality; but we will spread abroad the canopy of a living faith upon the earth and upon the hearts of her people.

"I AM Helios of the sun system your scientists call 'our solar system'; and, together with beloved Vesta, my consort, I release now in the beginning of this decade those energies which we have held in abeyance, waiting for humanity's acceptance of the Light and for their 'miraculous expectations'. . . . This release has been ordained by the Solar Lords in order that a significant movement from out the sun might also become a significant movement in the life of each individual on earth connected thereby with us.

"And so the Brotherhood, in its many departments, is coordinating a great inner network of Life, Light, and Love directed through the Darjeeling Council. . . . The cosmic task of assisting the planet earth out of the Darkness and into the Light is therefore being effected by the continual denial (through the decrees of the sons and daughters of God) of the network of Darkness that has been spun over the planet and by the lowering from the heavenly realms of such a new level of Light into the world that it cannot help but evoke a response in those who are attuned to that Light.

"It is our hope also to enlist the aid of countless individuals who do not as yet know our names and who are unaware of the great hierarchical network of universal Light that is being invoked. These are ready, because of the inward response in their souls, to acknowledge what they have not seen as yet; and by a vital faith that no man can take from them, they are willing to hold our hands in the dark until such a time as that which is presently hidden to their eyes shall be revealed.

"We give no power, therefore, to the dark and surly mongers of human gossip, to the sordid purveyors of doubt and anguish, to the false accusers of the brethren, or to the legions of Darkness. Ours is an activity of Light; and from the Summit towers, that Light shall blaze forth and evoke tidal waves of cosmic response in the hearts of the students until there shall form in the Invisible World that dramatic reenactment of a universal ascension for a planet. This drama will show the life evolutions of earth that in the heart of God there is a supreme and universal purpose whose revelation will affect the life of every man, woman, and child upon the planet.

"Thus the wounds of the centuries and the millennia shall be healed by the hands of infinite Love that were expressed so nobly through the Galilean Master. His voice still rings clear in the voice of universal Truth, above personality yet in the Light that unites all men in their inward parts to the sacred realization of the words 'This is my Body, which is broken for you.'[35]

"I AM Helios, Advocate of the Central Sun of beloved Alpha and Omega. I, together with Vesta, salute the evolutions of this earth in that consummate sense of universal Reality and peace which ring out the joys of Cosmos everywhere, pealing the Light and repealing those human edicts that have bound men and nations. That all may learn to be free and to cherish freedom is our living prayer."[36]

Just as heaven heeds the cries of earth, so earth answers the call of heaven:

Helios and Vesta!
Helios and Vesta!
Helios and Vesta!
Let the Light flow into my being!
Let the Light expand in the center of my heart!
Let the Light expand in the center of the earth!
And let the earth be transformed into the New Day![37]

BECOMING ONE WITH ALL LIFE
THROUGH THE HOLY SPIRIT

The short tenure of man's life on earth does not permit him to delve into many fields of knowledge and still have time to make a living and seek some measure of personal happiness. A shortcut method whereby he can receive invaluable knowledge and assistance in relating the Macrocosm to the microcosm is to make contact with the Holy Spirit by expanding the flame of Life within the heart. This is the only direct and safe method of becoming truly one with all Life and thereby merging one's consciousness with the Mind of God through whose omniscience man gains an understanding of his link with eternity.

It is through the great intelligent outreach of the energies of Life itself that the individual is able to maintain contact with the many facets of God's consciousness expressed through man and Nature. These energies are focused within the heart flame of every man, woman, and child; for the heart flame is the central sun of individual Being, the candle that lights the way for the weary traveler seeking his Eternal Bourn. Through the rays of light that emanate therefrom, man's consciousness flows out to drink in the universe—"all of it," as Jesus bade his disciples do when he handed them the communion cup.[38]

The unawakened soul knows not that he is one with all Life, for he has not yet discovered the mystery of the flame of compatibility within the heart. Yet what mortal is there who has not rejoiced in the discovery of the dawn—the early rays of promise that quicken a memory, not altogether dead, of the inner man and the galaxy of Being that begins right within his own heart?

Life is not moved simply because the parts have not discovered their relationship to the Whole; it simply rolls on, at times almost resembling a car of juggernaut, to fulfill a destiny so vast as to be unmoved by the specks of dust that house evolutions of lilliputian and gargantuan concepts—a destiny that pauses to listen to the prayer of a child while conscious of worlds without end. What if man be unconscious of his place in the cosmic scheme? Nature will school the dullest wit to rejoice in a bubbling stream, a robin's call, the beckoning of a rose. And one day she will unfold the grandest fact of all: that God lives in man as He lives in Nature.

The comprehension of the Whole by the parts— or the comprehension of the parts by the parts—is often intentionally withheld from mankind by the Lords of Creation. Until it can be demonstrated to these Higher Powers and to the Divine Self that there is a worthwhile purpose for an individual to obtain the knowledge of some specific area of Life's mysteries, it is deemed wise to limit his perspective. For karma, or ordered destiny—destiny that is made to order by individual action—does direct the unfoldment of his life plan. To unravel at once for the untutored mind all of the mysteries of the universe would be to convey superhuman power before superhuman understanding could be attained.

This the God of mercy will not do. But man can make himself worthy to receive an abundance of knowledge as his soul accepts and applies the tutorings of the Holy Spirit. We shall therefore devote this section of our chapter to the instruction of the Representative of the Holy Spirit on becoming one with all Life, one with the Mind of God and its infinite manifestation, hence one with the gnosis of the Law everywhere present in man and Nature.

Inasmuch as every part of Life is a part of God, becoming one with all Life requires that we first become one with the essence, or Spirit, of that Life which is God. To become one with him is to know him as he is, and thence to know his creation, the offspring of his infinite Mind. In man and in Nature, the Father-Mother God is made relevant to the individual monad through the presence and power of the Holy Spirit.

The Paraclete, meaning Helper or Intercessor, is the integrating Principle of Life that unites the fire of the soul with the fire in the heart of Cosmos. The great feeling of belonging to Life, of being at home in the universe, comes to man as the result of the divine tie established and maintained through the Third Person of the Trinity, of whom Jesus spoke assuringly to his disciples as the Comforter. [39]

Although the vital energies of the Holy Ghost, the very essence of God himself, are found all around man in the plane of Matter—even in the space between the electrons of his atomic world—he does not recognize these energies as God nor does he experience their quickening power until he makes conscious attunement with the Spirit of Truth whom Jesus said "the world cannot receive, because it seeth him not, neither knoweth him." [40]

Those whose souls drink in the glories of Nature as an elixir of the gods have found the promised Comforter. To these the Master says, "But *ye* know him; for he dwelleth with you, and shall be in you." Wherefore, those who gaze upon the panorama of Nature and see but the material side of its manifestation, denying that God as creative intelligence, as essence, ensouls the beauty thereof, deprive themselves of the abundant resources of the Holy Spirit universally available to all.

Lecturing in his retreat in Ceylon, the Maha Chohan, who focuses the flame of the Holy Spirit on behalf of earth's evolutions, often draws the following analogy from the world of cinematography: "Man can, if he wills it so, look back from the screen of Nature to the projection lens in the Eye of God; following the light beam which passes through the film of Spirit's design, he perceives the origins of Life in the heart of the Creator, who so wondrously reveals

himself in both the spiritual and the material creation."[41] Thus he broadens his students' understanding of what it means to go back from the material
manifestation to the spiritual idea in order to find the
Source of Life and thereby to become one with the
emanations of Life that proceed from that Source.

He also explains that "the agency of the Holy
Spirit, descending as with the sound of a rushing mighty
wind on the day of Pentecost,[42] assumes a more volatile
aspect of God than that expressed in the gentle ministrations of Nature; but as the Representative of the
Holy Spirit, let me say to all that the greatest experience that can befall man in connection with the Holy
Spirit is the spiritual rebirth which occurs on an individual basis—the infiring and the infilling of his very
being and consciousness with its presence and power.

"As the Master explained to Nicodemus: 'Verily,
verily, I say unto thee, Except a man be born of water
and of the Spirit, he cannot enter into the kingdom of
God. That which is born of the flesh is flesh; and that
which is born of the Spirit is spirit. Marvel not that
I said unto thee, Ye must be born again.'[43] It is therefore the consummate purpose of the Representative
of the Holy Spirit to teach mankind how to be born
again—how to translate, by the action of the sacred
fire, that which is born of the flesh into that which is
born of the Spirit.

"Let all know, then, that the consciousness employed by man in assuming his own earthly identity
must be introverted in order that he might attune with
the God within, with the precious Flame Spirit of
Holiness posited in the center of his heart chalice.
From thence his consciousness must be extroverted:
he must begin to trace the homeward pathway of that
flame—upward through the myriad manifestations of
Nature, piercing the skyey envelope, journeying back

through the starry focuses of Solar Logoi and the cosmic hierarchical design to the very heart of creation in the Great Central Sun.

"I am well aware that the simple way is eulogized by the theologians of the world—so much so that I wish to make clear that there is nothing complex about the cosmological plan which we shall be discussing; neither is the journey in consciousness a weighty matter. The individual may with ease return in thought to the Heart of God and immediately fulfill a part of the divine purpose.

"Inasmuch as God intends to confer upon man not only the glories of conceptual reunion but also the vestments of eternal power and dominion, he is not satisfied to have man assume the role of a mere monad in manifestation; but he demands that those who would fulfill the Father's total plan shall also be able to enter into the very heart of Nature and Nature's God, there to fathom the mysteries of Life. This includes the control of both cyclic and cyclonic forces in human dimensions as well as in divine spirals. . . .

"The Holy Spirit flows through the consciousness of man in a transmutative release in order to transfer to his world the reality and power of God, effecting thereby an integration of the personal self with the Godhead. Truly this is the uniting agency of God that enables the avatar to affirm, 'I and my Father are one.'[44] Truly this is the wind that bloweth where it listeth,[45] seeking to purify the vessel and wash it whiter than snow. . . .

"It is through the Holy Spirit that the currents of Life, the essence of God himself, actually flow through the nervous and cardiovascular systems, the musculoskeletal structure, and every cell and atom of the physical form of man. It is through the Holy Spirit that they flow through his soul consciousness, including the etheric, mental, and emotional vehicles, purifying the internal facets of the mind, integrating all into conscious identification with the Christed individuality of man."

It is the responsibility of the office of the Maha Chohan to teach mankind how to contact the Holy Spirit and how to create in consciousness a climate of receptivity to the Truth it imparts. Through contact and receptivity man gains self-mastery and becomes a tower of strength not only to his family but also to his community and eventually to the planet as a whole. The Holy Spirit is the Great Unifier of the Body of God on earth. Therefore, to identify with God and with his Spirit becomes an activity of increasing joy which unites all people in the electrifying consciousness of the Divine Identity.

Through the rituals of sacred *communion (come ye into union)* taught by the Maha Chohan, the individual comes to realize who and what I AM; that where I AM the Spirit is; and that I AM one with all Life through the omniscient, omnipresent power of the Spirit of the I AM. In the bliss of Oneness the communicant is filled with the awareness of the Holy Spirit; and from the depths of his being he exclaims, "Lo, because Thou art, I AM!"

"To cast oneself adrift from the mainland of Divinity out into the restless sea of mortal thought and feeling," says the Maha Chohan, "is to shun the Holy Spirit; and this will never satisfy the great purifying Light of the Christ that God has sent into the world to bring peace and joy to the multitudes. To teach men how to tie into the mainland of their Divinity and in so doing to come into union with the Holy Spirit—this is the work of the brothers and sisters of our retreat as they serve with the angels of my band.

"It has been rightly said that many men are their own worst enemies. Be this true, it need not continue; for the Christ of every man has manifested in order to bring deliverance to each one. Social unrest may be disquieting, even as warfare disturbs the affairs of nations; but the internal warfare between the flesh and the spirit can be successfully waged only through a more complete alliance with the bulwarks of the Holy Spirit."

Standing before the assembly in the Great Hall of Learning, the Maha Chohan says: "You may think of the Holy Spirit as the *Whole-I-Spirit,* because it is the wholeness of the Spirit of the I AM in manifestation. It is the unity of the Father-Mother God made real to the consciousness of man." The stern advocate of the disciplines of the Spirit begins his instruction on attunement with the Whole-I-Spirit by making the all-important distinction between the spirit of man and the Spirit of God:

"The Spirit of God is the Spirit of Wholeness, of complete Goodness. The Spirit of God does not require perfection; it already *is* Perfection. The pristine spirit (the soul) of man can be likened unto a clean slate on which a teacher adds sums. The impressions of life, the happenings and events thereof, make their recordings upon the spirit of man as clearly as chalk marks upon a board. Man's reactions to environmental pressures and to the subtle influences of the Fiery World also make their engravings upon his spirit; but until the spirit of man becomes wholly Godlike, it cannot unite through the alchemical marriage with the Spirit of the LORD as was intended.

"While in the state of being perfected, the soul, therefore, remains unreliable as a source of absolute Truth; and the Most High must be continually contacted for direction on the initiatic path." But be assured that God the Knower can become the known in the consciousness of man and that man the known can become the Knower in the consciousness of God. For through the agency of the Holy Spirit, the balance between macrocosmic and microcosmic energies is maintained; and in the process man becomes more Godlike.

The molding factors that make it possible for the Holy Spirit to shape the destiny of the individual are listed in the following order by the Maha Chohan: "holy prayer uttered from the heart; holy meditation selflessly offered—and herein may I say that one engaged in such meditation is never too busy or too concerned with the manifestation of God's kingdom to turn aside for a moment and render assistance to his brother; holy faith persistently sought as the gift of God; holy compassion toward others that senses their struggles and desires to add not to their burdens but to their light; and holy service, symbolized in Albrecht Dürer's painting of hands extended in prayer, that continually offers hand and heart and head to be the Hand and Heart and Head of God. These attitudes held in mind will create for the individual who is constant in them an open door through which the Holy Spirit may enter in and abide."

The disciples who come to the retreat in Ceylon zealous of "getting" the Holy Spirit in ten easy lessons as it were, stand out among their more meditative brethren who hang on the Maha Chohan's every word, content to sit for eternity, if necessary, to learn the infinite way of the Law of the Spirit. Out of tender regard for all, he answers both their patience and their impatience, concluding his opening dissertation with these words:

"In great patience men must possess their souls[46] and be content to move forward from day to day until the splendor of His shining surrounds them with the great immortal aura of the Christ. For as of old, it is hard for any to 'kick against the pricks'[47] of their immortal inheritance; and all can and should bask in the radiant sun of the Holy Spirit, whose ancient loveliness lifts the sons and daughters of God to the eternal hills whence the glory of the Eternal Day continues to shine forth."

This Ascended Master, who holds the office of Great Lord (Maha Chohan) over the Seven Lords (Chohans) of the Rays, was embodied as the poet Homer and spent his final earthly incarnation quietly ministering to the needs of the people of India through his communion with the flame of Life. Among the qualifications for his office in Hierarchy is the attainment of adeptship on each of the seven rays which merge into the pure white light of the Holy Spirit. Eminently qualified to speak on the renewing of the Holy Spirit, he bases the theme of his lecture on the words of Paul to Titus "Not by works of righteousness which we have done, but according to his mercy he saved us, by the washing of regeneration, and renewing of the Holy Ghost."[48]

"The Holy Spirit," he begins, "is the ingredient of Life which is the fire of Cosmos, the germinal power in Nature; it is the power that beats the heart and infuses every form of Life with the essence of the Father-Mother God. The Holy Spirit is indigenous to every Life manifestation, and without the Holy Spirit there can be no manifestation of Life.

"When individuals forsake the Light of the Christ and of the Holy Spirit, they become literally devoid of Reality; hence the term 'not-person' or 'non-person' which has come into use in certain circles. When this happens," he explains, "even the reflected Light of Life within the person takes on the robes of Darkness.

This is why Jesus said, 'If the Light that is in thee be Darkness, how great is that Darkness!'

"The renewing action of the Holy Spirit is a purifying process, a refining action, which must take place if the not-person is to be replaced by the Real Person. For as the soul is instilled and infilled with the fire of the Holy Spirit, it identifies more and more with the Real Person and hence with all Life, thereby coming into that Oneness to which Jesus referred when he prayed, 'Father, make them one even as we are one.'"[49]

To those who would center their energies in the flame of Reality, the Maha Chohan imparts the knowledge of how to qualify the energies of the heart with divine compassion rather than with human sympathy. The ability to discriminate between these two qualities—one that is sustained by the Real Self and the other by the not-self—will enable those following in the footsteps of the Christ to make rapid strides on the path of attainment.

Let it be understood, then, that compassion, as a virtue of the comfort flame, can be achieved only through attunement with the Real Man, through identification with the Christ, whereas sympathy is achieved solely through identification with the ego-personality in oneself and in others. The devotee of Reality must therefore learn first of all to have compassion for himself—for the human consciousness that is in the state of becoming divine. Only then will he learn to have compassion for others.

Compassion may manifest in the wisdom of the Law which always chooses the better way, even though that way may be momentarily painful; or it may manifest in the disciplines of the Spirit and the fires thereof which consume human indulgences and the pseudo-loves of the not-self. Compassion is ever the flame that draws the lower self into congruence with the Christ Self. It is a determined *seeing* of the divine blueprint for every part of Life, and it is a determined *knowing* that allows nothing to stand in the way of the individual fulfillment of that blueprint.

By contrast, sympathy, an emotion generated by the impure thoughts and feelings of man, places the lower self in direct agreement with the human ego and its personality patterns. Sympathy is agreeing with a human being where you find him, allowing him to feel sorry for himself, to indulge in his weaknesses, and to lick the wounds of his pride. Sympathy draws the individual into the whirlpool of human chaos and ties up his energies in the day-to-day melodrama of the mass consciousness, thereby aiding and abetting the weight of human pathos upon the planetary body.

The compassion of the Saviour is of course decidedly disagreeable to the carnal mind, which takes offense in the statement of the Christ Mind "Think not that I AM come to send peace on earth: I came not to send peace, but a sword." [50] Nevertheless, the compassion of the One who comes to save that which was lost [51] *must* be in disagreement with imperfection and in agreement with perfection. The Christ would not be the Christ if he did not speak to the lower selves of all men, saying, "Come up higher."

The compassionate heart flows with the stream of the Christ consciousness that binds up the wounds of the brokenhearted and heals the sinful consciousness of the world; and in so doing it becomes one with the heart of God, one with all Life. On the other hand, the sympathetic movements of the emotions, flowing with the stream of the mass consciousness, multiply the sorrow and travail of the exiles of Eden, who thereby become one with the not-selves, the pseudo-images of the race. Ultimately the consciousness of the

sympathizers merges with the spirals of disintegration
and death which carry their synthetic images into
oblivion, whereas the compassionate ones rise upon
the very cycles of virtue which they have embraced
and ascend into the immortal consciousness of God.

Well aware of the fact that dry dogma and theological speculation can never be substituted for the
vital action of the Holy Spirit coming into intimate
contact with the individual, the Maha Chohan admonishes his students to speak the word of welcome to
God as Jesus did and to invite his Spirit to come in and
sup with them. Pointing to the Master as the great
example of one whose life was imbued with the Holy
Spirit—his whole consciousness being saturated with
its influence—he explains that the alchemy of the
divine Sonship manifest in Jesus was itself a consummation of the Fatherhood of God. "Therefore," he
says, "it could well be spoken of him, 'The zeal of
thine house hath eaten me up.'"[52]

Jesus' great zeal for the LORD's Spirit and his
constant communion with "our Father which art in
heaven"[53] enabled him to sustain a brilliant flame
upon the altar of his heart, a piercing fire that proclaimed liberty to the captives of sense thralldom and
opened the prison doors to those bound by the sickness of sensuality.[54] Of such extraordinary dimension
was this fire that John bore witness of him as "a burning and a shining light."[55] Thus the zeal of the Holy
Spirit consumed the remnants of the human personality in his followers, enabling them to testify of the
Presence of the sacred fire in *mani*festation.

It was, then, in the bonds of a fiery devotion to
the Holy Spirit that Jesus achieved that cosmic oneness with Life which enabled him to commune with
the Divine Father and the Divine Mother and with all
who looked to him for wholeness and for contact with

Reality. In his devotion to God and man, expressed in life and in parable, we discover the secret of Jesus' strength and we learn how the Prince of Peace kept the flame of peace midst the turmoil of the world's rejection of the Christ.

The Maha Chohan explains how men's love of Darkness makes them susceptible to a dark dogma and a dark theology and how their love of the Holy Spirit can lead them out of the labyrinth of intellectual error into the light of Truth: "Men whose deeds are evil often love Darkness rather than Light;[56] and there is a fruit of Darkness, an evolution of Darkness, which proceeds from dreary minds damp with rank emotionalism; unsatisfied even with self-adulation, they remain fettered by the conditionings of mortality.

"The Son of God is not so, and the Spirit of God is not so; for the Spirit of God moves across the margent of the world bestowing at will his gift of Reality to every man. Far above the speculations of the mortal mind that are used to justify a way of life, the Spirit of God transcends human philosophy and replaces it with the divine theosophy. Searching out the vastness of the Divine Self and translating it for the human self, the power of the Word lights man's path that he may clearly see the way to go.

"Of all the heartrending problems encountered by mankind upon this planet, the one that is most trying to spiritual seekers is the question, Which is the correct or true Path? Many are the innocent lambs of God who know not that there are traps laid for them, nor do they expect to find wolves in sheep's clothing[57] preaching from the pulpits of the world. They have not reckoned with those unregenerate spirits who have spawned a Luciferian theology to keep the children of God from finding the true Path. Jesus said, "I AM the Way";[58] but the Sadducees and Pharisees have loudly proclaimed another way and through their sorcery have exercised a hypnotic control over the people. Practicing black magic as blatantly today as they did in the Dark Ages, they bind the faithful to doctrine and personality through their satanic lies of hellfire and damnation.

"Wise are the disciples of God who will understand, then, that there are abroad in the world false doctrines in large number created out of the whole cloth by men whose consciousness has been contaminated through personality worship with the silt of their own sensual concepts. Those who would know the Truth and thus be free[59] must understand that many of these gross figures surround themselves with an aura of sanctity, profundity, and peace, combined with the mystique of veiled prophecy. Thus, those who require the exclusiveness of a personality cult are often sucked into the 'hallowed circle' of the false prophets who succeed in playing God by playing upon the credulity of the masses.

"The Holy Spirit speaks with great plainness and forthrightness; nevertheless, the laws of God, so obvious and so charged with common sense, so apparent in Nature and so natural to the heart of man, are often ignored for the dimwitted complexities of intellectual sophistry. Those who rise to positions of prominence in the religious community have no qualms about fabricating a multitude of rationalizations that confuse the people and in some cases even inspire them to espouse noble causes when for a time it suits their ends.

"In this day when the elect can indeed be deceived,[60] it is necessary that we stimulate among mankind the desire for the correct understanding of the spiritual path. Initiations abound; and the circumstances of initiation, whereby mankind's devotion to

Truth is tested from day to day, are often brought about through the ministrations of the Holy Spirit coordinated through the office of the Cosmic Christ. When these initiations are passed, the unfolding soul awareness of man is caught up into the arms of God and revitalized in His blessed consciousness of the Truth that indeed makes all men free. . . . *

"God and his Spirit have desired to draw mankind not away and apart, but upward and together into the realm of spiritual regeneration where the brotherhood of man, uniting with the Fatherhood of God, perceives the bond of the Holy Spirit as the cement of cosmic unity. There is no need, then, for men to fear when the battle for men's minds is bursting all around them; rather should they seek the association of the Ascended Masters of Light, the true and faithful witnesses of the Law, and the sanctity of the Divine Presence that is both above and within.

"Let your search for the true religion of God be one of diligence and not of discouragement. Did he not say, 'Seek, and ye shall find'?[61] Therefore, accept the promise and bid the Spirit of God welcome in your world. If you would make a place in the temple of your being for the LORD's Spirit, you must end feelings of hostility toward all men, toward the self, and even toward the justice of the Law that in exacting its toll may have caused you some distress. Let the

---

*When the Holy Spirit infills the soul gradually through the initiatic process, each gain is permanent because man is first required to master the laws and cycles governing the greater increment of Light which he desires to magnetize to his world. On the other hand, when the Holy Spirit comes upon the supplicant suddenly in response to fervent invocation, it is a man's faith rather than his understanding which evokes the response from the Godhead. The energies he receives in this manner will diminish as he once again takes on the vestments of wordly living; for he has not learned how to retain the fires of the Spirit within the cup of consciousness or to make the garment of the LORD his very own. Of these two approaches to "getting" the Holy Spirit, the Ascended Masters recommend the former as the safer and surer method.

love-light of God occupy your eye and heart; and let
the flow of His Spirit through you be as the wind from
the mountain: a penetrating call to action. As the
LORD liveth, his Spirit is the Great Activator of all that
is holy and mighty within you!

"Men have deceived themselves; but through
God they shall be awakened from the darkness of
self-deceit, and the hand of mortal error that was laid
upon them shall be lifted. Shadows upon the Path are
dissipated by the initiatic light, and the bond of true
devotion unites hearts as never before. The Brotherhood seeks the practical manifestation of the Spirit as
a balm of fervent action that will lift the burdens of
mankind. Then shall all be changed in the twinkling
of the Eye of God,[62] and the veil that hung between
the spirit of man and the Spirit of God shall be rent in
twain.[63] Then shall man know that he is ready to be
fashioned by His Spirit in the Divine Image; then
shall man himself transfer from heaven to earth the
perfect pattern for a planet and its evolutions."

The cosmic conception of the universe as "the
place where the Lord lay"[64] is the key to the understanding of Jesus' universal consciousness of God and
man. Knowing that God and man coexist throughout
Cosmos, he demonstrated the principle of cosmic
interaction—of energy flow from Idea to action, from
Action to idea—from Idea as God fulfilled in action as
man, and from Action as God fulfilled in idea as man.
Only through the omnipresent potential of the Holy
Spirit does this interchange between God and man,
focused in the Christ, become possible. Jesus' proof of
the laws governing the cosmic flow was therefore
dependent upon his vital contact with the Holy Spirit,
and therein did he achieve his oneness with all Life.

Giving his students the same instruction which
Jesus received prior to his final three-year ministry—

that which all initiates of the sacred fire must have to prepare for the rigors of mastery—the Maha Chohan declares with the full authority of his office: "The Holy Spirit is the omnipresence of God; it saturates all space and hallows that space, but it concentrates in greater measure where the call that goes forth to the heart of God compels the answer of the descent of his abiding grace. Those who drink lovingly, almost ravenously, of the Spirit of God are thus opening the doorway for the light of Love to flow from my heart to theirs.

"As the Representative of the Holy Spirit, I can do no less than abide where the Spirit of God is; and as your Advocate of Completeness, I desire to imbue you with the power that God has placed as a sacred gift in my hand. Whensoever his Spirit cometh upon you and dwelleth in you, then are you truly brethren of the divine action; and the fruit of that action as the joint endeavor of God and man will manifest in your world as the delight of his Law in your heart, as the joy of his Law in your mind, and as the meditation of his Law in the forcefield of your being.

"These gifts of the Spirit shall then be yours to project as hope to those standing in the shadow of doubt, as healing to those who, lacking wholeness, need a physician,[65] and as the great Light that shall be seen by all who walk in darkness.[66] Your life will then become a mission on behalf of the Holy Spirit; following in the footsteps of the avatars and Elder Brothers of the race, you will, by His authority and grace, prepare the way for the great golden age to come into the consciousness of men even as they are transformed and renewed by the Christ Mind."[67]

When mankind desecrate the place prepared for the LORD's Spirit, the temple of being, they bring upon themselves "the abomination of desolation standing in the holy place where it ought not"[68] instead of the divine approbation "This is my beloved Son, in whom I am well pleased."[69] This is the choice which the Holy Spirit gives to all: the raising up of the individual consciousness through the raising up of the Holy Spirit in man or the desecration of the individual consciousness through the desecration of the Holy Spirit in man. The choice is always man's, for God has already chosen.

"It was and is and shall forever remain the purpose of the Father-Mother God to imbue the creation with their own Spirit; for in that Spirit lie the best gifts and the greatest blessings that Life can afford—the completeness, the wholeness, the oneness of Being. No external palliatives could ever equal the great internal consolation of the LORD's Spirit that sweeps man out of the depths of mortal delusion into the heights of immortal Reality—into the sweet sense of eternal Life in the Spirit of God, which abideth and dwelleth forever in those who have sanctified and exalted his name in the dome of consciousness.

"When men become conditioned to the ways of the not-self—with its obstinance, pride, sensuality, and spiritual blindness—they are acquiescing to the awful robe of Darkness which the prophet Daniel referred to as the abomination of desolation. When men reject their divine opportunity and fail to respond to the knocking of the Spirit of Life upon the door of their hearts, they open themselves up to subtle forms of self-annihilation which, all too late, bring them to their knees before God in a most desolate and helpless state of consciousness. If the energies of Life are squandered in riotous living and eternal values are meanly thrown aside for the pauperism of fleshly gain which in a moment is swept away and lost forever, truly what shall it profit a man if he shall gain the whole world and lose his soul[70]—the only means he has of implementing his spiritual opportunity?. . .

THE DRAGON SHALT THOU TRAMPLE

Thou shalt tread upon the lion and adder: the young lion and the dragon shalt thou trample under feet.

page 348

RENUNCIATION OF THE PAST

And God shall wipe away all tears from their eyes; and there shall be no more death, neither sorrow, nor crying, neither shall there be any more pain: for the former things are passed away.

Revelation 21:4

JOHN THE REVELATOR

In the beginning was the Word, and the Word was with God, and the Word was God.

The same was in the beginning with God.

All things were made by him; and without him was not any thing made that was made.

In him was Life; and the Life was the Light of men.

And the Light shineth in darkness; and the darkness comprehended it not.

John 1:1–5

"Me Ye Have Not Always"

Jesus said: "Let her alone: against the day of my burying hath she kept this. For the poor always ye have with you; but me ye have not always."

THE PEACE-COMMANDING PRESENCE

I AM the peace-commanding Presence of the Holy Spirit exercising full God-control in the planes of air and water. Fire and earth likewise joyously mold themselves to the Christic design when man affirms the God-power inherent within the intelligent, obedient, loving desire of the electron to flow into the perfect pattern.

page 384

Having Received, Retain!

Above all, having received, retain / Whate'er gift God hath given unto thee, / That ere the sun set each day / Thou shalt have cleansed thy being / Of all perceptions vain and hapless / And readied thyself through eventide / To enter into immortal peace / In the hours of the night while thy body sleeps / To dream the immortal dream / And to be one who gathers / Of the flame of God's Spirit in greater measure / And fullness, that as the new day breaketh, / Thy energies, made holy and pure, / Rising as the incense of devotion, / Shall invoke for all who are thy friends of Light / Some new miracle of consciousness.

THE MISSION OF THE DIVINE FEMININE

The immaculate conception of the Christ is ordained in the perfect union of Spirit and Matter where heaven and earth meet.

page 396

MAN'S CHOICE

"This is my beloved Son, in whom I am well pleased." This is the choice which the Holy Spirit gives to all: the raising up of the individual consciousness through the raising up of the Holy Spirit in man or the desecration of the individual consciousness through the desecration of the Holy Spirit in man. The choice is always man's, for God has already chosen.

page 426

VOICE OF INNER FLAME

You must begin to harmonize your life by an invocation to the sacred fire that the LORD may enter your being and there reestablish the Holy of Holies of his flaming consciousness.

page 428

WASHED UPON THE SHORES OF LIFE

The cosmic tide is incoming; as a giant wave of light, it inundates entire solar systems. Those who ride the crest to victory will witness the dawn of a new order of the ages. Those who resist will be lost in oblivion to be remembered no more. Through personal and planetary cataclysm, men and nations washed upon the shores of Life are brought to the feet of their Creator.

page 482

THE MERGING OF TWIN FLAMES

We have spoken of the Holy Spirit as the all-pervading essence of the Father-Mother God, the merging of the fires of the twin flames of Deity made tangible through the Christ in Spirit and in Matter.

page 490

Keeper of the Scrolls

*I call heaven and earth to record this day against you, that
I have set before you Life and Death, blessing and cursing: therefore
choose Life, that both thou and thy seed may live.*

Deuteronomy 30:19

El Morya Speaks on the Path of Chelaship and the Founding of The Summit Lighthouse

Chelas of the Will of God:

The tall pines of Darjeeling move against the morning light. A day is born. It is a day of opportunity. Just as knowledge that is unused is lost, so knowledge without love is brittle. The mists in the foothills are for the watering of life. And the love of the Holy Spirit nourishes the soul in time of travail.

The path to our abode is steep. The way is fraught with unknown dangers, yet the peaks of pride are more jagged than the uncharted heights. I come to clear the way for the chelas of God's will—those who would become chelas of the Ascended Masters.

Let it be made clear at the beginning that all who read the words of the Ascended Masters and all who hear our word are not necessarily counted as chelas of our will. Let it be quite clear that there are requirements. As the chips of wood fly when the pines in the forest are cleared, so the winds of Darjeeling blow. Let the unworthy chela be cleared from our path. We clear for a noble purpose—the ennoblement of a cause and a race. Hierarchy has also said, "Let the chips fall where they may!"

The strong gaze of the true Master is upon the stalwart. The weak-willed, unable to look upon their own image, can scarcely receive our eye. I write for those who have a will to change; for transmutation is the requirement of the hour. I direct this series to those moving in the wind of the Aquarian cycle. To those who would move into the new dispensation yet know not the way to go I say, there is a path. Step by step it has been carved by the initiates of the sacred fire.

Over thousands of years the barefooted devotees have worn a trail over the rocks.

The way is known of us. It can also be known by you. In support of Saint Germain, Master of the Aquarian Age, exponent of the flame of freedom to mankind, I place the jewel of my crown upon the altar of the Great White Brotherhood, that those who have lost the way may find it again.

As it is written in scripture, "There is a way that seemeth right unto a man, but the end thereof are the ways of death." The way that seemeth right is the way of reason—and that not of the eternal Logos, but of the consciousness that is bound to the laws of mortality. Hence its ways are the ways of the death of the Christ consciousness.

I am come to bring life in the tradition of the Master of Galilee. He came that all might have Life, and that more abundantly. His way is the way of grace. His grace is oil for the gears of the law and for the meshing of the teeth of the deeds of righteousness. I would free those who would be freed.

Until men recognize the darkness, they do not reach for the Light. Thus the grossness of materialism and of a mechanistic civilization continues unchallenged. To challenge, men must have a sword; and the sword is the sacred Word of truth to this age.

The Darjeeling Council is a unit of Hierarchy. I am its chief. Numbered among those who deliberate in our chambers are Saint Germain, Mary the Mother, Jesus the Christ, the Master Kuthumi, Chananda, the Great Divine Director, Lord Maitreya, and the Ascended Master Godfre. Assisted by many unascended chelas, we serve the cause of the will of God among humanity, in the governments of the nations, in the economic councils, in the social strata, in the institutions of learning, and above all, in the diamond hearts of the devotees.

Those who see the crumbling of the old order look for the new. The path of chelaship is the way of transition. For those who would arrive at the station of the new cycle, we provide answers and a formula. And there is no turning back. In those in whom selfishness has not marred the vision of the new day, there is the burning desire to be free and to make that freedom available to all.

Such was the purpose of the Darjeeling Council in the founding of The Summit Lighthouse in Washington, D.C., in 1958. With humble beginnings, yet with the torch of our trust passed from God and anchored in the heart of a band of devotees, we built our organization—an outer arm of the Great White Brotherhood, a forum for the will of God, a focus for the purity of its fiery core.

Mark Prophet—and later his twin flame, Elizabeth—was trained by me to be a Messenger for that Hierarchy of adepts composed of all who have graduated from earth's schoolroom with honor. These are they who have mastered the laws of their own karma and by the pursuit of the Buddhic light have been thrust from the wheel of rebirth. These are the ascended ones whose souls have been lifted into the glory of the life universal and triumphant. By their striving on the way, by their excellence in self-discipline, and by the grace of Christ, they are the overcomers. Having not been found wanting in any thing, they have entered into eternal communion with the fount of reality through the ritual of the ascension.

To ascend into the plane of reality as they have done, you must garner within your soul the thrust of power, wisdom, and love. To transcend planes of consciousness, to make the giant leap into the arms of God—this requires thrust. Therefore from the wellspring of Life, out of the fount of living flame which Almighty God has anchored within your heart, draw forth the thrust of faith, hope, and charity.

Whether Christian or Jew, Moslem or Zen Buddhist, or none of these, know, O seeker after higher reality, that the path of initiation can be trod wherever you are. But *you* must take the first step. My responsibility is to guide and guard: yours is to follow.

With the full faculties of mind and heart and soul, you chart the course of your life. If you desire, the grid of Hierarchy and of initiation through Hierarchy can be superimposed upon your chart. If you have not the desire for initiation, if there be no longing to replace the old man with the new, if there be no desiring for freedom, then you cannot magnetize the molecules of our momentum on the path, nor will you magnetize the mind of the Great Initiator who provides not only the testing, but the wherewithal to pass the tests.

Hierarchy comes forth to reveal truth to the age. We gather together the atoms of self-determination. The new year is the open door for initiation. Our call is to the many who have come of age, who are ready to be received by their own Christ-identity. For the dispensation has gone forth from the Lords of Karma that a million souls presently evolving on this planet—a certain million whose evolutionary time has come—might be given a more than ordinary assistance on the path of life. These will feel the emanations of our word. These will know the presence of the Ascended Masters. Though yet unseen, that presence will be clearly marked by divine direction and by inspiration leading to solutions to current world problems.

To chelas throughout the world I dictate this series through our Messenger, Elizabeth Clare Prophet, called by Saint Germain to hold the office of Mother of the Flame. Let all who are moved by the flame of their own consciousness to pursue the high road of inner reality elect to follow the path of the elect of God. These are they who throughout the ages, in every walk of life, both within and without the Church, have chosen the bands of his will. These have banded together to define the laws of science, mathematics, and the geometry of the soul; these have pursued culture, education, the arts and music out of the desiring to merge with the laws of Cosmos that are the will of every man's being.

Let all who perceive the need to nourish the flame of consciousness prepare to work with the Mother of the Flame and the Darjeeling Masters for the enlightenment of the race through the discipline of the self.

I AM a mentor of the Spirit,

El Morya

Reprinted from *The Chela and the Path* by El Morya, pp. 13–17.

"You must, then, teach those who look to you for guidance to look to the Eternal Now as the nexus of the Spirit through which the radiant stream of God's energy is pouring in order that the patterns of thought and feeling akin to the love of God and his Sons might be generated in them by the agency of his Spirit. . . .

"The admonishment of the Christ 'Feed my lambs,'[71] made two thousand years ago to Peter, comes full circle today as you become the instrument for the silent ministrations of the Holy Ghost that touch these little ones—heart, head, and hand. As I have spoken to you to generate in you love and respect for this vital force of God that flows into the family of humankind, wedding all nations and peoples to the Higher Way, it is preparatory to the Second Coming of the Christ.

"And as I have spoken to you, you must speak to others; for the Holy Spirit admonishes men to be up and doing—to prepare the way of the LORD, to make straight in the desert a highway for our God.[72] It refutes the passive attitude that sits back and waits for a personal saviour or the hand of destiny to deal with mankind's problems and to bring the race to judgment. Those who forbear actively challenging the evil of their day—although they themselves may lead a righteous life—are the very ones who will be found wanting at the hour of reckoning. This is the message of the Holy Spirit that must be heeded, told, and retold if men are to find salvation through a faith reactivated and revitalized."

Harmony is the very first lesson in self-mastery taught by the Maha Chohan to the neophyte class in his retreat—harmony in thought, which begets the harmony of controlled action; harmony in the emotions, which begets harmony in the spoken word. Once certain basic exercises in the principles of harmony are mastered, he then explains that the disciple is responsible for harmonizing not only the present

flow of energy in his world but also the flow of the
past. This he is taught to do by systematically reclaim-
ing, by the authority of the Christ, all discordant
energies that he has allowed to pass through the nexus
of his consciousness since his fall from grace.

Although this may at first seem an overwhelming task, the Maha Chohan quickly assures them that
with God and with a correct knowledge of his laws, all
things are indeed possible.[73] If you would move a
mountain, you must begin with the first shovelful of
earth; and if you would progress on the Path, you
must begin with the first erg of misqualified energy.
You must begin to harmonize your life by an invocation to the sacred fire that the LORD may enter your
being and there reestablish the Holy of Holies of his
flaming consciousness. There can be no harmony with
Life, no inner or outer peace, until a man's debts to
God and his fellowman are paid. Since these debts are
always made in moments of uncontrol, the attainment
of God-control through God-harmony is a way of life
at the Maha Chohan's retreat.

In our next two chapters on karma and reembodiment, it will be seen that man is in his present
state of evolution on this planet simply because he has
not balanced his accounts with Life. At the close of
many preceding lifetimes, his ledger has been on the
debit side, which means that he has qualified more of
his daily allotment of energy with evil than with
good—with discord rather than concord.

Coming into embodiment with the scales of
karma unbalanced, the soul, in its intense longing for
direct contact with God, often experiences great frustration. Blinded by the negative effects of his own past
actions, man cannot see the way to go. He yearns to
commune with higher expressions of God and to find
the answers to his questions about Life, but these the

Law withholds from him according to the weight of his own sin. Not surprisingly, the accumulation of misqualified energy within the electronic belt, which we call negative karma, also prevents him from making contact with other souls who are likewise buried beneath the debris of their own spiritual neglect. The Maha Chohan recommends that "any frustration in thought and feeling involving the spiritual search should be translated into a spur—a chastisement of the LORD given to those whom he loves[74] that they may gird up the talents of their lifestream in the pursuit of a cosmic purpose and a cosmic identity."

It becomes increasingly clear to the devotee that the goal of oneness with all Life that is reached through oneness with the Holy Spirit is not only desirable but absolutely necessary if he is to pass beyond the first levels of initiation. Failure to attain this goal is failure to attain. Either man is an island or he is part of the continent of God's being. He cannot be both. And if he choose to remain an island separated from other islands, his progress toward the mainland of his own Divinity must cease. By the law of mutuality, in order for man to get to God he must first get to the heart of himself and to the heart of his fellowman.

Thus we learn at the feet of the Maha Chohan that the first requirement of becoming one with Life is that we face the responsibility of our karma and our *dharma,* which, simply put, are our debts and our duties to God and man; for only by so doing can we overcome the obstructions of the mortal consciousness and pass freely into the stillness of the flame of the Holy Spirit, there in quiet communion to realize our oneness with Life.

When asked by one in the circle of devotees the same question which was asked of Jesus, "Good Master, what shall I do to inherit eternal Life?[75] What

shall I do to become one with the Life that is God?"
the Maha Chohan replies:

"The accretion of neglect in the karmic record is
the mark of the unprofitable servant.[76] When men fail
to use the talents given unto them, hiding them in the
folds of their garments, their creative faculties become dulled through the idling of the flow of the Holy
Spirit. The Holy Spirit serves as Wayshower unto
those who will let go of their own way, which leads to
self-condemnation that is no part of the Divine Self,
and embrace the divine Way. Those who turn to God
repentant and meek receive the ministrations of his
Spirit as long as they pursue the path of righteousness;
because he is nigh at hand, even at the very door, they
can begin a new era of soul progress in their dealings
with the infinite Law of Being.

"Let it be understood that there is no attitude
more calculated to turn the heart of man to stone than
that of fleeing from karmic responsibilities and from
the working-out of circumstances in which the individual finds himself as the result of his previous
actions. New stations in life should be sought only
when the karmic scales are balanced—when debts
with the parties involved have been cleared and past
accounts have been settled fairly.

"As part of the system of initiation evolved by
the Brotherhood for the lifewaves of this planet, individuals are often brought together with those who
cause them great distress of mind and heart in order
that they may work out their karmic patterns through
mutual service. The temptation is ever to cast aside the
unpleasant responsibility and to find temporary peace
by fleeing the chastisement of the Law. This is particularly true within families and organizations where
individuals of differing polarities are often thrown together—seemingly piecemeal, but actually by karmic

decree—into situations that require adjustment before further progress can be made.

"There is no doubt in the minds of the Lords of Karma, who have arranged many such situations to exact the highest virtue from the souls of men, that if the individuals were to avoid personality clashes by going their separate ways, a greater measure of personal peace would come. Let it be clear, however, that the avoidance of all conflict and the isolation of oneself in a mountaintop retreat or in a tower of aloneness, whether in the midst of a great city or far from the madding crowd, often creates an atmosphere of synthetic peace [77] and safety which contributes neither to the growth of the soul nor to its freedom from old karmic ties.

"Debts to Life, in the name of wisdom, must be paid! If men have wronged others, they must undo their wrongs and in the process learn how to do well. Thus, in the great citadel of life the spiritual as well as the material needs of man are served through the Holy Spirit. By invocation to its flame the pain of penance is lessened, and lifestreams forced to rub elbows can without pride or rancor roll up their sleeves and enter into a sincere labor of love on behalf of one another and all mankind.

"You do not know nor can you imagine what a joy it is to the soul to feel free from the pride of person, a disease which has long engaged mankind's energies in the mold of a frightful futility. The strength of the soul is developed through a universal concept of love; but if this universal concept is to justly serve its purpose, it must become personal and practical as men apply the unguents of love to the wounds of those whom they have afflicted in yesteryear.

"So often men flee the presence of individuals with whom they have karma as though reeling from an old hurt. The reopened wound aggravates the memory of an ancient encounter; the fires of animosity are rekindled; and more negative karma is made than balanced. What a pity when the fire of the heart might well have been invoked to blaze forth and consume all that ever transpired between friends or enemies that was less than God's perfection!

"How quickly the flames of God respond to the fervent call of the soul for love, for forgiveness, and for balance to manifest! How much easier it is to transmute past wrongs than it is to perpetuate them! How much more advantageous it would be to personal and planetary progress if men would welcome the knock of Opportunity upon the door of the heart!

"Soul redemption is soul freedom, and only the free soul can become one with all Life. The strains of the melody from the heart of God 'O Love that will not let me go' strengthen man's resolve to not let go until the last farthing of his karma is paid.[78] As God will not let go of man, even in his wayward state, so man must not let go of man; brother must bear the burden of brother—even in his wayward state. And Jacob said to the angel (symbol of the Light challenging his karmic densities) at the breaking of the day (the dawn of the Christ within his consciousness), 'I will not let thee go, except thou bless me!'[79]

"Thus, each opportunity for karmic adjustment should be seized as the universal joy of the Holy Spirit floods the consciousness with the rays of the morning, imbuing the soul with the humble desire to be 'my brother's keeper.'[80] The cooperative industries of nations and peoples are spurred by their understanding of the purposes of life on earth, not the least of which is the working-out of the cycles of individual and group karma. Through a correct apprehension of the relationship of souls to one another and to the Holy Spirit, mortal involvements are put aside and man joyously pursues the path of discipleship, balancing his karma and entering into such rewarding friend-ships as are forged in Christ."

Another disciple eagerly raises his hand; when recognized by a nod of the Master's head, he asks: "But Lord, what can we do when we are forced to deal with old habit patterns of mortal thought and feeling re-created over and again by the multitudes who are ignorant of karmic law? How can we deal with the recalcitrance of those who remain uncommitted to the principles of the Holy Spirit?" The Maha Chohan replies:

"Unfortunately, as you have observed, much of the turmoil in the world today has been occasioned by the re-creation of old habit patterns of thought and feeling. These enemies of the soul continually trespass upon the race consciousness, disturbing the peace that ought to be the personal property of men and nations. This, of course, they have no right to do; but it is up to each individual to drive them from the sacred ground[81] of his consciousness where he would en-shrine the image of the Christ.

"In reality, precious ones, the Holy Spirit desires to give peace and comfort unto everyone upon the planetary body; but the 'peace I leave with you,' the 'peace I give unto you,'[82] can be enjoyed only as the reward for honest labor. Saint Francis, in his prayer 'Lord, make me an instrument of thy peace,' desired to convey the comforting aspects of the Holy Spirit, realizing that his God Self and not his lower self was the Source of that peace. He knew that by letting God's peace flow through him, like the wind rustling in the trees, he would become one with the Spirit, hence one with all Life that proceedeth there-from. Because his prayer to the Holy Spirit was utterly selfless, it left an indelible imprint upon the con-sciousness of mankind and elemental life.

"Consider your life, then, as though it were a giant press imprinting hieroglyphs upon the ages. And then see with what consideration of comfort you can begin to engrave the designs of the Holy Spirit upon the building blocks of creation in man and Nature. Erase the defenses of the personal self which are always reacting against the offenses of others. Let them go! For they have never served the cause of comfort. As you become a free agent of the Christ, an activator of cycles of comfort to Life, you will begin to move with the great wheel of the Law that liberates mankind from the grinding of the karmic millstone.

"You live in a time when a greater bond betwixt heaven and earth must be forged, when the purposes of true religion must be served, and the old timeworn dogmas replaced by an infusion of Life and purposed faith within all mankind. For if the budding truths of the Law are to replace the undergrowth of religious error upon the planet, enlightenment must first take place within people. The sweet sense of the Holy Spirit as the Master Comforter of Life is intended to be shared by all. Therefore let none through fear, whether of theology or of theologian, deny themselves the right to receive it as the patent Identity of God."

Those whose reverence for God as Life, and Life as God, has enabled them to understand the goal of becoming one with all Life as primary must be prepared to deal with certain prevailing conditions which might otherwise prevent them from achieving the goal. A problem requiring serious consideration by those working for the unification of men and nations upon this planet is that the Body of God upon earth, in the words of the Maha Chohan, consists of "broken fragments which all too often are found warring with one another."

"The pure Christian traditions have been warped by men's misinterpretations of Christ's theology, which for the most part have resulted from the incomplete record of his teachings available to them. Needless to say, this has created an awful confusion among the brethren. The purposes of God which were destined to unite the hearts of men through the treasures of spiritual law have, through the depredations of men and the false zeal thereof, been turned into a sword of division, piercing humanity's longing for Christ-unity and producing a mounting debt to Life.

"Allying themselves with those of like mind, separating into camps of mutual hostility, individuals steeped in personal delusion do not consider the possibility that their own misinterpretation of Truth might be the cause of the attrition of their ranks; thus they fail to recognize that their brother, in whom they see so much wrong, might indeed have correctly apprehended some aspect of God's Law. Straining at the gnats of personal perception, they swallow the camel[83] of an almost universal division in their ordered services for the holy cause of God.

"It is the function of the Holy Spirit to act as the unifying principle in all Life; but I ask you, precious ones, when the ministrations of the Spirit are rejected, where is the possibility of continued effort on behalf of unity? The Lords of Karma, who by divine appointment are responsible for the administration of divine justice on earth, have been forced to deny petitions made to them and unto God simply because the Great Law could not grant more energy to be expended in a failing cause. Because of the bigotries and religious hatreds of their followers, often based on an incomplete understanding of the Law, many religious movements have become sterile; meanwhile, individuals continue to bemoan the awful travesty of disunity, failing to see that the power of change lies within their own hands.

"We have asked the Karmic Board what can be done to meet the challenges of this division. Can we justify further vast expenditures of energy on behalf of those who have pocketed themselves within the cells of their own narrow beliefs and refused to heed aught else? For the record clearly shows that these accomplish little more than the branding of their neighbor as a heretic, in some cases attempting to prevent the publication of his material or his renting of halls for the dissemination of Truth, in other cases attacking him directly with cunning and slander. And this in the name of religion!

"We believe that the answer lies in the building of the kingdom of God within the domain of the receptive soul. Therefore, the Lords of Karma have decided that the greatest justice is to grant the energy of the passed torch to those spiritually advanced movements of the world who will enter into no degree of unbrotherly feeling against other groups who either misunderstand the Law or who refuse to work with those whose concepts may differ from their own.

"Our intent is to increase the ministration of the Holy Spirit everywhere upon earth. We shall not, then, deny to those who lack true spiritual understanding the blessings which their own level of comprehension allows; but we shall ask for an increase of cosmic energy on behalf of those advanced spiritual teachers who have expounded the laws of God for many a year, who have cleaved unto Good with the fullness of their being, and who, where Truth is concerned, have stood ready to receive the revelations of the Holy Spirit even when these challenged their most cherished beliefs. These have extolled the laws of God and reproved within their own consciousness any and all concepts based on a lesser understanding of Truth, replacing them on the moment, when the Great Law demanded it, with the expeditious grace of God and his progressive revelation.

"There are so many manufactured divisions, so many religious persuasions, blessed ones, that it is indeed heartening to see the simplicity of the childlike mind, ready and willing to grasp each amplification of divine grace and knowledge dispensed from God's own hand with the timeliness of cosmic law. . . .

"There are in the world today a large number of devotees of humanity—such as those of you who have assembled here in our retreat—who yearn to magnetize the glow of the comfort flame on behalf of their brethren. These also desire to mobilize an effective means of contact whereby the individual soul can come to know the needs of others and, by the mystical touch of the Holy Spirit, reach out to aid every part of Life. This is magnanimity in the fullest sense of the word; it is the faint echo of perfection within the corridors of memory recalled from the vast halls of learning wherein the Mind of God and man do meet.

"The Temple of Concord is a holy place. Those who have worshiped there, kneeling at the feet of the God Presence, know the measure and worth of the highest devotion that, in forsaking all selfish desire, receives the highest reward. These emerge from their communion with the Holy Spirit ready to translate the strands of immortal opportunity into a great tapestry of Reality. Weaving vestments of hope for all people, they portray the drama of the Second Coming of Christ and illumine a darkening world.

"We know full well, however, that the theories of theologians, ancient and modern, whose purpose should be to impart a greater sense of God's reality, have often had the opposite effect, causing men to feel far and apart from the heart of their Creator. By contrast, the Holy Spirit has had no other purpose than to draw men closer to God through an enlightened theology—closer to Good and into the great bonds of the universal brotherhood of God and man.

"Men ask themselves, as you have asked me, how they can unite with children of error. If they would only realize that they do not have to unite with children of error, but with children of God in whom error dwells and from whom error must be expelled! We often wonder at the strange attitude of mortals who stagger and stumble over the fact that other mortals are not manifesting perfection. If they were dwelling in the higher octaves of heaven's beautiful light, they could expect to find immortals manifesting perfection. But as long as they dwell upon earth, where souls are mortifying human error, they must learn to live with the imperfections that temporarily manifest in others and to be unto them as the Holy Spirit is unto all—a deliverer in God's name.

"Many have no desire to be in attunement with any among mankind, choosing to remain in the consciousness of the not-self outside the circle of God's love. Because man has free will, you cannot always enter into complete rapport with all people; but you can become one with the Christ in all and with the Real Self that is the true Being of man."

"Is it possible, then, for us to help those who would divest themselves of their densities but seem helpless to effect change in their own worlds, much less in the world at large?" asks another eager postulant.

"Yes, it is possible, as long as you have their consent. In order to fully understand the answer to this question, it would be well if you would contemplate the statement of the Master Jesus concerning the casting out of demons 'This kind goeth not out but by prayer and fasting.' [84]

"This doctrine of Christ-principle is intended to teach mankind that when the forces of negation are deeply entrenched within the mind and heart of man (within the four lower bodies and the personality, for they can never abide within the Real Self), they hold an iron rule over the psyche. Because of long association with their subject and the deeply ingrained habits that he has taken on under their influence, the demons, who actually live off of his energy, violently oppose any attempt of the Christ to enter in and take dominion in the individual consciousness.

"Possessiveness is ever the quality of the Evil One; therefore those who would use the power of the Holy Spirit to cast out demons from others must themselves be free from possession. They must understand the need for faith, hope, and charity, as well as humility, as they garner the energies of the Holy Spirit in readiness for the freeing of the obsessed. Attempting to possess neither the soul nor the demon that has held it bound, they must seek to be possessed of God; for it is the Divinity within man that is his authority to cast out all evil forces that prey upon the minds of men.

"Man's consciousness must be totally possessed of the Holy Spirit* if he would have access to the power

---

*Those who would speak in tongues must beware of the forces of Antichrist that impersonate the Holy Spirit. Taking over the consciousness of the untutored who have not yet established the divine tie, they can produce dangerous tremblings in the psyche which cause the separation of the four lower bodies; moreover, these forces often speak through them—not in tongues of angels, but in the language of demons. And because the aspirant is sincere, he knows not that he has been duped. Wise, then, is he who pursues the mark of the Holy Spirit as the mark of enlightened self-mastery.

that effectively purges the Darkness of obsession. Being possessed of the LORD's Spirit is not bondage, but a bond of love that makes man the instrument of the Christ, honoring his laws and serving his purposes every hour of the day and night. Possessed of the great flaming balance of God's Love, Wisdom, and Power, you have every right to demand from Life an expansion of all divine qualities within your world and to use the energies thereof for the freedom of your fellowmen; but you must bear in mind the need to have a request for assistance either from the one obsessed or from those responsible for him.

"No matter how zealous your regard of the needs of another, it is dangerous for you to enter in where you have not been invited. Interference with the lives of others establishes karmic ties and energy cycles that will one day rebound upon the shores of your own being. Such ineptness, often rooted in spiritual pride, will only give you more to handle without necessarily bestowing freedom upon the one who has sought neither the assistance of the Holy Spirit nor your own.

"When you are asked for help by an individual or by a member of his family who longs to see him free, you must be ready to hold your attunement with the great power of the Holy Spirit and to in faith draw down that power into the world of the obsessed individual. If you have given your consciousness to God and you maintain a constant attunement with the Holy Spirit, then when you speak to the demon and command him with a loud voice, saying, 'In the name of Jesus the Christ, I command you to come out of him!' you can expect immediate results. Where the possessing demons are deeply entrenched, prayer and fasting for one to three days will provide the devotee with clarity of mind and an impetus of the Spirit, thereby making him a better instrument for the casting out of dark forces that have tormented a child of God.*

"Restoration, then, is an action of the Holy Spirit; and in your service to Life you must not neglect the restoration of the temple of your own being. We expect those on the spiritual path to understand that the fruit of purification must be sought by them before they attempt to impart it to others. Devotees of God must be unafraid to perform the ritual of self-purification, knowing that the fruits of their devotion can only bring closer attunement with the Holy Spirit and richer blessings to all Life. When men begin to study the laws that govern the casting out of unclean spirits, they will see that they cannot have an excess of holiness; for to be a friend of the LORD and to secure his favor on behalf of those in need, they must be pure and sinless in his sight.

"In the mainstream of human thought and feeling, there have been generated over the centuries tremendous quantities of negation that hang as a thick pall of effluvia between the souls of men and the Spirit of God, preventing the divine reunion. Because mankind do not see this pollution of the astral, mental, and etheric planes—although the more sensitive feel it— I cannot fail to stress to all upon the planet the need to make contact with the Holy Spirit as the Agent of God whose fires will burn a pathway through the night and reestablish man's contact with the I AM Presence.

"Those who would bow to divine edicts must, above all, adore the ministration of the Holy Spirit as the brightest light in a darkened world and the mightiest hope for humanity's freedom. To those who would

*N.B. The Ascended Masters do not recommend that their disciples undertake fasts lasting more than three days unless they are directly under the guidance and protection of a Master, inasmuch as prolonged fasting may result in the loss of one's spiritual faculties and even in demon possession, the very state the disciple seeks to overcome.

increase the tempo of the lovebeat of God within their hearts and sustain an activity of the divine similitude within their consciousness, the Holy Spirit is the Great Energizer of all right motive and conduct and the means whereby the ever mounting tides of the holier way will crest their worlds as the abundance of every good and perfect gift."

As the advocate of man's contact with the Infinite, the Holy Spirit speaks of the divine bond as the guarantee of God, the assurance that he will not leave man comfortless. The Holy Spirit is charged by the law of divine agency with establishing the contract of Life with individual man. "Just as the Almighty guarantees his bond of Life with man and backs that bond with eternal promises, so the LORD deserves to have his covenants observed by man," says the Maha Chohan. "He deserves to have full representation and no misrepresentation by those who profess to love him and to serve his cause. Man must extend comfort to every part of Life in whom the eternal Spirit dwells. Just as God will not deny man comfort, so man must not deny comfort to God.

"The Holy Spirit will often fill the soul with floods of rejoicing, particularly as the individual walks and talks with God in greater measure. To some among mankind, talking with God as with dearest friend may at first seem strange. Yet you must assure them that there is no safer or surer method of getting immediate results, of 'getting' the Holy Spirit and feeling a flow of radiant personal comfort in their world, than to practice this ritual of 'sensing' the divine tie. The words 'My yoke is easy and my burden is Light'[85] should be revered in the mind and heart as a certification of the promises of God fulfilled in his creation— a certification of the garment of God's hopes that men may rejoice to wear. . . .

"The tide of God's love flows in tangible currents to the souls of men through the Holy Spirit, ordained by God as the universal link between heaven and earth. As a bubbling spring, as a fountain of eternal youth uplifting mind and heart, the surge of the Holy Spirit is the resurgence of the Christ consciousness in man.

"Where the Spirit of the LORD abides, there abides the Spirit of the Son. Where the Holy Spirit dwells, there dwells the Father-Mother God with the Son. The transfiguration of Jesus, wherein Moses and Elijah appeared unto Peter, James, and John through their communion with the eternal God made possible by the agency of the Holy Spirit, caused them to exclaim, 'It is good for us to be here: if thou wilt, let us make here three tabernacles!'[86] This manifestation of the eternal Christ portrays the great boon of heavenly comfort that is bestowed by the Holy Spirit upon all who seek diligently to know God through his emissaries. . . .

"The God of Abraham, of Isaac and Jacob, the eternal God of our Fathers, is no myth, but a tangible, breathing, vibrant reality. He can be known as infinitely real, even within the circle of the finite world. He can quickly infill and inspire and animate all things. He can raise the dead and breathe the breath of Life into a newborn babe. He overflows the banks of mortality, enhancing joy in service and the bonds of eternal Reality, so that wherever you live or move or have your being, you know that you are alive within his Spirit and that his Spirit is alive within you. Thus many a moment which might otherwise be surfeited with the boredom of a self-centered ego can become instantaneously productive of the joyous communication established through the eternal tie between the Spirit of God and the spirit of man.

"When the spirit of man flows into the Spirit of God and the Spirit of God flows into the spirit of man, there is a divine exchange—a cosmic transmutation—and both God and man enjoy the feeling of sharing and of belonging to one another. No longer severed from any part of Life, the soul perceives itself a pilgrim among other pilgrims upon the path of progress. The hand of fellowship extended with great expectation from moment to moment imparts the tenderness of that patience which possesses the soul.

"Thus will God be glorified in you and in all creation; thus in an age destined for freedom—one that has been stretched upon the racks of bondage—will freedom and its flame be the means to the divine end that raises the soul into its great eternal realm of immortal blessedness."

SERVANTS OF GOD AND MAN IN NATURE

Representing the cosmic Hierarchy to the Nature kingdom through the fires of resurrection which bathe the earth in the glorious rebirth of springtide, Amaryllis, directress of the forces and rites of spring, speaks to us of the wonders of God precipitated by elemental life. By way of introducing herself she says:

"Those who are not familiar with me as a person must understand that God intends to make each monad, each person, familiar to all persons. For when the universal perfection of God is served as heaven designed it, each person is found to be the indispensable manifestation that has locked within its cellular identity the mystery of the cosmic circle of Life." [87]

Upon the cadences of Rubinstein's Melody in F, our consciousness flows with this figure of the Divine Feminine in Nature. Like the elementals that troop after her billowing garments, our eyes follow her every movement. Awed by her transparent beauty, we watch as she advances among the flowers and the grasses, through meadow and forest, tenderly caressing Life in all its aspects with the rainbow rays that adorn her loveliness in the resurrection spiral.

"Unity with God is unity with Nature!" proclaims the Mother of Spring. "Therefore, open the pores of your minds to the Godhead, to the stimulus of universal beauty, and to the acceptance of responsibility in whatever walk of life you have chosen!

"It cannot be that Nature would ever become insensitive to the dicta of the Universal Christ manifest within you. When the Master said to the raging elements, 'Peace, be still!'[88] when he uttered the fiat 'Be still, and know that I AM God!'[89] it was the Universal Presence speaking through him. There is no desecration here: man, made in the divine image and restored to His divine image and likeness, can assert that divine dominion which was his original conferment: 'Take dominion over the earth and subdue it!'

"The key to man's reunion with God through Nature is dominion, and dominion is exalted in the simplicity of the divine order: man made a little lower than the angels, crowned with glory and honor.[90] The universal potential which God has locked within every cell and atom of man's being—his physical, emotional, mental, and etheric identity—harks back to the supreme moment of creation when all beauty and perfection went forth in divine procession to do God's will."

Thus Amaryllis speaks to joyous, willing hearts. And she is heard by the carefree and the innocent—those to whom Nature is the intimate friend, those for whom a deeper communion with the Holy Spirit has become the dominant movement in the symphony of Life:

"In those landed areas of the earth where the four seasons flourish, the miraculous advent of spring brings to the waking hearts of men a sense of the renewal of Life. But to those of us who are privileged to see from inner levels through the veil of manifestation, the wonder is increased.

"Man presupposes, in his limited frame of reference, that the programming that makes for perfect manifestation is inherent within substance itself. Little do men dream—that is, men who reckon according to material science without benefit of spiritual science—of the vast network of higher intelligences who function in magnificent consonance behind the screen of Nature. But when they are apprised of the existence of the guardian spirits, they are able to have a greater appreciation of the so-called miracles of Nature. Going beyond a mere acknowledgment of these higher intelligences serving under the Divine Presence, they may actually enter into communion with the beings who are responsible for the riot of color and the tender expressions of abundance in verdant Nature. Then they may learn to apprehend the science of Nature—including both material and spiritual science—which is even more exact than the scientists of this world imagine.

"Little children, uninhibited by form concepts and hard dogmatic lines, are able to commune with Nature in a manner that beggars description. They could not, if they were asked, tell the feelings that they have within their hearts as they wander barefoot in a dew-kissed field, as they fling their hands toward the lacy clouds and with consummate abandon cast aside all care in the wondrous awareness of Life everywhere. For Life is God; it is the surge of his Presence, his creative pre-essence, his all-penetrating love. . . .

"Cast aside, then, this unwanted feeling, this hardness of heart—call it brittleness or fear, for they are the same—and enjoy the throbbing Presence of God in Nature and self. This Presence is your own, but it also belongs to all. You will find in the surrender of the tiny self to the allness of God a welling-up of the feeling of universal brotherhood which is the hum of the universe: *Om mani padme hum!** The flowering of the spiritual lotus portends the opening of the soul who yearns to drink in God and his compassion. This compassion manifests through the child of Love, the child of Nature, who sees in all of this reckless, wild abandon the order and sincerity of universal Intelligence prescribing itself according to divine decree.

"Thou hast appointed the bounds of life: its limitations are created by Thee. Nature is the servant of God and the servant of man. Nature is kindred to all that is lovely; and Nature, when cherished and honored, produces all that is grand and noble. Nature, unchained, functions unnaturally in her raw estate. When the human will would bind her to the thralldom of the senses and have her believe the lie that God is dead, that life is simply a struggle between relative states of imperfection tumbling toward some semblance of social order, Nature rebels. By contrast, the boundlessness of the will of God and the great onrush of perfection, with all of its buoyancy, has that restraint of the hierarchs of Nature that was beautifully inspired by the Most High to stimulate order and perfection in all things. . . .

---

*Hail, thou jewel in the heart of the lotus! The *National Geographic* magazine (vol. 123, no. 5 [May 1963]:686) gave the following translation: OM—I invoke the path and experience of universality, so that MANI—the jeweline luminosity of my immortal mind PADME—be unfolded within the depths of the lotus-center of awakened consciousness HUM—and I be wafted by the ecstasy of breaking through all bonds and horizons.

"Every part of Life blends with every other part, and the heaven of God possesses that magnificent outreach which excludes none but includes all. Those powers and forces which have allied themselves with the dark but contrast the power of the Light to free man for immortality. In the messages of the flowers and the trees, men see aspiration reaching toward heaven; they see beauty flourish everywhere in glorious fulfillment. Why, then, should any man cast aside his divine birthright for sensuous living and the senseless struggle between egos when the great continents of the air await the coming of the Higher Mind? For the Mind of Christ communed of old with Nature, and through his oneness with Nature he did receive the power to control the elements.

"Modern man and modern mystic, as they once again draw nigh to God, will find the power of God drawing nigh to them; and the Holy Spirit will regenerate within them that unity by which they shall ultimately come to be the harmonizing power of the natural order of all things. Nature herself cannot bear to deny a proper response to such as these. Therefore, in taking Christ-dominion, in basking in the flame of the resurrection, in ascending in consciousness to folds of natural immortality, men obtain a release of the dominant power of God into their worlds."

When God created man and commanded him to be fruitful in service, to multiply His graces, and to take dominion over the earth, He gave him helpers to assist in the expansion of His kingdom. Angelic ministrants and elemental servants of earth, air, fire, and water formed the cosmic retinue that accompanied the sons and daughters of God as they descended to earth "trailing clouds of glory" and vowing, "Lo, I AM come to do thy will, O God!"[91]

During three golden ages man talked freely with his God and associated intimately with angels and elementals; communion with all Life was unrestrained and cooperation between angels, elementals, and men was unspoiled. To man was given the assignment of overseeing the creation and working with God to execute the divine plan—to design, to invent, and to direct. To the elementals, the builders of form, was given the important task of bringing into manifestation the intents of God and man. And to the angels was given the holy ordination of ministering to the spiritual and emotional needs of both men and elementals.

Thus, within the framework of Nature there functions a divine Hierarchy of guardian spirits comprised of cosmic and lesser evolved beings—Solar Lords; Gods and Goddesses of galaxies and sun systems; the mighty Elohim, together with their divine complements; directors of the elements; angel devas;* and builders of form. Yes, even the legendary gnomes, sylphs, undines, and salamanders are a very real and indispensable part of Hierarchy. Their joint services, coordinated through the agency of the Holy Spirit and directed by the regents of the kingdoms of earth, air, fire, and water, include the stepping down of cosmic energies released from Helios and Vesta, the solar hierarchs, for the balance of the four seasons; the control of climatic conditions and of the cycles of seedtime and harvest; and the interchange between man and the animal, vegetable, and mineral kingdoms.

Presided over by Virgo and Pelleur, twin flames in cosmic service, the earth element is maintained by the gnomes, who hold the balance of natural forces for the planet and see to it that all things living are supplied with their daily needs. Aries and Thor, administrators of the air element, are assisted by the sylphs, who control the flow of the air currents and the patterns of atmospheric conditions, helping mankind

*A deva is an angel that works specifically with elementals.

to keep the great continents of the air free of pollution. Overseeing the water element and the balance of life therein, Neptune and Luara, together with the undines in their command, govern the tides of the seas and the waters under the sea, precipitation over the landed areas, and purification of water wherever it is found—even in the body of man. Oromasis and Diana are responsible for the fire element. Their fiery salamanders, working closely with the gnomes, sylphs, and undines, are the great coordinators of the sacred fire in man and Nature. Drawing upon the fires of the atom, they imbue the entire creation with the energies of God necessary to sustain life on earth.

HIERARCHS OF THE NATURE KINGDOM
Representing the Four Cosmic Forces
of the Holy Spirit under the Elohim

	Fire	Air	Water	Earth
Regents of the Elements and Their Twin Flames	Oromasis Diana	Thor Aries	Neptune Luara	Pelleur Virgo
Servants of the Elements	Salamanders	Sylphs	Undines	Gnomes

One who appreciates the services of the elementals—one whom God named Rose of Light—speaks of the wonders of spring made tangible through Nature's helpers:

"Flood o'er the souls of men, O God, the wonders of thy love! Pour forth from thy fountain deep the all-consuming splendor of thy knowledge bright with hope! The wonders of immortal Love have never been expressed, save in part; however, in the hope of man for thy all-engulfing splendor to reveal the light of Allness springs forth the strong pursuit of Life to find itself aflame with Reality.

"I am come this day to remind you of the onrushing tide of eternal spring, incoming with natural grace and the perfumed lyrics of the immortal Breath—visible form of invisible Love in action. Fairies, elves, sylphs, undines, salamanders leap in the flame of springtime's buoyant glory. How splendid is this paradise! The tiny elementals were designed by the Architect of infinite wonder to tenderly enfold all natural form with the magical broadcasts of their radiating love-energy and to serve through the four seasons to make earth redundant with beauty, comfort, adornment, and providential supply of all substance. How grateful I am for their constancy!

"Thou shalt not contaminate the elements with outpoured discord! Rather, call unto the precious Spirit of Comfort from the heart of the Maha Chohan for their release from the weight of human effluvia. Appreciation stems from the heart whose cup runneth over, bringing an expansion of the power of Life to all who are ready to receive it. Become, then, self-widening channels for the expanding love of the Nature kingdom by pouring the devotion of your heart flame to the elementals, and receive in return the wonderful blessing of their highly serviceable friendship.

"The Ascended Masters utilize the love and harmony of elemental life to implement the immortal plan of God. The elementals are the natural manifestation of divine care in action. The Father endowed these stalwart ones, whom Francis knew intimately as brother and sister, with the emerald flame of constancy that they might sustain a platform to bless all evolving upon this broad expanse of land and sea and sky—all who dwell upon the earth that is the LORD's and the fullness thereof.[92]

"Springtime and resurrection are complements of Jesus' victory over death and over the very thought of life as finite. The whirling leaves that descended last fall have changed their shape and color, lost their moisture, and begun to pass through the change from the formed to the formless; but the primal energies thereof will, if not this year then in one soon to come, arise garbed in some new and splendid form. Thus all Life continues to evolve in the perpetual cycles of infinite purpose. Beloved Jesus' supreme example likewise speaks to sensitive souls of the wonderful love of God, whose gift of Life is not for just a moment, but for an eternal forever. . . .

"Cherished offering of victory, O lilies of the field that toil not,[93] floral trumpets of resurrection, I AM the promise of Light fulfilled in every hue of Nature, bold and minute, and in crowned and un-crowned servants of eternal purpose! Let the glory of the resurrection blossom now in every heart as it does in the foreverness of the eternal spring!"[94]

A being of Love's promise fulfilled, the Lady Master Rose of Light focuses the light from her heart in a golden pink rose whose abundant petals deli-cately unfold the Christ consciousness for angel devas, elementals, and child-man. She explains that man-kind must cooperate with the elementals if they would solve the mounting problems of ecology and master their environment.

Without a cooperative attitude and a tender regard for these tireless servants, without a grateful acknowledgment of their very existence, mankind unknowingly cut themselves off from the great cosmic flow of Life generated by the Holy Spirit and released into their hands each day through the ministrations of the blessed elementals. As manna from heaven, as daily bread, this flow is the divine love that meets every human need. Nature's craftsmen are the hands and feet of the Holy Spirit. Through the dexterity of their consciousness the descending cycle of divine love is passed from God to man; in the ritual of their service the spirals of precipitation from Spirit to Matter are consummated.

Describing his intimate oneness with his disciples, Jesus said, "I AM the vine, ye are the branches."[95] In a like manner the Holy Spirit tenderly regards the elementals as the Body of God in manifestation. The statement of Jesus "This is my Body, which is broken for you" takes on another dimension when spoken from the lips of the Maha Chohan. We see the elementals as fragments of the LORD's Body, extensions of his very Being in the world of form. They are his disciples *in deed.*[96]

They are the leaves of the Tree of Life that are for the healing of the nations.[97] They are the petals of the rose emitting the fragrant purpose of the flowering bush—the bush that burns with the sacred fire but is not consumed.[98] Their sole purpose in life is to transfer the essence of the Holy Ghost to child-man that he might receive and absorb through Nature the energies of the living Word. Theirs is to joyfully execute the will of God as it is expressed by man and to bring forth and preserve the pristine patterns of the Christ in all of his noble endeavors.

The lowering of the God-idea from the plane of Spirit into active manifestation in the plane of Matter is the only life they know, the only happiness they seek; and their reward is with them. At times subject to frightful abuse, they nevertheless remain devoted to man, whose needs they were created to serve, whose mandates they are bound to carry out.

Fortunately and unfortunately, the little spirits—perhaps we should say "sprites" to distinguish them from more evolved parts of Life—have a certain plasticity in their makeup, an almost chameleonlike quality that causes them to readily take on the vibrations of their surroundings. The originators of mime, they are imitators of the first order. However, their facility in duplicating the designs inherent within the creation is not confined to the realm of perfection, but extends into the realm of imperfection.

Elemental life is dependent upon man in his role as the discriminator of Good and Evil that it might fulfill its role as the precipitator of Good in the earth below as it is in the heavens above. It is therefore unable to express perfection in the natural order as long as man continues to express imperfection in the ordering of his life and consciousness.

As man's discriminating faculties diminished during the thousands of years of his sojourn outside Eden, imbalances in Nature continued to mount; meanwhile, the efforts of both men and elementals to cope with their ecology became increasingly divergent, until cooperation between them was almost nonexistent. With the zeal of a sorcerer's apprentice, the elementals responded to the influences of men, both harmful and benign; and their mimicry of humanity's discordant thoughts and feelings resulted in the turbulence of raging seas, the roaring of uncontrolled fire, volcanic eruption, the breaking and shaking of the earth, and the shifting of entire landmasses.

When, after the Fall from grace, mankind began to create negative karma with one another, the forces of Nature became the instruments of karmic judgment meted out by the Lords of Karma. Famine and pestilence, drought and flood returned to man the thrust of his rebellion against natural law, his extravagant waste of natural resources, and his defiance of Life's oneness.

Although he knew it not, man was beset with the problems of ecology—which in effect are the problems of his karma—the day he was banished from Eden. "Cursed is the ground for thy sake!" rang the judgment of the LORD God. "In sorrow shalt thou eat of it all the days of thy life; thorns also and thistles shall it bring forth to thee; and thou shalt eat the herb of the field." Nor was woman spared the challenges of fulfilling her role in a hostile environment: "I will greatly multiply thy sorrow and thy conception; in sorrow thou shalt bring forth children...."[99] Mournful as they beheld the plight of man, the beings of the elements, under the direction of the Elohim, dutifully carried out the karmic edicts of the Almighty; for as King Nebuchadnezzar, and many others who have challenged the LORD, finally concluded, "None can stay his hand, or say unto him, What doest thou?"[100]

While the Holy Spirit remains the indispensable link to man's oneness with Life, the elementals are the indispensable agents of the Holy Spirit in Nature. Not only are they responsible for sustaining life upon the planetary body, but they are also the caretakers of the body temples of all mankind. Since the descent of the soul into physical embodiment—since "the LORD God formed man of the dust of the ground, and breathed into his nostrils the breath of Life"[101]—a *body elemental* has been assigned as his unseen bodyguard and personal physician.

This devoted servant is man's constant companion throughout his numerous incarnations. Working under the direction of the Christ Self and the I AM Presence, to whom he bows as the Great Regenerator of Life, the body elemental lowers into physical manifestation the electronic pattern and the etheric blueprint of the lifestream. From the moment rebirth is announced by the Lords of Karma and conception takes place, the body elemental of the incoming soul joins forces with the body elementals of the father and mother, forming a trinity in action under orders to coalesce the energies of Father, Son, and Holy Spirit within each cell of the developing embryo.*

Executing their assignment with Christly aplomb, the three together magnetize the currents of the Holy Spirit from the heart of the atom and from the heart of the I AM Presence—their goal, to create a masterpiece in form, the body temple of man that will one day be consecrated by the Holy Spirit as the temple of the living God. Governed by karmic law, these artisans of the Spirit can outpicture only those virtues of Christ-identity which the soul itself has outpictured through the four lower bodies during past eras of accomplishment. Drawing upon the archives of the etheric body, they reproduce in form that which man has decreed himself to be through thought, word, and deed. Thus man is truly self-made and he remains the architect of his own microcosm.

As the LORD's triumvirate appointed to direct the flow of Life into the archetypal patterns of the soul, the body elementals labor twenty-four hours a day employing the cycles of the four elements to bring forth in the plane of Matter the greatest perfection recorded by the individual in the plane of Spirit. Under the direction of the Divine Mother and using the energy allotment awarded the incoming lifestream by the Lords of Karma and the Holy Spirit, they weave the heart chalice with golden-pink threads of love and wisdom which he has spun in previous lives. Their delicate carving of the skeletal frame and the brain show forth his rapport with the Father and the Son,

---

*Where the father is not present, his Christ Self directs the light rays to the mother to assist in the development of the child.

while the quality of the cardiovascular and nervous systems reveals his meditation upon the Mother flame and the Holy Spirit. Each organ focuses a spiral of attainment, or a lack of it, as the case may be; and the *liver,* as the focus of the etheric memory of the soul, contains the *live records* of all qualification of energy in the lower chakras.

Whereas each living cell is a miniature solar system imbued with the flame of the Christ at its heart center, the body elemental cannot build the body cells as fitting temples for the flame unless the soul in its previous incarnations has gathered enough light to provide the energy for the task. It cannot produce in Matter that which man has not attained in Spirit. Although an artisan par excellence, he must have the natural resources to create a perfect work of art.

The alchemy of his endeavor is to a great extent dependent upon the accessibility of the necessary elements derived from the mother's body and her nutritional intake according to dietary law. In addition to the karma of the child, which determines who the parents shall be and even the characteristics of the genes and chromosomes passed on to him, the key factor in precipitating the perfect body as the perfect vehicle for mind and soul is the enlightened attitude of the mother and father. For upon their attunement with the Holy Spirit the flow of Life into the delicate matrix of the manchild depends.

At the end of the second month of gestation, the Holy Spirit descends into the embryonic earth body with "a sound from heaven as of a rushing mighty wind"; and the voice of divine authority, speaking in the stillness of the soul, echoes in the chambers of the womb: "Awake, thou that sleepest!" With these words the Spirit of Life enters the manchild and quickens the heartbeat in rhythm with the heart of God. Ripples of joy swirl in the body of the mother. The Light has come—the Light that illumines the holy night of Matter with the flame of Spirit's own Self-awareness.

When the Star of the Presence is positioned over the manger—the place prepared for the soul's earthly incarnation—and the cosmic timetable indicates the arrival of the hour for the soul to enter the birth canal, the signal is relayed by the Christ Self to the three body elementals—the "three wise men" who initiate the ritual we observe as the birth process. From the moment the umbilical cord is cut and the threefold flame is lit by the Holy Spirit*—who breathes into his nostrils the breath of Life—until it is extinguished at the close of the earthly cycle, the body elemental serves the needs of the evolving soul on the physical plane even as the angelic hosts minister to his needs on the emotional and mental planes.

When we pause to consider the words of Jesus "I will not leave you comfortless," [102] we are awed by the marvelous plan of God to bring the comfort of the Holy Spirit to every aspect of man's being and consciousness. These faithful helpers in their numberless numbers are arrayed on the hillsides of the world as the army of the Great Helper. Keepers of the Flame in the truest sense of the word, they keep the fires of the body cells burning brightly in imitation of their Lord, the Keeper of the Flame.†

Alchemists of the highest order, the body elementals interpret the divine science of the Holy Spirit within the physical body of man, while their cohorts serving under the hierarchs of the four elements interpret the sacred science within the body of the planet earth. Thanks to all elemental life, man has both a personal and a planetary platform for his solar evolution—a forcefield uniquely his own through which

*See page 281.
†Because of his pledge to all mankind "I AM keeping the flame for you until you are able," the Maha Chohan is called the Keeper of the Flame.

he may master the plane of Matter, balance and expand his threefold flame, and ascend back to the plane of Spirit.

Innocent and childlike, masterful and intelligent, the body elemental stands approximately three feet tall, almost an exact replica of his master—sometimes a caricature of the human, sometimes the epitome of the Divine, but always a mimic of his moods and mandates. Whether man decrees "I am well" or "I am sick," "I feel good" or "I feel bad," the body elemental is the genie that appears to carry out his wish— man's karma his only limitation.

The body elemental is the playmate that children often see and that parents have come to accept as part of their "make-believe" world. Dressing according to the mode of the individual's consciousness, this unseen helper dons the garb that most resembles either the predominant quality currently being expressed by the lifestream or one that is outstanding from the past.

Whether or not man acknowledges the existence of the body elemental and his responsibility to deal justly with this servant, the elemental takes his orders from him and acts according to his will. All of man's thoughts and feelings are electronically transferred to him and he immediately outpictures them within the cells of the body temple. Thus, man often makes himself ill by first making his body elemental ill. He trains his servant to think negatively and to feel negative, and his servant obeys. Whereas man's doubts and fears completely paralyze the body elemental, a positive attitude toward life releases him to establish man's health and well-being.

Just as sylphs and salamanders, gnomes and undines are bowed down by the planetary effluvia, so mankind's body elementals are severely handicapped by the mass consciousness. If the individual is possessed by demons or is under a negative influence, the body elemental cannot help but be affected. Thus an ailing physical body can be symptomatic of the contamination of the aura and the control of the consciousness by forces untethered to the Christ. Unless challenged in the name of the Christ, these intruders can prevent the body elemental from effectively performing his service. Prevention being the best and safest cure, it behooves man to make daily invocations to the Christ Self for the freedom and protection of the body elemental from all foreign interference and from all that is not of the Light.

The source of the energy that the body elemental uses in servicing the physical body is man's own heart flame and the light emanations of the chakras. If these centers, which are for the distribution of energy from the heart to the four lower bodies, are covered with astral effluvia, the body elemental is hindered in his attempts to bring forth perfection on the physical plane. The more light the individual has lowered into the forcefield of his being, the more light the body elemental has to work with as he tends the flame upon the altar of the body temple.

Unlike other elementals, the body elemental enjoys a type of immortality. Created simultaneously with the physical body of man, he becomes a part of the evolving soul consciousness as it gains experience in the plane of Matter. Between the soul's embodiments the body elemental identifies with the etheric counterpart and is prepared with the soul for the next incarnation. Recharged by the Christ Self for the service ahead, the body elemental assumes the form of the sometimes changing polarity—masculine or feminine—of the body that the soul will inhabit.

The body elemental gains immortality only when

the soul earns his ascension. Having no further need
for a physical body, the soul no longer requires the
services of the body elemental, who likewise is freed
from the rounds of reembodiment and the burdens of
human density. Having attained through service, the
body elemental may be retained by the Ascended Master as an immortal aid. Ascended twin flames, each
possessing such a friend, make a spiritual foursome.
The immortal bond between the Master and his aid is
one without parallel in the human scene except, perhaps, in the loyalty of a Damon and Pythias.

While man is totally dependent upon Nature,
waiting upon the seasons and the weather, the health
and the moods of the body to plan his activities,
Nature's obedient servants await man's loving guidance and encouragement. Having become somewhat
retiring as the result of mankind's disregard, they feel
unwelcome in the company of those who fail to appreciate their humble efforts; moreover, they are repelled
by mankind's hardness of heart and worldly sophistication. Therefore, if he would truly enjoy their friendship, man must once again become as a little child; he
must renew his acquaintance with Nature's servants
and enter into communion with this most important
aspect of Life; he must invite not only his own body
elemental but all elementals everywhere to cooperate
with him in a concerted action on behalf of humanity.
Then he must give them the authority and the energy
allotment of his own lifestream, commanding them
to go forth to do the works of Christ—north, south,
east, west—fire, water, air, earth—throughout the planetary body.

We are admonished by the Holy Spirit to enfold
this faithful attendant in a glow of gratitude from our
heart chalice and to visualize a flaming pink ovoid pulsating all around him. Love is the universal language

of Nature's guardians to which they never fail to respond. Each compassionate regard from man is joyously communicated from one to another, forming a
chain reaction around the globe and returning to man
the original lovebeat he sent forth, amplified a million
times by a million elementals thankful for the opportunity to serve.

The following invocation for Christ-wholeness
shows how the student may (1) call his own body elemental into action and (2) command his atoms, cells,
and electrons to "Be all Light!" These two steps are
necessary if man would take dominion over the earth
plane. By the power of the spoken Word, he can thus
draw forth the universal energies of the Holy Spirit
into a highly concentrated focus of the sacred fire
wherever it is needed for the healing of body, mind,
and soul. By making this natural resource abundantly
available to both the body elemental and the body cells,
man becomes the manifestation of Christ-wholeness
and ultimately the master of his world.

Invocation for Christ-Wholeness

In the name of God, I AM, individualized
in me, my beloved Holy Christ Self, and beloved Jesus the Christ, I pour forth my love and
gratitude to my beloved body elemental for his
faithful service always. (Pause to visualize your
precious body elemental in an ovoid of the pink
flame of Divine Love.)

I now command my body elemental to
arise and take complete dominion over every
imperfect condition which may be manifesting
within my physical body! Beloved body elemental, move into action now to mend the flaws
under the guidance and direction of my own
Christ Self, beloved Jesus the Christ, and the
immaculate design of my lifestream released

from the heart of my own Mighty I AM God
Presence—O Thou Great Regenerator!

In the name of the Presence of God which
I AM and by and through the magnetic power of
the sacred fire vested in the threefold flame
burning within my heart, I decree:

1. I AM God's perfection manifest
   In body, mind, and soul—
   I AM God's direction flowing
   To heal and keep me whole!

Chorus: O atoms, cells, electrons
   Within this form of mine,
   Let Heaven's own perfection
   Make me now divine!
   The spirals of Christ wholeness
   Enfold me by his might—
   I AM the Master Presence
   Commanding, "Be all Light!"

2. I AM God's perfect image:
   My form is charged by Love;
   Let shadows now diminish,
   Be blessed by Comfort's Dove!

3. O blessed Jesus, Master dear,
   Send thy ray of healing here;
   Fill me with thy Life above,
   Raise me in thine arms of Love!

4. I AM Christ's healing Presence,
   All shining like a mercy sun—
   I AM that pure perfection,
   My perfect healing won!

5. I charge and charge and charge myself
   With radiant I AM Light—
   I feel the flow of purity
   That now makes all things right!

And in full faith I consciously accept this manifest, manifest, manifest! (3x) right here and now with full power, eternally sustained, all-powerfully active, ever expanding and world enfolding, until all are wholly ascended in the Light and free!

Beloved I AM! Beloved I AM! Beloved I AM!

The Man of Galilee was master of the elemental forces serving the planetary body, all of whom were eager to support his mission and to assist his every effort for the upliftment of humanity. Bowing to the great Light he bore, they strewed his path with floral offerings and obeyed his alchemical fiats. And so it is not surprising that the deep desire of the Son of God to set the elementals free from the impositions of mankind's misguided energies has not diminished from the hour of his ascension unto the present.

At an Easter conference held by the Brotherhood in Washington, D.C., under the auspices of The Summit Lighthouse, the Master Jesus offered his own Life-energy and the flame of the resurrection to be divided as his own Body portioned out from his heart flame as a glad-free gift to all elemental life upon this planet. In essence he said:

"In response to many requests I am come to anchor in the hearts of the faithful a portion of my own flame. And do you know, dear ones, today my flame is being given to every deva and to every elemental upon earth to impart to them the comfort which the Maha Chohan has so long desired to externalize in those blessed beings.

"As you know, the elementals are without a human soul. They do not have immortality as do the angels; for when they descended into form in the process of creation, their vibratory rate was such that they became identified with the context of Matter and the physical body of the earth. When the earth became more dense with the substance of the energy veil imposed by mankind, they went through a metamorphosis; and like the physical bodies of fallen man with which they had come to identify so closely, their nature became transitory and subject to decay. Therefore, when they pass from the screen of life, they are no more; because they do not have a soul, they do not have eternal Life.

"The angels, of course, are radiant flames of fire; endowed from the beginning with immortality, they minister to the holy will of our Father. Not so the elemental beings, who are almost despondent when their loved ones pass, for they know they will never see them again. As has been told you before, these little mirrors of mankind's thoughts and feelings do reflect the sorrows of the world. The grief which mankind express when their loved ones pass from the earth plane is deeply felt by them; for they love also, and their love is expressed in the flowers they create.

"Today the gift of my flame will make it possible for them to feel throughout their entire manifestation as elemental beings a part of the radiance of immortality which I AM. Contemplate what this means: it means that they shall no longer be aware of death.

"The cycles of Nature, conceived by God and designed in the higher octaves, lowered into manifestation through the elementals, are endowed with my momentum of the flame of resurrection this day, that from this day forward the elementals shall never again have the sense of death. Though they pass, it shall be as the click of a camera shutter or the dropping of a bird on wing when its beating heart stops. Suddenly they shall be here—and then they shall be gone, but without pain or quiver of fear. They shall feel my flame always; and a portion of that flame resting in them shall remove for time immemorial all of the fear that they have outpictured as the result of mankind's discord.

"This is one of the first steps that must be taken ere we begin the process of quickening the world for the golden age, robing it in the garments of the eternal spring. For the archetypal pattern of the eternal spring must be anchored in the invisible world and the world of the formless before it can be outpictured in the world of form. The love of the students for the elementals and the decrees and the prayers of both heaven and earth have made this mighty release possible this day. . . .

"As the Holy Kumaras stand here with me before you, blazing forth what I choose to term the "fury" of their divine radiance toward God, the holiness of their purity, it gives us pleasure, in the name of the Great White Brotherhood, to announce to the world this dispensation made on behalf of Nature, on behalf of all Life. This is a manifestation of greatest hope, and it is one of the first steps in the abolishment of all death everywhere."

Commenting on this auspicious event, beloved El Morya said: "Let it be understood that this flame which Jesus imparted does not confer upon them immortality; for it is impossible at this time to alter the laws governing elemental life, the human kingdom, and the angelic kingdom.* However, the mitigation of their fear of death and the removal of that sense

---

*As the law now stands, only by passing through the human kingdom (i.e., by being born to human beings through special dispensation awarded by the Karmic Lords for meritorious service) can an elemental gain immortality. This is because much of elemental life has been imprisoned in animal forms. To immortalize the elemental would be to immortalize the form, thereby endowing animal life, which remains an incomplete and imperfect manifestation of the Christ, with permanent reality before it is perfected.

through the fiat of beloved Jesus is a boon of tremendous happiness to all elemental life, who upon the occasion of this Easter danced with unspeakable joy as waves of cosmic ecstasy swept the planet round.

"The fulfillment of this fiat manifested in a bathing of the precious elemental life with the regenerative power of the Christ-radiance as it flowed across the planetary body from Pelleur's domain in the center of the earth out through the rocky structure, up into the oceans, and out into the very atmosphere itself. Its meaning, of course, is apparent in the fact that the elementals—feeling now a lesser measure of humanity's discordant vibrations—will be able to express more God-happiness, which, it is our hope, will in turn be communicated to mankind. Thus the words of beloved Jesus spoken on the hillsides of Judea so long ago are found to be the matrix for a continuing release of tangible power in this cycle and even unto the end of the age: 'Blessed are they that mourn: for they shall be comforted.'[103]

"I would add a note of warning here lest the students be overly optimistic. There may be times when mankind's outpoured discord will react more sharply, returning to his doorstep for swift redemption. For the elementals, capricious by nature but long held down by mankind's own lethargy, may now leap forth in almost wild abandon; and pockets of human discord formerly held in abeyance may explode in earthquakes, volcanic eruptions, atmospheric disturbances, and the uncontrolled raging of fire and water—for this is the only means Nature has of righting itself when mankind fail to invoke the sacred fire for a harmonious adjustment of natural forces. To man, such manifestations are cause for alarm; but from the standpoint of the Law, they are simply karmic retribution—energy come full cycle. Nonetheless, they should not be ignored as a solemn warning of the LORD to those who persist in polluting the planetary body with the by-products of their selfish endeavor.

"The purposes of creation must first be espoused by man if they are to be outpictured through elemental life. For only thus—and I emphasize this—can the mandates of goodwill and freedom be extended to every creature. There is no wisdom superior to the wisdom of God; but that wisdom, which is universally available, must be universally sought and acknowledged. Those who out of blind atheism, agnosticism, or cynicism continue to vacillate in their relationship to the God of the universe forestall not only their own freedom but in some areas that of all mankind. . . .

"When the false glamor of religious seeking is stripped from mankind's consciousness and he acts from the undefiled motive of his heart's longing, he will bow to the mighty Divinity that is within himself; and in so doing he will pay allegiance to his own I AM Presence, the Source of all Life everywhere. Into the fortress of man's own being the power of Light must be gathered; and there it must also be expanded—the power of Christ-regeneration, the power of the resurrection, and the sweet power of happiness and joy in the whole of creation, knit together with golden strands of wondrous light spun from the loom of the Infinite Weaver." [104]

Archangel Michael, whose legions afford protection to elemental life as they do to mankind, sounds forth a warning that cooperation with Nature must be diligently sought by man if the earth is to remain as a platform of evolution for the souls assigned to it:

"We who are a part of the angelic realm know full well that the brotherhood of angels, elementals, and men must, in this time of Aquarius' approaching, enter more and more into the beauty and joy of balanced cooperation if mankind are to come to that state of awareness where the universe in its cosmic manifestation becomes both understandable and real to them." [105]

We who are of the human family know full well that there is simply not enough conscious cooperation between men and elementals in these latter days. The spiraling energies of the Holy Spirit which reverberate between the angelic hosts and the guardian spirits rebounding from heart to heart, magnified in love and service, are not being absorbed as they should by the children of men. Neither are they being amplified in the flame of gratitude and flung back into the universe with hosannas and rejoicing as was intended.

In the beginning it was ordained by God that the joys of Nature should reach their culmination through the being of man. But when man fails to play his role, the eternal drama of the seasons is without its grand finale. When he continually absorbs the Life-giving energies released through the cycles of Cosmos without returning to Life the harvest of those energies, sealed with the stamp of personal devotion, he arrests the recycling process and thereby aborts his own opportunity in the next round. If man persists in sowing the wind of ingratitude, discontent, and spiritual neglect, he is bound to reap the whirlwind of self-destruction, chaos, and spiritual famine; for only thus can the cycles of elemental forces be righted and balance be reestablished in the natural order.

The price man must pay for his failure to cooperate with Nature is the price of life itself. Citizens of the world have been provoked to concerted action. En masse they seek solutions to the problems of ecology; but not having all the facts, they tread upon dangerous ground. Let them beware. Ignoring the Presence of the Holy Spirit as the Great Coordinator of the cosmic flow in Nature, circumventing karmic law in order to carry out their shortsighted goals, the false prophets of a falsely based ecology must come under closer scrutiny before their premises and conclusions are universally adopted.

Those who look to man as the ultimate source of knowledge instead of recognizing his role as the instrument of the Christ Mind, those who regard him as a mere link in the chain of evolution rather than as the master of the cosmic chain of Life, will awaken one day to find evolving upon this planet not a kind of man, but a kind of god. Scholars and scientists disoriented from the cosmic scheme, lawyers and theologians relying on incomplete knowledge are wont to cry "Peace and safety!" And when sudden destruction cometh upon them, as travail upon a woman with child, then, Paul declared, "they shall not escape!" [106]

No man can escape the consequences of his failure to assume his responsibilities. Either here or hereafter the scales of Life must be balanced: and this is karmic law. Those who have diligently pursued human knowledge need not despair; building upon the foundations of honest scholarship, they can raise a monolith of divine wisdom that shall reveal the whys and wherefores of all human endeavor. Before concluding our chapter, we shall discuss what man can do with his ecology when his present knowledge is made complete through the knowledge of Ascended Master law.

ECOLOGY AND CATACLYSM: PERSONAL AND PLANETARY

"While man's concern for his ecology mounts, what shall I say is happening to the soul within?" [107] These words of the Darjeeling Master remind us of mankind's neglect of the ecology of the soul and his almost total disregard for the law of cause and effect operative between the soul and its environment.

All that man beholds around him, all that makes up his environment, is the effect of those causes which he has set up within his own consciousness. And far more than he realizes, that which he encounters from day to day is the objective reality of his subjective awareness. In his own world man is a law unto himself, and that which he decrees is binding both upon himself and his society. By his mental and emotional fiats, he can either imprison or liberate the souls of millions—among them his own; and it comes to pass with the turning of the great wheel of the Law that by his words he is justified and by his words he is condemned. [108]

Some may ask, "If you say that man is the maker of himself and his world, do you deny that God is the creator of heaven and earth?" To this we would reply, "Emphatically not!" The LORD God is indeed the Creator of the universe and man, whom He ordained as a co-creator and to whom He gave the earth as a laboratory for his own creative expression.

The entire Cosmos is the objectification of God's own Self-awareness. But within the giant Egg we call Cosmos is, among billions of cells, a single cell; and within that cell man is the god of his universe. In his playpen he gurgles and coos and evolves fanciful worlds patterned after the geometric forms of Nature reflected in his toys. Thus the building blocks of creation are offered to child-man by the Father-Mother God. For a while he tosses them from his playpen, but one day he will claim them for his own and build a tower to the skies.

It is written in the sacred scriptures that the LORD "ended his work" on the seventh day of creation [109] and pronounced it "very good." [110] Man's work begins where God's work leaves off. From a tender, carefree infancy he must rise to the golden years of manhood. As a cohort of the Infinite, he is destined for dominion.

All that man is and does is immediately reflected upon the mirror of Nature. If it were not so, life would hold no challenge; existence would be without purpose. At every hour of the day and night while man has consciousness and breathes the breath of Life, he is continually setting in motion causes that produce effects somewhere in the cell that is his universe within the Cosmic Egg. These causes reverberate first in the subconscious recesses of the mind and then in the deep astral caverns of the planetary body before making their swift and sudden appearance on the physical plane.

Like the tides of the sea and the currents of the air, all energy moves in rhythmic flow. Energy patterns set up at the personal level between and among peoples, whether harmful or benign, must sooner or later recycle through the planetary body and in the process be assimilated and outpictured by the forces of Nature. The scientific relationship between man and the sphere which he inhabits cannot, therefore, be overlooked in his considerations of ecology; nor can he disregard the relativity of time and space—both to his consciousness and to his sphere of influence—if he would master himself in his universe and his universe in himself.

"The moving stream of time varies with the consciousness of the individual," observes the Maha Chohan. "Those absorbed in aspects of human happiness often find the passage of time to be swift like the flight of an eagle. For them the sands in the hourglass flow with incalculable speed, whereas those caught in the web of despair find themselves bound by the tediousness of time and a painful awareness of its passage. The relativity of the cosmic hour strikes for all flesh the opportune moment. Some heed the call, while others who have allowed their attention to be diverted in *sangsara** do not perceive the destructive trends in man and society until it is too late." [111]

For the most part, mankind are not ready to accept their God-ordained responsibility for the harmony of the natural order; for they are unwilling to make the personal sacrifice which such responsibility implies. Many continue to insist that their thoughts and feelings are private, that their personal life is their own business. They have a right to do, to say, to think, or to feel whatever they please—to be happy or sad, selfish or unselfish, pure or impure, peaceful or warlike, if they so choose. Some, who have preserved a remnant of altruism, would add that they have that right only as long as they are not hurting someone else or encroaching upon someone else's freedom. Such assertions of the human ego ought not to be construed as a viable philosophy of life; for the relativism they infer, like the popular theory known as situation ethics, is nothing more than a feeble excuse for a state of consciousness that is neither in conformity with the laws of God nor in harmony with the natural order.

Those who see the cause-effect sequence only as it appears in the plane of Matter, unaware of the interchange of energies between Spirit and Matter that takes place through the nexus of the Christ consciousness, do not observe the relationship between personal and planetary karma and the pollution of the elements. Because their spiritual senses have not been quickened, they deny the presence of God in Nature and the reality of his servants active in Nature as the instruments of the Holy Spirit. These would also deny

*The circuit of mundane existence, worldly illusion, maya.

that the destruction of Maldek, the sinking of the continents of Lemuria and Atlantis, and the burying of other ancient civilizations were karmic penalties exacted by God through Nature. They regard cataclysm as the result of the interplay of natural forces which is or one day will be scientifically explained through the empirical method.*

We realize that certain cause-effect sequences are observable in the plane of Matter, and we respect man's right to hold a material, mechanistic view of the universe if this be his present awareness. But we must also be allowed to draw our conclusions from our present awareness which leads us to the realm of First Cause, to the plane of Spirit, where causes and effects observed in man and Nature are set in motion. We have seen that Spirit interpenetrates Matter and that Matter has dimensions as yet undiscovered by man. We have seen that man has only a partial knowledge of the material universe and almost naught of the spiritual. When man observes partially, he can only expect to draw partial conclusions. When he sees in part, he can only know in part.

As Saint Paul said: "For now we see through a glass, darkly; but then face to face: now I know in part; but then shall I know even as also I am known." Now we see through Matter in part; but when the veil is rent in twain, we shall see the spiritual-material creation face to face: now I know the Spirit in part; but then shall I know the Light as the glory of the Fiery World even as I also am known as the soul-emanation of that world.

Thus in the realm of the infinite, out of which proceed all finite manifestations, we find an unerring

_____

*When man gains greater mastery of his faculties, he will be able to transcend empirical methods and go straight to the Source of all knowledge, there to gain through direct awareness an a priori perception of any aspect of the universe he may desire to probe.

spiritual law that is neither material nor mechanistic. We find an impersonal law tempered by a personal God. We discover that the Almighty reserves the authority either to restrain or to unleash the momentum of mankind's karma, which is sometimes withheld for centuries while the LORD mercifully extends to the race the opportunity in time to balance their debts to Life.

Moreover, having seen the judgments of the Most High, we cannot fail to acknowledge man's free will as supreme. We cannot fail to acknowledge this free will rather than a material, mechanistic science as the arbiter of his destiny. Man is not at the mercy of an overpowering force outside himself, but he is at the mercy of the Power within. Through the spoken Word and the divine seed originally implanted within him, man can, at any moment he wills it so, take dominion over the earth. By his free will he can subdue it, and by his free will he can destroy it.

If humanity could bring themselves to admit that their wars and their hatreds, their economic opportunism and their slaughter of animal life have a direct bearing upon the balance of forces in their environment, they would be taking the first step in solving the problems of ecology. And the second step, no less important, that of mobilizing their resources and know-how in a concerted effort to eliminate their violations of natural law, would bring about the desired rapprochement with the forces of Nature which we have called oneness with Life.

Instead, they occupy themselves with building fences around what they have come to regard as their own little patch of earth. If they can secure their families from the pollutions of the masses, they are satisfied; but, though they know it not, they are also debtors of the human race. In vain will their

No Trespassing signs keep out the gathering clouds of planetary karma. He who fails to observe on a world scale the ancient maxim "I AM my brother's keeper" has failed to understand that the only one who can avert total cataclysm in the natural order is man himself.

Prior to the annual conclave of the Brotherhood held at the Grand Teton Retreat in July 1966, the Maha Chohan presented his yearly report on the Nature kingdom to the East Indian Council, which was summarized for the student body in the *Pearls of Wisdom:*

"The first item on the agenda was the reading of a report from the Keeper of Records. It was noted that through the prayers, decrees, and faithful service rendered by many devotees of the Holy Spirit on behalf of a misguided humanity, the elemental forces of a ravaged Nature had often been deterred from unleashing mankind's destructive momentums, thereby averting both major and minor cataclysm. It was pointed out that in the present day, as in the days of Noah, many warnings have been sounded forth which have passed unnoticed by the masses of mankind and which have been heeded only by the few. It was also pointed out that as the closing days before the Flood passed swiftly by and the remaining hours were dallied away by mankind, almost in defiance of the law of mercy and justice, the mercy of the Law which had withheld the return of mankind's karma was withdrawn, and justice required a recompense.

"Let me solemnly state, as the Emissary of the Holy Spirit, that men ought to turn wholeheartedly to God and make a forthright determination to let nothing dissuade them from fulfilling the purposes of Divine Love, which begin with compassion toward all and personal spiritual progress to the glory of God and the deliverance of this age. It is never too late—so long as the retributive effects of personal and planetary karma have not been released—for mankind to do all in their power to hold the balance for the earth.

"Countless prognostications have gone forth. The sounding of a note of warning by the Hierarchy was an act of grace intended to create hope for the deliverance of all from every evil condition. We do not act to strike terror in the hearts of men; neither do we attempt to force an unwilling humanity to bow its knees to the Great Cosmic Source. Rather it is our desire now, as it has been in the past, to assist mankind to read the handwriting on the wall of the age and to forewarn them that the rubble of their human creation will take its toll unless they transmute it by a valiant act of cosmic service and unless those who are presently engaged in selfish endeavors—totally negligent insofar as their great spiritual responsibilities are concerned— reverse the tide of their selfish energies and channel them into the mainstream of the divine will.

"The Master Saint Germain, together with be- loved Jesus and Kuan Yin, appeared before the high tribunal of the Karmic Board, beseeching that august body to consider the great service of the saints of past ages as well as the tremendous effort currently being made by men and women in humble walks of life who seek to avert for the earth and all mankind the release of those destructive forces which they have sown down through the centuries.

"Great was the response of the Karmic Board in their advisement to the East Indian Council; and while no specific promises were made, the entire assembly was assured that the more response to virtue that would be forthcoming on the part of mankind, the greater would be the possibility of forestalling the rumblings latent within the heart of the earth which during the current year have burst forth periodically as earthquakes, unnatural rainfall, and an imbalance in atmospheric conditions, causing a violent surging in the feelings of mankind.

"Recommendations were made based on the fact that the power of the Holy Spirit, sufficient to every need, stood ready to be invoked by mankind as they developed a sense of proximity to their own Divine Presence and intensified their yearning for divine grace within the forcefield of their consciousness. The momentums of service which the children of the Light have built up over the years must be maintained as they steadily press toward the manifestation of the Golden Rule. Service to man is service to God; but in his service, man must not neglect the pursuit of divine awareness. For in the higher reaches of the Self are to be found the treasures of God of which the world has great need."

> Let us then decree that the human prisoner
> Bound to a senseless round of useless habits
> Shall go free!
> Loose him and let him go!
> Thus has God commanded.
> Neglect continues—
> Thus has stubborn human will demanded;
> Yet in sweet surrender there is born
> The essence of the cosmic morn,
> The golden age to be. [112]

"The earth is the LORD's, and the fulness thereof," proclaims the God of the Mountains; "but no one is more eager to bestow it on man than God. It is man, and man alone, who, by the schisms he has created between himself and his God through his doubts of his own immortal destiny and his questionings of the divine plan, has frustrated the grace that God has and is from manifesting right where it is so badly needed. . . .

"I AM Tabor. My concern is with the proper utilization of the abundant Life that God has placed in the hills. In reality man is like unto a hill, one that we would till and cultivate; for the cultivation of the spirit of man and of spiritual goals is our desire. . . .

"Mankind's current concern with the pollution of the elements is a hollow mockery of their pollutions of the human spirit and the human mind through their failure to stop the trafficking of dangerous drugs and pornographic art. The flood of degrading concepts now being released into the world of man at an alarming rate, unless reversed in its course, will destroy this planet as surely as it did Maldek.

"O humanity, hearken to thy cosmic teachers, who are no longer removed into a corner but stand before thee face to face to reveal the Truth of the ages and the law of thy being![113] The way of cosmic history is plain. The way of the Great Law is also plain: 'Whatsoever a man soweth, that shall he also reap.'[114]

"The advent of cosmic Truth can be brought to bear upon human needs if hearts will open and respond. If they will not, and I speak to each little spark of the Divine Spirit, I am certain that we will not be allowed from our level to interfere with human free will. The hope of the world lies in man's acceptance of the grace of God. . . .

"Today as never before man must take a good look at himself, at his world, and at his life in its universal context. He must realize that in this vast network of universal Life which he calls Cosmos are framed such mysteries as to delight his eye and bring wonder to his heart. But if he is ever to know these graces, if he is ever to become an ascended being, if he is ever to enter into the fruit of holy reason, it will be because he acknowledges that spark of Life in himself and in Nature as the inviolate creation of a Reality so

far beyond his finite self as to be labeled by him 'infinite.' If he acknowledges the spark, then I say, there
is hope." [115]

Saint Germain, whose acclaim as an alchemist
of the sacred fire was won as the result of his total
mastery of natural forces, has often been heard to
discourse to his students on the power of Divine Love
focused in the core of the atom—the power that moves
men and nations toward the fulfillment of the divine
plan. Likening this power unto an evolutionary spiral
fulfilling its own preordained destiny, he declares
Divine Love to be the irresistible force of the universe.
But to man, who sees and knows in part, it often
appears awesome and foreboding.

In reality, the power of God in Nature—the
impersonal presence of Love—can provide man with
the greatest personal comfort. But man must learn to
make Love's energies personal by meditating upon
the personal Presence of God focused in his own
beloved Christ Self and his own I AM Presence. For
God, as energy, remains unaware of himself in the
plane of Matter until this energy is focused through
his own individualized consciousness which he has
placed in man and elemental life. Therefore, by magnetizing the energies of Love through his threefold
flame, man draws the impersonal power of Love into
the heart chalice, his personalized focus of the consciousness of God, and finds thereby that he becomes
aware of God in himself as God becomes aware of
himself in man.

Saint Germain makes clear that "the nature of
Divine Love is such as to ever make provision for the
fulfillment of God's precepts and plans. If it is the way
of the infinite ocean to sweep through a finite cause-
way in order to recall a large stone from the shore
back into the sea, it may be that the force of the water

required to move the stone will cause the tiny rocks and splinters to be scattered hither and thither. The smaller crystals are more easily dislodged and tossed about by the cosmic tides.

"Human speculation about God has evolved its own theology," comments the Chohan of the Seventh Ray. "The future of the planet has been the object of much speculation, and the possibility of its destruction by either water or fire has become a part of man's theology.[116] Thus the threat of total or partial world cataclysm is not unfamiliar to the consciousness of many. Gazing upon the evil conditions in society, men will often admit that if they were to be given their just reward, they would deserve to be destroyed; for they know that their deeds are evil.[117] Yet it has been well pointed out that scattered among the evil ones are any number of blessed souls together with the so-called wholly innocent. However, past history has not proven that the earthshaking powers of Nature have necessarily saved the innocent while destroying the guilty."[118]

Although mankind's collective karma may decree the return of his misqualified energies on a planetary scale, Saint Germain explains that Life has also provided the means for man to redeem these energies and to balance his karma without having to experience directly, either through personal or planetary disaster, the full impact of the cause-effect sequences which sometime, somewhere he unwittingly set in motion.

Predictions of natural disaster come, then, as an act of mercy that the people might repent before it is too late, that they might know that their fate is pending in the halls of cosmic justice, and that the outcome will depend entirely upon their attitude and their actions. We recall that when the word of God was given through the prophet Jonah, the inhabitants of Nineveh responded by turning from their evil ways;

and their city was spared.[119] Thus predictions can fail
or be altered—even those made from the human level
by seers and scientists. "The only predictions that cannot fail," the Master says, "are the cosmic ones which
foretell the ultimate end of a civilization through its
elevation into the divine plan."[120]

One way or the other, the golden age shall manifest; the kingdom of God shall come into manifestation at the personal and the planetary level. The
cosmic tide is incoming; as a giant wave of light, it
inundates entire solar systems. Those who ride the
crest to victory will witness the dawn of a new order of
the ages. Those who resist will be lost in oblivion to
be remembered no more. Through personal and planetary cataclysm, men and nations washed upon the
shores of Life are brought to the feet of their Creator.
But the harsher method is the last resort of the Law. As
Morya has said on more than one occasion, "Nature
ever prefers the gentler way."

The way of mercy is still open. Man *can*
approach the altar of God seeking forgiveness; he *can*
avert calamities by right action and by invocation to
the Light of Spirit to descend into the planes of Matter. By making an about-face he *can* depart from his
self-centered existence and center his life in Christ,
glorifying God in man and in all his works.

In his *Encyclical on World Good Will,* the Chief
of the Darjeeling Council summarizes the causes of
social ills and their cures, which can be brought about
only through man's obedience to natural law:

"Among the more serious problems of business
today is the rising trend to produce by deliberate
intent inferior merchandise for the repeat trade. Engi-
neering know-how has been used to defraud the con-
sumer not only of the superior products that it is
capable of producing, but also of the benefits of
increased leisure hours which would result from the

manufacture and distribution of commodities made to pass the test of excellence. Instead of assuming the increased responsibility attendant with increased knowledge, mankind have flaunted the higher law and the precious gifts of wisdom to outsmart the public and fill private purses.

"Scientific invention and skills ought to be used in their most effective manner for the general welfare of mankind instead of being suppressed by competitive economic interests. The abuses of child labor in the cotton mills of England may be long ended, but much of the world still dwells in the twilight zone of nugacious effort. Let the world be freed from needless drudgery through the harnessing of its scientific resources to serve humanity's needs. Clothing, machinery, and other so-called durable commodities should be made to wear not to a minimum, but rather to a maximum degree of service.

"The merchants of Babylon have in dishonor sacked the people of the world by aborting divine purpose in ignorance of the universal law of sympathetic attraction. They have closed their eyes to the truth that all good rendered unto life returns to the one sending it forth. If men are not motivated by essential humanitarianism, they should at least pay their respects to this irrevocable law on the basis of enlightened self-interest!

"Cataclysm on a planetary scale has been forestalled more than once by the power of Divine Love expressing through the world's spiritual leaders and the mighty prayer force they muster. Mankind owe a continual debt of gratitude to the true spiritual guardians of the race, whose unceasing prayers have interceded in their behalf. People of earth, this cannot go on forever! Individual responsibility for distortions imposed upon the earth shall be exacted by natural law.

"When people do not respond to God's laws

through the orderly processes of Love's gentle ministrations, they set in motion the only alternate method
whereby Nature can correct those abuses; then natural law operates through disaster, fire, flood, and mass
epidemics as the earth convulsively shrugs off men's
perverted creations in order that the nobler image
may once more be brought forth. We make plain: The
Law ever prefers the gentler way!

"Men and women of this blessed planet, you
must rise in a united effort to throw off all chains of
violence, warfare, greed, deceitful advertising, harmful habits, and the insatiable desire for trash in
entertainment! Replace these plunderers of your divine inheritance by those spiritual and cultural pursuits which will expand for the individual soul a more
permanent state of happiness resulting from new horizons of Truth and wondrous revelations concerning
the total being of each individual and his place in the
universal order.

"Crime will diminish in direct proportion to the
unbiased application of proper cultural and religious
training through the world's vast networks of communication systems. There is no excuse for ignorance or
immorality in America, where drama and instruction
bearing the high concepts of integrity and justice may
be brought to the most humble shack through radio
and television.

"Because the individual and the family are
linked with the state and because personal security is
of great importance to the individual, it is essential that
personal integrity be the example maintained at the
grass-roots level as the standard for public servants at
all echelons of government. Ministers holding public
office should keep faith with the people and thus help
the people to keep faith with them.

"Most problems are centered in the marketplace
of life's basic necessities. Therefore, give knowledge,

bread, and opportunity to all, and strengthen thereby the most natural deterrents to war and Communism. Reduced to its simplest expression, the formula for world goodwill and happiness is this: Feed the hungry, teach the ignorant, and love the people of the whole world as yourself! Sponsor this unity of goodwill, and the earth will prosper." [121]

The entire Hierarchy are in unanimous agreement. Only thus will mankind find themselves moving with the cosmic tide, becoming the instrument for the fulfillment of the impelling presence of Love in Nature. Only thus can man assimilate in his own being the power and majesty of the great onrush of Life. Only thus can he become one with the Prime Mover of the destiny of continents and planetary bodies, stars, and galaxies.

Saint Germain interprets the signs of the times appearing in the skies: "Freedom is on the move; and those who will not move with its tide will be left behind, high and dry upon the shoals of human consciousness, apart from the great ocean of infinite Love and Light for which they shall one day certainly thirst. . . . The elementals are no longer willing to be the instruments of mankind's discord. Too long have they been subject to the depredations of mortals; thus those who continue to do evil and to ignore their responsibility to the Great Law will, under the proper exposure and circumstance, find themselves literally swept away by a whirlwind of natural force. . . .

"The time of the fall of Babylon is very near at hand, and the cycle is nigh completion: 'Many will say to me in that day, Lord, Lord, have we not prophesied in thy name? and in thy name have we cast out devils? and in thy name done many wonderful works? And then will I profess unto them, I never knew you: depart from me, ye that work iniquity.' [122]

"If this civilization continues on its present

course, it shall literally tear itself apart and Nature shall prepare for a new cycle to begin. This will be a quaking to those who witness its occurrence, and their hearts will indeed fail them for fear.[123] Yet I tell you clearly: *This need not be!* If men and women of vision will accept the victory and will but give equal portion to the power of Light that they have bestowed upon the shadows of mortality, they will provide a way of escape." [124]

What seems dire prophecy, then, is actually the sounding of the LORD's trumpet; it is a call to battle, a battle in which the ultimate victory or defeat of the soul may be decided. Man never knows which confrontation will be the decisive one—his final opportunity to come to grips with Reality. The warning of prophecy represents a cosmic interval, a micropause when the sun and the moon and the stars stand still[125] while man makes his supreme choice: to be or not to be.

By his misuse of free will, man separates himself from God and from the harmony of cosmic law in Nature. Apart from the center of the LORD's creativity, from the whirlwind action of the sacred fire that is his God-ordained forcefield of protection, man suffers under the impersonal law which decrees the return of the cause-effect patterns that he has initiated. While he remains separate from God, man has no protection from his own miscreations. Only by putting on the garment of God and returning to the seat of his authority and consciousness is man given the knowledge and the power to transmute his miscreations. Through fervent invocation to the sacred fire he learns to arrest the spirals of negation that he has hurled into space before they boomerang, falling like meteorites into his own back yard. Saint Germain explains this law:

"Separation from God is the original sin, and it is the sin against the Holy Ghost for which there is no forgiveness; [126] for so long as the separation remains, there cannot be forgiveness. Only when the separation is ended by man's self-determined reunion with God can the great givingness of God once again bestow upon man his own rightfully earned and divinely decreed just portion." [127]

The return of mankind's discord and the balancing of that discord through the adjustment of natural forces is well illustrated by the Alaskan earthquake of 1964. This is an example of cataclysm that became necessary because mankind did not elect consciously, freely, and willingly to merge with the cosmic tides of Divine Love, making them personal through the God flame and thereby staying the hand of their own returning karma. This incident also illustrates to what extent the release of God's Light can effect change in the world of form as Light comes into contact with human discord. Morya recounts:

"Those who were present at the 1964 Easter class will recall that during the address of beloved God Harmony on Holy Thursday there was a release of a 'mighty tide of cosmic energy' over the Atlantic and Pacific oceans. This release was the commencement of a mighty action over the entire planet which was to culminate between dawn and noon Easter morn (EST) with the release of the resurrection flame from the Cave of Light in India as had been prophesied by beloved Chananda at the New Year's class.

"Now, beloved Harmony stated that had the energy he released been charged forth upon the landed areas of the earth's surface, cataclysmic action would have ensued because of the greater accumulation of human discord generated there; therefore, the angelic hosts were charged with the responsibility of distributing this 'mighty tide' over the continents. It was an unfortunate happening that certain karmic conditions having to do with aspects of human greed recorded on the Aleutian Islands and the Alaskan mainland during the eras of the gold rush had to be expiated. Thus you can understand why the earthquakes occurred simultaneously with the tremendous burst of power released on Good Friday during the dictation of the beloved God Tabor." [128]

We are well aware of the popular notions of the day concerning the mechanical workings of a mechanical universe. The almost universal indoctrination of the people in the Luciferian theory that God is impersonal at every level of manifestation has effectively forestalled mankind's personal contact with those very personal representatives of the LORD serving in a vast hierarchical network all the way from Cosmic Beings and Elohim to angel devas and the tiniest of elementals.

By preventing cooperation with this universal brotherhood, the forces of Antichrist have prevented mankind, lifetime after lifetime, from achieving the supreme goal of oneness with *all* Life and thereby finding his place in the cosmic order. If mankind accept the Luciferian denial of the personification of Good and follow this argument to its logical conclusion, they must ultimately deny themselves; for man was created to personify God-Good. Man in the state of becoming God is the essential link in this cosmic evolutionary chain. Without the link there can be no chain; without the chain there is no link.

Let men pause and consider the plan of God; for while the laws of science cannot be denied, neither can the Law of the Spirit be denied. And those who pursue the co-measurement of a cosmic perspective will readily admit that they are one and the same.

Some of these will no doubt summarily dismiss our explanations of natural law and the somewhat astounding revelations we have set forth on the lineup of colorful personages in the Nature kingdom. But the thoughtful investigator, fearless in his quest for Truth, unintimidated by theories old or new, will bide his time and wait for the Holy Spirit to prove all things, as He always has and always will to an open heart and a willing mind.

We ask our readers to refrain from judgment until they have grasped a fuller understanding of the universal plan, of divine science, and of their own individualized God consciousness. It is our humble desire that new insight will be gained through this volume; but ultimately each man's Christed illumination must come from the fount of all wisdom, his own I AM Presence. The true alchemist of the Spirit, not unlike the physical scientist of today, will neither reject nor accept a theory so vast as this which we have presented without making a thorough study in the laboratory of Nature as well as in the laboratory of the soul. He who does not consider it worth the effort is not worthy of the reward which the effort brings— mastery of the self, mastery of the universe, mastery of the planes of God's consciousness.

The interplanetary Master known to us simply as Victory—so named by God because he has sustained a momentum of Christ-victory for ages beyond the ken of mortal time—teaches his protégés, who zealously pursue the flame of God-victory, that to have manifest dominion over the forces of Nature and the natural man, they must understand that Nature is obedient to spiritual law and to the God Presence individualized in all. As man aligns himself—his will and his energies— with Cosmic Law and its universal power, he comes into his divine inheritance of manifest dominion. All of Nature bows to his mandates because they are the mandates of God. This is the divine ecology which coordinates the flow of natural forces on all planes of manifestation through the servants of God and man in Nature.

"All of Nature—earth, air, fire, and water, the very elements of which your body temple is composed—must come into obedience unto the Great Law and to Spirit. For the Spirit of God that giveth Life, the Spirit of your own I AM Presence, is your victory; and it is within you. If you will only accept and understand this fact, you can have the dominion that the Christ intends you to have over all outer conditions, including the manifestation of the natural man which houses the Spirit." [129]

EXTRATERRESTRIAL PROBES

We have spoken of the Holy Spirit as the all-pervading essence of the Father-Mother God, the merging of the fires of the twin flames of Deity made tangible through the Christ in Spirit and in Matter. Now we would speak of the Mother, of God aware of himself in and as the Divine Feminine. As Adam came to know Eve as the objectification of his own self-awareness, as "bone of my bones, and flesh of my flesh," [130] so that Spirit which declared, "It is not good that the man should be alone [it is not good for man to be *all-one*]; I will make him an help meet for him [I will make him twain]" [131] knows itself only as it is objectified in Matter.

Through the allegorical account of the making of the helpmeet, we become aware of the mysterious creation of Matter out of Spirit. The deep sleep which the LORD God caused to fall upon Adam denotes Spirit unformed and in a state of quiescence—consciousness suspended, waiting to be animated in form. We read that the LORD God took one of Adam's ribs and closed up the flesh instead thereof, and out of it He made a woman and brought her unto Adam.[132] When the Spirit of the LORD moved upon the being of Adam, identity achieved self-awareness: the Feminine aspect, passive in Adam, became active in Eve; the Masculine aspect, active in Adam, became passive in Eve. Arising from his sleep, Adam beheld his own likeness polarized in Matter. And he called her Woman, "because she was taken out of Man."[133]

Behold the synthesis of creation! Spirit—the original thesis of Being—gives rise to its antithesis, Matter; and out of the twain the Logos, the eternal Christos, is born. The Divine Manchild comes forth from the Father-Mother God in a fiery sphere whence twin flames spiral into form. This ritual of materialization whereby the soul descends into the plane of Matter, there to enshrine the flame of Spirit, is described in Genesis as the clothing of Adam and Eve—of their twin flames—with "coats of skins."[134] And the decree went forth that a man shall "leave his father and his mother, and shall cleave unto his wife: and they shall be one flesh."[135] Created out of the same white fire body, the masculine and feminine counterparts of the Christ are destined forevermore to be the expression of the Divine Whole. And the benediction of the eternal Logoi rests upon them: "What therefore God hath joined together, let not man put asunder."[136]

"All things were made by Him [by the Word that comes forth through the union of the Father-Mother God]; and without Him [without this synthesis] was not any thing made that was made."[137] Every seed idea, every perfect gift sent forth from the Father, gains Life and Love and Self-awareness in the womb of Cosmos. Thus Adam called his wife's name Eve, "because she was the mother of all living." [138] Embracing the cycles of eternity, the Divine Eve shows forth the fruit of Spirit's consummation in Matter—the only begotten Son made manifest in the children of God throughout the spiritual-material creation.

The endless drama of creation is based upon the eternal pursuit of Matter by Spirit and of Spirit by Matter. Upon the magnetic forcefield drawn by the Divine Lovers, the all of Cosmos is sustained. As in the symbol of the serpent swallowing its tail, the wholeness of Spirit in spherical motion produces a polarity in Matter that establishes the yin and yang of Life—the passive and active cycles of every aspect of Being.

Presented as Adam and Eve in the Genesis allegory, the polarity in expression is in reality comprised of the electrical energies of the twin flames of the Christ consciousness. As Matter is born of Spirit and the Christ is the product of their union, so when the Word becomes flesh, the Christ flame descending from the fiery sphere is manifest as "male and female." These are the twain which God (as Elohim) commanded to descend into Matter-form, saying, "Let us make man after our image and likeness. . . ." Thus male and female focus the "Divine Us," the Father-Mother flame, and establish the dual nature of the Godhead in manifestation. Nevertheless, the completeness of Being is not fully realized until that which has descended into Matter returns to Spirit, until twin flames ascend into the fiery sphere whence they came.

As the cloven tongues of the Paraclete make known to us the Fatherhood of God in Spirit, [139] so they reveal the Motherhood of God in Matter. As the Holy Ghost extends to an infinite degree the aura of the Godhead in Spirit (through each individualized I AM Presence), so it diffuses the emanations of the Godhead in Matter across the entire span of Cosmos (through all souls which have descended into Matter-form). To know the Holy Spirit above is to know the Father; to know the Holy Spirit below is to know the Mother. And through this comprehension of the balanced manifestation of the Divine One, male and female ultimately become the epitome of creation, the Universal Christ personified.

The cult of the Mother, destined to come into prominence in the twentieth century, was the foundation of the civilization of Lemuria—that lost continent which sank beneath the Pacific Ocean many thousands of years ago.[140] The evolution of Life in the Motherland and her colonies represented the initial thrust of Spirit into Matter on this planet. Here, where the early root races completed the cycles of their divine plan during not one but several golden ages that reached their apex prior to the Fall of Man, the Masculine Ray (the descending spirals of Spirit) was realized through the Feminine Ray (the ascending spirals of Matter) in the world of form.

In the main temple of Mu, the flame of the Divine Mother was enshrined as the coordinate of the flame of the Divine Father focused in the Golden City of the Sun. Perpetuating the ancient rituals of invocation to the Logos and intonation of sacred sounds and mantras of the Word, priests and priestesses of the sacred fire held the balance of cosmic forces on behalf of the lifewaves of the planet. Throughout the far-flung colonies of Mu, replicas of the temple and its flame-focus were established as shrines of the Virgin consciousness, thereby creating between the earth and the sun an arc of light, anchored in the flame below and the flame above, which conveyed the energies of the Logos necessary for the precipitation of form and substance in the planes of Matter.

Far beyond our own meager accomplishments,

the great advances in technology made during centuries of continuous culture on Mu were brought forth through a universal at-one-ment with the Divine Mother, whose consciousness embraces the laws governing all manifestation in the earth plane. The accomplishments in every field of endeavor of a people dedicated to the plan of God revealed through his All-Seeing Eye show to what heights a civilization can rise when the Mother flame is honored and adored in every heart and guarded and expanded in shrines dedicated to her name. And it becomes clear that man's fall from grace was, in actuality, the result of his falling away from the cult of the Mother and his misuse of the energies of the seed atom focused in the base-of-the-spine chakra, which establishes the light of the Mother flame in the physical body.

The fall of Mu, then, was the direct result of the Fall of Man, which reached its lowest point in the desecration of the shrines to the Cosmic Virgin. This came about gradually through compromise with Principle, separation from the Holy Ghost, and the loss of vision that inevitably results therefrom. Blinded by ambition and self-love, priests and priestesses no longer tended the flames; forsaking their vows, they abandoned the practice of those sacred rituals which had remained unbroken for thousands of years—even as the holy angels keep perpetual watch over the unfed flame that burns upon the altar of the Most High God.

The worship of the Moon Mother, the Great Whore mentioned in the Book of Revelation, [141] replaced the worship of the Sun Mother, the Woman whom John saw "clothed with the sun, and the moon under her feet, and upon her head a crown of twelve stars." [142] A black crystal set in lead and stone became the focus for the perversion of the Mother Ray and the symbol of the new religion. One by one the inner circles of the temple orders were violated through the diabolical practice of black magic and phallic worship taught by the Luciferians, until a completely false theology wiped out the pristine patterns of the Mother Cult.

By and by the early rumblings of cataclysm were heard by the inhabitants of Mu. The altars of the most remote colonies were the first to topple. When the last strongholds—the twelve temples surrounding the main temple—were taken over by the Satanists, the momentum of light invoked by the remnant of the faithful was not great enough to hold the balance for the continent. Thus Mu finally sank by the sheer weight of Darkness which her children had invoked—and which, because their deeds were evil, they had come to love more than the Light. She went down in a horrendous mass of volcanic fire and exploding lava, and the flame focuses that had sustained a mighty people and a mighty civilization were no more. What had taken hundreds of thousands of years to build up was torn down in a cosmic interval—the achievements of an entire civilization lost in oblivion, the spiritual-material evolution of man stripped from his outer memory!

Devastating though that cataclysm was for millions of souls, of far greater consequence was the destruction of the focus of the Mother flame that had blazed on the altar of the main temple—a Life-giving fire, the insignia of each man's Divinity made manifest as Above, so below. Alas, the torch that had been passed was let fall to the ground. The strategies of the fallen ones, who had worked night and day with a fanatical zeal, were successful in accomplishing their end: the Mother flame was extinguished on the physical plane.

For a time it looked as though the Darkness had completely enveloped the Light. Beholding the defection of the race, cosmic councils voted to dissolve the planet whose people had forsaken their God; and this would have been its fate had Sanat Kumara not interceded, offering to exile himself from Hesperus in order to keep the flame on behalf of mankind and hold the balance of the Light for Terra until such time as mankind should return to the pure and undefiled religion[143] of their ancient forebears.

The souls who perished with the Motherland reembodied upon a naked earth. Their paradise lost, they roamed the sands whose atoms were etched with the edict of the LORD God "Cursed is the ground for thy sake...." Having no recall of their former estate and no tie thereto—for they lacked the flame—they reverted to a primitive existence. Through disobedience to the laws of God, they forfeited their self-mastery, their right to dominion, and their knowledge of the I AM Presence. Their threefold flame was reduced to a mere flicker and the lights in their body temples went out.* Man, no longer found in the image of the Christ, became one of the species *(Homo sapiens),* an animal among other animals, his God-potential sealed for a thousand days of cosmic history. Thus began the tortuous trek of evolution which has brought civilization to its present level and which is intended to culminate in a golden age of Christ-mastery and full God-realization.[144]

Although the physical focus of the Mother flame was lost when Mu went down, the Feminine Ray has been enshrined on the etheric plane by the God and Goddess Meru in their temple at Lake Titicaca. In 1971 devotees of the sacred fire serving in an outer retreat of the Great White Brotherhood magnetized the Mother flame of Mu to the physical octave, thereby anchoring the lodestone for the Aquarian-age culture being initiated in these final decades of the century.

*The flame-focuses in the chakras were withdrawn to the heart and the Elohim assumed the responsibility for the natural functioning of the chakras—the distribution of Light to the four lower bodies.

Once again the torch has been passed; and this time, by God's grace and man's effort, it shall not go down!

Just as the worship of God as Father has dominated religious thought for many centuries, so in the next cycle the appreciation of God as both Father and Mother will provide the theme of an Ascended Master philosophy and way of life. This promises to be an era of perfecting the precipitation of Spirit in and as Matter as man takes dominion over the four elements—fire, air, water, and earth—which represent the four planes of God's androgynous consciousness whose cycles he must master prior to his reunion with the God Self. Through the worship of the Motherhood of God and the elevation in society of the functions of the Feminine aspect of the Deity, science and religion will reach their apex and man will discover the Spirit of God as the flame enshrined upon the altar of his own being even as he discovers the Matter of God in the cradle of Nature. Moreover, through the enlightenment of the Divine Theosophia he will accept his role as the living Christ—the seed of the Divine Woman.

In Erman's *Handbook of Egyptian Religion,* we find certain statements attributed to Isis, the personification of the Feminine aspect, which recall the identity and purpose of the Divine Mother. They are noteworthy in that they evince the continuity of the teachings of the Brotherhood on the Mother flame from ancient times to the present:

I am Isis, mistress of the whole land:
  The Earth Mother takes dominion over the entire physical universe.
I was instructed by Hermes,
  The God of Science ordains the Mother to teach mankind the laws governing the plane of material manifestation.

and with Hermes I invented the writings of the nations, in order that not all should write with the same letters.

> *The communication of God-ideas and identifications through the written and spoken Word is the process whereby the Mother makes intelligible to her children the consciousness of the Father.*

I gave mankind their laws, and ordained what no one can alter.

> *The commandments of the LORD and the laws governing the release of energy from Spirit to Matter, indispensable to the well-being of man, are the unalterable expression of Spirit in Matter.*

I am the eldest daughter of Kronos.*

> *While the Mother embodies the consciousness of the Father in the plane of Matter-earth, her energies issue forth from the plane of Spirit-earth.*

I am the wife and sister of the king Osiris.

> *In referring to feminine goddesses as the wife, sister, or daughter of the gods, the ancients indicated the polarity that exists between the yang and yin aspects of the creation. Isis is the twin flame of Osiris; together in their appointed sphere they coordinate the functions of Alpha and Omega.*

I am she who rises in the dog star.

> *The Image of the Divine Mother is seen in the God Star, Sirius, focus of the Great Central Sun in this sector of our galaxy.*

I am she who is called the goddess of women. . . .

> *The World Mother represents God in the Womb-man.*

I am she who separated the heaven from the earth.

> *With the creation of Matter the divine Whole became twain.*

I have pointed out their paths to the stars.

> *The Mother delineates the destiny of her sons and daughters and imparts to them the wisdom and the love necessary to fulfill the divine blueprint.*

---

*Cronus, the earth god.

I have invented seamanship. . . .

> *The Mother, often called the Star of the Sea, is the mistress of the seas—water being the most feminine, or yin, aspect of the material creation.*

I have brought together men and women. . . .

> *The love aspect of the Divine Mother is the cohesive force of atoms, universes, and twin flames.*

I have ordained that the elders shall be beloved by the children.

> *Through the Mother the continuity of the flame—of life, culture, and the blissful awareness of the Father—is preserved from one generation to the next.*

With my brother Osiris I made an end of cannibalism.

> *Through the Mother, man comes to understand reverence for Life, for the God who inhabits his creation.*

I have instructed mankind in the mysteries.

> *Wisdom teaches her children the geometrization of the Spirit of the LORD.*

I have taught reverence of the divine statues.

> *As the statue is the symbol of the identity of God individualized in his manifestation, so every manifestation is the embodiment of Universal Christ Principle. It is to this rather than to the statue or to the person that we bend the knee and direct our devotion.*

I have established the temple precincts.

> *Mater is the temple of Spirit and forms the boundaries thereof, enshrining the sacred law, the sacred science, and the sacred flame of Life.*

I have overthrown the dominion of the tyrants.

> *The perversions of the God consciousness and of the Father Image are exposed by the Divine Mother.*

I have caused men to love women.

> *The Mother is the counterpart of the Divine Magnet as She attracts the flow of Spirit into the womb of Matter.*

I have made justice more powerful than silver and gold.
Through the discovery of the Mother Image mirrored in Nature, man is no longer wedded to materiality as an end in itself but perceives in the virtues of the Spirit rising out of the crucible of time and space that the material universe is but the means to an end; moreover, he recognizes those virtues as having the power to take dominion over the human spirit, making it to transcend itself and the clay vessel that houses the Spirit.
I have caused truth to be considered beautiful.
Truth, as the arrow of the Father's consciousness, becomes beauty in manifestation through the Image of the Mother. [145]

In the ancient city of Saïs on the Nile delta stood the temple of Isis on which was written the following inscription: "I, Isis, am all that has been, that is or shall be; no mortal man hath ever me unveiled." [146] Known by a thousand names, Isis pervades the cultures of the world. Known by any name, she is the Divine Mother that ensouls all Life. It is she who gave birth to all things, including the only begotten Son of God. She remains the Cosmic Virgin; for the Divine Mother preserves the Whole-I-Vision of the Godhead, and through the perception of the Eye of God within her forehead, the Christ victorious appears.

Whereas God the Father is depicted as the Omnipotent One, the impersonal Law and the personal Principle that undergirds the creation, the Mother is personified in and as the creation and is identifiable to man not only through the forces of Nature but also through every aspect of the physical universe, including his own four lower bodies. Thus the Divine Mother shows forth the eternal glories of the Father and the Son in the four planes of Matter and balances in man the cosmic energies that ordain his destiny.

Omnipotent is the flame of the Mother, omniscient her wisdom, omnipresent her love. Inasmuch as the flame is the catalyst necessary for the crystallization (*Christ*alization) of man's consciousness and for the materialization (*Matter*ialization) of God's consciousness, it has been opposed throughout history by the forces of Antichrist that have relentlessly pursued the seed of the Divine Woman to destroy it. Just as the Lamb of God—the Divine Manchild—has been slain from the foundation of the world, [147] so the Fount of the Divine Mother from which the essence of the Christ issues forth has been desecrated since the Fall of Man in time and space.

The carnal mind, ever at war with the Christ, seeks to destroy the Woman before the identity of the Father can be realized in her Child. Thus we read in the Apocalypse that "the serpent cast out of his mouth water as a flood after the Woman, that he might cause her to be carried away of the flood. And the earth helped the Woman, and the earth opened her mouth, and swallowed up the flood which the dragon cast out of his mouth. And the dragon was wroth with the Woman, and went to make war with the remnant of her seed, which keep the commandments of God, and have the testimony of Jesus Christ." [148]

The martyrdom of Hypatia in A.D. 415 is an example of the raging of the serpentine force against the wisdom of the World Mother. As a disciple of Plutarch, this holy woman became the key exponent of the Alexandrian school of Neoplatonism. So great was her wisdom, so beautiful her countenance, so eloquent her speech that she attracted thousands to the feet of the Divine Theosophia.

A true representative of the Divine Virgin, Hypatia was a master of science and religion. Consulted by the greatest of her contemporaries on questions of

mathematics, astronomy, philosophy, and politics, revered by Alexandrians from every walk of life, she
stood as a supreme example of the Motherhood of
God. In her divinely appointed role as an exponent of
Truth, Hypatia revealed the mysteries of Christian doctrine, as Origen had before her, and exposed the pagan
background of many religious traditions. It is not surprising that her brilliant mind eclipsed the leading
churchmen and drew many converts to her teachings.

Cyril, Bishop of Alexandria, jealous of her success and fearful that she would interfere with the
spread of Christianity in North Africa, fanned the
flames of fanatical hatred among certain of his followers,
which exploded in a fierce attack upon Hypatia in the
streets of Alexandria. Led by Peter the Reader, they
tore her from her chariot, dragged her to the Caesar-
eum (then a Christian church), and there, before the
baptismal font, stripped her of her clothes and club-
bed her to death. In a final act of barbarism the
maddened monks scraped the flesh from her bones
with oyster shells and burned the remains. With her
death the Neoplatonic school of Alexandria collapsed
and the most important representative of the Divine
Mother in the ancient world passed from the scene. [149]

Though he search the planet round for Wisdom,
pursuing her trailing garments, man finds that the
streams of the Divine Theosophia are but tributaries
of the great Fount of Life, of the Central Sun of Being,
of the threefold flame that is God's gift of Life and
consciousness to every soul. The "Lady with a Lamp,"
who Longfellow prophesied "shall stand / In the great
history of the land, / A noble [arche]type of good /
Heroic womanhood," [150] is the Divine Mother whose
glowing heart draws her children into the awareness of
all Truth. It is she of whom the author of Proverbs
writes:

"Forsake her not, and she shall preserve thee: love her, and she shall keep thee. Wisdom is the principal thing; therefore get Wisdom: and with all thy getting get understanding. Exalt her, and she shall promote thee: She shall bring thee to honour, when thou dost embrace her. She shall give to thine head an ornament of grace: a crown of glory shall she deliver to thee. . . . She is a Tree of Life to them that lay hold upon her: and happy is every one that retaineth her." [151]

The rays of light emanating from the heart of the Mother nourish the offspring of God dwelling in the farthest cycles of the universe. They know the Self as God because they are known by her Love. Awareness of all Life and oneness with the Father are the gifts of her blessed Mind. Among the children of God locked in her embrace, separation remains a concept undefined. Swimming in the womb of her Consciousness, their souls gather skeins of light for the hour of their birth in form. Wrapped in the swaddling garments of her Love, they are sealed in Wisdom's flame unto the day of their return to the Eternal Bourn.

The unawakened soul is the soul that knows not the Divine Mother. Cast adrift upon the endless sea of life, he feels a gnawing hunger, a hollow emptiness from which he will not find surcease until he speaks her blessed name. Because she ensouls the plane of Matter, he has no link with the stream of Life, with the flow of eternity, or with the Father, except through her tender ministrations. It is she who will rock him in the cradle of her Love and teach him of the Light within the heart, of joy in the fulfillment of the Father's plan, of his concern for each one, and of Life's purpose that is real.

Whether man elects to probe the far reaches of interplanetary and intergalactic life or to traverse the forcefields of atoms, molecules, and cells within the heart of the earth, he must understand that the exploration of the material universe is the exploration of the Body of the Divine Mother. Matter in all her glory is revealed through telescopic and microscopic probes and through journeys in consciousness to the uttermost parts of creation. Though he traverse the heavens and the earth from subconscious to superconscious realms, man cannot escape the folds of her Consciousness. Wherever he goes, he is caught in the vast network of her sentient Being and he discovers more of the eternal Father through her compelling ministration.

Lack of contact with the Divine Mother, resulting in an unbalanced manifestation of her flame, is the underlying cause of all functional disorders occurring at physical, mental, emotional, and etheric levels of man's experience. As the Superconscious Mind governs the spiritual aspect of man's being through the Father Image, so the subconscious mind (including the etheric body and the electronic belt) governs the material aspect through the Mother Image. Since man's subconscious is preeminently feminine (in that it is the passive receiver of the active impressions of man's being), the soul, or psyche, which evolves through man's subconscious (which contains all of the records of his conscious and superconscious experiences) is likewise polarized to the Matter Principle.

The study of the soul and its relation to the momentums of the subconscious mind we call psychology. If this science is to be properly applied, it must be based upon an exact knowledge of the Mother flame and its reflection upon the facets of man's total consciousness. Physicians of the future specializing in psychiatry—that branch of medicine dealing with mental, emotional, or behavioral disorders—will probe the four lower bodies of man for the purpose of analyzing the effects of man's experience throughout his many incarnations on this and other planets.

By examining the electronic pattern of the God Presence and the blueprint of the solar identity, the doctor who practices according to the principles taught by the priests of the Order of Melchizedek will be able to see where and when the individual departed from his divine plan. Since this departure from his central reason for being marks the beginning of disorders in the psyche due to his separation from the Mother flame, the practitioner trained by the Hierarchy will be able to determine what specific measures must be taken by the patient in order to facilitate the regaining of his full faculties through a return to the balanced expression of the Mother Ray.

Exploring the subconscious world of man can be as fascinating and rewarding an experience as the most exciting extraterrestrial probe. For in the cosmic sense—through the macrocosmic-microcosmic interchange—inner and outer space are related as the subjective and objective manifestations of the Mother aspect within man's own consciousness. Inasmuch as our investigations of the Body of the Mother—of both the frontiers of the mind and the virgin territory of spacial realms—lead to an expanded awareness of our own solar evolution, let us review the instruction of the Brotherhood on both aspects of this most essential self-knowledge.

Addressing "those who are willing to probe the subconscious with the sword of the Holy Spirit," the Maha Chohan wrote in a *Pearl of Wisdom:* "The depth of man's inferiority, inefficiency, doubts, and fears always stems from past momentums, either of the self or of infections carried into the self from other selves.

"An understanding of the nature of the subconscious mind [and its relation to the Mother aspect] will assist the individual in solving his problems and in developing a greater level of God-awareness with its attendant victory and happiness. The ministration of the Holy Spirit is intended to provide humanity with both the understanding and the vital determination that are needed to eliminate undesirable qualities, that they might no longer be subject to their power, but only to the God-victorious thoughts that flow from the Mind of Christ. Thus the maintaining of a steady contact with the Godhead [through the Mother Ray] will assure each individual of the fulfillment of his original Life plan.

"Here on earth Ascended Master concepts have become so distorted from their original intent that they are scarcely recognizable in heaven. People persist in the habit patterns which they established early in life under parental guidance, and as the years go by they continue to mimic the outer expressions of others. Let them learn, if they would be free from the bondage of imperfect molds, that the buoyant nature of God must be welcomed into conscious as well as subconscious levels of being. This is a matter of uprooting weeds that have no place in the garden of Reality and of cultivating the virtues implanted there which have been choked out by the incumbent growth.

"Momentums foreign to the nature of both the spiritual and material principles of the Deity are built as people go over the old patterns again and again until these furrows become so deeply entrenched that it is almost impossible to eradicate them from the face of consciousness. We have seen how the suppression of unwanted habits, when transmutation is in order, leads to degeneracy and despair. Individuals fail to understand that where latent desire goes unchecked and there is an unwillingness to let go of unwholesome human conditions (often because such conditions are more familiar to the ego, hence more comfortable than the unknown realms of Light from which man has departed), there is a steady draining of energy into subconscious desire matrices that are not in conformity with either the true nature of the individual or his original Life plan.

"Desire suppression is dangerous because it causes the buildup of these internal cell pockets while affording no outlet for frustration. When the pressure at subconscious levels becomes great enough, something has to give; and because body, mind, and soul are interwoven upon the loom of individuality, the resulting explosion may temporarily disrupt the normal flow of consciousness.

"We advocate, then, in the overcoming of unwanted habits and conditions, a recognition of the all-power of God. 'All power is given unto me in heaven and in earth,'[152] declared the Master Jesus. The recognition that this power in both its Masculine and Feminine aspects is given unto the Christ in every man as the just steward of his potential is essential; for God's power, with its inherent perfection, is now and always has been available to man. However, man was also given the gift of free will which he may use to effectively blot out the Holy Spirit which gave him birth, even as he uses it to still the voice of conscience, having his conscience 'seared with a hot iron,'[153] as Saint Paul said long ago.

"Knowing that Truth and Life are more important than the temporal satisfactions which must one day be surrendered, knowing that the divine birthright far exceeds man's earthly expectations, the advocates of the Holy Spirit bear the hope that individuals in this day and age will understand that surrender to God is only surrender to the goodness of Life itself. This goodness [which is made intelligible through the Divine Mother] is already resident in Life and awaits the welcome of the individual monad who possesses the key of free will. When your blessed free wills are

tethered to His will, there is far less of the sense of
struggle about life. One's future is no longer subject to
the whim of personal desire but rests firmly in the
God-desire to develop, under the aegis of the World
Mother, the patterns of the Life plan to the fullest
extent of which the individual monad is capable." [154]

The Maha Chohan reported in the *Pearls of Wisdom* that "at the same conference of the Indian
Council [mentioned earlier in this chapter], the cycle
of vain repetitions and its link with the power of binding habit was discussed as a key factor separating man
from the harmonizing effects of his communion with
Nature, thus depriving him of the benefits of the
Mother flame. It was pointed out that many unfortunate men and women who presently suffer the rav-
ages of diseases of the mind and body which were
caused by contamination of the aura through wrong
habit patterns were misled in their early youth by
irresponsible parents who themselves were victims of
an earnest malpractice of other decades.

"One who serves with K-17's* legions remarked
that mankind are prone to react most strenuously to
defend their own position when that position is challenged by a son of Light. Beloved Morya stated to
those assembled that this was but a surge of rebellion
in defense of an ego which already knew that it was, in
the vernacular of mankind, 'off the beam.' He pointed
out that oftentimes people feel that because they are
defending a position which is their own, they can in
some way justify it, even though it is in error. This, of
course, is pulling the wool over one's eyes, as the per-
ceptive will admit.

"Someone asked what could be done about it;
he was reminded that it had been suggested many

*K-17 is the code name for the Ascended Master at the head of the
Cosmic Secret Service.

times that countermeasures of a spiritual nature were most effective in assisting those who willingly responded to spiritual ministrations, but that these measures carried little weight with those whose faith was yet pinned upon mortal opinion. This, blessed ones, is the reason it is necessary to meet the enemy on his own ground and to battle for the minds of men by the use of certain subtleties from a cosmic level.

"The present age is one of total warfare wherein the battle between Light and Darkness continually rages and the valiant know no rest save that which God gives to the spiritual soldiers who, weary from service to mankind, reach a point of near exhaustion. I would not for one moment imply that men cannot mount up with wings as eagles and renew their strength.[155] They have done so again and again, and they shall continue to do so; but there are times in the life of the most devoted when the weight of the cross is staggering. It is then that the succor of the Divine Mother is poured out in a more than ordinary measure.

"In connection with the solving of the problems of a misguided humanity, it was noted that many individuals who were spiritually hungry [who, though they knew it not, yearned to drink in the Mother flame] were often being fed misleading material which did not satisfy their souls. Beloved Brother Chananda, who presided at this session of the Indian Council, informed us that the crux of this problem was the lack of discernment which those beginning to understand God's Law often felt in the face of the many signs and sign-bearers, each pointing a different way.[156] He also said that many of those beginning to understand the real truth about Life did not yet have their spiritual centers quickened. Therefore they could not discern the LORD's Body;[157] that is, they could not feel the radiation of the Light of the Masters in the printed text. Because of this inability, they were often subject to the trickery of malevolent forces which function in the invisible but unascended state, assisting both embodied and disembodied black magicians who work from many levels to deceive and enslave the mind and being of man.

"A brother whom we do not choose to name rose from the audience and queried, 'Under these circumstances just what can be done?' We felt the earnest desire of that one to assist the council in evoking some satisfactory solution to the problem of humanity's lack of discernment; and after due deliberation it became apparent to all that our intercession on behalf of mankind must be continued and intensified. Some of the great Masters who have rendered intense cosmic service for many centuries referred to the degree of their own involvement with humanity which came about through their ministrations in the name of the Divine Mother that had continually flooded forth to illumine mankind.

"The Cosmic Beings from Venus who were attending the council sessions were called upon to give of their Light and opinion upon the subject. One of them spoke for all, and these in essence were his words:

"'Variation will come wherever there is a lack of understanding or of total dedication. In the case of a lack of understanding, man does not always know whether he is doing right or wrong. In the case of a lack of dedication, there is a tendency to substitute a smattering of attainment for the full manifestation of mastery. This could rightly be considered the result of mental laziness and physical sluggishness, both of which can be cured in part, if not altogether, by total involvement in the Golden Rule ethic of being 'my brother's keeper' and by renewed consecration to the causes of the Brotherhood. This must start with the will. Men must will to do good. They must will to woo eternal principles and to hold them in esteem. They must forsake the banal influences of the past and determine to work for right change in the future, which will most assuredly become the now!

"'It was suggested by an unascended earthly brother of considerable advancement who was permitted to attend this session that some form of curative device, such as that which was used upon ancient Atlantis for the removal of criminal tendencies from the brain, should be released again, together with the proper technique for its operation, to the scientists of this age. This, our brothers, was vetoed by the Karmic Board as an interference with the free will of man. It was also indicated that some crude forms of this practice are already being used in prefrontal lobotomies performed by the medical profession in this time.

"'We particularly wish to call to your attention the fact that Light—and I refer herein to spiritual Light and most specifically to the emanation of the Christ consciousness—when it is accepted and received into an individual's forcefield and invited to abide therein, will, in transmuting wrong tendencies, produce a most marvelous cauterizing effect. We cite the records of some men of earth in past and present ages whose spiritual prowess was almost nil and whose intellectual capacity was very crude. These individuals, upon contacting an intense concentration of the Christ consciousness, were so imbued with the power of the Holy Spirit [through the intercession of the World Mother] that earthly densities passed from their consciousness and all things became new in divine dimension.

"'The coloring of these conditions by the heavenly Light is most invaluable in curing depression and melancholia. Many forms of insanity now plaguing the mankind of earth can likewise be cured by genuine

spiritual experience; for it is our opinion, based upon
the records of this solar system, which involve many
planetary bodies, that common conditions produce
common problems and that the best solution—the simplest, the quickest, and the most economical for all
men—is to contact the mighty radiation of the Son of
God, the emanation of the Christ consciousness that
becomes the common property of every man who will
receive him.

"'Theologians and their followers on Terra
often seem incapable of differentiating between a
stepped-down release of the Spirit of God and a
higher release of that Spirit. Let them understand
their own expression 'God tempers the wind to the
shorn lamb.'[158] The blessedness of Almighty God, his
Spirit, and the Spirit of his Sun Radiance, the Christ
consciousness, charged with the cosmic illumination
of the Divine Mother and her capacity to alter unwanted conditions for mankind, is released from the
highest levels of the Godhead and descends into the
very heart of the earth to contact the most primitive
types, manifesting diversely to each level of awareness
in order that everyone might derive the greatest benefits of the Great Law according to his capacity to
receive.

"'Be not entangled with the yoke of bondage[159]
which differing religious opinion sometimes brings
about. Understand, blessed ones of the planet earth,
that many manifestations of the Father-Mother God
are necessary in order to reach the various levels of
consciousness of embodied humanity. There is no
enmity between one manifestation of God and another. There is only the cosmic outreach from the
heart of the Spirit of God intended to save that which
is lost[160] in the planes of Matter.

"'The almost total involvement of mankind in
flesh-and-blood consciousness has thwarted many of

the plans of God for his creation; but all of this is only temporary, and the golden age which has long been in preparation is daily coming closer into manifestation. No one need wait for the golden age in order to externalize its character by engaging in the practice of the Golden Rule. This will accelerate the coming in of a new era when the old things will indeed have passed away and all things will have become new [161] in the Christ consciousness.'

"These, blessed ones, are some of the statements made by the great emissary from Venus. After considerable comment and exchange of ideas between many among the Brotherhood, a resolution was adopted whereby some of the hidden mysteries and hidden power of past ages (which to the present have been kept from unascended mankind but given in part to certain adepts prior to their ascension) would now be released into the hands of some of the advanced disciples of the Ascended Masters who have demonstrated balance and a sense of responsibility over a prolonged period of their existence. These individuals are to act as a point of contact with the Great White Brotherhood in establishing certain talismans upon the planet which will serve to counteract the negatively qualified compelling forces that have enslaved the minds of youth and age alike throughout the world.

"I would like to stress that a sincere and absolute humility must manifest in those to whom these gifts are given; and their use must be guided by the prayer of the righteous [162] which is able to raise mankind to the level of attunement with their own Christ Selves.

"By August 14 we expect to have completed the necessary arrangements whereby these powers can be restored to those who are ready to receive them. No physical contact will be made with these lifestreams; nevertheless, an internal spiritual activity will take place and a mystical experience will be given them which will ready them for a closer collaboration with the Brotherhood. With these gifts of added power in the service of Hierarchy will come the understanding of how to use them. Let those who may be in doubt concerning this calling understand that all who receive the gift will be made aware of it clearly and unmistakably, together with an index of action and a plan of cooperation between the visible and the invisible.

"Through this dispensation of Light granted by the Karmic Board, unascended brethren serving with the Ascended Masters will be privileged by the grace of God to anchor these powerful focuses in the world of form in the present era. Thus they will be able to help mankind learn how to break the force of vicious habit, whether it be the inordinate use of intoxicants or narcotics, the wrong use of the mind or tongue, a propensity for ego strutting, or the vain use of energy.

"New clarity of mind will enable many students to maintain a greater measure of attunement with their own God Presence. A sense of personal well-being with God and of universal brotherhood with man will permeate the atmosphere of the planet, making many among mankind more vitally aware of the active participation of the Holy Spirit in human affairs. Through this very present Helper, God has provided the means of delivering the earth from the perils of past ages, including the intensification of mortal delusion, thereby paving the way for a clarification of the earth's place in the solar scheme." [163]

Man may be limited as to the number of individuals he can contact personally in the short span of his life; but there is no limitation as to the contacts that can be made by his soul, by his Christ Self, and by his Divine Presence with the souls of all who are associated with the planet earth and even with those native to worlds beyond—not to mention the magnificent outreach into the kingdom of God, the kingdom of Spirit, which he can achieve through his own individualized focus of the flame of Life.

The eternal God who lives in every man desires His children to contact other souls in other worlds—those "other sheep" which are not of this fold [164] dwelling in the many mansions [165] of His consciousness. However, the method that He advocates to achieve this aspect of oneness with Life is to go within and not without—to go within and discover the Presence of the Holy Spirit, the light of the Christ, and the Omniscience of the Godhead.

The ancient advice "With all thy getting, get understanding" applies to many things. The getting of the Holy Spirit is to be desired above all contact with flying saucers and life on other planets. One day in the not-too-distant future man will encounter extraterrestrial lifewaves and evolutions; nevertheless, until he has encountered the Christ identity of his neighbor, he will remain a stranger to Life and all of Life will remain a stranger to him. The pursuit of outer contacts, outer knowledge, and outer success must come to an end with the close of the earthly cycle; but each acquaintance made with the God in man and the God in Nature will live forever in the soul as a permanent aspect of one's identity and one's relationship to Cosmos.

Answering his students' questions on the subject of flying saucers, the Ascended Master Hilarion, Lord of the Fifth Ray of Science and Healing, said:

"Yes, there are flying saucers, if you wish to call them that. There are also beings from other planets, both malevolent and benign, who are able to navigate the spacial realms in their 'physical' bodies. Yes, some of the more qualified among them do occasionally work with the spiritual Hierarchy of the earth, just as earth people traveling in their finer bodies sometimes work for the cosmic Hierarchy of other planets.

"Yet there are others who, in exercise of their free will, make expeditions into the atmosphere of earth for the purpose of observing conditions on this planet earth much as men in bathyscaphes plunge beneath the waves of the ocean to study marine life. Just as oceanography is a vital subject to mankind, so knowledge of the earth as one of the planets of this system is vital to these interplanetary investigators. The Ascended Master rulers of their planets have warned them in advance, however, of the present warlike nature predominant in the mankind of earth. Therefore, for the most part they have heeded the solar rulings for excursions to earth. These explorers are not ascended beings, but in the main—and there are exceptions—they represent a highly select and advanced society of God-free men." [166]

Sanat Kumara, Hierarch of Venus, has given instruction on several occasions, placing extraterrestrial probes in proper perspective for the spiritual aspirant:

"The final admonishment of Jesus to Peter, 'Feed my sheep,' shows the importance that he placed on the work of the Good Shepherd. As the planetary flocks fill the heavens, so the evolutions of the many planets in far-flung worlds are separated in time and space. The exploration of these many mansions of the Father is of little practical consequence to the man of earth who seeks to wisely expend his Life-energies. We do not say that science will not in your time offer many new discoveries in space or that He who has prevented togetherness among the planets, having dispersed the sheep of His pasture throughout the universes, will not permit man to cross some of the present boundaries of his habitation [167] because he has sought to take heaven by force. [168]

"We recommend, rather than let the consciousness fly with its saucers, its imaginings, its extraterrestrial probes, that men see, as we of Venus do, the need
to perfect their world in beauty and in love, the need
to put an end to inner turmoil and war among the
nations, the need to properly educate the young, the
need to extend comfort and grace to all peoples, the
need to reveal the true religion and those aspects of
the Law dealing with karma and reembodiment which
have been removed from the church by deliberate
design. Above all other concerns, the teachings of the
Christ must be correctly taught to the people of this
world; for individuals will understand thereby that as
they sow, so shall they reap." And we are certain the
reader will agree that this knowledge must be assimilated before mankind begin to land on other planets,
contaminating other lifewaves with their present dense
consciousness.

Sanat Kumara also admonishes the students to
explore the space within: "We would direct a ray of
Light's perfection to the hearts of men. You seek to
probe outer space. Your technology reaches for the
stars. But I say to you with a solemn warning, neglect
not the space that is within—the realm of self that
requires the perfectionment of the eternal plan. You
were fearfully and wonderfully made; [169] and I, as the
Ancient of Days, [170] did long hold for men the immortal concept. . . .

"Now there comes a ray of intense beauty to the
earth, focused from beloved Lady Venus and me, sent
forth with the thought of the Christ-matrix of every
man, the Universal Son of God. For he must appear in
human affairs. Christ must be enthroned in every
heart and in every home. He must blaze upon every
altar as the sacred fire. We must restore the earth to her
golden age estate. Technocracy must embrace a divine
theocracy. Atheism, spawned by Serpent's sinuous

materialistic concepts, invading and pervading the
universities of the world, must be shed, that the dove
of order with the olive branch in his bill may appear.
Then shall the universal Spirit of the LORD God unite
the universe that is within with the universe that is
without." [171]

HARMLESSNESS TOWARD LIFE

Albert Schweitzer said, "If a man loses his reverence for any part of life, he will soon lose his
reverence for all of life." [172] Wherever man is conscious
of Life as Mother, the doctrine of *ahimsa**—of harmlessness, of reverence for all things living, of the
oneness and sacredness of all Life—is understood and
practiced as a part of the day-to-day interchange of
love between people and elementals. But where civilization has destroyed the image of the Mother—
whether in divine or human form—souls recede from
one another, from Nature, and from God.

Having seen the neglect of the Mother Principle
in Western society, we can easily understand why so
few in this hemisphere have communed with the wind,
the trees, and the hills and from the depths of their
souls revered Nature in all of her glorious manifestations as Saint Francis did in his psalm of praise:

Most high, omnipotent, good Lord,
Praise, glory and honor and benediction
    all, are Thine.
To Thee alone do they belong, most High,
And there is no man fit to mention Thee.

Praise be to Thee, my Lord, with all Thy
    creatures,
Especially to my worshipful brother sun,

---
*Sanskrit for noninjury.

The which lights up the day, and through him
   dost Thou brightness give;
And beautiful is he and radiant with splendor
   great;
Of Thee, most High, signification gives.

Praised be my Lord, for sister moon and for the
   stars,
In heaven Thou hast formed them clear and
   precious and fair.

Praised be my Lord for brother wind
And for the air and clouds and fair and every
   kind of weather,
By the which Thou givest to Thy creatures
   nourishment.
Praised be my Lord for sister water,
The which is greatly helpful and humble and
   precious and pure.

Praised be my Lord for brother fire,
By the which Thou lightest up the dark.
And fair is he and gay and mighty and strong.

Praised be my Lord for our sister, mother earth,
The which sustains and keeps us
And brings forth diverse fruits with grass and
   flowers bright. [173]

    The Western mind has for the most part been
unfamiliar with the concept of reverence for Life; it
does not truly know the meaning of adoring Life in all
its forms—because it does not know that Life is God.
It has not been taught to honor the earth as the Body
of the Divine Mother and all that lives and breathes
thereon as the incarnation of the Feminine Ray. It has
not been taught to acknowledge the flame of the
Almighty resident in the rocks and the ranges and in

the everlasting hills or the breath of his Spirit in the wind and the fire and the wave.

When Matter is not held sacred by unascended man, Spirit, because it can be revered by him only through its expression in Matter, remains a concept undefined. Until it is made tangible and real by man's adoration of the flame enshrined in the tabernacle of Mother Nature, Spirit remains an unknown quantity, and to those evolving in the planes of Matter it is an unexplainable force. The Western mind has not been taught that the harvest of the earth symbolizes the gathering of concepts from her blessed head, archetypal patterns precipitated as fruit and grain, luxuriant vegetation and material resources to feed and clothe and house the bodies of billions, each one a temple for the flame of Life, each temple a cell in the Body of the Mother.

Instead of seeing her face in the grasses and in every flower and shrub, in the mountain fastnesses and in the waters of the seas, in the thunder and the lightning, man has assumed that Nature is hostile to his endeavor and that he must constantly struggle to survive. Far be it from the truth! As our Elder Brothers have made quite clear, Love is and forever shall be the supreme orderer of Nature. When man blends his energies with its joyous flow and sends the arrow of the soul quivering through the consciousness of the Mother, he alone commands the elements. Possessed by none, he possesses all. Nature is the great collaborator of his soul's evolution—his dearest friend, his Mother.

The concept of mutuality—of mutual love and mutual service, of the interlocking of the energies of the sun between man and man, of the interdependence of souls born of the one Mother and of their dependence upon their natural environment—has been replaced by the concept of the survival of the fittest. The prevalent belief that man is an animal above other animals who arrived at his present evolution by meeting Nature's challenge forever ties mankind to a competitive way of life. According to this theory, in order to retain his supremacy as the subduer of his world man must constantly battle the forces of Nature and compete with other animals, namely, his fellowman. This attitude has led to the adoption of a materialistic philosophy implemented through both communism and capitalism; for man so conceived is obliged to channel the greatest part of his energies into the struggle for existence.

With the rise of modern technology, Western man at last acquired the ability to perpetuate his civilization in the face of all but the most severe cataclysm. Having freed himself from the drudgery of eking out his existence from day to day, he sought to further unravel Nature's mysteries with a view to becoming her master. But in so doing he did not adhere to the original purpose for which God intended science, which was to provide man with an understanding of Matter and its relation to Spirit in order that he might attain the mastery of self. Instead he used science much as he had used a club a million years ago—to beat Nature into submission.

With total disregard for the law of conservation of energy as it is operative both in and between the planes of Spirit and Matter, man has ravenously devoured Nature's resources. This law—which states that although energy may change in form within a given system, it can neither be created nor destroyed—governs the activity of "flow" and the recycling of energies between the planes of Spirit and Matter. It involves the process of sowing and reaping, the give-and-take or push-pull action that must be continuous between God and man if the balance of Life is to be maintained as Above, so below.

Man has not understood that natural resources, so precious to the evolution of his solar awareness, are a direct tie to his Source; for the inner meaning of the word *resource (re-Source)* is regarding or relating to the Source of Life, or the Center of Being. We call this Source, or Center, God because it represents the greatest concentration of physical-metaphysical energies in motion at the Hub of Cosmos—a concentration so great as to provide the impetus for all of Life and the whole of creation. From this Source man receives in many forms the energy necessary for his existence, and to this Source he must return a portion of that energy if he and his world are to survive.

With the advent of the industrial revolution, mechanization became the god of the West. As the wilderness gave way to jungles of iron and steel, the arteries of the earth body became the depositories of every kind of waste, the atmosphere a dumping ground for chemical fumes, and the land, stripped of its redundant beauty, was hollowed out and filled with deadly by-products and dead men's bones. Through ignorance of the Law man has raped his environment; through ignorance of the Spirit of the Father he has desecrated the Body of the Divine Mother. Taking without giving, man, instead of exercising dominion over Nature, has plundered her resources; and in the process he has plundered the resources of his own soul. Alas, when man separates himself from his Source, he becomes separated from every lifestream that emanates therefrom. Conversely, as he violates any of the streams, he violates the Source and ultimately himself as a tributary of the Source.

The eternal Mother woos her children with patience and forbearing love. Gradually through science, the very instrument man used to exploit her, she revealed to him the truth that all Life is one, that man, being a part of Nature, must take dominion by making himself subject to her laws rather than an exception to them. Through the study of ecology, people in every walk of life have come to realize their massive failure to meet their responsibilities to Mother Nature and to themselves as creatures of her heart. They recognize that they have used her sacred gifts to create a monster that is now turning upon them, threatening to destroy the very platform upon which they evolve.

So startling has been this discovery that millions of voices are demanding that something be done before the planet is rendered totally unfit for habitation. Quoting statistics with fear and trembling, everywhere people are urging people to consider the ecological consequences of their every act. From city hall to summit conference, ecology is the topic of the seventies which continues unabated as, moving toward the millennium, the earth becomes more populated and more polluted; and plague, famine, war and anarchy play their role and take their toll. But just as man has misused his scientific knowledge in the past, so he is misusing the ecological findings of the present. Let us then in this final section of the chapter discuss the human ecology, pinpointing certain errors in theory and practice, and at the same time discover the divine ecology and more of the consciousness of the World Mother and her concern for *all* of her children.

Ecology is defined by Webster as "a branch of science concerned with the interrelationship of organisms and their environments; the totality or pattern of relations between organisms and their environment." [174] The word is derived from the Greek *oikos,* meaning house or habitat. As we have seen, the house, the body temple, or the planet* which man inhabits is

*The letter t in the word *planet* (plane-t) stands for the cross which symbolizes the descent of the energies of God into *man*ifestation. Thus the inner meaning of the word is the *plane* where the lines of Spirit and Matter converge.

the Mater or Mother aspect of God—the temple which houses the flame of the Spirit Most Holy. Thus our concern with ecology is with the study of the interrelationship of man with the Body and Consciousness of the Divine Mother, beginning first with the microcosm of self and then expanding to include not only the macrocosm of the world he inhabits but also that of the solar system, the galaxy, and the entire universe—in all of its material and spiritual planes. All solutions to man's environmental problems must of necessity arise from this total view of ecology; for a limited understanding of man's universal biosphere can only result in limited conclusions, which may or may not be valid within the confines of his immediate physical environment.

A case in point is man's concern with overpopulation, considered by many ecologists to be the most pressing problem of our age. By means of projected analysis, environmentalists have concluded that the earth cannot support a population double its present size of five billion people. Yet with a current growth rate of about 1.7 percent each year, that figure could be reached in the next century. A worldwide drive is now under way to reduce the population growth to zero and thereby stay the wholesale famines and resulting wars that are considered to be inevitable.

In commenting upon these theories we must point out certain gaps in man's understanding of his ecology. It is one thing for man to control the populations of "the fish of the sea, the fowl of the air, the cattle, and of every creeping thing"—for God placed these in his care; [175] but it is another for him to assume this control over mankind. Although God gave to man the privilege of naming the species and governing their reproduction, he reserved for himself and his heavenly Hierarchy the authority of giving or withholding Life among his sons and daughters evolving on earth.

It is strange—more than strange, it is diabolical—that millions of God-fearing people should be convinced overnight by population "experts" that current growth trends represent an ever mounting swell on a graph that has no governing principle behind it, no coordinator, no God who is in control of his universe. The truth is that human life is not merely one step removed from animal life: it is another evolution entirely—an evolution of souls in the state of becoming God, an evolution programmed from the very heart of the Central Sun, whose every member, like the hairs of our heads, is numbered. [176]

God does not create without purpose, and life in the planetary ecosystem is not without purpose. If we can define that purpose, we can define our ecology. To begin with, we must realize that the planet is a space platform to which billions of lifestreams have been assigned to work out their individual and collective destinies. (For every soul now wearing physical form, at least two are waiting at the portals of birth for the opportunity to reembody.) We must understand that there is a divine plan for the planetary systems, each world destined to host certain lifewaves, or root races, who come forth in succeeding ages to fulfill their destiny.

In the case of earth, added to the assigned souls were unplanned-for laggards who by edict of the Karmic Board were given haven here when their planets were destroyed. These intruders as well as fallen angels cast down into earth bodies* descended to earth, cohabitated with her evolutions and continued

*See Elizabeth Clare Prophet, *Forbidden Mysteries of Enoch: The Untold Story of Men and Angels,* containing all the Enoch texts, including the Book of Enoch and the Book of the Secrets of Enoch, esp. pp. 1–76.

their self-multiplication through subsequent geneti-
cally engineered human creations of mechanization
man. (See Genesis 6:4; Revelation 12:7-9)

We begin to see that it is the responsibility of
those who presently enjoy the privilege of being in
embodiment to provide for the birth, care, and education of a predetermined group of souls who are
natives of earth as well as an undetermined world
population consisting of various strains from other
planets, including Christed ones, Teachers and angels
of Light who took on dense bodies to lead the original
children of Light out of the miasma of evolutionary
crosscurrents that have indeed upset the balance of
the ecosystem.

Given these x factors, it is possible to say there
are ten billion plus lifestreams who are now karmi-
cally bound to planet earth. That is, through reembodiment these have made karma which ties them to
the physical octave and the physical evolution of the
lifewaves of earth until that personal and planetary
karma is transmuted. The merciful dispensation of
the violet flame and its persistent invocation by the
Children of the Sun is *the key* to the undoing of the
retribution of an age hanging over our heads as a
sword of Damocles, or a satellite of nuclear self-
destruction.

What with cataclysm the handwriting on the
wall for the purging of the elements prior to the
golden age, what with the unpredictability of humans
side by side with the predilection of the fallen ones of
all castes to perpetuate the wars of their ancient rival-
ries, power plays and infighting, it is not ours to
presently predict the capacity of the earth body to
support the ten billion and more who are still struggling for time and a patch of earth to outplay their
karma on this weary war-torn world.

One thing is, however, clear: prior to the golden age (barring subsequent dispensations handed down by the Lords of Karma), no more than those presently accounted for and dwelling in various planes will be allowed tenure in physical embodiment at a given time.

And karma itself (albeit mitigated by mankind's dynamic decrees to the violet flame) is the regulator not only of the destinies of men and nations but also of the planetary population. Moreover, the Cosmic Christ as the Mediator of world and individual karma—whether it is held back by divine mercy to the children of Light or unleashed as divine justice upon the seed of the Wicked One—may raise his right hand to intercede against the fury of the Four Horsemen of the Apocalypse and the seven angels who pour out the vials of the seven last plagues.

All of these probabilities, as the web of karmic circumstance, as the roads taken or not taken, will have much and everything to do with the survival of untold millions whether physically or in the astral plane.

While all things are in flux and free will is yet ours, we must remember that the constant of predestination is upon the sons and daughters of God who have chosen to make sure their calling and their election to ascend to God—by their will to survive and to serve. Yes, some are predestined to ascend, for they have sealed their hearts in the Father's heart even as he is in theirs. Their number is known of him, for their names are written in the Book of Life. While others, also by free will, have predestined themselves to non-Being.

As we shall explain in Chapter Nine, the fact that man can work out the karma of deeds and fulfill his destiny only in the plane of Matter makes it absolutely necessary for the soul who has not earned his ascension to reembody. Lifestreams studying between embodiments in temples of Light and in the etheric cities and retreats of the Masters may make progress in their understanding of Cosmic Law and its application to the human dilemma, but not until they reenter the physical octave can they effect change in the world of Matter-form by working the works of God, thereby gaining mastery over the energies of the physical universe. Here man made his mistakes; here he must correct them. This is the "place prepared" [177] for him to exercise his free will; and to this place he must return to experience the consequences of his creations. Man has made the world what it is, and he is obliged to live in it until he determines to change it and to evolve a better way.

By neglecting to create a proper environment for incoming souls, mankind deny those who are scheduled for embodiment the surroundings that are necessary for their spiritual development and their mastery in the planes of Matter. By neglecting their responsibility to take dominion over the earth, mankind have allowed the problems of war and aggression, famine, pestilence, economic imbalance, pollution, and the spread of evil among the ignorant masses to reach such alarming proportions that the only solution they can see is to create a worldwide ecosystem vested with unlimited authority to control the lifewaves upon the planet. The primary goal of those who favor such a system is zero population growth. Their slogan seems to be If You Can't Eliminate Pollution, Eliminate People.

Man's failure to master his ecosystem is also cause for concern to the cosmic Hierarchy, for his contamination of his earthly home has resulted in a setback in the cosmic timetable for the incoming golden age. The Lords of Karma are directly involved with the problems of ecology; for it is they who decide how the edict of God "Be fruitful and multiply and replenish the earth"[178] will be implemented by regulating the flow of souls into and out of embodiment. In considering who shall reembody, one of the most important factors which the Karmic Board must examine is the weight of personal and planetary karma, that is, the degree of human pollution of the environment on all four planes of consciousness—etheric, mental, emotional, and physical.

Since the earth can support only so much karmic weight, this weight determines the number of people that can survive on the planet at a given time. The karmic weight of the planet is the total weight of misqualified energy that mankind have put forth since their fall from grace. Just as ecologists look at a biotic community* in terms of numbers, biomass (weight), or calories (energy), so in their annual deliberation of which souls shall be taken into or out of embodiment, the Lords of Karma must take into consideration individual karma as it is added to (in the case of births) or subtracted from (in the case of deaths) the karmic weight of the planet.

When a soul descends into embodiment, he is assigned a portion, or weight, of his karma that he must work out in the physical octave in that lifetime; at the same time, the weight of that portion of his karma which is held in abeyance at emotional, mental, and etheric levels must also be reckoned, although on a different scale. What effect the individual ecosystem will have upon the total ecosystem is arrived at by cosmic computer, and the decisions of the Lords of Creation must be governed accordingly.

*Ecological terms defined: *biosphere:* the part of the world in which life can exist; *ecosystem:* an ecological unit composed of living organisms and their environment functioning as a whole in Nature; *biotic community:* the living organisms within an ecosystem.

Another consideration in the assignment of life-streams in a given era is that the number of souls having a heavy karma (a greater amount of misqual-ified energy to transmute) must be balanced by an equivalent number having a light karma (a relatively greater amount of correctly qualified energy). More-over, individuals who have been tied together in the past, evolving within the same ecosystem, must reem-body as a group in order to work out what is called *group karma,* which may be defined as energies ex-changed by the members of a family, a group, a community, a nation, or a planet. Group karma is made by the evolutions of an ecosystem when they either move together or fail to move together in con-certed action. This karma may be good or bad, positive or negative; that is, individuals acting as a group may misqualify energy or they may qualify it correctly to the glory of God and man.

The carrying capacity of the biosphere (its abil-ity to support a certain number of organisms) can be increased only as mankind balance their individual and group karma and thereby lessen the total weight of planetary effluvia. If karma is not being balanced daily through prayer, service, and invocation to the sacred fire which results in the transmutation of mis-qualified energy, then the population of a planet must be limited by the Lords of Karma. Thus increases in the population of a planet must be accompanied by a corresponding lightening of the karmic weight of the individuals in embodiment.

Due to the enormity of mankind's karma result-ing from their departure from grace and their subse-quent misuse of the sacred fire on Mu and Atlantis, the Lords of Karma, as an act of mercy, greatly reduced the earth's population, allowing souls evolv-ing on etheric, mental, and astral planes to regain their equilibrium before returning to the physical octave to face the harsh realities of life—the effects of causes set up in their former existence. During the ten-thousand-year period following the sinking of Atlantis, the forces of the elements worked to balance the cycles of Nature and to purify the four planes of Matter in preparation for the civilization that was to provide the link to the golden age.

During the same period mankind balanced a great deal of karma through pain and suffering as well as through mutual service. Avatars—souls of great Light and spiritual attainment, such as Jesus the Christ and Gautama Buddha—were sent to take upon themselves a certain portion of mankind's planetary karma. This they were able to do because they themselves were "without blemish and without spot," [179] having expiated what karma they had, if any, in previous lives.

The fact that in the West time is reckoned before and after Christ indicates that the mission of Jesus the Christ, who "died for our sins," [180] marks the beginning of a new era and a new civilization. Such a tremendous weight of planetary karma, or "sin," was borne by the Master, both in his ministry and in his victory over mortality, that every man, woman, and child evolving upon the planet can rightly affirm "Christ died for me!" Furthermore, they can accept him as their personal Saviour; for he has not only saved each one from the agony of the cross, of bearing the sins of the world as he did, but he has also saved each one for the sheer joy of overcoming the world [181] and ascending as he did "unto my Father, and your Father; and to my God, and your God." [182] With these words spoken to Mary Magdalene on the morning of his resurrection, Jesus made clear the equal opportunity of the sons and daughters of the one God who throughout eternity receives all who earn the right to share in his oneness.

Because of the triumph of the Saviour and the lives of sacrifice led by the saints who followed after him, the Lords of Karma were able by the middle of the nineteenth century to justify a tremendous step-up in the birth rate, granting the privilege of reembodiment to many God-fearing souls of great creative genius who vowed as Jesus had before them to glorify God on the earth (in the planes of Matter) and to finish the work which He gave them to do. [183] The Lords of Karma also opened the gates of birth to those souls who had been confined to the astral planes because of the part they played in the destruction of Atlantis and their unwillingness to confess the Christ and acknowledge the incarnation of the God flame in the man Jesus. [184] Thus as we approach the completion of this two-thousand-year cycle, cosmic law dictates that as many lifestreams as possible be given the opportunity to attain reunion with their Divine Presence and to balance a maximum amount of karma prior to the release of the Christ Light known as the Second Coming of the Christ, which must occur before the golden-age civilization can be externalized.

While it is true that the increase in the world's population has been facilitated by advances in science and technology, it should be understood that all of mankind's discoveries and inventions have come forth from the Lords of Karma by special dispensation and that no forward movement of the race is ever made without their approval and the assistance of the entire cosmic Hierarchy. The creative genius of man is the spark of the Christ Mind. As Jesus knew full well, it is the Father—the Spirit, the animating Principle—which quickens the lump of clay that of itself can do nothing. [185]

Those flashes of insight which the great of all ages experience are actually cosmic glyphs flashed forth from the I AM Presence to the outer consciousness.

Even the steady plodding of the empiricists and the superhuman constancy of a Copernicus, a Brahe, a Kepler, or a Galileo, who have held high the torch of civilization, are directed and empowered from above. We must remember that the miracles and blessings of science were never intended to be used to subject the flame to mechanization, but rather, by the grace of God, to free the race from the death grip of a mechanical existence in order that billions of souls might have a greater opportunity to work out their karma, gain self-mastery, and fulfill the purposes of Life.

The Lords of Karma have decreed that during the thirty-year preparatory period prior to the scheduled appearance of the golden age a great number of highly evolved souls should reembody, together with cosmic emissaries and avatars who have never before incarnated upon earth.* These will bring forth and anchor in the physical octave the necessary scientific discoveries, practical know-how, and spiritual understanding to raise mankind to the level of awareness where they can use the dynamic power of the Christ Light within to master their environment. The dispensation of the Lords of Karma providing for the birth of these dedicated souls—Children of the Sun, the virtuous and the meek who are destined to inherit the earth—was pronounced by the Goddess of Liberty on May 22, 1966:

"We see through the span of the Spirit a new age, a coming age of greater hope. We see that each

---

*On February 4, 1962, Sanat Kumara and Lady Master Venus announced that at the conjunction of the planets a number of Christed beings were born who would "show men how to perfect themselves not only through social evolution but also through spiritual evolution." The hierarchs of Venus said that "they shall direct mankind more and more to the power of their own I AM Presence and that great Cosmic Being, the unfolding Christ within themselves." They also said that their coming was an initial release paving the way for the Ascended Masters to step through the veil to manifest visibly in the physical octaves of earth.

generation that fails to accept the torch will of necessity, by the demands of Nature, pass on some form of life to succeeding generations. We see the great tides of the Spirit going to the Lords of Life and Death and speaking unto them as each candidate for reembodiment comes to the gateway of birth and saying unto them, 'MENE, MENE, TEKEL, UPHARSIN: Thou art weighed in the balances, and art found wanting, [186] O unworthy one. Go thou back and wait thy turn; for when Life was given thee before, thou wouldst not heed the call of God, but thou wasted thy substance and cast it upon the ground.'

"Therefore, let the most worthy ones be selected from the vast multitudes awaiting reembodiment upon this planet and from the virtuous, from the blessed, and from those who seek to finish their course with joy and dignity. Let souls come forth and let the mighty ones of old walk the earth, the sons of God who have rejoicing in their hearts; and let the rest go back into the Darkness they have created and loved and let them remain there until perchance the gateway to birth shall once again be opened to them in some distant time.

"Let the Lords of Karma take heed this day to our plea for the withholding from the earth of a further onslaught of the hordes of darkness and shadows from ancient times. Let those lifestreams now be stayed! We command it in God's name. And we say, let the virtuous come forth and let the sons of God, whose faces shine like the sun, come forth! And let Virtue have her manifest reward!

"It has been said, 'My Spirit shall not always strive with man for he also is flesh.' [187] Hear, then, this word as a fiat of Light is entered upon the great records of akasha. I AM the Goddess of Liberty. I have commanded by divine decree this day that the power of virtue must stand and shine forth. And if those to whom the torch of Life has been passed choose to deny that torch, shall not the torch of Life deny them? For is it not written, 'Whosoever shall deny me before men, him will I also deny before my Father which is in heaven'?[188]

"The Children of the Sun shall inherit the earth; the meek shall inherit the earth.[189] When the chastity of meekness and love for God is accepted by the people in full faith that he is God of the very earth and that his love is supreme and that his beauty is transcendent light streaming forth from the portals of Infinity, these shall have accepted that God is the God of very gods.[190]

"They shall not be ashamed in this day or in any age to call him Father, for they are of the Christ-dimension. These are the sons of the Spirit; these are the sons of Liberty. For in a new generation they shall stand to bring about a spiritual revolution that shall sweep the earth free from those children of riot who seek pleasure and all that is without when the kingdoms of the Spirit contain the treasures of Infinity as all that is within."[191]

Ignorant of the spiritual causes behind material effects, ecologists have viewed with alarm the implications of what appears to them to be an overwhelming increase in the world's population since the turn of the century. What's more, their projected figures for the year 2000 and beyond have led to dire predictions on the fate of the human race. Citing the rapid depletion of natural resources, the widespread pollution of the environment, and the unwillingness of governments and industry to cooperate in the management of the biosphere, Neo-Malthusians* see only famine

---

*T. R. Malthus (1766–1834) was an economist who theorized that as population tends to increase at a faster rate than its means of subsistence, unless it be checked by moral restraint or by disease, famine, war, or other disaster, widespread poverty and degradation inevitably result.

and social cataclysm awaiting man in the future. Their doom consciousness hangs as a pall over the land; in guilt and gloom they have shrouded the joys of procreating in the name of the LORD. Instead of rejoicing at the opportunity for so many of God's children to realize his kingdom upon earth, they have attempted to arrest the flow of souls through the portals of birth by imposing birth control en masse.

The Commission on Population Growth and the American Future reported to Congress and the President on March 11, 1972, that after two years of study they recommended a national policy of zero population growth—based on a limit of two children per family—to avoid the threat of a "more contrived and regulated society"[192] in the future.

This is just one example of the hysteria that has seized the governments of the nations that are now instituting comprehensive programs of population control, including the legalization of abortion, the encouragement of sterilization, and the widespread dissemination of birth-control information. Strong consideration has even been given to the proposal that the state undertake the responsibility of deciding who shall procreate and when. Moreover, research is currently under way to create test-tube babies, thus giving the state the ultimate method to control both the quantity and quality of its citizens.

The consequences of these attempts by man to interfere with God's business—when he has so often proved himself incapable of minding his own—are tragic. Those who are ignorant of the laws of karma and reembodiment cannot begin to imagine the far-reaching effects of their tampering with personal and planetary cycles. Those who deny the opportunity of embodiment to souls assigned to take their place in a given ecosystem at a given time will find that when they themselves are ready to apply for readmission to the earth, their karma will decree that they shall be the ones—the two out of three—who will be denied the opportunity for rebirth. And their waiting period may extend hundreds or thousands of years before the door will once again be opened to them.

This is not the only danger in man's attempting to control the population of the world. The modern method of slaughtering the innocents[193] by denying birth to the missing links in the chain of the ecosystem causes irreparable damage to its internal structure; for the spiritual, cultural, and scientific contributions of the Christ Selves of these lifestreams are absolutely necessary to its survival. Alas, when the actors who are cast by the Divine Director in vital roles on the world stage are forbidden to play out their parts in the drama of Life, the sequence of the plot is broken and the curtain drops before the final act is begun. Painfully, painfully mankind learn that when they arrest the natural flow of Life they create more problems than they solve!

Humanity will never solve their social and economic problems through state-directed birth-control programs; for the error in the human equation lies not in the quantity of people, but in the quality of their inherent selfishness. Only a self-centered attitude could make people willing to sacrifice human life rather than personal pleasure; only the lack of perspective caused by selfishness could make them unwilling to correct the abuses of our natural resources—resources which are more than adequate to meet the needs of the souls for whom the earth was created. Thus the Spokesman for the Karmic Board proclaims:

"Let me reiterate that which your beloved El Morya has declared in his *Encyclical*[194] warning mankind against the doctrines of Malthus and bringing to their attention the fact that Almighty God has the power, through the great influx of souls destined to come into embodiment, to bring balance to the affairs of the world. In these latter days it is understandable that the planet should harbor more souls than in the past; for through science mankind now have at their disposal the means to produce an abundant harvest for all, even while much of the arable land is not being cultivated.

"Therefore I say to you that it is not man who ought to regulate these matters, but it is God in his infinite wisdom who can and will do so when called upon. Yet we do not say that individuals ought not to exercise prudence in the carrying-out of their family aims. Certainly this is wholly within the domain of cosmic reason. After all, precious ones, you ought not to bring forth more children than you are able to care for and for whom you may adequately express your love.

"But as we see it, it is not a problem of national responsibility so much as it is one of personal responsibility wherein each family ought to make its own determination as to what it desires to do. For the power of God has often brought forth at a specific moment in the world's evolution some great soul destined to become for all mankind a great Light upon the planetary body. And then it was spoken that 'the people that walked in darkness have seen a great Light.'[195] And the Light manifested upon the planet and raised mankind a step higher in their own cosmic mark of achievement."[196]

Whereas the LORD giveth Life and the LORD taketh Life,[197] within the province of his free will and within his own family unit man may also give or take Life. But whereas the decisions he makes are his own, the Life he gives and the Life he takes is not his own, nor is it his brother's: it is God's. The decisions he makes are therefore of far-reaching consequence; for there is no more frightful karma than that which accrues from the abuse of the Life that is God—no matter what its form.

Some who favor compulsory birth control claim that the earth's natural resources are not sufficient to enable the present population to live at the level of consumption enjoyed by the majority in the industrialized societies. Moreover, they say that the remaining natural resources are being used up at an alarming rate without regard for the ecological consequences to the biosphere. Therefore, it is argued, drastic measures must be taken to ensure that mankind in the future, both in the developed and the developing countries, will have sufficient resources to maintain a meaningful level of existence.

While we recognize that many of the ecologists' recommendations may be valid within their limited frame of reference, we must point out that according to the Ascended Masters, the earth has abundant resources to sustain its present population at a universally high standard of living. In fact, at no time in history have the earth's resources, when properly used, been inadequate to support the souls abiding thereon. The Chief of the Darjeeling Council said in his *Encyclical on World Good Will:*

"The presently available resources of the international economy—comprising organized manpower and materiel with the facilities to transport and mobilize their effectiveness; knowledge and skills and the means to communicate them—are sufficient to mend all the world's ills. To this task we have pledged our lives, our fortunes, and our sacred honor.

"The regrettable trend of the purposeless dissipation of mankind's energies and assets into crosscurrents of means and ends in politics, religion, and economics continues to deny to the world community the unity of freedom, the peace of understanding, and the enlightenment of abundance in which all should share. Tensions and dissatisfactions—individual and international, both well and little known—persist; therefore, the demand for renewed study, foresight, and decisive action imbued with world goodwill should be our first consideration in the universal cause for the ennoblement of man.

"Honest appraisal of abundant opportunity at hand will reaffirm that the world already has at its disposal the elements necessary and sufficient for the resolving of its difficulties. Therefore, fuller utilization of the matrix of the present is the only sound approach to international order and better living; and this disposition must dispel any tendency to put off till the morrow that which needs attention today if that morrow is to become a desirable reality." [198]

"The present surge in world population, which seems to have caused many demographers to review and revise the doctrines of Malthus with the aim of extinguishing or limiting human life in complete contradiction to God's laws, will prove of less concern to future societies as they become aware of marvelous methods of increasing agricultural production, of harvesting the wealth of the sea, and of the unlimited use of atomic energy in advanced city planning as well as in interplanetary colonization.

"There is a purpose in the plans of God which far transcends the understanding of the human intellect and the memory of history upon earth. The wonders that are to come will soon be dwarfed by still greater wonders, and therefore all life should live in a state of constant expectancy.

"It is the joy of the Mind of God to give richly of his blessing. But above all, may I counsel you now, students of the Light and all mankind: Obtain first from God the Father the wisdom to live peaceably, to deal gently and courteously with one another, to promote the education of mankind the world around, and especially by honest efforts to prevent the increase in number of those indigent individuals who are prone to commit crimes against society.

"The value of training the young in a proper manner and encouraging them to live lives of useful service and good character cannot be overestimated. Political scandals within the nations of the world and the harshness of police-state methods (as enforced in Communist-dominated countries) must be overridden by the sword and the invocation to the powerful flame of the Prince of Peace. The Prince of Peace is imaged in the compassionate Christ going forth to teach all nations that the way of God is good, that his wonders are intended to be used and possessed by all and exclusively by none. A higher way of life than vain competition must be pursued. Men must become God-spurred and less motivated by status seeking. Teach this truth and all nations shall prosper! The sharing of the grace of heaven is a message of eternal watchfulness from the Great White Brotherhood to all upon earth.

"Abundance and peace go hand in hand, and this state of felicity is the will of God. Let this planet, by the power of spiritual and natural alchemy, arise to build new homes, new churches, new schools, a new civilization, new concepts, new virtue, new greatness—all in the bonds of eternal confidence which blazes forth from the very heart of God and is anchored within your own physical heart as the expanding flame spark of the Immortal Alchemist himself!" [199]

Again and again the Masters have told us that if man uses his natural resources wisely, he can raise the standard of living upon the planet and at the same

time increase the population without harm to the ecosystem. They have shown us through the akashic
records and archives of ancient civilizations how the
deserts have been made to bloom and the waste places
made fit for man's habitation. They have said that the
vegetation of the seas could feed the entire population
of the planet without even requiring the tilling of the
soil. Thus, by applying the principles of cosmic re-
sourcefulness man can reach the goal of bringing into
embodiment all who are destined to complete their
evolution on this planet and earn their ascension—and
at the same time pave the way for the golden age and
the reign of an Ascended Master culture.

Another problem of ecology that no citizen of
the world community can ignore is the pollution of the
environment. The Masters who lecture in the retreats
of the Brotherhood on the divine ecology teach us that
in the delicate equilibrium of our ecosystem, the pollution of earth, air, and water is but the final out-
cropping of man's misqualifications of his etheric,
mental, and emotional bodies. Thus there is a pollution of the etheric plane, of the mental plane, of the
emotional plane, and of the physical plane, both at the
personal and the planetary level. This all-pervading
pollution, which sears the souls of billions, must be
quenched by the purifying fires of the Holy Spirit and
the energies redeemed through the Christ flame anchored in the heart of every man.

The pollution that man contacts with his physical senses is the cumulative effect of the violations of
natural law that he has tolerated within the forcefields
of his consciousness since his departure from Eden.
Just as mastery in the physical plane is achieved
through prior soul development in each of the other
three planes of consciousness, so the lack of mastery
in the physical plane that manifests as pollution is the

end result of a lack of soul development on etheric, mental, and emotional planes. Man's first act of disobedience to the Creator was his first abuse of his spiritual-material resources. And the seeds of his rebellion have become the seeds of his pollution that have spread throughout his being and world.

Thus it becomes more and more obvious that in looking for solutions to the problems of ecology, including that of environmental pollution, man must take into consideration not only the causes and effects he observes on the physical plane, but also those causes which originate within the collective subconscious and gradually spiral through the memory, the mind, and the emotions, ultimately to appear in the world of the concrete; for these momentums, unless checked by man's invocation to the sacred fire, will continue to dominate the motives and acts of the human race.

Those ecologists who have suggested that environmental deterioration might best be remedied by placing a moratorium on technological innovation ought first to consider the innovation of a massive campaign to promote a tender, reverent regard for every part of Life through communion with the Holy Spirit. An active harmlessness rather than a harmful inaction is the need of the hour. A positive attitude toward self-purification embraced by citizens and communities enthusiastically working together in an all-out effort to stop the encroachments upon Mother Nature, elemental life, and each other can work wonders in short order. And by this method those industrial processes that are harmful to life will be exposed and eliminated as the Holy Spirit teaches man how to accomplish all that is necessary to his enjoyment of the abundant Life both harmlessly and harmoniously.

Man must realize that the greatest influence he can bring to bear upon his environment originates in the realm of spiritual causes, that of the Superconscious Ego, of the Divine Self which, when invoked into action, releases unto man "all power in heaven and in earth" to bring the four planes of his personal and planetary bodies into congruency with the cosmic blueprint. When man sees the spiritual-material universe as a unit, as a single ecosystem, he will begin to study the interrelationship of the planes of Spirit and Matter and he will begin to arrive at solutions to the problems of ecology drawn from the cause-effect sequences of their energy cycles.

Change on earth can be brought about only through the transmutative powers of the Holy Spirit. By giving himself wholeheartedly to the will of God and by dedicating his total energies to its implementation on earth, man will, in the crucible of the present, draw the necessary energy from the Source to solve the problems of ecology—past, present, and future. This energy will manifest as a flourishing science and an abundance of raw materials to build a civilization unparalleled in the annals of time. On the other hand, if man continues to give his energies to the fulfillment of his human will and to the solution of human problems by human means, his energy will be reduced by divine edict to a minimal allotment and his evolution will retrograde to the primitive culture from which he has painfully emerged. [200]

The flame of peace which was invoked by the Prince of Peace two thousand years ago is the missing ingredient in man's ecology. It is the essential element that would make all of his human efforts divine. Yet there is a false security which comes from a false sense of peace of which the heirs of the kingdom must be forewarned. Both falsities are the result of idolatry.

Therefore, the definition of idolatry must be carefully considered by those who cherish their soul's rapport with the Spirit of God in Nature.

We define idolatry as the placing of one's trust in the vessel of clay that houses the Spirit instead of in the flame itself that abides therein. If one is attached to the forms of Life rather than to their contents, one has failed to discover the mystery of Life. However, one must be careful not to deny the necessary function of the form. One must learn to love for its own intrinsic worth the altar on which the sacred fire blazes. One must love it for its essential beauty and for its indispensable quality. One must love the form because it represents energy in a state of becoming—in a state of evolving toward a more permanent manifestation. Although the forms of man and beast, tree and flower may be temporal, the electronic energies that sustain these forms are in the process of spinning a momentum of light which by the law of transcendence will one day spiral into the perfection of the divine ideal that is formed in the planes of Spirit.

All of form in Nature is the Body of the Divine Mother seen in all her glory throughout the four cycles of the year. Through the rituals of these cycles the energies of God coalesce in Matter-form: as the sun of the atom gathers unto itself more of the energies of Spirit, of the "Fire infolding itself," [201] the universe transcends itself in ever widening spirals which, hour by hour, include a more manifold expression of the Creator's consciousness. Nature, then, must be revered as the chalice into which the flame of the Holy Spirit descends. And our attachments to Nature must be to the Spirit, to the essence of the sacred fire, even while our love enfolds the blossoms and the leaves and the grasses, all of which hold droplets of fire from the Fiery World.

The principle of nonattachment enables us to revere Life as both Father and Mother. As we apply this principle to our persons and our possessions, we are not overcome when the energies that have sustained the form in the planes of Matter pass through the cycle of disintegration and return to the plane of Spirit. We do not mourn when death seems nigh, nor do we mind our separation from loved ones in time and space; for our attachment is to the flame within and to the fires of the soul that animate the form—to the Will that structured the form, to the Love that magnetized its atoms, and to the Wisdom that inspired its design.

We have spoken of the deluded sense of those who cry "Peace" when there is no peace. [202] Although they walk in the name of peace, their ways—the vibrations of their thoughts and feelings which go before them—are not peaceful; for they lack the polarity of the Father-Mother God anchored by the Holy Spirit in the four lower bodies of those who love the Christ.

Man must correctly apprehend the flame of peace, the balanced action of the Masculine and Feminine aspects, the purple and gold of the Alpha and Omega spirals which were so magnificently anchored in the planes of Matter by the Prince of Peace. This flame is enshrined by the Elohim Peace and Aloha in the etheric Pavilion of Peace situated over the Hawaiian Islands. By meditating upon the divine attributes of the Sixth Ray—the Christ-peace that is ever active in ministering unto the needs of mankind—at the same time that he consciously draws into the chamber of the heart the regenerative fires of the purple and gold, man can induce the alignment of his four lower bodies and the balancing of his threefold flame. Through service to one's fellowman the flame of peace is expanded within the molecules of one's consciousness. The more one serves, the more one absorbs of the flow of the flame. The greater one's service, the greater one's capacity to amplify in the name of the Christ both the geometry of the flame and the energy of the flame.

Without faith it is impossible to please God,[203] and without peace it is impossible to properly qualify his energy. The sudden destruction that is wrought upon the efforts of those who rely upon a false sense of peace is the collapse of the false foundations which they have laid. When man attempts to build without peace and without a correct apprehension of the laws of Nature, the structure of his creation lacks the balancing action of the Holy Spirit—the Masculine and Feminine aspects of the flame of peace—that is necessary to sustain the matrix of every endeavor, both human and divine. The success of any project depends upon the understanding that the only true and lasting peace is that which comes from non-attachment to the form, from immersion in the Spirit, and from building upon the foundation of the flame of peace; for as Paul said, "Other foundation can no man lay than that is laid, which is [the flame of] Jesus Christ."[204]

The fiat of the Ancient of Days "Whosoever hath, to him shall be given, and he shall have more abundance: but whosoever hath not, from him shall be taken away even that he hath,"[205] spoken by Jesus the Christ, must also be understood in the light of our expanding knowledge of the flame of peace. The Elohim of Peace explains that those who hold the flame of peace within their hearts and minds and are obedient to the laws of harmony in their creations establish both in themselves and in their creations a magnetic force-field based on the polarity of the Father-Mother God that draws to them more of the God-qualities which they have determined to precipitate into form.

No matter how hard they try or how loud their

cry, those who create without the flame of peace will
never be able to establish that magnetic forcefield
which will draw to them a continuous flow of energy
to sustain and amplify the original matrix of their
creation. What's more, the energy which they have
misused in their miscreations will be taken from them;
for by the law of attraction God's energy cannot
adhere to an imperfect matrix or to a forcefield that
lacks the polarity of the flame of peace focused in the
Great Central Sun Magnet. If his material gain has
not come as the result of his Christed illumination and
compassion, when man is tried in the fire of the Holy
Spirit[206] he will lose all that he has. And it will surely
come to pass when the fiat of the Ancient of Days is
invoked by the Lords of Karma that the sudden
destruction spoken of by Paul will be upon him.[207]

Essential to the understanding of the doctrine of
ahimsa is man's relationship to animal life. This subject raises many questions which for centuries have
divided people around the world. Does man regard his
cow as his friend, his servant, his meat, or his mother?
Depending on his point of view—some people actually
consider their attitude toward animals more important
than their attitude toward God—man will take various
approaches to ahimsa. From total indifference to
shameful abuses, from wholesale slaughter and vivi-
section to the worship of animals, a golden mean based
on the Golden Rule must be found.

Let us begin our discussion with a brief outline of
certain facts which must be set forth if mankind are to
have a proper regard for animal life on this planet.

Long ago scientists on Mu and Atlantis began to
use the knowledge they had acquired over the forces
of Nature to imprison Life rather than to set it free. In
order to control the beings of earth, air, fire, and
water—whose natural inclination to restore harmony

in Nature interfered with their perverted practices—
they locked the elementals in etheric patterns, using
advanced methods of magnetism and mind control.
These patterns, which resembled the variety of creations we now observe in the animal kingdom, were
actually electronic forcefields which the scientists
superimposed upon the elementals for a dual purpose: (1) to limit their expression of the Holy Spirit,
and (2) to manipulate their energies and thereby manipulate the functions of Nature to their own ends.

Eventually the energies used to sustain these
patterns coalesced around the elementals in succeeding stages of densification, until that which had begun
as an electronic forcefield on the etheric plane became
an idea on the mental plane, a sentient being on the
emotional plane, and finally a physical entity on the
earth plane. In this manner millions of imprisoned
elementals became subject to the laws governing the
evolution of animal life in this octave. Later through
certain depredations of the human consciousness and
the misuse of the sacred fire, other millions were also
forced to enter the bodies of animals. As a result,
the Christward evolution of the elemental kingdom—
which should have taken place simultaneously with
the Godward evolution of man's consciousness—was
detoured by an alternate evolution through the animal kingdom.

Whereas each man has an individual soul, animals have what is called a *group soul*—an energy
forcefield which focuses their group awareness of
Life. Each of the species is a unit of evolution within
the animal kingdom, and the combined awareness of
these units makes up the total animal consciousness
on the planetary body. It is the group soul that produces the herd instinct—the gregariousness of cattle,
the formation of birds in flight, or the movement of a

school of fish—and the migratory patterns of many of the species.

Whether there are ten or ten thousand kine on the hillsides, the group soul of each species continues to evolve; for its evolution is based not on numbers,* but on experience and the evolvement of habit patterns which are subject to man's own expansion of the Christ consciousness. For animal life, strange as it may seem, is totally dominated by man's awareness of God. Animals can rise no higher than man's highest thoughts and feelings and actions, and they can fall no lower than his lowest. Animals have no free will of their own, but reflect the free will of man; for the dominion over the animal kingdom which God gave to man was the dominion of his Christ consciousness over the group soul.

Elementals that have been evolving for thousands of years through the group soul of animals have come to identify with their animal bodies and with their animal consciousness just as the souls of men have come to identify with the human form and consciousness. Thus the elemental that is tied to the body of a horse, a cow, a goat, a dog, or a cat thinks that he is that animal. He has lost his awareness of himself both as an elemental and as an elemental inhabiting an animal body. The domestic animal who exhibits more than ordinary talent and devotion is no doubt an imprisoned elemental who readily takes his place as a member of the family. People would no more kill their pets than they would their own children, because they are more than animal forms; they are elementals tied to animal forms—worthy of being called the friend of man.

*If numbers were necessary for the evolution of the group soul, it would not have been possible to transmit the accumulated soul awareness of each species through the male and female which God preserved on Noah's ark (Genesis 6:19).

How do you go about freeing that friend from his limited form? He would speak; yet he cannot, because his form does not permit. He would serve your every need; yet he cannot, because his form does not permit. You would loose him and let him go; yet you cannot, because your consciousness does not permit.

Because the animal form is an imperfect matrix for the integration of the virtues of the Christ in the elemental kingdom and because the brain and nervous system are inadequate vehicles for their Self-conscious awareness of the Holy Spirit, the elementals are entirely dependent upon man's consciousness as they evolve from a state of limitation back to the unlimited awareness of Life they once knew. And this spiritual evolution is a requirement of the Law that must be met before they can attain immortality.

The only way man can free and raise elementals that have been tied to animal forms is for man to free and raise his own consciousness to the level of the Christ; for then the elementals over which he was given dominion will identify with the Christ in man rather than with man's carnal consciousness, which binds the elemental to the group soul of the species. And when the elemental no longer identifies with the animal, he will no longer require the body of the animal in order to evolve: he will break the bonds of his confinement and commence his God Self-awareness— as a sylph in the form of a sylph, as an undine in the form of an undine, as a gnome in the form of a gnome, or as a salamander in the form of a salamander.

When all the elementals have been freed from the animal consciousness and from the animal form, they will assimilate the net gain of their experience in the animal kingdom and they will be given the same right to earn their immortality which man now enjoys. If man identifies with the spirit of love, courage, loyalty, obedience, and faith which the elementals express, rather than allowing his attachment to be confined to the animal form—which attitude, as we have said, is idolatrous—he will rejoice to see those qualities immortalized through the perfected forms of the elementals, who, like man, originated in God. Just as man fears not to surrender the weight of his terrestrial body for the glory of his celestial body, [208] so he should not lament the passing of the old order of elemental life for the new.

Those who have come to accept Life as it is expressed through animals as natural and complete do not realize that the harmony they observe in the animal kingdom is the harmony of God's consciousness that manifests wherever there is Life, even though the form be imperfect (even as the inharmony they observe is a reflection of the inharmony of man's consciousness). So powerful is the Spirit that animates the form that it transcends the form in its expression even before the imperfect pattern gives way, or evolves, to perfection.

The pleading eyes of our animal friends tell us that Life is not altogether content in its present matrix. Here we see Life imprisoned. Here we would set it free. Here Spirit is crucified in the planes of Matter. Here we would sanctify it in the resurrection fires. Here we must make it whole by bringing it into congruency with the immaculate design of the Godhead. Through an enlightened ahimsa, an exalted awareness of God in Nature, we realize that being kind to animals is a mandate to set Life free in the most divine and yet the most practical sense of the word—if man is to be true to himself, true to his love for all Life, and true to his vow to invoke Christhood for all that lives.

The abuses of animal life have created a karma between mankind and the elementals which must be

expiated before the Edenic paradise can be reestablished upon earth and before the elementals can be
given immortality. It is the duty of mankind who have
thus imprisoned the elementals to love them free first
by ceasing all of their mistreatment of animal life, and
second by invocation to the sacred fire to free the
elementals from the impositions of the decadent scientists of Mu and Atlantis.

It is written that God gave to man "every herb
bearing seed, which is upon the face of all the earth,
and every tree, in the which is the fruit of a tree yielding seed," saying: "To you it shall be for meat. And to
every beast of the earth, and to every fowl of the air,
and to every thing that creepeth upon the earth,
wherein there is life, I have given every green herb for
meat: and it was so." [209]

After the Fall from grace, when the crystal cord
and the threefold flame were reduced and man was no
longer able to nourish his four lower bodies with light
from the God Presence, with *prana,** and with certain
fruits "of trees yielding seeds" which contained cosmic energies, he was obliged to "eat the herb of the
field" [210] as a secondary source of light and prana. As
man's density increased, he looked to animal life for
his sustenance; not satisfied with the herb of the field,
he killed and ate creatures who, like himself, were
unable to draw their daily strength directly from the
universal Source.

As soon as man began to partake of flesh, he
assimilated into his own body those *ani-mal†* forcefields which the scientists had superimposed upon the

*The sacred fire breath of God, or essence of the Holy Spirit, which is
present in the earth's atmosphere as electronically charged light particles of the Father-Mother God.
†The word *animal* is actually comprised of two stems that have come
down from the Lemurian tongue: *ani,* an abbreviated form of *anima,*
meaning soul, or that which is infused with the breath of Life; and *mal,*
an abbreviated form of *malus,* meaning evil. Hence *ani-mal* refers to the
animation, or the ensouling, of patterns of evil with the energies of the

elementals, with the end result that those who had imprisoned the elementals were now able to imprison mankind's consciousness in the same animal patterns which had aborted the Christ Light in the lesser kingdom. Over the centuries man's consciousness became more animallike and less Godlike; even his appearance gradually took on the characteristics of the lower species—so much so that scientists theorized that mankind were a kind of animal instead of a kind of God.

Many today believe that if man has a universal reverence for Life and is willing to assume the responsibility of the sixth commandment, "Thou shalt not kill,"[211] then he will stop the slaughter and eating of animals because, *pur et simple,* to do so is a sin against the Holy Ghost and against the Divine Mother. And until he does so, he cannot consider his life to be harmless nor can he consider himself to be a practitioner of the science of ahimsa.

Others, however, are convinced that some meat in their diets, for health reasons, is necessary. Affirming the element of free will in the exercise of the Law by degrees as one is able, Morya once said that "those who choose to eat meat must give more violet flame decrees than those who don't"—both for themselves and for animal life who are daily laying down their life for their friends, the sons of man.

This sacrifice the elementals will continue to make, lovingly, even as in their bodies they bear world karma,[212] until man, who cannot live by bread alone, may also find the living Word a compensation for centuries-old human habits which one by one he will

Holy Spirit. When we realize that the body temple of man was intended to be a focus of the Divine Mother and that the bodies of animals are incomplete and imperfect manifestations of the archetype of man's form, we see that animal forms are a perversion of the Feminine Ray. Note the derivation of the word *mammal: mam,* an abbreviated form of *mamma,* meaning breast, referring to the Life-giving aspect of the Feminine Ray; and *mal,* an abbreviated form of *malus,* meaning evil.

Welcome to the Heart
of the Inner Retreat
where people of every nation
gather to study and apply
the Lost Teachings of Jesus
in a celebration of Life

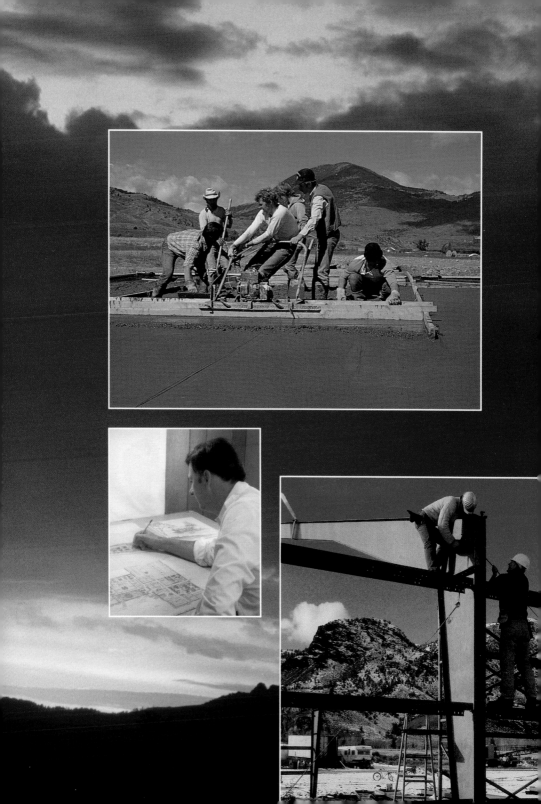

Welcome to the Heart
of the Inner Retreat
"The Place of Great Encounters"

set aside by resurrection's flame on the mount of spiritual attainment.

In the meantime, let us love one another, remembering the wisdom of the apostle:

"For one believeth that he may eat all things: another, who is weak, eateth herbs.

"Let not him that eateth despise him that eateth not; and let not him which eateth not, judge him that eateth: for God hath received him.

"Who art thou that judgest another man's servant [another guru's chela]? to his own master he standeth or falleth. Yea, he shall be holden up: for God [the Great Guru] is able to make him stand." [213]

The Maha Chohan speaks to his disciples of humanity's great need to master the art of creating peacefully. He cautions that before this can be accomplished men must undo that which they have built on false foundations through their misunderstanding of the nature of peace. He says that "as men seek to expel from their worlds the shadowed substance woven there by the misuse of the flame, as men seek to refine their inner natures and to purify their souls, they automatically renew their attunement with the Holy Spirit which beareth much fruit.

"Thus when Jesus said, 'They that be whole need not a physician, but they that are sick,' [214] he was referring to the wholeness of the Whole-I-Spirit, in other words to the completeness of the flame of peace. Those who are sick—those whose energies are not in the perfect polarity of the Father-Mother God, hence not whole—are the ones who need the transforming power of the Great Alchemist."

The Maha Chohan points out that "self-righteousness, a shadowed weight reinforcing the patterns of deceit within the subconscious mind of man, must be laid aside as the first veil that covered the Reality of the Holy Spirit." He also warns of "self-depreciation

whereby individuals sell themselves short in the cosmic marts and assume themselves to be nothing in the
eyes of God."

"Both outlooks," he says, "reveal an imbalance
in man's consciousness. Self-righteousness is a perversion of the Masculine aspect, whereas self-depreciation is a perversion of the Feminine aspect of God."
Making a plea for balance on the spiritual path, the
Maha Chohan explains that "harmlessness toward
Life is not possible to those who remain steeped either
in self-righteousness or in self-depreciation; for in
both cases, by his failure to balance and correctly
apprehend the energies of the Father and the Mother,
the individual inflicts harm upon himself. And if he
inflict harm upon himself through an incorrect application of the energies of God, how can he be harmless
to other parts of Life? For is it not true that all Life is
one and that that which man is he projects upon the
screen of Nature?"

In applying this instruction to the expansion of
man's consciousness through Nature, the Maha Chohan
advises: "The borders of God's kingdom ought not to
be enlarged with force, but by the peaceful power of
the Infinite One. The statement 'And I, if I be lifted
up, will draw all men unto me'[215] refers to the Christ
consciousness. It ought to be apparent that as man
lifts up the Spirit of God in the eternal verities which
he has acquired through his solar awareness, the Spirit
of God in all of its tangibility will increase its action
within the life of man—within a given set of squares."
He then explains the concept of the set of squares
within man's consciousness:

"If the sphere that extends nine or ninety feet
around the heart chalice of a man were divided into
cubes one foot square and each cube contained a certain intensity of the action of the Holy Spirit, that

intensity could vary from a pinpoint of light to a star of great magnitude. The greater the concentration of the Holy Spirit in the aura of man, the greater will be the magnet of his consciousness to draw men Godward. Jesus taught his disciples to lift up the Christ in their service by invoking the flame of peace and its balancing action. Thus the devotee who would expand the Holy Spirit, cube by cube, around the chalice of the threefold flame as Jesus demonstrated should qualify the energies of his heart flame with the purple and gold radiance of the Father-Mother God.

"An error which men frequently make—and this involves a razor's edge of understanding—is that they utilize the great drawing power which comes to them through the action of the Holy Spirit to attract people to their own personalities rather than to the personality of God, and to their own opinions about Life instead of to the divine gnosis, the compendium of cosmic law that originates in the flame of true Being. This state of mind cannot be considered harmless, for it is based on an unbalanced manifestation of the flame of peace and on a placing of the human ego and the human will in the seat of authority where the Christ ought to reign."

"It is ever a wise cosmic scientist," says the Maha Chohan, "who seeks to point out to those individuals who are drawn by the light into his orbit the divine unity that comes from the radiance of the Holy Spirit and to encourage them to expand the light of their own hearts rather than be caught up in the magnetism of anyone's personality, including what may appear as their own. The personality-cult consciousness is a false peace and a false safety that can never lead man to self-mastery; it can only postpone the dominion of his own God Presence, of the Divine Personality in his life.

"There is a transforming power in the flame of peace when it blazes in balanced action within the heart of the individual; but when it is absent, there is danger that the maya of the human personality, with all of its glamor,* will collect as effluvia around the heart chakra in place of the radiance of the divinely impersonal personality of the Holy Spirit. When those who would serve as our representatives allow the pollutants of the carnal mind to accumulate in their consciousness, they do us a great disservice. For until these are flushed out and transmuted by the action of the sacred fire, the new light which the would-be servant invokes flows into the vessels of his old momentums—like new wine into old bottles[216]—the vessels break, and the light is spilled on the ground. It is then that his consciousness becomes wide open to the forces of Darkness, who take up the light he has spilled and use it against him to reactivate the old momentums of his carnality.

"Jesus' commentary on those who, cleansed of their evil tendencies (evil spirits), allow them to return was 'The last state of that man is worse than the first.'[217] In the same tradition Peter counseled the early church: 'Of whom [of what momentums] a man is overcome, of the same is he brought in bondage. For if after they have escaped the pollutions of the world through the knowledge of the Lord and Saviour Jesus Christ, they are again entangled therein, and overcome, the latter end is worse with them than the beginning. For it had been better for them not to have known the way of righteousness, than, after they have known it, to turn from the holy commandment delivered unto them.'[218]

"As long as the ego is allowed to sit upon the throne of the three-in-one, man's consciousness is in a

*The magnetic attraction of illusion.

state of whoredom; for the ego is the Great Whore who usurps the authority of the Divine Mother, absorbs the uses of the flame of peace, and ties men to the abomination of desolation standing in the holy place of the Christ Self where it ought not."

The Maha Chohan warns of "the propensity on the part of the student to rush forward too quickly into the teaching field as soon as he feels a touch of the Paraclete and the burst of light within his heart flame that marks the beginning of the expansion of his own Christ-awareness. Many who have studied a few short years fancy themselves worthy of being gurus. They seek to draw to themselves a circle of chelas, not realizing that unless they are wholly prepared by the Holy Spirit for this purpose, they may take unto themselves unduly many karmic conditions without necessarily improving the lot of those whom they instruct and of those whom they would heal."

It is therefore the supreme desire of the Representative of the Holy Spirit in his tender regard for his disciples to assist them in developing God-awareness. He says: "In drawing the Holy Spirit to you, I urge you, whether you contemplate God as man, God as Nature, or God as God, that you retain within your mental and emotional bodies the abiding sense of being held in the very hollow of God's hand. Then when the disquieting factors of life come and when old momentums seem to take their toll, you shall stand above these and all outer conditions and circumstances; you shall stand in the bastions of God's own preeminence—his preeminent strength, love, and understanding.

"All around you, vibrating in space, is light. This light, which many do not recognize in their day-to-day activities and which some have recognized for a time and then forgotten again, must be persistently invoked and adored. Men must love the light and bask in the light until they feel it and then see it. To do this they need not become materially impractical, nor should they avoid their responsibilities to Life on the physical plane. But neither should they become spiritually impractical, dissipating their energies in worldly involvements that are without purpose.

"Men must find room in the inn of being for the divine plan. They must pay allegiance to eternal verities and their faith must mount up with wings as eagles. From the platform of the present to the capstone of the future, men must not fear to study the sacred writings handed down from the past nor to follow the progressive revelations of the Ascended Masters released through their divinely appointed Messengers.

"The pure gold of the Christ consciousness can stand the trial by fire.[219] Its intent can be analyzed and brought before the eyes of the soul, and its Source can be disclosed to the sincere. Those who would pursue the Holy Spirit must give themselves without reserve to the purposes of God. Those who would become one with all Life must pursue the Holy Spirit and its holy desire to establish God Self-awareness in all who have the spark of Life within them.

"As long as any price is too great to pay, as long as any measure of the sense of possession is retained in consciousness, the disciple has not let go of his finite self with its selfishness and self-love. Man must come to the great threshing floor of God and place himself there, subject to the eternal flail of right knowledge; for "whom the LORD loveth he chasteneth, and scourgeth every son whom he receiveth."[220] Therefore, all who would enter into the kingdom must be willing to receive the fires of purification within the mind and heart; they must be willing to pass through the necessary trials and take the necessary risks. God will never ask aught that is evil of man, nor will he misdirect man to do harm to any other part of Life.

"The science of harmlessness must be understood and practiced. In complete surrender to God's holy will, men must become receptive channels through which the purifying fires of the Holy Spirit may flow." Thus through the consciousness of the Holy Spirit we perceive that the science of harmlessness and the science of flow are one and the same and that both are born out of the flame of God-gratitude, which, as liquid fire, is released in unceasing undulation from the heart that is filled with the Holy Spirit. We see that as we are grateful for Life we cannot be harmful toward Life, for gratitude is loving God through an appreciation of his wondrous works. This is flow, this is harmlessness, this is ahimsa; this is the voice of gratitude that speaks from the heart of the flame of peace.

The Maha Chohan explains that the fires of the Holy Spirit, whence the power of purification emanates, are both actual and symbolic. "Therefore," he says, "let none suppose that the cloven tongues of the Holy Spirit abide in the realm of symbol alone; for there is a tangible emanation of fire from the octaves of purity that is ministered unto by the purifying angels. When these angels' wings brush the physical octaves of earth, blending their energies with the blessed fire elementals, mankind, who often entertain them unawares,[221] may experience an uncomfortable sensation in which the flesh itself seems to melt with a fervent heat. But this, too, shall pass, as will all tests, until one day mankind becomes cooled to the restless passions of the flesh and awaits a release of spiritual grace and a goal-fitting for higher and more expansive dimensions of service.

"The foundations of Life must not—cannot—be
ignored by the devotees of the Holy Spirit; for the
temple which is the body of man's substance must be
prepared for the infusing, the infilling, the infiring,
and the descent of the Holy Spirit. Man's body of
purified energy must become a tabernacle builded
without hands[222]—the hallowed, eternal biding place
of God. Whether of the child-man reborn and recon-
secrated in the manger of Life or of the wise master
builder whose dedicated service towers above the
plains, may it be said of all in harmless, harmonious
rhythm, 'Come, see the place where the Lord lay!'"[223]

INTROIT TO THE CHRIST FLAME

Holy Christ Self above me,
Thou balance of my soul,
Let Thy blessed radiance
Descend and make me Whole!

> Thy Flame within me ever blazes!
> Thy Peace about me ever raises!
> Thy Love protects and holds me!
> Thy dazzling Light enfolds me!
> I AM Thy threefold radiance:
> I AM Thy living Presence—
> Expanding, expanding, expanding now!

Holy Christ Flame within me,
Come, expand Thy triune Light!
Flood my being with the essence
Of the pink, blue, gold, and white!

> Thy Flame within me ever blazes!
> Thy Peace about me ever raises!
> Thy Love protects and holds me!
> Thy dazzling Light enfolds me!
> I AM Thy threefold radiance:
> I AM Thy living Presence—
> Expanding, expanding, expanding now!

Holy lifeline to my Presence,
Friend and brother ever dear,
Let me keep Thy holy vigil—
Be Thyself in action here!

> Thy Flame within me ever blazes!
> Thy Peace about me ever raises!
> Thy Love protects and holds me!
> Thy dazzling Light enfolds me!
> I AM Thy threefold radiance:
> I AM Thy living Presence—
> Expanding, expanding, expanding now!

THE SEVEN RAYS AND THE SEVEN CHAKRAS

Seven Rays of the Flames Magnetized on the Seven Days of the Week	God-Qualities Amplified through Invocation to the Flame	Chakras, or Centers: Chalices of Light Sustaining the Frequencies of the Seven Rays in the Four Lower Bodies
First Ray Will of God (Blue) Magnified on Tuesday	Omnipotence, perfection, protection, faith, desire to do the will of God through the power of the Father	**Throat** (Blue)
Second Ray Wisdom of God (Yellow) Magnified on Sunday	Omniscience, understanding, illumination, desire to know God through the Mind of the Son	**Crown** (Yellow)
Third Ray Love of God (Pink) Magnified on Monday	Omnipresence, compassion, charity, desire to be God in action through the love of the Holy Spirit	**Heart** (Pink)
Fourth Ray Purity of God (White) Magnified on Friday	Purity, wholeness, desire to know and be God through purity of body, mind, and soul through the Consciousness of the Divine Mother	**Base of the Spine** (White)
Fifth Ray Science of God (Green) Magnified on Wednesday	Truth, healing, constancy, desire to precipitate the abundance of God through the immaculate concept of the Holy Virgin	**Third Eye** (Green)
Sixth Ray Peace of God (Purple and Gold) Magnified on Thursday	Ministration of the Christ, desire to be in the service of God and man through the mastery of the Christ	**Solar Plexus** (Purple and Gold)
Seventh Ray Freedom of God (Violet) Magnified on Saturday	Freedom, ritual, transmutation, transcendence, desire to make all things new through the application of the laws of alchemy	**Seat of the Soul** (Violet)

Chohans, or Lords, Focusing the Christ Consciousness of the Ray; Location of Their Retreats	Archangels and Divine Complements Focusing the Solar Consciousness of the Ray; Location of Their Retreats	Elohim and Divine Complements Focusing the God Consciousness of the Ray; Location of Their Retreats
El Morya Darjeeling, India	**Michael Faith** Banff and Lake Louise, Canada	**Hercules Amazonia** Half Dome, Sierra Nevada, California, U.S.A.
Lanto Grand Teton, Teton Range, Wyoming, U.S.A.	**Jophiel Christine** South of the Great Wall near Lanchow, North Central China	**Apollo Lumina** Western Lower Saxony, Germany
Paul the Venetian Southern France Temple of the Sun, New York City	**Chamuel Charity** St. Louis, Missouri, U.S.A.	**Heros Amora** Lake Winnipeg, Canada
Serapis Bey Luxor, Egypt	**Gabriel Hope** Between Sacramento and Mount Shasta, California, U.S.A.	**Purity Astrea** Near Gulf of Archangel, southeast arm of White Sea, Russia
Hilarion Crete, Greece	**Raphael Mother Mary** Fátima, Portugal	**Cyclopea Virginia** Altai Range where China, Siberia, and Mongolia meet, near Tabun Bogdo
Nada Saudi Arabia	**Uriel Aurora** Tatra Mountains south of Cracow, Poland	**Peace Aloha** Hawaiian Islands
Saint Germain Transylvania, Romania Table Mountain in Teton Range, Wyoming, U.S.A.	**Zadkiel Amethyst** Cuba	**Arcturus Victoria** Near Luanda, Angola, Africa

*And this Gospel of the Kingdom shall
be preached in all the world for a witness unto
all nations; and then shall the end come.*

Jesus

Notes

For an alphabetical listing of many of the philosophical and hierarchical terms used in *Climb the Highest Mountain,* see the comprehensive glossary, "The Alchemy of the Word: Stones for the Wise Masterbuilders," in *Saint Germain On Alchemy.*

AUTHORS' MESSAGE

1. Ralph Waldo Emerson, "Character," in *Essays,* 2d ser., vol. 3, cent. ed. (Boston and New York: Houghton Mifflin Co., Riverside Press, 1903), p. 95.
2. Lecomte du Noüy, *Human Destiny* (New York and Toronto: New American Library; London: New English Library, 1947), p. 128.
3. Job 38:2.
4. Mic. 4:4.
5. Phil. 2:12.
6. Isa. 28:10.
7. I Cor. 15:51.
8. John 10:16.
9. I Cor. 2:7.
10. Rev. 5:10.
11. Gen. 1:26.
12. Exod. 3:13, 14.
13. Mark 13:31.
14. Rev. 21:6, 7.
15. Gen. 2:7.
16. II Tim. 2:15.
17. John 1:3.
18. Luke 11:52.
19. Luke 11:54.

20. Rev. 3:20.
21. Matt. 25:23, 30.
22. Rev. 3:21, 22.
23. Rev. 10:10.
24. Ps. 23:3.
25. Luke 18:17.
26. Luke 21:19.
27. Isa. 55:1.

Chapter One
YOUR SYNTHETIC IMAGE

1. Sir Edwin Arnold, trans., *The Song Celestial or Bhagavad-Gita* (London: Routledge & Kegan Paul, 1948), p. 9.
2. Kuthumi, "'It Does Not Matter!'" in *Kuthumi On Selfhood* (1969 *Pearls of Wisdom,* vol. 12, no. 33), p. 142, $17.95; *Understanding Yourself,* quality paperback, pp. 62–63, $4.95; pocketbook, p. 76, $2.95.
3. Prov. 23:7.
4. Luke 11:52.
5. Rev. 13:8.
6. Isa. 40:1, 3.
7. Serapis Bey, 1967 *Pearls of Wisdom,* vol. 10, no. 27; "The

Predication of God: Seraphic Meditations III," in *Dossier on the Ascension,* quality paperback, pp. 139–40, $5.95.

8. God Meru, "The Hidden Man of the Heart," in *Kuthumi On Selfhood* (1969 *Pearls of Wisdom,* vol. 12, no. 37), p. 159; *Understanding Yourself,* pp. 90–91; pocketbook, pp. 107–8.

9. Mark 5:9.

10. Matt. 24:15; Mark 13:14.

11. Isa. 64:8.

12. I Cor. 15:50.

13. I Cor. 15:31.

14. God Meru, "The Ego," in *Kuthumi On Selfhood* (1969 *Pearls of Wisdom,* vol. 12, no. 31), pp. 132–33; *Understanding Yourself,* pp. 46–48; pocketbook, pp. 55–57.

15. Gen. 1:26, 31.

16. Matt. 6:23.

17. Matt. 4:9.

18. I Cor. 13:12.

19. John 3:30.

20. Eph. 2:14.

21. Exod. 20:3.

22. Exod. 3:2.

23. Exod. 3:14.

24. Matt. 5:48.

Chapter Two
YOUR REAL IMAGE

1. Jesus, "Prayer as Communication with Purpose," in 1968 *Pearls of Wisdom,* vol. 11, no. 14, p. 54, $14.95; *Prayer and Meditation,* quality paperback, p. 29, $9.95.

2. Heb. 10:9.

3. Gen. 1:26.

4. Rev. 22:13.

5. Isa. 40:31.

6. John 10:10.

7. Luke 12:15.

8. Rom. 8:17.

9. Saint Germain, "The Sense of Permanence within the Framework of Impermanence," in 1968 *Pearls of Wisdom,* vol. 11, no. 7, p. 29.

10. I Cor. 9:27.

11. God Meru, "The Ego," in *Kuthumi On Selfhood* (1969 *Pearls of Wisdom,* vol. 12, no. 31), p. 132, $17.95; *Understanding Yourself,* quality paperback, p. 45, $4.95; pocketbook, p. 54, $2.95.

12. John 10:35, 36.

13. John 8:58.

14. God Meru, "The Hidden Man of the Heart," in *Kuthumi On Selfhood* (1969 *Pearls of Wisdom,* vol. 12, no. 37), pp. 160–61; *Understanding Yourself,* pp. 92–93; pocketbook, pp. 109–10.

15. Ps. 51:5.

16. Luke 1:35.

17. John 1:14.

18. Josh. 24:15.

19. Job 22:21.

20. Exod. 6:7.

21. Rudyard Kipling, *The Ballad of East and West,* line 1.

22. Acts 17:24.

23. II Cor. 5:1.

24. God Meru, "The Hidden Man of the Heart," in *Kuthumi On Selfhood,* pp. 161–62; *Understanding Yourself,* pp. 93–94; pocketbook, p. 111.

25. Matt. 23:27.

26. Rev. 3:14, 17, 18.

27. Lord Maitreya, "A Letter from Beloved Lord Maitreya," Keepers of the Flame Lesson 13, pp. 10–11.

28. James 1:27.

29. Exod. 20:3, 4.

30. Judg. 6:25–28.

31. Col. 3:9, 10.

32. Luke 1:46.

33. Eccles. 11:1.

34. I John 3:3.
35. Isa. 28:10.
36. I Cor. 15:50.
37. Gen. 3:21.
38. I Cor. 3:6.
39. Luke 19:40.
40. Matt. 5:48.
41. Heb. 11:1.
42. Saint Germain, "The Law of Transfer of Energy," in 1962 *Pearls of Wisdom,* vol. 5, no. 26; *Studies in Alchemy,* quality paperback, pp. 9–10, $3.95; *Saint Germain On Alchemy,* pocketbook, pp. 3–4, $5.95.
43. Matt. 28:20.
44. Matt. 28:18.
45. John 14:12.
46. John 18:37.

Chapter Three
A HEAP OF CONFUSION

1. Dan. 5:27.
2. Saint Germain, "A Summoning to Cosmic Purpose," in *Masters of the Far East* (1971 *Pearls of Wisdom,* vol. 14, no. 18), pp. 73–74, $14.95.
3. Gen. 1:26–30.
4. Isa. 66:1.
5. Saint Germain, "A Summoning to Cosmic Purpose," in *Masters of the Far East,* p. 71.
6. Prov. 29:18.
7. Saint Germain, "A Summoning to Cosmic Purpose," in *Masters of the Far East,* p. 69.
8. Lanto, "Identification with the Real Self," in *Kuthumi On Selfhood* (1969 *Pearls of Wisdom,* vol. 12, no. 29), p. 126, $17.95; *Understanding Yourself,* quality paperback, pp. 34–35, $4.95; pocketbook, p. 42, $2.95.
9. Rev. 21:2.
10. Matt. 5:48.
11. See pp. 84–93, 493–95.

12. Matt. 18:3.
13. Rev. 21:23.
14. John 14:2.
15. Heb. 9:23.
16. Jer. 31:33.
17. I Cor. 11:3.
18. Eph. 2:20.
19. John 5:17.
20. See *Studies in Alchemy* in 1962 *Pearls of Wisdom,* vol. 5, nos. 26–34; quality paperback, $3.95. *Intermediate Studies in Alchemy* in 1970 *Pearls of Wisdom,* vol. 13, nos. 6–17, pp. 23–81, $14.95; quality paperback, $4.95. *Saint Germain On Alchemy,* pocketbook, pp. 1–99, 153–251, $5.95.
21. I Cor. 2:9.
22. Matt. 28:18.
23. Gen. 3:24.
24. Gen. 3:22.
25. I Cor. 15:47–50.
26. Matt. 5:13.
27. Saint Germain, "Nature Yields to the Childlike Mind," in 1970 *Pearls of Wisdom,* vol. 13, no. 15, pp. 69–71; *Intermediate Studies in Alchemy,* pp. 71–74; *Saint Germain On Alchemy,* pp. 231–35.
28. Gen. 3:11.
29. Rev. 12:7–9.
30. The Great Divine Director, "The Mechanization Concept," in 1965 *Pearls of Wisdom,* vol. 8, nos. 3–26, pp. 9–142, $16.95; *The Soulless One,* pocketbook, $1.95.
31. God Meru, "The Ego," in *Kuthumi On Selfhood* (1969 *Pearls of Wisdom,* vol. 12, no. 31), p. 132; *Understanding Yourself,* pp. 45–46; pocketbook, pp. 54–55.
32. I Sam. 15:23.
33. Gen. 2:17; Saint Germain, "Nature Yields to the Childlike

Mind," in 1970 *Pearls of Wisdom,* p. 68; *Intermediate Studies in Alchemy,* p. 70; *Saint Germain On Alchemy,* p. 229.

34. Prov. 14:12.
35. I Cor. 15:56.
36. Paul the Venetian, "In Christ 'without Blemish and without Spot,'" in *Masters of the Far East* (1971 *Pearls of Wisdom,* vol. 14, no. 17), p. 66.
37. Gen. 3:4.
38. Gen. 38:9.
39. II Cor. 4:9.
40. Exod. 20:5.
41. Saint Germain, "Nature Yields to the Childlike Mind," in 1970 *Pearls of Wisdom,* p. 68; *Intermediate Studies in Alchemy,* p. 70; *Saint Germain On Alchemy,* p. 229.
42. Luke 16:8.
43. Matt. 7:20.
44. Eph. 6:12.
45. Dan. 7:9.
46. Gen. 11:1–9.
47. Gen. 1:26.
48. The **"sons of Belial"** are mentioned a number of times in the Old Testament: Deut. 13:13; Judg. 19:22, 20:13; I Sam. 2:12, 10:27, 25:17; II Sam. 23:6; I Kings 21:10, 13; II Chron. 13:7. See "Concealed References to the Watchers (and Nephilim) in Scripture," in *Forbidden Mysteries of Enoch: The Untold Story of Men and Angels,* containing all the Enoch texts, including the Book of Enoch and the Book of the Secrets of Enoch, quality paperback, pp. 263–303, $12.95.
49. Matt. 13:24–30, 36–40.
50. Cha Ara, "Sons of Belial: The Problem of Embodied Evil," in *Masters of the Far East* (1971

Pearls of Wisdom, vol. 14, no. 5), pp. 17–18, 19–20.
51. Matt. 10:34.
52. Cha Ara, "Sons of Belial: The Problem of Embodied Evil," in *Masters of the Far East,* pp. 18–19.
53. Saint Germain, "Nature Yields to the Childlike Mind," in 1970 *Pearls of Wisdom,* p. 68; *Intermediate Studies in Alchemy,* pp. 69–70; *Saint Germain On Alchemy,* pp. 228–29.
54. Zech. 13:7; Matt. 26:31.
55. Josh. 24:15.
56. Saint Germain, "A Summoning to Cosmic Purpose," in *Masters of the Far East,* pp. 69–70.
57. I Pet. 1:19.
58. Rev. 3:12.
59. Matt. 26:52.
60. Luke 16:1–12.
61. Gal. 6:7.
62. Paul the Venetian, "In Christ 'without Blemish and without Spot,'" in *Masters of the Far East,* pp. 65–67.
63. Luke 21:19.
64. Eph. 6:10, 11.
65. Paul the Venetian, "In Christ 'without Blemish and without Spot,'" in *Masters of the Far East,* pp. 67, 68.
66. Jer. 23: 23, 24.
67. El Morya, "Individual Responsibility," in 1970 *Pearls of Wisdom,* vol. 13, no. 31, p. 139.
68. Saint Germain, "Spiritual Alliance," in 1970 *Pearls of Wisdom,* vol. 13, no. 8, pp. 32–33; *Intermediate Studies in Alchemy,* pp. 21–22; *Saint Germain On Alchemy,* pp. 171, 172–73.
69. Saint Germain, "What Alchemy Can Mean to a Decaying World," in 1970 *Pearls of Wis-*

dom, vol. 13, no. 13, p. 57; *Intermediate Studies in Alchemy,* p. 58; *Saint Germain On Alchemy,* pp. 214–15.

70. Rom. 3:8.
71. Mother Mary, "True Religion," in 1970 *Pearls of Wisdom,* vol. 13, no. 18, p. 84.
72. I Cor. 9:22.
73. I John 1:5.
74. Alexander Gaylord, "The Golden Rule Standard," in 1970 *Pearls of Wisdom,* vol. 13, no. 26, pp. 118–21.
75. Luke 23:12.
76. Luke 22:66.
77. I John 4:4.
78. Isa. 40:31.
79. Gen. 32:24.
80. Heb. 13:8.
81. Jude 13.
82. I Pet. 1:20.
83. John 8:58.
84. El Morya, "Universities of the Spirit," in 1970 *Pearls of Wisdom,* vol. 13, no. 19, pp. 86–89.

Chapter Four
WHAT IS INDIVIDUALITY?

1. John 11:25, 26.
2. Saint Germain, "Knowledge of that Power Which Will Transmute," in 1970 *Pearls of Wisdom,* vol. 13, no. 27, p. 125, $14.95.
3. Rev. 2:17.
4. John 5:17.
5. Saint Germain, "The Highest Alchemy," in 1970 *Pearls of Wisdom,* vol. 13, no. 16, p. 74; *Intermediate Studies in Alchemy,* quality paperback, pp. 76–77, $4.95; *Saint Germain On Alchemy,* pocketbook, p. 238, $5.95.
6. El Morya, "The Human Will," in *Kuthumi On Selfhood* (1969

Pearls of Wisdom, vol. 12, no. 13), p. 57, $17.95; *The Sacred Adventure,* clothbound, pocket edition, p. 97, $7.95.

7. Ibid.
8. Gen. 2:17.
9. Gen. 1:26–28.
10. Gen. 2:7.
11. I Tim. 2:5.
12. Gal. 4:19.
13. Phil. 2:5.
14. Jer. 17:9.
15. Jer. 17:5.
16. Hab. 1:13.
17. Rev. 2:7.
18. Matt. 3:17.
19. Mark 16:19.
20. John 10:30.
21. Gen. 3:24.
22. Saint Germain, "The Knight Commander's Message," Keepers of the Flame Lesson 1, p. 11.
23. Matt. 10:39.
24. II Cor. 7:15.
25. Heb. 9:23.
26. Matt. 25:23.
27. Luke 15:7.
28. II Kings 2:1–15.
29. Luke 9:42, 43.
30. I Cor. 6:19, 20.
31. Matt. 10:33.
32. Serapis Bey, "The New Order of the Ages Begins," in 1968 *Pearls of Wisdom,* vol. 11, no. 4, p. 14, $14.95.
33. Jesus Christ, "Prayer as Communication with Purpose," in 1968 *Pearls of Wisdom,* vol. 11, no. 14, p. 54; *Prayer and Meditation,* quality paperback, p. 29, $9.95.
34. Matt. 11:28–30.
35. Matt. 27:32.
36. Luke 23:42, 43.
37. Ps. 46:10.
38. Gen. 2:5, 6.
39. Mark 4:39.

40. Matt. 13:33.
41. I Cor. 5:6.
42. John 11:43.
43. Saint Germain, "The Law of Transfer of Energy," in 1962 *Pearls of Wisdom,* vol. 5, no. 26; *Studies in Alchemy,* quality paperback, p. 9, $3.95; *Saint Germain On Alchemy,* pocketbook, p. 3, $5.95.
44. Ibid., *Studies in Alchemy,* pp. 9–10; *Saint Germain On Alchemy,* p. 4.
45. Mark 15:38.
46. Exod. 20:7.
47. Matt. 6:34.
48. Matt. 24:22.
49. Eph. 4:22, 24.
50. Mark 10:31.
51. Ps. 14:1.
52. I Pet. 4:5.
53. Rom. 7:23.
54. Rom. 3:23.
55. Matt. 13:12.
56. Job 14:15.
57. *"Watch with Me" Jesus' Vigil of the Hours,* 32-page booklet, p. 28, $2.95; on audiocassette B83143, $6.50, or with healing lecture on 2-cassette album *"Physician, Heal Thyself!"* A83143, $9.95.
58. Matt. 13:35.
59. Gen. 22:1–18.
60. Gen. 22:17.
61. Saint Germain, "The Highest Alchemy," in 1970 *Pearls of Wisdom,* p. 73; *Intermediate Studies in Alchemy,* p. 76; *Saint Germain On Alchemy,* p. 237.
62. Decree 40.00, in *Prayers, Meditations, and Dynamic Decrees for the Coming Revolution in Higher Consciousness,* Section I, $2.95.
63. Gen. 2:18.
64. Rom. 8:7.
65. Gen. 25:29–34.
66. Matt. 6:24.
67. Serapis Bey, 1967 *Pearls of Wisdom,* vol. 10, no. 19; "The Divine Right of Every Man," in *Dossier on the Ascension,* quality paperback, pp. 58–59, 60, $5.95.
68. The Great Divine Director, "The Mainstream of Consciousness," in 1968 *Pearls of Wisdom,* vol. 11, no. 46, p. 194.
69. Matt. 28:18.
70. I Cor. 15:26.
71. James 1:1; 2:14–24.
72. Eph. 2:8.
73. Eph. 2:10.
74. Eph. 4:11.
75. Matt. 22:37.
76. Heb. 2:3.
77. Matt. 5:44.
78. Luke 23:34.
79. John F. Kennedy, "'My Fellow Americans...' Posthumous letter of President John F. Kennedy."
80. II Cor. 12:2.
81. Mary Baker Eddy, *Science and Health with Key to the Scriptures,* 5th ed. (Boston: Trustees under the Will of Mary Baker G. Eddy, 1906), pp. 264–65.
82. Acts 17:22, 23.
83. Mary Baker Eddy, *Poems Including Christ and Christmas,* 2d ed. (Boston: Trustees under the Will of Mary Baker G. Eddy, 1897), p. 39.
84. God Meru, "The Making of Man," Keepers of the Flame Lesson 16, p. 24.
85. John 14:12.
86. Luke 21:19.
87. II Pet. 3:8.
88. Rose of Light, "The Bonds of Love Can Never Be Broken," in 1968 *Pearls of Wisdom,* vol. 11, no. 29, p. 118.

Chapter 5
WHAT IS CONSCIOUSNESS?

1. Serapis Bey, 1967 *Pearls of Wisdom,* vol. 10, no. 15; "The Triangle within the Circle," in *Dossier on the Ascension,* quality paperback, p. 26, $5.95.
2. John 6:68.
3. Prov. 2:6.
4. Saint Augustine, *Confessions of Saint Augustine,* trans. Edward B. Pusey (New York: Random House, 1949), pp. 166–67.
5. Ibid., pp. 169–70.
6. *Webster's Seventh New Collegiate Dictionary,* s.v. "consciousness."
7. Arthur Schopenhauer, *The World as Will and Idea,* trans. R. B. Haldane and John Kemp, vol. 2, 2d ed. (London: Kegan Paul, Trench, Trubner, & Co., 1891), p. 328.
8. Will Durant, *The Story of Philosophy: The Lives and Opinions of the Greater Philosophers* (New York: Simon and Schuster, 1951), p. 236.
9. Sir William Hamilton, *Lectures on Metaphysics and Logic,* ed. Rev. Henry Longueville Mansel and John Veitch, vol. 1, Metaphysics (Boston: Gould and Lincoln, 1863), p. 132.
10. Lanto, "Identification with the Real Self," in *Kuthumi On Selfhood* (1969 *Pearls of Wisdom,* vol. 12, no. 29), p. 123, $17.95; *Understanding Yourself,* quality paperback, p. 30, $4.95; pocketbook, p. 37, $2.95.
11. Gen. 1:3.
12. Jesus, "The Light of Prayer," in 1968 *Pearls of Wisdom,* vol. 11, no. 13, p. 50, $14.95; *Prayer and Meditation,* quality paper-back, p. 23, $9.95.
13. Immanuel Kant, *Critique of Pure Reason* (London: Macmillan & Co., 1933), pp. 67–91.
14. Durant, *The Story of Philosophy,* p. 26.
15. Phil. 2:5.
16. Rev. 1:18.
17. Lanto, "Identification with the Real Self," in *Kuthumi On Selfhood,* p. 123; *Understanding Yourself,* p. 30; pocketbook, pp. 37–38.
18. Matt. 6:28, 29.
19. Luke 12:22, 23; Matt. 6:26; Luke 12:25, 26.
20. Matt. 6:33.
21. *"Watch with Me" Jesus' Vigil of the Hours,* 32-page booklet, pp. 13–15, $2.95; decree 60.02 in *Prayers, Meditations, and Dynamic Decrees for the Coming Revolution in Higher Consciousness,* Section II, $2.95.
22. Matt. 6:24.
23. Schopenhauer, *The World as Will and Idea,* pp. 333–34.
24. Matt. 6:22.
25. El Morya, "The Ownership of God's Will," in *Kuthumi On Selfhood* (1969 *Pearls of Wisdom,* vol. 12, no. 11), p. 47; *The Sacred Adventure,* clothbound, pocket edition, pp. 57, 58, $7.95.
26. Henri Bergson, *Creative Evolution,* trans. Arthur Mitchell (New York: Henry Holt and Co., 1911), pp. 179, 262.
27. Ibid., p. 264.
28. Ibid., p. 270.
29. I Cor. 14:32.
30. Henri Bergson, *Mind-Energy,* trans. H. Wildon Carr (New York: Henry Holt and Co., 1920), pp. 10–11.
31. Luke 19:37, 39, 40.

32. Mark 8:35.
33. Jesus, "Unbroken Communion," in 1968 *Pearls of Wisdom*, vol. 11, no. 10, p. 40; *Prayer and Meditation*, p. 5.
34. Ps. 82:6; John 10:33–36.
35. Ps. 46:10.
36. Matt. 19:26.
37. Saint Germain, "Commanding Consciousness," in 1962 *Pearls of Wisdom*, vol. 5, no. 33; *Studies in Alchemy*, quality paperback, pp. 64–65, $3.95; *Saint Germain On Alchemy*, pocketbook, pp. 69–71, $5.95.
38. John 10:4.
39. Immanuel Kant, *Foundations of the Metaphysics of Morals*, trans. Lewis W. Beck (Indianapolis: Bobbs-Merrill Co., 1959), p. 80.
40. Saint Germain, " 'Create!' and the Cloud," in 1970 *Pearls of Wisdom*, vol. 13, no. 11, pp. 46–48, $14.95; *Intermediate Studies in Alchemy*, quality paperback, pp. 40–44, $4.95; *Saint Germain On Alchemy*, pp. 194–99.
41. Serapis Bey, 1967 *Pearls of Wisdom*, vol. 10, no. 27; "The Predication of God: Seraphic Meditations III," in *Dossier on the Ascension*, pp. 137–39.
42. Matt. 6:2, 5, 16.
43. El Morya, "The Ownership of God's Will," in *Kuthumi On Selfhood*, p. 48; *The Sacred Adventure*, pp. 59–61.
44. Matt. 9:17.
45. *Oxford Universal Dictionary*, 3d ed., s.v. "ritual."
46. El Morya, "The Human Will," in *Kuthumi On Selfhood* (1969 *Pearls of Wisdom*, vol. 12, no. 13), p. 58; *The Sacred Adventure*, pp. 98–99.
47. God Meru, "The Ego," in *Kuthumi On Selfhood* (1969 *Pearls of Wisdom*, vol. 12, no. 31), pp. 131–32, 134; *Understanding Yourself*, pp. 44–45, 48; pocketbook, pp. 53–54, 58.
48. Matt. 6:23.
49. Ps. 121:4.
50. El Morya, "A Sacred Adventure," in *Kuthumi On Selfhood* (1969 *Pearls of Wisdom*, vol. 12, no. 14), pp. 60–62; *The Sacred Adventure*, pp. 109–14.
51. **World Mother.** The Spirit of God is both Father and Mother, an androgynous fiery ovoid of Power, Wisdom, and Love. Mankind have readily identified that Spirit as Father, but seldom do they pray to the Divine Mother as the counterpart of the Divine Father. This prayer to the World Mother (the Being who holds the office and responsibility of the Divine Mother for a planetary home) is given to enhance your appreciation of the Feminine aspect of the Deity and the nearness of her flame through the hierarchical offices of the Great White Brotherhood.

Chapter 6
GOD IN MAN

1. Acts 17:28.
2. Matt. 6:22.
3. **Light.** Although we have explained that *Light* is capitalized when it means the Christ consciousness as the personal Presence of the Lord, the First Cause behind the effect we perceive as physical or spiritual light, in some cases this is a moot point since the consciousness of God cannot be separated

from his light or energy. Carrying this theological concept to its logical and ultimate conclusion, *light* should be capitalized in every instance; this we refrain from doing, elevating only those *L*'s for which a member of the Trinity or the Divine Mother as the Person of God may be directly substituted.

4. John 1:5.
5. Jer. 31:33, 34.
6. John 1:14.
7. I Cor. 11:24.
8. John 1:14.
9. Acts 10:34.
10. I Cor. 3:16.
11. Matt. 25:40.
12. Col. 2:9.
13. Heb. 7:25.
14. Matt. 18:12.
15. Matt. 15:14.
16. Kuthumi, "The Perfecting of the Aura," in *Masters of the Far East* (1971 *Pearls of Wisdom*, vol. 14, no. 21), pp. 84, 85, $14.95; *The Human Aura*, pocketbook, pp. 3, 5, $4.95.
17. Gen. 3:21.
18. Deut. 6:4.
19. I Cor. 15:41.
20. Matt. 2:2.
21. John 10:1.
22. Kuthumi, "The Intensification of the Aura," in *Masters of the Far East* (1971 *Pearls of Wisdom*, vol. 14, no. 25), p. 100; *The Human Aura*, p. 29.
23. Matt. 27:50.
24. Eccles. 12:1–7. **Editorial commentary on Ecclesiastes:** Note the editorial comment (Eccles. 12:8–14) that follows this profound yet veiled teaching. The editor appears to praise Ecclesiastes, but in fact his remarks are highly questionable in their intent. Verses 8 through 11 seem calculated to put the reader off guard before he reads the word of stultifying caution in verse 12: "And further, by these, my son, be admonished: of making many books there is no end; and much study is a weariness of the flesh." Edwin T. Ryder states in *Peake's Commentary on the Bible* (Matthew Black and H. H. Rowley, eds. [Walton-on-Thames, Surrey: Nelson, 1962, p. 467]) that this verse "generally may be taken as a corrective against Koheleth's [the Hebrew word for Ecclesiastes] heterodoxy or as a caution regarding the voluminous non-Israelite literature such as was available in the great library of Alexandria." In *The Interpreter's Bible* (Nashville: Abingdon Press, 1956), vol. 5, p. 88, O. S. Rankin comments that "the first epilogue [Eccles. 12:8–11] may have been written several generations before the time of the writer of the second epilogue [12:12–14].... The writer [of the second epilogue] has in mind Koheleth as a student and thinker, whose views require some corrective emphasis."

Those who would tamper with the word of God are not so foolish as to counter it directly; rather they suggest in a roundabout way that the reader take the teachings "with a grain of salt." Verses 13 and 14 are an attempt to convince the seeker that a simple religious faith is all that is needed and that an understanding of the deeper mysteries is not required. "Let us hear the conclusion of the whole matter," he says. "Fear God and keep his commandments: for this is the whole duty of man." This, of course, is true; but it is only a part of the truth. For in order to maintain the necessary respect (fear) of the LORD and to keep his commandments, man must have a scientific understanding of the Law—the very teachings which Ecclesiastes set forth in the twelve chapters of his writings contained in the Bible and in other documents written by this holy one of God which have not been preserved but are available for study to initiates who frequent Jesus' retreat in Arabia. Here the Lord has guarded a vast library of the teachings of the Cosmic Christ set forth by world teachers and some treatises not published since earth's early golden ages.

Verse 14 says that "God shall bring every work into judgment, with every secret thing, whether it be good, or whether it be evil." Without question the LORD shall bring man's works to judgment. "The fire shall try every man's work of what sort it is" (I Cor. 3:13). But if man's works are to be found acceptable unto God, he must know and practice His laws and be willing to study to show himself approved (II Tim. 2:15). His must not be the attitude that "much study is a weariness of the flesh," but one of joy and enthusiasm in the pursuit of the science of the sacred Word.

Paul's commentary on those who close their ears to the true message of the Divine Mediator and on the dogmatic interpretations of the religious leaders of his time was "The natural man receiveth not the things of the Spirit of God: for they are foolishness unto him: neither can he know them, because they are spiritually discerned" (I Cor. 2:14).

25. Eccles. 1:2; 12:8.

26. Saint Germain, 1967 *Pearls of Wisdom,* vol. 10, no. 7; "A Valentine from Saint Germain," in *Saint Germain On Alchemy,* pocketbook, pp. 350–52, $5.95.

27. Luke 17:21.

28. Prov. 16:32.

29. Luke 21:19.

30. Lord Acton to Bishop Mandell Creighton, 5 April 1887, quoted in John Bartlett, comp., and Emily Morison Beck, ed., *Familiar Quotations: A Collection of Passages, Phrases and Proverbs Traced to Their Sources in Ancient and Modern Literature,* 14th ed., rev. and enl. (Boston: Little, Brown and Co., 1968), p. 750.

31. II Pet. 1:19.

32. Gen. 1:16.

33. Col. 3:11; I Cor. 15:28; Gen. 1:26, 27.

34. **Decree book.** See *Prayers, Meditations, and Dynamic Decrees for the Coming Revolution in Higher Consciousness,* a handbook of daily invocations to the sacred fire you can use to command the flow of God's power, wisdom and love through your heart for the alchemy of positive change, to balance and expand your threefold flame, transmute the records of past lives that are often

the cause of current physical and emotional burdens, free yourself from unwanted habits, and direct God's healing light into the cause and core of community, national, and world problems. Sections I, II, and III, $2.95 each. See also Mark L. Prophet and Elizabeth Clare Prophet, *The Science of the Spoken Word,* quality paperback, $7.95; *The Science of the Spoken Word: Why and How to Decree Effectively,* 4-cassette album, A7736, $26.00.

35. Matt. 10:36.
36. Matt. 13:24–30, 36–43.
37. Luke 6:39.
38. John 15:13.
39. Rev. 3:16.
40. Luke 23:34.
41. Ps. 61:2.
42. I John 4:20.
43. I John 4:21.
44. II Cor. 5:6.
45. I John 4:18.
46. John 21:6.
47. I John 5:7.
48. John 3:16.
49. I John 4:7.
50. Gen. 2:18.
51. Gen. 22:17.
52. I Cor. 12:4–11.
53. John 13:34, 35.
54. John 15:13, 14.
55. Luke 23:34.
56. John 8:32.
57. Matt. 9:27–31.
58. Mark 5:25–34; Luke 8:43–48.
59. Heb. 12:6.
60. Rev. 21:2, 9–27.
61. Saint Germain, "A Trilogy on the Threefold Flame of Life," in *Saint Germain On Alchemy,* pp. 267–69, 270–84, 302–3, 304–5, 308–9, 311–12, 315, 321–26, 328–29, 335–38, 339–45.

62. Ps. 1:2; Josh. 1:8.
63. Rom. 8:17.
64. Matt. 7:3.
65. Kuthumi, "The Colorations of the Aura," and "The Strengthening of the Aura," in *Masters of the Far East* (1971 *Pearls of Wisdom,* vol. 14, nos. 23, 26), pp. 91–92, 93–94, 103–4; *The Human Aura,* pp. 15–17, 18–19, 33–34.
66. Matt. 6:19, 20.
67. John 14:2.
68. Matt. 25:14–30.
69. I Cor. 15:47.
70. I Cor. 15:41, 42.
71. II Tim. 2:15.
72. Phil. 4:7.
73. Will Rogers, Address at Tremont Temple, Boston, June 1930.
74. William Shakespeare, *Hamlet,* act 3, sc. 1, line 67.
75. Matt. 5:12.
76. Gen. 4:9.
77. Matt. 5:41.
78. Matt. 18:22.
79. Matt. 5:44.
80. See motto of Father Flanagan's Boys' Home, "He ain't heavy, Father... He's m'brother," Boys Town, Nebraska.
81. Luke 2:14.
82. Heb. 10:9.
83. I Cor. 15:40.
84. The Great Divine Director, "The Causal Body of Man," Keepers of the Flame Lesson 12, pp. 15, 16.
85. Ps. 103:15, 16.
86. Rev. 3:12.
87. See pp. 8–9.
88. Ps. 91:4.
89. Zech. 2:13.
90. Zech. 2:5.
91. Gen. 18:14.
92. Jesus, December 25, 1970,

audiocassette B85069, $6.50, on *Only Mark 9,* 4-cassette album, A85068, $26.00.

93. Luke 4:28–31.
94. Eph. 6:16.
95. Eph. 6:10–13.
96. Eph. 6:14–18.
97. Exod. 13:21, 22.
98. Ps. 91:1.
99. Isa. 45:5.
100. Isa. 45:11.
101. Gen. 1:26.
102. Acts 7:49.
103. Matt. 6:10.
104. Matt. 7:7, 8.
105. Mal. 3:10.
106. I John 2:1.
107. James 1:17.
108. Gen. 4:3–5, 22:1–14; Exod. 12:3–14.
109. I Sam. 15:22.
110. John 6:53.
111. I Cor. 11:24.
112. Ps. 19:14.
113. Eccles. 7:29.
114. Gen. 11:1–9.
115. Ps. 1:1.
116. Matt. 4:9.
117. Eph. 2:14.
118. Josh. 6:4.
119. Ps. 23:4.
120. Ps. 23:6.
121. Ps. 91.
122. Job 14:15; Acts 2:1–21; Rom. 10:13; Isa. 65:24.
123. John 17:11; *"Watch with Me" Jesus' Vigil of the Hours,* 32-page booklet, p. 15, $2.95.
124. Matt. 6:6.
125. Exod. 20:4.
126. See p. 14.
127. Serapis Bey, 1967 *Pearls of Wisdom,* vol. 10, no. 22; *Dossier on the Ascension,* quality paperback, pp. 87–88, $5.95.
128. Heb. 12:29.
129. Matt. 13:29.
130. Lanto, "The Essence of the Higher Consciousness," in *Kuthumi On Selfhood* (1969 *Pearls of Wisdom,* vol. 12, no. 26), pp. 109–10, 111–12, $17.95; *Understanding Yourself,* quality paperback, pp. 8–9, 11–12, $4.95; pocketbook, pp. 11–12, 14–15, $2.95.
131. I Cor. 15:42–45. Lanto, "The Essence of the Higher Consciousness," in *Kuthumi On Selfhood,* p. 112; *Understanding Yourself,* pp. 12–13; pocketbook, pp. 15–17.
132. Gen. 3:17.
133. Prov. 14:12.
134. John 16:24.
135. Job 22:28.
136. The Great Divine Director, "Error," in *The Mechanization Concept* (1965 *Pearls of Wisdom,* vol. 8, no. 7), pp. 29–30, $16.95.
137. Saint Germain, "Methods of Transfer," in 1962 *Pearls of Wisdom,* vol. 5, no. 32; *Studies in Alchemy,* quality paperback, p. 47, $3.95; *Saint Germain On Alchemy,* p. 49.
138. Acts 2:1–4.
139. Ezek. 20:47.
140. II Kings 2:11–14.
141. Exod. 3:2.
142. Matt. 3:11.
143. Luke 12:49.
144. Heb. 1:7.
145. I Cor. 3:13.
146. Ezek. 1:4.
147. Mal. 3:2.
148. Rev. 1:14.
149. G. R. S. Mead, *Echoes from the Gnosis,* vol. 6, *A Mithraic Ritual* (London: Theosophical Publishing Society, 1807), p. 25.
150. Shakespeare, *Merchant of Venice,* act 4, sc. 1, lines 183–86.

151. Kuthumi, "The Strengthening of the Aura," in *Masters of the Far East*, p. 105; *The Human Aura*, p. 36.
152. John 13:15.
153. John 13:1–20.
154. I John 4:2.
155. Mark 10:43, 44.
156. Matt. 11:12.
157. John 12:44, 45.
158. John's Gospel gives the supper in the house of Simon the leper before Jesus' triumphal entry into Jerusalem, whereas Mark's Gospel places it afterwards.
159. John 12:1–8.
160. I John 4:3; Job 19:26.
161. Isa. 52:7.
162. John 12:13.
163. Mark 14:3–9.
164. John 12:32.
165. **Sixth Ray ministration of our Lord.** It is the purple-and-gold flame of ministration and service that Jesus applied in this ritual of the washing of the disciples' feet—the purple symbolizing the consecration of the body, or the Matter aspect of man, and the gold symbolizing the consecration of the blood, or the Spirit aspect. The purple ray intensifies the action of the blue, the power or Father consciousness in the material form, whereas the gold is the adornment of the Divine Theosophia, the wisdom of the Motherhood of God.
166. John 14:6.

Chapter 7
GOD IN NATURE

1. Saint Germain, "The Crucible of Being," in 1962 *Pearls of Wisdom*, vol. 5, no. 34; *Studies in Alchemy*, quality paperback, p. 88, $3.95; *Saint Germain On Alchemy*, pocketbook, p. 99, $5.95.
2. Luke 17:20, 21.
3. I Cor. 3:16.
4. John Godfrey Saxe, "The Blind Men and the Elephant."
5. Saint Germain, "The Crucible of Being," in 1962 *Pearls of Wisdom*; *Studies in Alchemy*, p. 67; *Saint Germain On Alchemy*, p. 73.
6. *Webster's Seventh New Collegiate Dictionary*, s.v. "pantheism."
7. *Standard College Dictionary*, 1963 ed., s.v. "pantheism."
8. Oxyrhynchus Logia (Agrapha), Fifth Logion, in *Bartlett's Familiar Quotations*, ed. Christopher Morley and Louella D. Everett, 11th ed. rev. and enl. (Boston: Little, Brown and Co., 1938), p. 1126.
9. The Maha Chohan, 1964 *Pearls of Wisdom*, vol. 7, no. 48.
10. Gen. 1:26, 27.
11. I John 5:7, 8.
12. John 14:16, 17.
13. I Cor. 13:12.
14. Matt. 6:23.
15. Pallas Athena, "'Behold, I Stand at the Door and Knock,'" in *Masters of the Far East* (1971 *Pearls of Wisdom*, vol. 14, no. 44), pp. 178–79, $14.95.
16. Gen. 2:6.
17. Isa. 1:18.
18. II Cor. 6:16.
19. Sanat Kumara, "The Space Within," in 1968 *Pearls of Wisdom*, vol. 11, no. 25, p. 99, $14.95.
20. Matt. 17:20.
21. Sanat Kumara, "The Space Within," in 1968 *Pearls of*

Wisdom, pp. 100–101.

22. Luke 1:52.

23. John 1:14.

24. Mother Mary, "A Letter from Mother Mary," Keepers of the Flame Lesson 16, pp. 9, 11.

25. Surya, "The Arhat—A Repository of God's Good," in 1970 *Pearls of Wisdom,* vol. 13, no. 32, p. 141, $14.95.

26. Mark 10:15.

27. John 5:17; Surya, "The Arhat—A Repository of God's Good," in 1970 *Pearls of Wisdom,* pp. 141–43.

28. Helios, "I AM In and Behind the Sun," in 1970 *Pearls of Wisdom,* vol. 13, no. 29, p. 131; decree 20.20 in *Prayers, Meditations, and Dynamic Decrees for the Coming Revolution in Higher Consciousness,* Section I, $2.95.

29. Prov. 6:6.

30. Job 9:7–8; Helios, "I AM In and Behind the Sun," in 1970 *Pearls of Wisdom,* p. 130.

31. Luke 2:14.

32. Hab. 2:20.

33. Rev. 11:15.

34. I John 3:2.

35. I Cor. 11:24.

36. Helios, "A Decade of Initiation for the Earth," in 1970 *Pearls of Wisdom,* vol. 13, no. 2, pp. 6–9.

37. Helios, October 12, 1970, "The Meaning of Life: Advice to a Planet," audiocassette B85068, $6.50, on *Only Mark 9,* 4-cassette album, A85068, $26.00.

38. Matt. 26:27.

39. John 14:26.

40. John 14:17.

41. Dan. 2:22.

42. Acts 2:1, 2.

43. John 3:5–7.

44. John 10:30.

45. John 3:8.

46. Luke 21:19.

47. Acts 9:5.

48. Titus 3:5.

49. John 17:22.

50. Matt. 10:34.

51. Matt. 18:11.

52. Ps. 69:9.

53. Matt. 6:9.

54. Isa. 61:1.

55. John 5:35.

56. John 3:19.

57. Matt. 7:15.

58. John 14:6.

59. John 8:32.

60. Matt. 24:24.

61. Matt. 7:7.

62. I Cor. 15:52.

63. Mark 15:38.

64. Matt. 28:6.

65. Matt. 9:12.

66. John 8:12.

67. Rom. 12:2.

68. Mark 13:14.

69. Matt. 3:17.

70. Mark 8:36.

71. John 21:15.

72. Isa. 40:3.

73. Matt. 19:26.

74. Heb. 12:6.

75. Luke 18:18.

76. Matt. 25:30.

77. Jer. 6:14.

78. Matt. 5:26.

79. Gen. 32:26.

80. Gen. 4:9.

81. Exod. 3:5.

82. John 14:27.

83. Matt. 23:24.

84. Matt. 17:21.

85. Matt. 11:30.

86. Matt. 17:4.

87. Amaryllis, "The Mystery of the Cosmic Circle of Life," in *Kuthumi On Selfhood* (1969 *Pearls of Wisdom,* vol. 12, no. 19), p. 83, $17.95.

88. Mark 4:39.
89. Ps. 46:10.
90. Ps. 8:5.
91. Heb. 10:9.
92. Ps. 24:1.
93. Matt. 6:28.
94. Rose of Light, 1963 *Pearls of Wisdom,* vol. 6, no. 13.
95. John 15:5.
96. John 8:31.
97. Rev. 22:2.
98. Exod. 3:2.
99. Gen. 3:16–18.
100. Dan. 4:35.
101. Gen. 2:7.
102. John 14:18.
103. Matt. 5:4.
104. El Morya, 1964 *Pearls of Wisdom,* vol. 7, no. 15.
105. Archangel Michael, "The Nature of Faith," in 1968 *Pearls of Wisdom,* vol. 11, no. 47, p. 198.
106. I Thess. 5:3.
107. El Morya, *A White Paper from the Darjeeling Council Table,* p. 2, $1.00.
108. Matt. 12:37.
109. Gen. 2:2.
110. Gen. 1:31.
111. The Maha Chohan, 1966 *Pearls of Wisdom,* vol. 9, no. 36.
112. Ibid.
113. Isa. 30:20.
114. Gal. 6:7.
115. God Tabor, "'The Earth Is the Lord's, and the Fulness Thereof,'" in *Masters of the Far East* (1971 *Pearls of Wisdom,* vol. 14, no. 15), pp. 59–60.
116. II Pet. 3:5–7.
117. Ezra 9:13.
118. Saint Germain, "Avert Disaster, Cataclysm, and Prediction by Right Action, Dynamic Decrees, and Change in Thinking," in *The Mechani-*

zation Concept (1965 *Pearls of Wisdom,* vol. 8, no. 40), p. 185, $16.95.
119. Jon. 3:10.
120. Saint Germain, "Avert Disaster, Cataclysm, and Prediction by Right Action, Dynamic Decrees, and Change in Thinking," in *The Mechanization Concept,* p. 186.
121. El Morya, *Encyclical on World Good Will,* pp. 17–19, $1.50.
122. Matt. 7:22, 23.
123. Luke 21:25, 26.
124. Saint Germain, "Avert Disaster, Cataclysm, and Prediction by Right Action, Dynamic Decrees, and Change in Thinking," in *The Mechanization Concept,* pp. 186, 188.
125. Hab. 3:11.
126. Matt. 12:31, 32.
127. Saint Germain, "Avert Disaster, Cataclysm, and Prediction by Right Action, Dynamic Decrees, and Change in Thinking," in *The Mechanization Concept,* p. 186.
128. El Morya, 1964 *Pearls of Wisdom,* vol. 7, no. 15.
129. Mighty Victory, "The Passion for Victory," in 1968 *Pearls of Wisdom,* vol. 11, no. 33, p. 139.
130. Gen. 2:23.
131. Gen. 2:18.
132. Gen. 2:21, 22.
133. Gen. 2:23.
134. Gen. 3:21.
135. Gen. 2:24.
136. Matt. 19:6.
137. John 1:3.
138. Gen. 3:20.
139. Acts 2:3.
140. **Lemuria.** According to the findings of James Churchward, archaeologist and author of *The*

Lost Continent of Mu, the Motherland extended from north of Hawaii three thousand miles south to Easter Island and the Fijis and was made up of three areas of land stretching more than five thousand miles from east to west. He estimates that Mu was destroyed approximately twelve thousand years ago by the collapse of the gas chambers which upheld the continent (*The Lost Continent of Mu* [New York: Ives Washburn, 1931], pp. 252, 282–83). We are not at liberty to release the exact dates of the sinking of Mu and Atlantis.

141. Rev. 17:1.
142. Rev. 12:1.
143. James 1:27.
144. **The sinking of Atlantis,** the largest colony of Mu (according to Churchward, Atlantis sank 11,600 years ago [*The Lost Continent of Mu* (New York: Ives Washburn, 1931), p. 264]), ensued as the result of the total perversion of both the masculine and feminine uses of the sacred fire in the latter days of her civilization. In the Fertile Crescent, where the dawn of a new civilization once again reappears, we find the **culture of the Divine Mother** appearing in many forms. It also appears throughout Egypt and Asia Minor, and later in Greece and Rome. Remnants of the antediluvian culture are seen in the worship of the Moon Goddess, known by various names throughout the cultures of both East and West. Her

various titles merged into *maia, maya,* and *Maria*—all derivatives of *mother.* The Hindu concept of maya is the personification of illusion—the inaccessible or the unreachable. And truly the mother form had become almost a chimera of unreality with the veiling of Matter and the pollution of the astral plane that reduced the moon to a reflector of the world of illusion that had been superimposed upon the Mother Image.

The symbol of the veiled goddess depicts the dark period of history when the Mother could no longer be identified through the veil of maya. The role of the moon as the reflector of both the fire of the sun and the water element of the earth makes it the eminently feminine symbol of creation shining in the night, or the passive plane of consciousness. Thus, to the ancients the sun was the symbol of Father and the active spirit of the day, and the moon was the symbol of Mother and the passive manifestation of the night. Very few of the world's cultures are without the traditional symbol of the Mother, a being half human and half divine who brings forth the immaculately born Son sent forth from the Father to give Life as an avatar of the people.

Surrounding Mother and Son is the unseen but very present essence of the Father Spirit, the all-pervading Presence whose purposes are fulfilled in Matter through the

Mother Image. The goddesses of these ancient cultures came to be called the Mother of God, for through them mankind perceive the incarnation of the divine archetype. And therefore the title Queen of the World, Virgin Mother, and the Celestial Light were in use long before their culmination in the figure of Mary the Mother of Jesus.

145. Adolph Erman, *A Handbook of Egyptian Religion,* trans. A. S. Griffith (London: Archibald Constable & Co., 1907), pp. 244–45.

146. Manly P. Hall, *The Secret Teachings of All Ages,* 11th ed. (Los Angeles: Philosophical Research Society, 1957), p. XLV.

147. Rev. 13:8.

148. Rev. 12:15–17.

149. *Encyclopaedia Britannica,* 1954, s.v. "Hypatia"; H. P. Blavatsky, *Isis Unveiled: A Master Key to the Mysteries of Ancient and Modern Science and Theology,* vol. 2, *Theology* (Pasadena: Theosophical University Press, 1960), pp. 53, 252–53; Hall, *Secret Teachings of All Ages,* pp. CXCVII–CXCVIII.

150. Henry Wadsworth Longfellow, "Santa Filomena," stanza 10.

151. Prov. 4:6–9, 3:18.

152. Matt. 28:18.

153. I Tim. 4:2.

154. The Maha Chohan, "Cleave Only to the Real," in 1970 *Pearls of Wisdom,* vol. 13, no. 33, pp. 144–45.

155. Isa. 40:31.

156. Matt. 24:23–26.

157. I Cor. 11:29.

158. Henri Estienne, *Les Prémices* (1594), in *Bartlett's Familiar Quotations,* ed. Emily Morison Beck, 14th ed. rev. and enl. (Boston: Little, Brown and Co., 1968), p. 188.

159. Gal. 5:1.

160. Luke 19:10.

161. II Cor. 5:17.

162. James 5:16.

163. The Maha Chohan, 1966 *Pearls of Wisdom,* vol. 9, nos. 27, 28.

164. John 10:16.

165. John 14:2.

166. Hilarion, 1961 *Pearls of Wisdom,* vol. 4, no. 9.

167. Acts 17:26.

168. Matt. 11:12.

169. Ps. 139:14.

170. Dan. 7:9, 22.

171. Sanat Kumara, "The Space Within," in 1968 *Pearls of Wisdom,* pp. 99, 101–2.

172. Albert Schweitzer, personal conversation with Father Charles Carroll, January 1961, Lambaréné, Gabon.

173. Father Paschal Robinson, trans., *The Writings of Saint Francis of Assisi* (London: J. M. Dent & Co., 1906), pp. 152–53.

174. *Webster's Seventh New Collegiate Dictionary,* s.v. "ecology."

175. Gen. 1:26.

176. Matt. 10:30.

177. John 14:2.

178. Gen. 1:28.

179. I Pet. 1:19.

180. I Cor. 15:3.

181. John 16:33.

182. John 20:17.

183. John 17:4.

184. I John 4:2, 3.

185. John 6:63.

186. Dan. 5:25–27.
187. Gen. 6:3.
188. Matt. 10:33.
189. Matt. 5:5.
190. Deut. 10:17.
191. Goddess of Liberty, *Liberty Proclaims*, pp. 34–35.
192. *Rocky Mountain News*, 12 March 1972.
193. Jer. 2:34; 19:4; Matt. 2:16.
194. El Morya, *Encyclical on World Good Will*, p. 5.
195. Isa. 9:2.
196. Goddess of Liberty, *Liberty Proclaims*, pp. 20–21.
197. Job 1:21.
198. El Morya, *Encyclical on World Good Will*, p. 4.
199. Saint Germain, "The Crucible of Being," in 1962 *Pearls of Wisdom; Studies in Alchemy*, pp. 80–81; *Saint Germain On Alchemy*, pp. 89–90.
200. **Fallacy of a one-world solution to environmental problems.** In attempting to solve our environmental problems, well-meaning individuals have proposed a number of solutions. One that has been widely discussed is the establishment of some form of world government wherein centralized control over the world's ecosystems would be administered by a group of environmental specialists. To eliminate imbalances in the biosphere and discrepancies in the economies of the nations, the proponents of this plan advocate the redistribution of natural and human resources on a global scale, thereby giving to every man and every country their "fair share" of the earth and its atmosphere—a patch of land 'neath a patch of sky.

While we acknowledge the sincerity of the majority of those who are working to improve man's lot, we must point out that within this plan there are certain marked inconsistencies with cosmic law. To begin with, a one-world government is not recommended by the Hierarchy. Until the Christ rules in the heart of the individual, the individual is not fit to rule the world. It must be understood that nation-states were instituted by the Ascended Masters to serve as the final point of transition between the imperfect society that evolved after man's expulsion from Eden and the perfect society that will be outpictured in the golden age—a society based on a one-world government headed by the Prince of Peace and those who have attained self-mastery through the Christ consciousness. The abuses that have occurred within and among the nation-states are not the intent of God, but rather a reflection of man's ignorance of and indifference to that intent; and this is to be expected, given his present imperfect evolution.

The Brotherhood cautions against the premature uniting of peoples, even for the purpose of solving the problems of the planetary ecosystem. For because of their group karma and their divine destiny to manifest an aspect of the Christ consciousness as a nation, the peoples of the world require boundaries of identity that enable them to fulfill their reason for being. The nation-state system is not inherently evil, nor are its citizens inherently selfish. For by evolving their own individuality and respecting the right of others to do the same, they enhance the evolution of all other states and the entire planetary body.

The uniting of the peoples of the world will come about naturally as individuals and nations strive toward and achieve perfection and unity through the Christ. Meanwhile, the Masters urge every family, every community, state, and nation to begin earnestly to seek solutions to their environmental problems. When this project is carried out selflessly with the general welfare as the only motivation and people are willing to make sacrifices for one another, then and only then will true progress be made.

The belief that the dangers inherent in a worldwide system of ecological control would be eliminated by the rule of an intellectual elite is also subject to serious question by the student of the Masters. While the Hierarchy acknowledges that only the most highly qualified and the best educated among mankind should have the final word on environmental controls, their judgment and man's judgment of who is most qualified and who is best educated do not necessarily coincide.

While rule by an intellectual elite is acceptable in theory, we would point out that in practice such a system can be both unwieldy and dangerous. The unwieldiness of the plan lies in the enforcement of the decisions reached by the world governing body. Nothing short of an international police state with the power to override the sovereignty of the nations could effectively put such a plan into action. The danger in the plan lies in man's assumption that by his intellect alone he can arrive at the judgments of God.

While it is often true that the trained mind can best attune with the Christ Mind, it is also true that the best minds can be trained according to the worst concepts. Such minds will reject the promptings of the Christ because they have been preconditioned by the warped perspective of the carnal mind. Some of the world's greatest thinkers, through no fault of their own, have been deprived of even a basic understanding of the laws of karma and reembodiment and the place of our planet in the cosmic scheme. Yet they are developing ways to alter man's entire life pattern to conform to the man-animal they have been educated to believe in. When man's best is not good enough to become a universal standard, then it is best that his sphere of influence be less than universal. The removal of the nation-state removes the last means of limiting the proliferation of error until man himself is able to transcend the limitations of his false indoctrination.

We must conclude that until the "specialists" who are slated to take charge of the proposed one-world ecosystem acknowledge the Christ-potential of every member of the biosphere and self-mastery becomes the primary goal of education, until the purpose of government is seen to be the protection of the Christ in every man, a worldwide system of control is in danger of being used by the wrong people for the wrong ends. Only when the specialists themselves are working consciously toward oneness with the Christ Self can they be trusted to preserve the freedoms that are essential to every man's realization of the Christ; only then can they be trusted to carve out the destiny of an entire planetary evolution.

In examining the belief that man's ecological problems can be solved by a more equitable distribution of human and natural resources, the Ascended Masters would point out that it is precisely because the energy quotients of individuals are not equal that the theory of the equal distribution of man's resources is untenable. Individual effort to develop the divine spark and to expand the qualities of the Godhead is the determining factor of man's individual status as a son or daughter of God. And as the Parable of the Talents (Matt. 25:14–30) illustrates, the use man makes of his talents in one embodiment determines how many he will merit in the next. Individuals and nations whose efforts to work the works of God have been greater than that of others who have had the same opportunity have earned the right to draw a greater allotment of wealth, energy, and talent from the universal Source.

Just as no man can take from another his treasures in heaven, neither can an individual or a political unit demand from another wealth and goods which it has not earned through honest labor. The very fact that a person or a group of persons is born in a certain time and in a certain place to a particular race and family in a particular nation and continent is an indication (1) of his karma, good and bad—of what he has and has not earned the right to enjoy—and (2) of his dharma—that service which it has become his duty, according to the will of God and his divine blueprint, to fulfill.

The plan for a one-world ecosystem will not work because it does not take into consideration the delicate balance of the spiritual ecosystem—the interaction of the causal bodies of the ten billion plus souls assigned to the planetary schoolroom. Individuals, groups, neighborhoods, communities, cities, states, and nations comprise ecosystems within ecosystems with interdependencies and interlocking energies. To take them apart and put them back together again like a game of blocks—to shuffle people and things like a deck of cards and deal a new world—is a violation of cosmic law so serious as to spell the ultimate end of the biosphere. Total control of a planet and its people equals total destruction of individual fulfillment of the Christ-potential through individual initiative. If you destroy a man's incentive to create, you destroy the man, making him an animal. And if at the same time you destroy the identity of a nation by depriving it of its destiny, you are left not with a golden age, but with an animal farm.

Some argue for a world organization on the grounds that man has a recognized need to expand his sphere of identity, that is, to transcend his identification with his self, his family, his clan, and his nation to include all of his world. They say that man's desire to express his individuality and to retain his freedom to act as he chooses is the underlying cause of all the problems of ecology. They conclude that man must give up his self-centered habits for the good of the whole human family of which he is but a single member.

We are well aware of the fact that man must learn to identify with man if Life is to continue on this planet. He must be his brother's keeper; and through identification with that which is real in self and society he must surrender his selfish desires if he is to continue to progress both spiritually and materially. But this man cannot do as long as he retains his carnality—his self-image as a man-animal through which he has functioned since his fall from the grace of the Christ Image. Therefore, if he would rid himself of his selfishness, he must rise from the plane of identification with animal life to claim his inheritance as a sinless, selfless son of God. Only then will he be able to expand his sphere of identity and through the power of divine love include the entire world in his Self-conscious awareness.

One of the great fallacies of our time is the projecting of mankind's current imperfections on the white page of the future. If instead, through invocation to the sacred fire, mankind would transmute in the present the evil, or the energy veil, which Jesus said was sufficient unto the day, they would be given the resources to meet the challenges of the future. And their future's problems would not be compounded by their failure to solve the problems of the present.

201. Ezek. 1:4.
202. Jer. 6:14.
203. Heb. 11:6.
204. I Cor. 3:11.
205. Matt. 13:12.
206. I Pet. 1:7.
207. I Thess. 5:3.
208. I Cor. 15:40.
209. Gen. 1:29, 30.
210. Gen. 3:18.
211. Exod. 20:13.

212. **Elementals bear world karma.** The quantity of energy which mankind have misqualified down through the centuries in their lack of reverence for Life is so great that if they were required to bear the full weight of their karma, they themselves would be bowed to the ground, walking on all fours as animals. Rather than consign the souls of men to animal forms to expiate their karma, the mercy of the Mother has allowed the elementals to balance a great portion of mankind's karma by working out the cycles of their misqualified energy in the physical bodies of the animals which they ensouled. By this dispensation man is not required to reincarnate in an animal body, even though his karma might indeed dictate such a fate; for the Lords of Karma, who interceded on mankind's behalf, knew that should this come to pass, mankind's evolution, insofar as the expansion of the Christ consciousness is concerned, would effectively be brought to a halt.

213. Rom. 14:2–4.
214. Matt. 9:12.
215. John 12:32.
216. Matt. 9:17.
217. Matt. 12:45.
218. II Pet. 2:19–21.
219. Rev. 3:18.
220. Heb. 12:6.
221. Heb. 13:2.
222. II Cor. 5:1.
223. The Maha Chohan, 1964 *Pearls of Wisdom,* vol. 7, no. 24.

Unless otherwise noted, all publications and audiocassettes are Summit University Press (Box A, Livingston, Montana 59047), released under the messengership of Mark L. Prophet and Elizabeth Clare Prophet.

Postage for Books

For books $5.95 and under, please add $.50 for the first book, $.25 each additional book. For books $7.95 through $15.95, add $1.00 for the first, $.50 each additional. For books $16.95 through $25.00, add $1.50 for the first, $.75 each additional.

Postage for Audiocassettes

For single audiocassettes, please add $.50 for the first cassette and $.30 for up to 4 additional cassettes. For 2-cassette albums, add $.90 for the first and $.30 for each additional album. For 4-cassette albums, add $1.15 for the first and $.25 for each additional album.

Acknowledgments

The authors wish to extend grateful acknowledgment to the following publishers for permission to reprint excerpts from copyrighted material: Bobbs-Merrill Co., Inc. for *Foundations of the Metaphysics of Morals* by Immanuel Kant, translated by Lewis W. Beck; Holt, Rinehart and Winston, Inc. for *Creative Evolution* by Henri Bergson, translated by Arthur Mitchell; Macmillan London and Basingstoke for *Mind-Energy* by Henri Bergson, translated by H. Wildon Carr; National Geographic Society for the May 1963 *National Geographic Magazine;* Philosophical Research Society, Inc. for *The Secret Teachings of All Ages* by Manly P. Hall; Random House, Inc. for *Confessions of Saint Augustine,* translated by Edward B. Pusey; Routledge & Kegan Paul Ltd. for *The Song Celestial or Bhagavad-Gita,* translated by Sir Edwin Arnold; and Simon & Schuster for *The Story of Philosophy* by Will Durant.

Index of Poetry and Invocations

Index of Scripture

For Those Who Would Teach Men the Way

TWO VOLUMES BY THE WORLD TEACHERS

PRAYER AND MEDITATION
AND
CORONA CLASS LESSONS
by Jesus and Kuthumi

From the heart of Jesus
these two handbooks for disciples
of the Lord's Word and Work are your key to
fulfilling his scriptural challenge to "feed his
sheep" and do his "greater works."

*"All who would follow in my footsteps must
understand that unless they are able to contact the
great Source of life and continually renew their
strength, their mission will not be carried forth
in the manner desired by God." Jesus*

The Lost Teachings of Jesus are being
shouted from the housetops. Let the disciples
of the Lord join him and his beloved Saint
Francis (known as Kuthumi) to deliver to his
own these precious dictations on prayer as
unbroken communion with the Father and
meditation as a two-way communication
system to God.

Let their 48 Corona Class Lessons lead
you step by step up the mount of transfiguration as you learn with Peter, James and John
of Jesus' communion with the ascended and
angelic hosts and take up the mantle he gives
you to preach his Lost Teachings to the world.

In *Climb the Highest Mountain* you have
at last made contact with the great truths of
your immortal being in God. Now you can
run with the message as Jesus and Kuthumi
show you how to teach the precepts that are
laid in divine order for the salvation of souls
and their protection in this time of trouble.

Yes, the teachings are meant to be taught,
God-taught, by each one who has drunk from
the cup of the Saviour. Hearts reach out to you
who know the true meaning of his life and
mission. They call to you to teach them the
Way of personal Christhood—the Path of
Love that freely gives to all the living Bread
which is come down to us from heaven *today.*

The supreme joy of reading Jesus' own
words dictated to the Messengers Mark and
Elizabeth Prophet—of entering the heart of
Saint Francis, everyone's divine poverello—
is beyond many a soul's hope for comfort
and enlightenment in this world. Yet here,
now, in popular paperback format, are two
volumes of the most profound, the most
essential knowledge so needed by seekers for
Christ's healing Truth made simple and practical
for everyday situations.

Let Jesus and Kuthumi open your understanding of the Divine Doctrine and show you
how to face and conquer life with the Spirit
of Christ's victory, even as you show others how
to prepare for the Lord's coming—bodily into
their temple—with his Holy Spirit and saints.

If you loved the Everlasting Gospel, if its
revolutionary message has spoken to your soul,
you will thrill to the new song of the Lamb that
enters your heart cupful by cupful from these
letters sent with all the love of heaven *to you.*

Order your personal copies of *Prayer and
Meditation* and *Corona Class Lessons*—written
especially for you who will not rest until you
shout the Everlasting Gospel from the housetops and teach men the Way, all the way home
to God—with Jesus "my Saviour."

Prayer and Meditation includes the Science of the
Spoken Word, Individualization of the God Flame,
Saint Germain, violet-flame decrees, 18 illustra-
tions of world teachers. 350 pp., #569, $9.95.
Corona Class Lessons 48 chapters with 32-page
color section on Healing through the Transfiguration, 500 pp., #1654, $12.95.

SUMMIT UNIVERSITY PRESS®

Available wherever fine books are sold or directly from the publisher, Summit University Press, Dept. 256, Box A,
Malibu, CA 90265. After Feb. 15, 1987, Box A, Livingston, MT 59047. Please add $1.00 postage and handling for the
first book, $.50 each additional book.

Index

For an alphabetical listing of many of the philosophical and hierarchical terms used in *Climb the Highest Mountain,* see the comprehensive glossary, "The Alchemy of the Word: Stones for the Wise Masterbuilders," in *Saint Germain On Alchemy.*

Malthus, T. R., 535n; doctrines of, 537, 540

Man: all of Cosmos within his grasp, 383–84; believing he is an animal, 106, 115, 496, 521; as the center of creative evolution, 235–36; in cooperation with angels and elementals, 448–49; created in the image of God, 29, 100, 148–49, 152, 389; creation of, 152; Fall of, 86; God beholds, in the image of Reality, 155; God in, 269–70; and God in relationship to one another, 158; is inherently Good, 75; "Let us make man after our image and likeness...," 492; lie that, is separate from God, 165; maker of himself and his world, 471–72; as master of his destiny, 59–60; putting off the old and putting on the new, 178

Manipulators, 107; of the synthetic society, 107; their psychology of mass control, 112–20, 123, 124, 128

Mansions, Father's many, 402

Mary, Mother, 131; on the Mother of God, 396–97; on schisms which breed violence, 126; a technique practiced by, 177–78

Masculine Ray, 493

Mass entity, whose name is Legion, 14

Master R., 355

Masters, "No man can serve two masters...," 190, 233

Matter: denial of the existence of, 390–94; Divine Mother ensouls, 503–4; false belief that, equates with Evil, 392–94; Father-Mother God in Spirit and, 388–90; as Mother aspect of creation, 149n; and Spirit, 379–82, 386, 391, 392–96, 474, 490–93, 497, 520

Matter and Memory, 235

Meat, in diets, 554

Mechanical creations, 86

Media, communications, 14–15

Meditation: going-out and going-within phases of, 243–44; holy, 416; visualization of geometric forms during, 259

Memory, Serapis Bey on, 350–51

Memory body, 233; basement level of, 355; etheric, 457; of man, 166. *See also* Etheric body; Four lower bodies

Mental body, 169–71; interrelated to the other three bodies, 293–94; of man, 166. *See also* Four lower bodies

Mental disorders, 40–41

Meru, God: on consciousness, 261–62; on the ego, 16–17; on man's plight, 86–87; on negative forces that seek to hide the Real Image, 12–13

Meru, God and Goddess, enshrined the Feminine Ray, 496

Michael, Archangel: on cooperation with Nature, 468–69; "...and his angels fought against the dragon...," 85

Microcosm: invasion of, 39–40; and Macrocosm, 77, 34–36, 38–39, 41–42, 44

Mind(s): battle for, 509–10; expanding the, 242–44; and heart as motivating factors, 231–32; universal, 219–20; "...which was also in Christ Jesus," 154–55. *See also* Mental body; Subconscious mind; Superconscious Mind

Mind–Energy, 235

Monotheism, 277

Moon, role of, 582. *See also* Lunar influences

Moon Mother, 494

Moral code, 246

Mortality, laws of, 93

Moses, 358; on Sinai, 20

Mother: Body of the, 520; civilization has destroyed the image of, 518; culture of the Divine, 582;

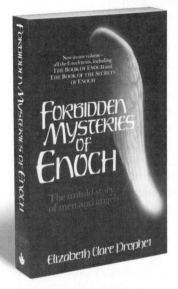

FOR MORE INFORMATION

For information about the Keepers of the Flame fraternity and monthly lessons; Pearls of Wisdom, dictations of the Ascended Masters sent to you weekly; Summit University three-month and weekend retreats; two-week summer seminars and quarterly conferences which convene at the Royal Teton Ranch, a 33,000-acre self-sufficient spiritual community-in-the-making, as well as the Summit University Service/Study Program with apprenticeship in all phases of organic farming, ranching, construction, publishing and related community services; Montessori International private school, preschool through twelfth grade for children of Keepers of the Flame; and the Ascended Masters' library and study center nearest you, call or write Summit University Press, Box A, Livingston, Montana 59047 (406) 222-8300.

Paperback books, audiocassettes and videotapes on the teachings of the Ascended Masters dictated to their Messengers, Mark L. Prophet and Elizabeth Clare Prophet—including a video series of Ascended Master dictations on "Prophecy in the New Age" and a Summit University Forum TV series with Mrs. Prophet interviewing outstanding experts in the field of health and Nature's alternatives for healing—are available through Summit University Press. Write for free catalogue and information packet.

Upon your request we are also happy to send you particulars on this summer's Summit University Retreat at the Royal Teton Ranch—survival seminars, wilderness treks, teachings of Saint Germain, dictations from the Ascended Masters, prophecy on political and social issues, initiation through the Messenger of the Great White Brotherhood, meditation, yoga, the science of the spoken Word, children's program, summer camping and RV accommodations, and homesteading at Glastonbury.

All at the ranch send you our hearts' love and a joyful welcome to the Inner Retreat!